Religion in Primitive Cultures

Religion and Reason 9

Method and Theory
in the Study and Interpretation of Religion

MOUTON · THE HAGUE · PARIS

Religion in Primitive Cultures

A Study in Ethnophilosophy

by

WILHELM DUPRÉ

MOUTON · THE HAGUE · PARIS

ISBN: 90-279-7531-0
Jacket design: Jurriaan Schrofer
© 1975, Mouton & Co
Printed in Hungary

Preface

We realize today that our attention must be focused more than ever on the historical character of our being. In and throughout the process of history, man's cultural situation has continued to gain new perspectives. It is only fair that we expect the same with regard to our own situation. Moreover, since we know about the historical condition of man, we are challenged to synthesize precisely this knowledge with the cultural consciousness by which we live today. We need to investigate the fundamental issues of culture again and again.

One of the fundamental issues of culture is without a doubt the significance of religion within the changing context of cultural and historical dynamics. If we study religion in primitive cultures accordingly, such a study becomes necessarily more than a repetition or reiteration of data already known. It becomes part of the unceasing question about the meaning of the present situation. In this sense, a study of religion in primitive cultures justifies itself.

The task of man's self-understanding as a historical being can never be fully completed, and its achievements will only be partial. But to the extent that it is successful it contributes to the on-going dialogue of reflective and reflecting beings. As such it is greatly indebted to many people. For this and similar reasons it is a pleasant duty to acknowledge the debt to all those authors mentioned in the text or the footnotes. Their works give a fair indication of the horizon wherein the study of primitive cultures has to be realized.

My thanks are especially due to those who fostered the growth of this study through their personal cooperation and assistance. Above all, I want to express my gratitude to the late Dr. Martin R. P. McGuire who instigated the study and who mentored its development.

I must also recall the memory of Dr. Paul J. Schebesta. Through the help of Dr. Gerald F. Kreyche, Chairman of the Philosophy Department at DePaul University, Chicago, and of Mr. Nicholas Thornton, Vice-President of Electronic Homes, Inc., Northbrook, Illinois, I was able to spend the summer of 1967 with

Father Schebesta, studying the religion and mythology of the Bambuti Pygmies. His firsthand experience with cultures that still existed in the full integrity of their traditions when he studied them was a most valuable guide for a philosopher who tries to understand ethno-religious data by integrating them into the world of reflection.

I would like to express my gratitude to my wife, Dietlind, who accompanied this study from first to last, giving many suggestions that have become part of the work.

I want also to say thanks to my friends W. Brennan, D. Duclow, H. Loiskandl, G. Remmel and B. Schreiter. Since we discussed many of the problems of this study with one another, their inspirations became part of what I have to say. In particular, I am most grateful to Bob for his unwearying help in giving the final touch to the English style.

Finally, I appreciate very deeply the assistance and efficient cooperation of Dr. Jacques Waardenbrug, general editor of RELIGION AND REASON, in offering me his series for the publication of this study.

Nijmegen/Chicago, 1974   WILHELM DUPRÉ

Contents

A Study in Ethnophilosophy

From an empirical point of view the following study falls within the province of cultural anthropology. It is concerned with the presentation and the analysis of *ethno*-religious data. To the extent, however, that it deals with *religious* phenomena and their interpretation, the study becomes a matter of the philosophy of religion.and culture. As such it belongs to the domain of philosophy.

A question that suggests itself in this context is that about the correlation between philosophy and cultural anthropology, or, as we might also say, ethnology. One could, of course, reject this question as irrelevant to the study of religion in primitive cultures. But then we have already decided that the relationship between cultural anthropology and philosophy is only an extraneous one, and we might rightly ask on what grounds such a decision has been made. On the other hand, if cultural anthropology and philosophy are intimately related with one another, we can expect that there will be a considerable difference both in the method by which we approach the data and the objectives that are pursued. Depending on whether we accept the first or the second possibility, the study has to be set up accordingly. In either case we become aware of a task that pertains to philosophy as well as to cultural anthropology or ethnology. Consequently, if an attempt is made to take up this task, we cannot restrict this effort to either philosophy or ethnology. Since both disciplines are concerned, we might express the particularity of this task by speaking of ethnophilosophy.

It goes without saying that ethnophilosophical problems are in one way or another present whenever and wherever we deal with the acquisition of cultural data and their interpretation. Beyond that, however, I would like to maintain that the ethnophilosophical aspect is nowhere as important as in the field of religious studies. What might be considered an interesting side issue in other areas becomes a methodological requirement when we turn to the world of religious phenomena.

By calling the present analysis of religion in primitive cultures a study in ethnophilosophy, I thus intend to bring the treatment of religion into a perspective that has been long overdue. I am convinced that such an approach can only benefit cultural anthropology as well as the philosophy of religion. Whether this objective will be achieved or not has to be left to the study and the judgment of the reader. At this point it seems to be appropriate to give at least a few indications of the meaning of ethnophilosophy as it will evolve in the course of this analysis.

There are three points that should be kept in mind when we speak of ethnophilosophy in the context of this study. In the *first* place we should pay attention to the fact that there are issues in cultural anthropology which cannot be adequately treated if we do not acknowledge their philosophical significance. We maintain that cultural anthropology, though an empirical discipline, will not gain its autonomy unless it recognizes the philosophical implications of at least some of its areas.

In the *second* place, there is the significance of cultural anthropology for philosophy in general and fundamental philosophy in particular. I am convinced that philosophy will not only miss an essential perspective in its quest for reality and meaning if it neglects to ask about the particular significance of the data provided by cultural anthropology, but that it will even be unable to accomplish the objectives of fundamental philosophy if it does not turn in one way or another to the ethnocultural and, especially, to the ethnoreligious data.

In the *third* instance I want to draw attention to the speculative character of cultural anthropology insofar as its genesis and specification is concerned. If we are to avoid the pitfalls of ideological distortion, we must not forget the transcendental conditions under which cultural anthropology originated. These conditions are not only relevant to the subject that understands but also to the object that is to be understood. A few examples will clarify these points.

If we follow the suggestion of the title of this study, we may expect a mere descriptive survey of religion in a particular group of cultures. But as we know from the experience of previous ventures in this direction, any attempt to follow such a suggestion will sooner or later be faced with defeat. An objective description of religious phenomena is a factual impossibility. One reason for this paradox of descriptive objectivity is the fact that the perception of cultural phenomena is not possible without the actuality of culture itself. The fact that man already has culture is the condition under which he becomes capable of seeing culture when it is there. In this sense it is not enough to say that 'culture produces culture', but one has to add that culture perceives culture.

In order to describe, we have to perceive. Perception in the field of culture, however, is in itself an act of culture. As such it presupposes understanding, while understanding implies conclusions about world, history and man that exceed the significance of the immediate perceptions. If we do not want to be lost in a chaos of impressions, we have to base our descriptions on conclusions that have a selective and ordering impact on the phenomena in question. While we may try to reduce the circles of interpretation or hermeneutics to a minimum, we cannot eliminate them altogether without at the same time eliminating the very perceptions that enable us to describe anything at all.

To get a better idea of this problem it may be of some help to construct a case of an ideal observation. For this purpose, let us imagine a small group of subjects that is to be studied from as many different angles and as exhaustively as possible. Moreover, since we know from our experience as attentive observers that one observer, even though our imagined group is small, will never be able to do this job alone, we propose that this study is done by a team of observers which will consist of as many people as are necessary to give a complete account of each individual subject in the group. Since the presence of so many observers is bound to disturb the ordinary course of actions and events, we even grant our team invisibility so as not to prejudice the activities of the subjects. Now we can be sure that the invisible team will not miss a single detail and that we will get a complete record on the subjects. And yet, we may ask, what will happen after the field work has been completed? We can begin with a totally synchronic inventory of all recordings. But unless we are willing to resign ourselves to becoming lost in a maze of divergent images and competing sounds, we will need a device that enables us to contrast and unite the acquired data within a common frame of reference which in turn will permit us to form a picture of the whole situation. Or, as an alternative to a synchronic presentation, we could place the recordings simply one after the other. But then we face the problem of recalling which instances belong together and of distinguishing those pertaining to a different context. In either case we will have to choose a principle for selecting and coordinating the data into some sort of perspective.

Even if we should try to use a computer for this purpose, we cannot disregard the fact that this machine has to be programmed before it can be set to work. But then we may rightly ask whether our data are still untainted and whether we are not taking away with the one hand what we gave – i.e., the provisions for a full and complete observation — with the other. Yet even in the most objective recording and reporting if no such coordination of the data takes place, we may seriously doubt whether the team produces any data at all. When it comes down to the processing or the description of their experiences, our invisible team will have to face the predicament of consciousness and 'observing reason' (*cf.* Hegel, 1952, p. 183 ff).

A second factor that aggravates the problem of a study such as the description of religion in primitive cultures is the meaning and the function of the term 'primitive' as it appears in the title. The application of this term to certain cultures necessarily presupposes a typology of culture. And this typology, in turn, is interwoven with patterns of orientation that have developed under the influence of circumstances which are both historical and, in some way, personal in nature. The very use of the term primitive implies (like its rejection) a theoretical stance that points far beyond the ideal construct of objective description.

Both these difficulties are underscored when we look at the relatively short history of cultural anthropology. Although the will to scientific and scholarly objectivity has always been firmly held as a fundamental principle among anthropologists, it was precisely the unrestricted and apparently self-evident devotion to this principle which in the name of scientific 'objectivity' made anthropologists fall victim to the dialectical ramification of various theories on the origin and nature of religion. Scholars such as Sir James Frazer and Father Wilhelm Schmidt, to mention only two among so many, tried to interpret the same ethnographic materials yet came to irreconcilable results. Scientific communication was stifled because of the positivistic prejudice that equated objectivity with objectification and therefore concealed the fact, central to hermeneutics or reflective understanding and interpretation, that subjectivity is primarily not a hindrance, but a necessary condition for research and understanding.

What needs to be kept in mind in this situation is the continuing interplay between the anthropological and cultural data, the description and interpretation of these data and the philosophy or *Weltanschauung* of the scholar who treats them. To do justice, then, to the ideal of a reflective and objective comprehension of world and reality, we must recognize this tripartite interrelation as a fundamental condition for a description that must simultaneously establish the data and, as an interpretation, decipher their meaning. And precisely because we want to come as close to the empirical data as possible, it will be necessary to develop a philosophical framework that not only provides a preliminary access to the phenomena in question but also serves as a basis for critically evaluating how they are interpreted. It is not sufficient to take an isomorphic and nominalistic view of reality for granted; nor is it enough to only point at this fallacy and to continue as if nothing had changed. The descriptive search for cultural data implies and, indeed, demands the articulation of the presupposed, underlying philosophy; and at the same time, the expression of this philosophy has to be conceived as an effort that gains its own structure in and by man's encounter with reality. As such it should not only be open to these phenomena but should be dependent upon them in such a way that this dependence will help us in becoming aware of the historical and cultural conditions both of the phenomena in question and of the process which enables us to understand them.

At any rate, for the sake of objectivity we must not forego an attempt at out-lining the scope of cultural studies by developing the principles of their procedure and verification in the light of a philosophy that meshes with the phenomena we would like to present. It is a demand brought forth by the facts of culture history and by the interest we take in their recording and understanding. The truth or validity of such a philosophy will be tested by its success in translating and communicating the phenomena in question. Even though we cannot know before-hand whether we will succeed, it would be an unforgivable offense against the integrity of both thinking and the empirically given were we to suppress the philosophical implications that are present in all acts of description and scholarly evaluation of cultural and, consequently, of religious phenomena. That such a philosophy can be developed is the implicit presupposition of anyone who addres-ses reality with the intention of learning and saying something about it.[1]

Of course, the hermeneutical problems of cultural anthropology just mentioned could be claimed for the second aspect of ethnophilosophy as well. But this is not precisely what should be emphasized in the second place. What we are concerned with in this instance is the universality of truth.

It makes no difference whether we follow the continental or the Anglo-Saxon line of thinking: In both instances we are in need of a method that permits us to understand the philosophical issues on their own grounds. Sooner or later we have to detach them from their historical settings and contingencies and, since this detachment cannot be absolute, to transfer them into the anticipated horizon of

---

1. For a further elaboration of these problems, *cf.* the various articles of R. A. Manners and D. Kaplan (1968). Furthermore, D. Bidney (1967); J. Fabian (1971); R. D. Baird (1971); and from a more philosophical point of view, F. Wiplinger (1961); H. G. Gadamer (1965); J. Haber-mas (1967); and E. Schillebeeckx (1972).

an entirely reflective culture. Within this context nothing can be more welcome than the experience of culture contrasts, for it is the difference they reveal which permits us to form the respective concepts. And while we agree that every history knows such contrasts both in the philosophies themselves and in the sequence of its epochs, we might add that any extension of the historical horizon can only further our understanding. Moreover, if we accept the significance of culture contrasts, we may say that philosophy must endeavor to get as comprehensive a concept as possible of culture history in order to fulfill its task of conceptual clarification and of comprehending reality.

This is all the more important inasmuch as we are always forced by the limitation of our capabilities to neglect certain aspects of man's cultural reality. We should, then, get an idea of what we are neglecting. Since this is not possible on purely empirical grounds, we have to succeed in bringing culture history into perspective. The process of empirical enrichment has to be complemented by the development of the *a priori* that keeps this process going. While we know what we have experienced, we have to clarify the perspective by which we approach reality to such an extent that the blind spots – 'by way of making progress towards mastering the whole' (Newman, 1959, p. 83) – begin to take shape in one way or another.

I need not belabor the fact that the general situation of philosophy is already reason enough to ask about the significance of those cultures that are of special concern to cultural anthropology. In addition, if it should turn out that the interpretation of ethnological data cannot be adequately realized without a theory of primitive culture, the import of cultural anthropology for philosophy shall increase considerably both because of the fundamental significance of the primum and because of the perspective that is brought upon the culture concept as such.

In terms of the present study we may describe this problem as follows. If it may be presumed that we do not reject the term 'primitive' outright, most of us are likely to use the expressions 'primitive religion' and 'religion in primitive cultures' interchangeably. Yet, if we are conscious of the words we use, the two expressions should be rigorously distinguished. For, while the question of 'religion in primitive cultures' refers primarily, as indicated by the plural form of this title, to an empirical problem, 'primitive religion' is above all a philosophical or speculative problem. The latter's meaning is correlated with the significance of the term 'primum' and the many words that describe the field of this concept. As such, primitive religion becomes a problem that is central to the general meaning of man as a cultural being. Its reality and significance does not, at least in principle, depend on any particular culture but belongs to the constitution of culture in general. On the other hand, if we call the question about primitive religion a speculative problem, we do not imply that this problem can be solved by mere thinking. On the contrary, we have to ask for those empirical instances that might be of special importance for the solution of this problem. Presupposing now that the more or less homologous use of the two expressions (as suggested by the employment of the term primitive in both instances) is not altogether wrong and that an adequate interpretation of ethnoreligious data implies the explicit development of a theory of primitive religion, we can definitely say that the philosophy of religion (and consequently, the philosophy of the primum) can no longer be indifferent to the data, the working and the results of the study of religion in primitive cultures. It is out of the question to speak of a unilateral dependence in this context. A philosophy of religion that wants to be fundamental[2] will have to acknowledge the essential character of its relation to cultural anthropology if it is to accomplish its objectives.[3]

As far as the third aspect of ethnophilosophy is concerned, I would like to emphasize the fact that the relationship between cultural anthropology and philosophy is not external but internal; or as one might also say, constitutive. This point resumes the previous arguments to the extent that they took reference to the speculative character of primitive culture. Even if we see no other meaning in cultural studies than the confrontation with reality (Weber, 1968, p. 24 ff.), we should well note that the object of cultural anthropology does not simply derive from the cultural data but from a synthetic judgment by which we 'discover' their coherence as elements of cultural reality.

When E. B. Tylor laid the foundation for cultural anthropology in 1871 he did this by coming to terms with two issues (*cf.* Tylor, 1958; Baal, 1971, p. 30 ff). On the one hand he succeeded in substantiating the mass of 'news' about man by

2. It should be worth mentioning that Hegel (no date, Works 16, p. 28) whose interest in fundamental issues is generally acknowledged came to the conclusion that 'philosophy develops only itself when it explicates religion, and while it unfolds itself, it is unfolding religion'.

3. If we are somewhat familiar with the history of ideas, we will know that this facet of philosophy is in want of systematic development. But it should also be noted that we do not have to start from scratch. Valuable work has been done so far by F. W. Schelling (no date, Works, Vol. XII), E. Cassirer (1953b), and M. Scheler (1960). The same holds true in part for the intention and method of E. Durkheim, L. Lévy-Bruhl and C. Lévi-Strauss. Also to mention are titles such as H. Frankfort *et al.* (1946), P. Radin (1937), M. Douglas (1970) and others.

introducing the culture concept 'in its wide ethnographic sense' (Tylor, 1958, p. 1). On the other hand he found a way of giving meaning and perspective to these data, that is, to specify them, by defining 'lower culture' or 'savagery' (Tylor, 1958, p. 32).

If 'Culture or Civilization' is indeed 'that complex whole which includes knowledge, belief, art, morals, law, custom, and any other capabilities and habits acquired by man as a member of society' (Tylor, 1958, p. 1), then we are justified to ask for the 'laws' that structure the complexity of the resulting reality. Mankind and history are no longer to be seen as the outcome of an haphazard summation of disparate beings, data, and events, but as an autonomous reality which can be approached by reason and reflection. Because of the culture concept and its cross-cultural implication it becomes 'the great task of rational ethnography' to investigate 'the causes which have produced the phenomena of culture, and the laws to which they are subordinate' (Tylor, 1958, p. 21). Because of the comprehensive and autonomous reality of culture, there is both the possibility and the need of a scientific program that inquires into the dynamics and structure of this reality.

Conversely, if the culture concept derives its 'ontological' status (i.e., its mode of reality and being presupposed while talking about it) from the total character and integrating function of culture, history may no longer be reduced to selected events, actions and ideas. There is more involved than past records and recorded deeds. 'Every possible avenue of knowledge must be explored, every door tried to see if it is open. No kind of evidence need be left untouched on the score of remoteness or complexity, of minuteness or triviality' (Tylor, 1958, p. 24). Since culture is a reality in itself it sets forth the rules that have to be followed if we want to understand its meaning and significance. We cannot dispose of culture, or substitute its reality by mere constructions. What is needed are 'broad views', a 'catholic sympathy' and, above all, the acceptance of the insight that 'savage' traditions are by no means 'superfluous to the rest of mankind' (Tylor, 1958, p. 22 f.). They bear their own significance within the larger context of mankind which is given to us and to them alike as the possible future of a particular situation. 'Not merely as a matter of curious research, but as an important practical guide to the understanding of the present and the shaping of the future, the investigation into the origin and early development of civilization must be pushed on zealously (Tylor, 1958, p. 24). On the basis of culture 'even the despised ideas of savage races become a practically important topic to the modern world, for here, as usual, whatever bears on the origin of philosophic opinion, bears also on its validity' (Tylor, 1958, II, p. 195).

Today we no longer agree with all of Tylor's hypotheses. In defending our stance we may appeal to data that were either partially or entirely unknown to him, or inadequately interpreted as far as we understand them. But even if we disagree we still are presupposing his culture concept in order to do so. For if such arguments are taken to be conclusive, they cannot be treated in isolation. They need the larger context of cultural reality in order to get hold of the 'shapes', 'colors' and 'properties' that mark the data in question. Without the culture concept the approaches to man and world are doomed to remain in essence unscientific. In this respect we may say that Tylor is as topical today as he was one hundred years ago, even though it may be fair to add that the culture concept needs further elaboration.

Matters become more difficult, however, if we ask about the specification of cultural anthropology as it has been carried out by Tylor. After he had discovered the principle of cultural studies, it was relatively easy for him to solve this problem. First, he lived at a time when many of the precolonial cultures still followed their own way of life. In fact, there still existed many peoples that had not come in contact with the technological culture of the West and its devastating effects as far as the integrity of tradition is concerned. In the second place, he experienced no difficulty in labelling the cultures of the 'lower races' as 'primitive culture' and in using this 'trait' as specifying difference for the new 'science of culture'. How deep this conviction was rooted becomes clear if we take into consideration that even as late as 1926 it was still possible for B. Malinowski to state in an essay on 'Myth in Primitive Psychology', 'I do, however, want to emphasize the fact that anthropology should be not only the study of savage custom in the light of our mentality and our culture, but also the study of our own mentality in the distant perspective borrowed from Stone Age man'. And a few lines farther, 'If anthropology could thus inspire us with a finer sense of humor, it might justly claim to be a very great science.' (Malinowski, 1954, p. 145). This is still in line with Tylor's approach. The 'specific difference' at least did not yet cause headaches.

In the meantime, most of these traditions upon which cultural anthropology based itself as a discipline have vanished; or, if they are still in existence, they have undergone changes of such far-reaching consequences that they are no longer the same. From the viewpoint of living traditions, cultural anthropology has thus lost its very subject matter. Moreover, the concept of 'primitive culture' or 'stone age man' can no longer be said to be as self-evident as it once was thought to be. If we add to these developments the new axiom that 'the teaching of anthropology must be reserved for eye-witnesses' (Lévi-Strauss, 1967, p. 370), one might even ask whether cultural anthropology has not suffered the same fate as the cultures whose existence brought this discipline into being. But no matter how we approach the issue, as far as the specific difference is concerned we cannot rely upon empirical criteria alone. If we assess the problem in terms of ethnological metatheory, there need to be ethnophilosophy if for no other reason than the specification of the subject matter of cultural anthropology.

One may surely not pass over in silence the fact that Tylor and many of his contemporaries could be criticized for remaining 'armchair anthropologists', and that this influenced the premises and philosophical presuppositions on which they worked. One should concede that there exists a relation between this fact and the philosophy to which they adhered. It would be wrong, however, if we applied this argument without bringing it into some sort of perspective. First, we have to note that the work of the field worker is not that of the cultural an-thropologist just as it is not the task of the historian to be a chronicler. There is, as we might also say, a particular meaning in the fact that field workers write about their experiences. In the second place, it should not be denied, however, that the acquisition of new data and the elaboration of the methods of meaningful field-work, their application and reevaluation, or, if this is no longer possible, the extension of these questions into the methods of sociology and the integration of sociological results into cultural anthropology, remains an ever-present and never-ending task. Since this task is in itself a rather complex matter, it may be fair to say that cultural anthropology is more than any other discipline dependent on joint efforts. Yet, if armchair anthropology is to be criticized, it should not be because of this type of work, but because sight is, or has been, lost of the task at hand and of the complexity of its realization. What should be criticized is the absence of reflection and self-relativation both with regard to the data in ques-tion and to the basis on which they are approached, deciphered and inter-preted.

Of course, there has been, and still exists, a temptation with cultural anthro-pology that threatens the scientific character of this enterprise and to which attention should be called for the sake of perspective and clarity. It is the urge to mythologize in the name and under the disguise of science. If we consider the historical situation in which cultural anthropology originated and which made it possible to study cultures on their own grounds, we encounter a process that points far beyond the interest of mere interpretation and impartial curiosity. When seen against the background of its historical setting, cultural anthropology turns out to be a concrete principle in the fashioning of a new planetary culture where the work of reflective thought plays a central role in the formation of tradition. From the viewpoint of its emergence, cultural anthropology reveals itself as a symptom of historical changes that touches upon the traditional substance of man. As in other instances of essential changes which in the continuation of history become a question of self-identity and psychic balance, we can expect that the line between reality and day-dreaming tends to evaporate. Since there is more at stake than a reflective understanding of reality, even reflective thought might easily turn to myth-making at a point where one still 'believes' to do the work of science. As Yasunari Kawabata says of Shimamura: 'Nothing could be more comfortable than writing about the ballet from books. A ballet he had never seen was an art in another world. It was an unrivaled armchair reverie, a lyric from some paradise. He called his work research, but it was actually free, uncontrolled fantasy. He preferred not to savor the ballet in the flesh; rather he savored the phantasms of his own dancing imagination, called up by Western books and pictures. It was like being in love with someone he had never seen' (Kawabata, 1968, p. 27).

Yet, if we believe that fieldwork experience is the remedy against this urge to mythologize, which doubtlessly can be recognized in 'armchair anthropology', we only have to read what Lévi-Strauss says about the 'training of research workers'. 'Only experienced members of the profession, whose work shows that they have themselves passed the test, can decide if and when a candidate for the anthropological profession has, as a result of field work, accomplished that inner revolution that will really make him into a new man' (Lévi-Strauss, 1967, p. 371).

As we know from the history of religions, the search for and the proclamation of a 'new man' is no less part of the mythological process than 'savoring the phantasms of one's own dancing imagination'. While the need for initiation rituals makes perfect sense from the viewpoint of personal and social identity, a statement such as that by Lévi-Strauss describes only one more facet of a problem that is intertwined with cultural anthropology as a historical and social phenomenon. Even if we disregard the predicament of a post-colonial world for a moment, it seems to me that the problems raised in this context are by far too complex to be solved in this manner. No matter if we sit in the chair or stay in the field, what is needed is a philosophical self-reflection which, in correlation with the data of cultural reality and with a growing awareness of cultural differences as well as of the similarities between men, brings perspective into our efforts to understand reality and to live by this understanding. Because of the implications of cultural anthropology with regard to existential issues and the culture of the future, we see again a fundamental need for ethnophilosophical reflection and a wide field for the activities and application of ethnophilosophy.

If we are to overcome the shortcomings of ideological restrictions we must not seek refuge on fabulous islands that exist only in our minds or in secret desires nor should we seek refuge in esoteric programs that defeat themselves in their unnoticed symbolisms. Rather, we should try to succeed in extending the paradigm of concrete and personal experience into the horizon of mankind where it can be synthesized with the data of culture history as they have been accumulated, though under varying circumstances, throughout the centuries.

Since this book is not intended to be a study *about* but one *in* ethnophilosophy, these few remarks may suffice. Their purpose has been to draw attention to the scope and the extent of the problems that await an analysis of religion in primitive cultures. I need not emphasize that I tried to organize this study accordingly.

In the first chapter I try to clarify the culture concept in general and that of primitive culture in particular. A short history of the studies on primitive religion(s) will serve both as background for the respective questions today and as horizon that permits us to contrast our own position with that of others. In the second chapter I will give a survey of the religious data as they can be found in the cultures of gatherers, hunters, planters and animal breeders. The wealth of ethno-religious data offered by these cultures shows the need for a more detailed study of religion in selected cases, in particular of cultural situations that comply best with the criteria set forth by the analysis of primitivity and the typology of primitive culture. I try to respond to this need by presenting and analyzing the religious data of the African Pygmies, of the Arctic hunters (Eskimos), of the Negritos on the Malayan Peninsula, of the totemistic hunters and gatherers in Australia and finally of the Kaingang, a group of gatherers and hunters in the highlands of Eastern Brazil (chapters four to six). Yet, before this program can be accomplished, it will be necessary to resume the theoretical deliberations set forth in the first chapter. By doing this in the form of a 'methodological inter-

lude' (chapter three) I want to underline the principle of phenomenological hermeneutics according to which theory should neither be developed prior nor merely
after the presentation of relevant data but with them. In chapter seven I then
will try to evaluate the data of the previous chapters by developing the idea of
primitive religion as a universal dimension of man and culture. Finally I will
discuss the significance of primitive religion for modern man (chapter eight).

I begin with the premise that religion must be approached as an aspect of
cultural reality (*cf.* James, 1938, p. 21 ff). In the course of the analysis however
I will come to the conclusion that religion and culture are closely interlinked
(*cf.* Van der Leeuw, 1963, II, p. 679), and that an understanding of their
reciprocal relationship is of utmost significance for man's ceaseless search to
discover what it means to be human. The present study on religion in primitive
cultures is an attempt to provide an interpretation of these interconnections. As a
study in ethnophilosophy it approaches religion as a cultural synthesis between
world and consciousness as it has been expressed and articulated by man living
in primitive cultures. The cultural differences that are brought forth in this
context are not to be considered as an end but as a different means for aiding
reflective beings in their pursuit of truth.

1

Primitivity, Culture and Religion

If we take the title of this study at its face value, the program seems to be plain and straightforward: We are to deal with religion as it appears in specific cultures. Such an apprehension of 'religion in primitive cultures' is certainly not wrong. We are indeed concerned with specific cultures and the respective phenomena of religion. On the other hand, if we reflect upon the principle by which we specify or select these cultures, matters begin to become complicated. In contrast to ordinary specifications we do not refer to particular and concrete features such as race, environment, economy, language, social and political organization, the possession of script and so forth. Instead, we use the highly theoretical, if not ideological, term 'primitive'.

Because of the particular circumstances of our own age one could ask whether it is justifiable to use the term primitive any longer, since it is so deeply implicated in the ideological restrictions of nineteenth century theories about man and the development of the human race. Would it not be better to abandon this term altogether as has been proposed by various authors? What sense does it make to cling to an inheritance that has become obsolete?[1]

The significance of these and similar questions becomes clear if we consider them in their historical and functional context. Traditionally, these have been indicated by such terms as primitive culture, protoculture, origins of culture and primitive religion. At any rate, the first problem we face in this study is not the meaning, the function and the significance of religion in general and of primitive

---

1. *Cf.* E. G. Parrinder (1971, Vol. II, p. 551): 'All races of man have had a long history, even if it is unrecorded, and many developments have occurred down the ages. Even "higher" religions contain survivals or revivals of ancient customs, though these are modified in changing contexts. The description "primitive" is misleading and should be abandoned.' Also H. Ringgren and A. v. Ström (1967, chap. V). On the other hand, the abandonment of a name is not necessarily identical with a change of mind, nor does it give us the guarantee that misconceptions have been overcome. In this respect I agree with M. Douglas (1970, p. 74) when she says: 'I suspect that our professional delicacy in avoiding the term "primitive" is the product of secret convictions of superiority.'

religion in particular but that of primitivity. We have to ask ourselves what reason do we have to speak of primitive cultures in the first place, or else, what is the methodological and theoretical significance of primitivity?

1. PRIMITIVITY AND THE STUDY OF RELIGION

The idea of primitivity as a significant category of the cultural process emerged during the Enlightenment. The various cultures first encountered during the Age of Discovery were, according to the general understanding of the epoch, not only different realizations of human life but, above all, representations of the early (or primitive) times of the human race. While this stage was idealized on the one hand as a state of freedom and equality, of virtue and simplicity,[2] it was interpreted as the embodiment of rudeness and savagery[3] on the other. This popular and subconsciously fostered attitude subsequently paved the way for the general acceptance of a unilinear and progressional evolutionism that tried to reconstruct the culture of early mankind by means of its survival in present-day cultures. 'Primitive Culture' not only became, as already mentioned, the title of E. B. Tylor's famous book, but also the cornerstone for modern cultural anthropology. Even the *Kulturkreislehre* in the conception of Wilhelm Schmidt, the strongest opponent of the evolutionistic interpretation of the Tylor form, remains for the most part in the grip of this scheme.

Without enlarging now on the concrete features of these theories, we may rephrase the previous question in a slightly modified form: Why should we not abandon altogether the concept of primitive culture and its derivates and redefine the different issues of cultural anthropology without referring to an obso-

2. See the projection of the 'noble savage' in the works of P. Martire (*Decades de Orbe novo*, 1511), B. de las Casas (*Historia de las Indias*, 1561), M. de Montaigne (*Des Cannibales*, 1580), and, J. J. Rousseau (*Essai sur les m œurs*, 1750).

3. The presupposition that peoples who did not conform to European cultural standards were 'savages' and 'primitives' is mirrored in the fact that the term 'primitive' was (and, unfortunately, still is) often used in a pejorative sense. This is even illustrated in the titles of early studies of non-European peoples encountered during the Age of Discovery, e.g., in Lafitau's *M œurs des sauvages américains comparées aux m œurs des premier temps* (1724). The 'primitives' are, as we may read in the French translation of F. Azara's *Voyage dans l'Amérique méridionale* (Vol. II, p. 44): such that 'Ils ne conaissent ni religion, ni culte, ni soumission, ni lois, ni obligations, ni récompenses, ni châtiments'. For a background analysis of this and similar topics *cf.* H. Loiskandl (1966, esp. p. 108 ff). Also, Th. P. van Baaren, (1960, in particular chaps. I and II).

lete scholarly inheritance? The difficulty with this solution, however, is that it runs the risk of overlooking and omitting a highly important point in the conceptual structure of terms that are essentially interrelated with man himself. For such terms as man, humanity, person, history, morality, God, and as we assume, primitivity, are not simply a matter of definition because it is through and in them that culture comes to rest in its search for being and subsistence. From the viewpoint of cultural dynamics, these words are interwoven with the symbolic life of man and mankind in such a way that they enjoy a kind of self-sufficiency which gives expression to the distinct reality of the symbolic itself. Even if their emergence in the consciousness of an epoch is surrounded by tacit presuppositions and prejudices, they bear a genuine meaning of their own because they are fundamentally related to the truth of man in his cultural existence. If we deal with such terms we have to recognize that there is a meaning which has to be traced out rather than dismissed dogmatically. In addition, because such terms are fundamental, no axiological replacement can clear the confusion. On the contrary, an uncritical and anticultural or a-historical complacency would only make matters worse, no matter how logical it seems to be. Consequently, instead of replacing such terms in a nominalistic fashion or of leaving them open, we have to find out the meaning they share and mirror in the process of cultural constitution. We have to get an idea of what they indicate, not only in the context of the restricted consciousness of the specific historical epoch in which they were first used, but also, and especially, in the general context of life and understanding. There they realize a logic of their own and a significance that has to be acknowledged in order to be grasped. We have to understand that there are words which are not empty signs but realities by which we live and through which culture itself maintains its being. They are the facts of cultural reality and have to be seen as such.

1.1 *The Problem of a Protoculture*

Returning to the problem of primitivity, we now can say that this question can no longer be dismissed by a simple abolition of the term primitive, presupposing that there is any probability in the assumption that this term is fundamentally significant and that word and culture are ontologically correlated. Instead we have to inquire about the proper context of this term itself. In order to comply with the demands of an open and unbiased search for cultural realities we thus have to ask: What does culture mean in the first place? In what sense is the idea of primitive culture, in relation to primitivity, originally significant for the meaning of culture in general?

One general feature of culture is indicated by its interrelation with totality. In nearly all attempts to define culture we find phrases that refer to culture as 'complex whole' (Tyler, 1958, p. 1), as 'totality' (Boas, 1938, p. 159), as 'sum total' (Kroeber and Kluckhohn, 1952, p. 43 ff, p. 88 ff), and so forth. A specific clue to the meaning of culture as a totality is given by the history of the word itself. 'Culture' derives from the Latin *cultura*; a word that was used in the context of such activities as the cultivation of the field (*agricultura*), the cultivation of the vine (*cultura vitis*) or the celebration of rites and rituals (*cultura dei, cultus deorum*). Accordingly we may interpret culture as the sign for the presence of that which distinguishes the human mode of being or living from (all) others. It is a symbol for *all* aspects of man's life, or better, of the life of mankind insofar as it concurs with humanity. In short, culture indicates the totality of the human *mode* of life insofar and inasmuch as it is *human*.

The same point can be made with respect to the traditional approaches that connect the total aspect of man's life with his social situation. Man, as a member of society, as a being who is integrated into the social process by education and politics, offers us the cultural point of view. At the same time, however, we become aware that it is not the fact of society as such (which can be discovered among all living beings) that renders man a cultural being but the modality of intersocial processes.[4] Culture emerges where living beings not only live together but also think and speak with one another and thus recognize one another as responsible entities, that is, as persons. The facts of life are transformed into cultural facts the very moment they become bound up with the symbolic dimension of man's existence. The mode of life becomes a mode of culture by entering into the symbolic processes of understanding and communicating or articulation.[5] What man does and says is surpassed and permeated by factors such as learning and teaching, value experience and value realization, agreement and disagree-

4. *Cf.* J. Fabian (1971, p. 26) where he speaks of society as 'a reality realized through communication'.

5. We touch here upon the problems of the philosophy of language which are dealt with by almost all contemporary trends in philosophy. As far as my own views are concerned I am indebted in particular to W. v. Humboldt (1836). See also F. Kainz's comprehensive study on language (1967, especially vols. 2 and 5), and J. Searle (1969).

ment, sympathy and apathy, memory and expectation, questioning and answering, truth and falsity. Culture means to live and to understand, or better, to live by understanding. As such it is the emergence and transformation of nature in and through the *logos* of man; the creative transformation of nature into the world of human existence, action and thought as well as the maintenance of this process. Within this process man becomes a symbol to himself. Even more, he himself turns out to be the most symbolic symbol of all, the situational unity of inwardness and outwardness which, by virtue of this unity, diversifies and unites both the reality of nature and that of culture. In being and becoming a cultural being man enacts a world of symbols and becomes capable of interpreting the world accordingly.

Culture, as a symbol for the totality of human life, includes, of course, all the different aspects of this life, the social as well as the individual, the spiritual or symbolic as well as the material or economic. However, because of the constitutive significance of 'being-with-one-another', culture implies a twofold structure: For man, culture reveals itself under the ontological modality of 'having' in such a way that it presents itself in the modality of 'being'.[6] While culture *is*, it is man who *has* culture. He takes part in it just as he shares the acts and possibilities of his whole life in a given moment. As nature, neither he nor human society, nor any of his deeds and actions, is simply identical with culture, though all he has is his because of culture. Consequently, if we are to avoid an interpretation of culture as illusion or as reality that levels any differentiation and personal responsibility – an interpretation which is equally illusionary – we must understand culture by and through the principle of participation, in which identity and difference are transcendentally united. To understand man in his humanity is tantamount to considering him and what he stands for according to the nature and function of this principle. Thus, it is culture that *makes* man by being *owned* by him.

We can clarify the meaning of these observations by analysing the most simple statement that *man has culture*. Although this statement seems vague and colorless, it nevertheless is the source of a series of highly important consequences which are subsequently verified by what they explain with respect both to the

---

6. For a metaphysical treatment of the categories of being and having, in which it becomes obvious that the problem of culture also includes that of bodily consciousness, see Gabriel Marcel (1951).

factual history and experience of man and to their own theoretical origin. The following points may help to make this clear.

1. Because man shares culture by reason of his humanity, culture becomes the principle binding mankind together. As such it maintains a kind of independence *vis-à-vis* individuals and societies, their cultural completion, as well as their attempts at cultural disintegration. The realization of culture proceeds under the condition of an unlimited completion. There are many cultures, but none of them *is all* that culture *could be*. The fact that man *is* man because he *has* culture reveals the reality of a *cultural difference*. As a result the relationship between the individual and his culture as the culture of mankind is a fractured or broken one. The integrity of culture as the concretion of humanity is bound up by an insurmountable distance. As such culture reveals the unity of finitude and infinity in the situational reality of progression and regression. The idea of an end of culture is a rational limitation that is true as long as it retains itself in the modality of inquiry.

2. On the other hand, when culture is seen from the perspective of interaction and communication, the fact that there are many cultures implies the principle of participation in order to make sense. It shows once more that this principle is fundamental. Consequently none of the existing cultures can be identified with culture as such. There are no strict boundaries between the different realizations of culture, nor is it possible to make a final judgment about cultures. There is the *one culture of mankind*, and this is both distinct from and realized by and in the many cultures of individuals, groups, historical epochs, peoples, which participate in it. As such, culture is always concrete and universal at once.

3. Synthesizing those two lines of reasoning, we can say that the principle of participation with respect to the one culture implies the reciprocity and comprehensibility of different cultures. Culture, as the humanity shared by the individual, the life-community, the society, an epoch, reveals the factual relationship of man to himself under and within the conditions of his situation. Therefore, culture has to be considered as the condition of understanding as well as of politico-historical self-consciousness in general. It enables man to *have* objects, i.e., to know and to understand, and to *realize* action and understanding in having these objects, i.e., to act through conscious interference with the emerging world of cultural objects. The diversity of understandable subjects and objects is mediated by the act of cultural participation. Consequently, a concrete culture as a mode of participation is to be seen as a definitive representation of humanity. As such it

is fundamentally open toward itself (in the sense of cultural and political processes) as well as toward other representations of cultures (in the sense of communication and personalization). Thus, the principle of cultural participation turns out to be both the principle of practical hermeneutics and the condition of theoretical hermeneutics. Comprehension is factually mediated by culture insofar as participation is realized while it is made a problem of culture insofar as participation is to be realized.

4. Because of the principle of participation, culture has to be understood as originating reality; that is, the concrete and the universal cut across and entwine with one another. Paradoxically, culture is both the horizon and the content that gains its features within this horizon. It is a measure as well as the measured. While it arises from the process of what actually is and was (culture as natural process) it points to what should and ought to be. Here the study of culture encounters a necessary feature of each cultural process, namely, the correlation between the implicit and the explicit, between beginning and end. But because neither the culture of the first nor of the last man, nor that of the first and the last society, would be the culture of mankind as such, this correlation is not simply a temporal one. Although the category of temporality cannot be excluded, since it is so intimately bound up with the whole of man's being, the correlation between the implicit and the explicit is not exhausted by temporality alone. Both an overemphasis on time (evolutionism, historicism) and its neglect (functionalism, structuralism) fall short of the universal meaning of culture. Consequently, the structural problem of culture – which necessarily appears, i.e., becomes graspable, on the temporal side of the cultural difference – is the problem of both a universal and morphological history.

5. The reality of culture within the tensions of a morphological history requests a final ramification of the study of culture: On the one hand it asks for something like a *proto-culture*, and on the other hand for the *final culture*.[7] Because it is

7. 'Final culture' is usually known as 'utopia', although it is understood here in a much larger, and, if we take K. Mannheim's definition (1936, p. 173) as a paradigm, more definite sense: 'A state of mind is utopian when it is incongruous with the state of reality within which it occurs.' I am convinced that the arguments around 'utopia' which belong to the larger field of eschatology (the science of the ultimate; or, if we think more in line with the history of ideas, the words about the ultimate) would improve considerably if they were handled in view of a theory of culture that is aware both of the constitutive significance and the logical character of the cultural primum and ultimum. See also M. Plattel (1970, p. 43 ff).

impossible to identify the beginning and the end in concrete terms, both conceptions are philosophical, and therefore they fall properly within the province of
philosophy. But because they are rooted in the empirical process of man's factual
history, they are empirical rather than speculative ideas, and as such, i.e., as
ideas of culture itself, they guide all of our studies in a manner that can be either
formally expressed or silently suppressed. Thus the final evaluation that takes
place in all cultural studies necessarily proceeds in the light of protocultural implications, and of final cultural expectations. Because their idea unites the empirical
and transcendental mode of culture, it is their reality that makes us see and identify the world of particulars with respect to their beginning and end and thus
enables us to know and to act by knowledge.

6. Since they are ideas of culture itself, the protocultural and final cultural
reality and their derivatives share the modality of the one culture. For this reason
they must never be equated with this or that culture. The protoculture as such is
not identical with the culture of any particular people, nor with any particular
instance of their culture. The same must be said about the final culture. For
utopia, as the full realization of a definite ideology, is a contradiction in terms,
even though each ideology is what it is only because of its participation in the
final culture. Similarily we can understand that even in the mode of theoretical
neglect the principles of cultural constitution are still operative. If we see anything
cultural at all, we see it because we are integrated into the play of protocultural
and final cultural conditions, even though none of the things we do see *is* proto-
or final culture. On the contrary, as in case of culture in general, their mode of
being is that of participation insofar as the concept of their genesis, and of
representation insofar as their empirical reality is concerned. If these different
points are considered as they were developed in the course of ascertaining that
man has culture, the question of what primitivity and primitive culture mean can
be given an adequate answer.

Although it is an empirical idea, the concept of protoculture is in itself not an
empirical datum, a kind of general denominator which can be extracted from the
available materials. Rather, it is the all-present beginning that sustains and permeates every cultural action and deed. Consequently the search for it may be
started, and its presence discovered, whenever culture appears, comes into being,
is there. In brief, protoculture (primitive culture) is both a theoretical condition
and a practical necessity that affects the totality of cultural phenomena, including
cultural studies themselves. Its immediate presence within the descriptions of

culture is in one way or another a matter of course. As such it shapes not only the content but also the form of the study of cultural phenomena.

Beginning with the historical fact that scholars considered certain cultures to be primitive, we can assert that the adequate interpretation of primitivity cannot be restricted to a definite set of objective data and their enumerative description. The concept of protoculture points to a meta-empirical reality and demands treatment as such. While the question for the beginning is necessary and fundamental, we have to attune the questioning process and the actual analysis to the logic of the very conception of this beginning (or end). Instead of asking for 'the' protoculture (or 'the' final culture), we must rephrase our question about the beginning and search for those cultural appearances that probably come closest to the protocultural conditions. Moreover, since such appearances are bound up within the morphological genesis of cultural types, the search for protocultural conditions merges with the methodological question of whether there may perhaps be certain cultures that offer us a more or less direct access to the structure and meaning of protoculture. As such they would be cultures which for this very reason revealed a typological structure that could be adequately described by the category of primitivity. Conversely, we can also say that in case such cultures do exist, their description has to proceed primarily along lines that concentrate upon protocultural implications. This approach would also explain why the question about the finality that is immanent in culture – we can also say that protoculture and final culture are the extremes of one and the same whole and unity – can be considered as secondary in the study of such cultures. However, if such a study would end up in identifying the idea of protoculture in a historical here and now, it actually would misapprehend the foundation upon which it is based.[8]

8. Though E. Durkheim, to whom I feel much indebted, has been aware of a significant or, as he says (*cf*. 1967, p. 20, footnote 3), of a 'relative sense' in the term 'primitive', he nevertheless fell victim to this fallacy. His break with contemporary ideas about the origin of religion was not radical enough. While he rejected the idea of 'an absolute beginning', he failed to notice that the root of the problem he was rightly arguing against was not primarily that of the beginning ('the most simple social condition') but usage and use of the term 'absolute'. The same holds true with regard to the Freudian myth of the initial patricide (*cf*. S. Freud, 1913, IV, 5), which was supposed to account for the beginning of culture in psychoanalytical terms. Freud himself does not disregard the fact that his 'report' of the patricide cannot be identified in a strict manner. But though one might agree with him about the meaninglessness of precision and certainty in this matter, one should and must not drop the question about the logical character of the 'indefiniteness' (*Unbestimmtheit*) that inheres this account.

This methodological and typological approach can be justified for two reasons. First, the idea of protoculture sheds light upon the data of this cultural type. Therefore, in order to comply with the scientific ideal of clarification, we have to proceed along those lines in case this cultural type does exist. The second reason concerns the conditions of cultural studies in general. Since the implicit and explicit dimensions are fundamental for the making and meaning of culture, and since interpretation and understanding are in themselves cultural realizations, they are always guided by one or the other of these two poles. However, the less one reflects on this guidance, the more it becomes subject to historical and ideological distortions. As the development of ideas shows, there is nothing worse than a study that is unaware of its premises and sources of evaluation. Thus a reflective integration of these poles is imperative for the sake of truth and objectivity. If modern man is to realize his very possibilities he has to search for the protocultural dimension of his being and for those empirical circumstances or situations which permit him an optimal realization of this task.

1.2 *Criteria of Primitivity*

If we grant the possibility of a cultural type that as a whole reflects the proto-cultural conditions more comprehensively than others, and which, for this reason, could be addressed as primitive culture, we must then ask for the criteria that permit us to speak of primitivity. In addition to the logical implication of our thesis concerning culture, this is necessary to delineate the scope both of the study itself and of the method used to study particular phenomena. Its validity, like the validity of every thesis, must be justified in and through the process of its realization.

The traditional criterion for the primitiveness of a culture has been lack of development. Economy, society and the symbolic culture were believed to be poorly developed, in a word, uncivilized and unspecialized. While we have already indicated the theoretical conditions under which it makes sense to speak of primitive culture(s), we will now examine this thesis by referring to two concrete examples with which we shall deal more intensively later in this study: They are the rain-forest culture of the Bambuti-Pygmies in the former Belgian Congo (Zaïre) and the arctic culture of the Eskimos. If we compare both cultures, and especially if we consider the economic situation, we become easily aware that they are not only quite different but also that the latter shows highly specialized features. When measured against these examples the interpretation and definition of development as the emergence of complexity and specialization, though theoretically correct, cannot be directly recognized in the pattern of these cultures. Obviously, either there is no primitivity at all,[9] or it has a somewhat different meaning.

In order to overcome this dilemma between theory and empirical data, we have to adopt a more functional view. We have to take into consideration that culture is not simply a kind of superstructure but the all-pervading otherness of man's natural life. The principle of participation which requires the independent character of the cultural dimension as such relies in this respect on constitutive, and in this sense, pre-cultural factors which are neither identical with the concrete person or personal reality for with an actual culture. Nevertheless they are real inasmuch as the process of cultural dynamics needs them in the objectivity of its constitution. These factors, which may be considered as the elementary units of the cultural process, can be seen in the demands of biological life, of the environment, and of the necessary nodal points in the social life – such as age, sex, neighborhood, kinship, disposition, emotionality, fantasy. They can also be seen in the demands of the symbolic life as expressed in phenomena like play, law, custom, language, consciousness and living for the sake of life. Their interplay within the uniting reality of the human situation constitutes culture with respect to its making in the concrete. Consequently if we ask for the criteria of primitivity we have to do it in the context of these elementary units. Accordingly we may apply the category of primitivity to that stage of cultural dynamics where those elementary units that are necessary for the cultural whole to come into being can be said to interact initially.

According to this point of view, primitivity has at least three different facets. First, it will be encountered as *primary simplicity* (with a possible secondary specialization[10]) with respect to biological and social needs. Secondly, we have to see it under the premise of *optimal and effective adaptation*. And finally, we have

9. In order to indicate the difference between a principle and its realization (*principium/ principiatum*), it seems appropriate to distinguish between 'primitivity' and 'primitiveness'. Thus primitivity here is understood as the condition that makes possible the apparent primitiveness of a culture. The latter might be understood positively as well as negatively, depending on the mode and the intensity of the realization of primitivity.

10. The distinction between primary and secondary specialization is related to a typological differentiation of themes which may either change or vary. If we examine the functional and structural process of social, poetic, technical and other themes, we can distinguish between funda-

to understand it as *total interrelation* with respect to the symbolic culture and the members of the group. The theoretical concept of simplicity is thus, empirically speaking, by no means a matter of poverty and absence of development (or even underdevelopment). Its meaning depends rather on the part of culture about which we are speaking and covers the whole scale from simple lack of specialization to complexity.

The usefulness and actual applicability of this theory of primitivity becomes clear if we confront it with the Bambuti and Eskimo culture. In both these cultures primary simplicity is characteristic for the accomplishment of the biological needs and demands. Food and shelter are not yet embedded into secondary systems of social stratification, which have to be observed in order to fulfill these primary needs. The society works largely on the basis of most simple conditions like the division of labor according to age and sex and the organization of mutual dependence in line with the fundamental demands of subsistence, child-rearing, and old age. There is no independent political superstructure. However, there are many secondary specializations, such as tools and techniques, especially in the world of the Eskimos. The complexity of the symbolic culture, due to a more or less complete interrelation of all one is conscious of, is also a common fact. Language, religion, law, are attuned to the experiences of their world. Finally optimal and effective adaptation is well corroborated by the fact that both cultures have survived in an environment that would be deadly for others, unless they either brought their own environment along or they adopted similar patterns of behavior.

If we resume the argument of the previous reflections we can say that the reality of the protoculture is not just a matter of historical or archaeological facts. On the contrary, it is present wherever and whenever culture *begins* to exist. In this sense we have to think of it not outside the field of the empirically given, even though we must not identify it with any concrete situation. Such situations are always both beginning and end, depending on how we look at them. Thus, if we are to speak logically about the idea and reality of the protoculture, we have

---

mental forms of differentiation (primary specialization) and more accidental ones (secondary specialization). There are changes that concern the whole of an existing pattern, and there are variations that affect the particulars and the details of a given pattern. The Australians, for instance, did not turn from a subpolitical to a political structure of social organization (which would have been a matter of primary specialization) although they developed a very complicated social system on the subpolitical level (secondary specialization).

to do it in such a way that we understand it on the one hand as the theoretical symbol of our search for the beginning, as a cipher for the most fundamental need of man to participate in the beginning of his own being and in that of others. On the other hand we have to think of it as a theoretical postulate whose empirical reality can be reached only by approximation. Theoretical postulation and empirical approximation belong together in such a way that the synthesis of both is marked by a transcendental difference[11] that enables us to coordinate the conditions of culture in general with the idea of a protoculture – i.e., to speak of the criteria of primitivity – while it forbids us to take the empirical concretion of these conditions in particular cultures as protocultural reality. As has already been said above, the empirical mode of the protoculture is that of representation; or, since this representative mode is marked by internal or structural correlation, we would better say, of analogous representation. Thus, if we speak of the empirical concretion of the protocultural conditions, we have to do it on a typological basis and with the expectation that the typological unity that results from this proto-cultural presence is marked by a thoroughgoing analogy.

So far we have shown that the protocultural presence, presupposing that it is treated as such, can readily be confirmed with respect to the biological, environ-mental and social situation, even if the entrance of the respective interaction into the cultural process is by no means an unequivocal affair. But can it also be con-firmed with respect to the symbolic data, and in particular to religion? There can be no doubt that religion must be seen within the context of culture. But is it possible to trace the emergence of religion to elementary units that have their irrefutable function in the initial constitution of culture? And if so, what are these elementary units or patterns of primitive religion? Are they only psychological needs, a modification of the biological, economic, or social conditions in the

11. The term 'transcendental difference' has been coined with reference to Kant's conception of the 'transcendental ego'. While reflecting upon the generalization process that marks the con-ceptualization of sense-perceptions, we discover a different meaning of universality if we turn to this performance and the reality of consciousness as it appears in it. While we know of objects, this knowing itself turns out to be 'something else'. It withdraws itself into the anonymity of an affir-mation that consists of the negation of this 'something else'. In other words, if we speak of a 'transcendental difference' we are reminded of the 'fact' that reality is not restricted to what we see and feel, but also present when and because we know by reflection. Thus, to the extent that knowledge has to begin with sense perception and to adjust to the logic of this beginning, it has also to take up with the 'workings' of transcendental reality and to follow its logic. For a further elaboration of these questions see E. Heintel (1958) and H. Krings (1964). Also J. Habermas (1967, p. 95 ff).

consciousness of man? Or are they truly autonomous and independent realities that contribute in their own way to the bare minimum of cultural existence and to the meaning of humanity?

These questions cannot be answered by a mere analysis of concepts because the existence or nonexistence of elementary units is directly concerned with life and fact. On the other hand there is an incontestable point of departure, if we truly try to answer these questions. There can be no doubt that the elementary units, no matter what they are, belong to a life that is realized through culture. Therefore, we must turn to the analysis of culture and see if this analysis enables us to get a better understanding of these questions as well as of the meaning of proto-culture with which they are interrelated. This analysis takes on all the more significance because not only the study of religion in general is dependent on it but also the actual and original truth of religion itself. If it should turn out that religion is only a secondary phenomenon, reducible to non-religious elementary units, then its truth would be only relative: The truth of religion would be a necessity for man and society at a certain stage of their development, but, in the name of truth, subject to rejection in an entirely humanized (or culturized) situation.[12] In this case the study of religion in primitive cultures would have to proceed in such a way that the description of the phenomena would point (at least in its final outcome) to the non-existence of religion. Or, to put the matter differently, the non-existence of religion would become the premise for evaluating what are improperly called religious phenomena in primitive cultures. At any rate, before we can answer these questions we have to deepen our understanding of culture especially with respect to the meaning and function of both the primum of the symbolic culture in general and that of religion in particular, even though the latter can only be anticipated hypothetically at this point of the investigation.

---

12. The concept of truth in this context is not that of conformity or functional isomorphy between the world of concepts and that of objects but that of relational proximity. Man as a cultural being integrates natural otherness in and through the modes of consciousness and thus becomes subject to a process of self-realization and 'illocutionary' (Austin) truth. Because and inasmuch as he is, he is subject to truth, while the problem of truth emerges in and through his being, assuming a variety of forms and modalities. For the same reason falsity is not understood only as a misinterpretation of phenomena in their objective setting but also as the estrangement and alienation that become manifest when biological, emotional, social and intellectual needs and demands lose, or are distorted in, their symbolic significance and value in the constitution of the human person as the 'concrete' universality of culture.

1.3 *Culture and Reflection*

Among the different topics of scientific interest, culture holds an exceptional position. For not only is it an object of scientific studies, but these studies themselves become a factor in the process of cultural realization. Furthermore, the kind of existence or reality possessed by culture is not comparable to the familiar modalities of being. It is neither real, as a stone is real, nor is it ideational and intentional, as is a concept or value. Culture is neither the sum total of all cultural objects, nor is it identical with the actual culture of an individual or group. Nevertheless, we are able to speak about culture and to know that this speaking is in itself an act of cultural realization. Culture is thus no empty word. On the contrary, the fact of speaking about culture reveals culture as the condition of the possibility to speak at all. And, whatever culture may be, it certainly exhibits circular patterns that bring it forth as a constitutive horizon, i.e., a horizon yielding content and structure at once, as was said with regard to the principle of participation in culture. That there is this horizon is ultimately due to the cultural difference we discovered in the same context. Because of its universal validity, being both immanent and transcendent, the latter corresponds with the conditions for becoming operative as a constitutive horizon wherein the empirically given is transformed into the otherness of cultural being while culture itself appears as the *hic et nunc* constellation of things natural and pre- and meta-cultural. In other words, since the factual character of the cultural horizon is constitutively caught by the cultural difference, we can also say that this difference becomes significant as the principle both of connection and of understanding. As such it relates actual cultures and cultural objects to one another by giving them their actuality as participated realities or cultural representations. In its continuing and durative presence as the difference between *culture* and *cultures*, it also provides the conditions for the possibility of understanding, since it is simultaneously both identity (culture as being) and difference (culture as having), and thus, not less than the inexorable and comprehensive presupposition of any knowledge by which we have objects without being identical with them. Since it is impossible to speak about culture as a definable, temporal entity, this statement is not a contradiction, as it may appear at first. When seen in the light of cultural differences, it is the one culture of mankind that connects whatever is human by temporal and metatemporal bonds. Yet, at the same time, this one culture of mankind is concrete only in the uniqueness of persons and their relations, or as we may also say, in singularized and differentiated entities. In the togetherness of both these aspects, the human being becomes capable of understanding as well as of interacting. While 'culture determines culture' it is man who is free and determined at the same time. Moreover, what seems to be a contradiction in terms becomes intelligible as the presupposition of the genesis and usage of just such terms and whatever is achieved through them. Because man has culture, he is capable of speaking about it. But while he speaks about culture, he is also realizing it. Within this circle we are what we can be: Beings that encounter a world in a variety of attitudes, thoughts, and actions.[13]

When we conceive of culture in terms of identity and difference, we can say that the former implies realization while the latter demands ideation. United in the cultural difference, however, both movements are interwoven with each other in such a way that we have to comprehend them as principles of being as well as of understanding. Through them culture comes into being. Because of them cultural beings can and must live by understanding. That, in turn, implies that the study of culture and all that is essential for it (its religious elements, for example) must be established within the horizon of these two principles, which synthesize empirical data as reality with their ideational structure as phenomenality. Only against this background of existing transcendentality (see Heintel, 1968, p. 178 or 219 ff) do description and interpretation become possible while we can understand them as realizations of culture as such.

According to the operational extension of these two principles of connection and understanding two different circles of interpretation or hermeneutics have to be distinguished in order to circumscribe both the theoretical and the practical fields of cultural processes. As such, they belong to all the branches of cultural studies. The first circle, which I would like to call the *intercultural circle of hermeneutics*, has to bridge the inter- or intra-cultural gap as far as the empirically given is concerned. Its counterpart on the ideational side is the circle of man's philosophical *weltanschauung* as a preconceived understanding of the world, its beginning and its end – an understanding that is continually enriched by experience. The second circle, which could be called the *inner-cultural circle of*

13. It seems that this ambivalence of the term culture not only explains why all ideas of metalanguages (as scientific tools) are nevertheless dependent on the so called ordinary (or pre-scientific) languages, but also why the human situation holds an irreplaceable priority in all cultural studies.

hermeneutics, has to bridge the different facts, deeds and actions in the unity of each human being or person with respect to the group's culture on the actual side. Its ideational counterpart is the systematic or theoretical circle; it is philosophy which, as the systematic reflection on the actual world, acts in search for and in interdependence on universal meaning and significance. Through the immanent creativity of the principles of cultural constitution, both circles are related to one another in a process of mutual transformation, which subsequently can be described as a process of both historical and 'creative hermeneutics' (see Eliade, 1967d, p. 26; 1967e, p. 505). The idea of historical and creative hermeneutics indicates that the first requirement of all cultural studies is the dialectical and dialogical demand for self-restriction, openness, communication and totality. If we reinterpret this in relation to the two circles of hermeneutics we can also say:

1. The intercultural circle of hermeneutics means that we have to start our investigations by basing them on, and developing them in, our own experiences and *weltanschauung*. We cannot, for instance, study the religion of another culture without referring to a minimum of religious consciousness of our own. We have to do it, however, in such a way that the interrelating process continues in a permanent and mutually limiting oscillation. Thus a permanent awareness of difference and distance becomes essential for the process of knowledge and understanding. As such it becomes hermeneutically significant. Accordingly we may speak here of the implication of a *hermeneutic difference and distance*.

2. The inner-cultural circle of hermeneutics means that each cultural fact has to be seen in the context of the whole culture in which it is functional. I cannot, for instance, take language or religion and separate them from the other 'parts' of my own or another culture, or from the whole context of interpretation. The inner-cultural circle insists, so to speak, on *the principle of completeness*. However, since the study of culture is always based on limited experiences, sources and reports, the principle of completeness merges with the idea of the hermeneutic difference.[14] As such any fact of culture becomes a sign for the material incom-

---

14. I am thinking here of the problem of an inner-systematic verification as it comes forth in the conception of 'learned ignorance' (Nicholas of Cusa). If we take the Socratic principle of not-knowing beyond the realm of modesty it becomes both a critique of intellectual endeavors and an impetus that presents continuously the idea of the whole as the only goal that is worth to be known. As Hegel puts it (1952, p. 21): 'The true is the whole.' But if we speak of the whole, we should also know that its concept is not this whole in itself (1952, p. 16). See also W. Dupré (1962).

pleteness of our studies, which in its reflective presentation is completed by the formal or ideational totality of an anticipated achievement. However outstanding a report, description, or study may be,[15] it retains its truth only to the extent that it is open to communication and critique, that is, only to the extent that it recalls the ideal of completion within the very process of its development.[16]

If we follow the logic of these reflections we can say that it is the prerogative of a cultural being to 'live' in these circles of hermeneutics. Yet, there still are two crucial and interrelated questions that have to be answered before we can 'work' with this insight. First, there is the question of how to enter the circles of hermeneutics reflectively. And secondly, how are we to find the actual crossing from one circle into the other in a way which will enable us to reach, above all, the primary conditions of the cultural process particularly with respect to its symbolic outcome? Perhaps the best way to answer these questions is by analyzing the concrete situation of one person speaking to another.

If persons speak with one another two factors constitutive for the process of communication and for the cultural meaning of this act are evident. One is the

---

15. See also P. Radin's (1950) distinction between 'report' and 'interpretation' with regard to the ethnological sources, which points to the same problem. The fact that both are very often imperceptibly interwoven in the ethnological sources reveals them as ideal types that in reality reflect the polarity of subjectivity and objectivity. Thus, it is not through the actual distinction of these types that we achieve truth, but through such an awareness of both aspects that this awareness becomes itself a methodological principle.

16. For a further elaboration of these problems see also the last chapter of J. J. Waardenburg (1969), especially p. 327. It should be noted that the language we are using when approaching and speaking about culture and religion is not that of the sciences, even if their methods may emerge during the process of investigation. Cultural phenomena and their linguistic representations, especially the term 'culture' itself, cannot be adequately defined in the same way as mathematical concepts can be. The terms ('figures', 'constants') we use are, and must be, guidelines rather than fixed signs; or, to speak more positively, they have to be understood and handled as conjectural terms. The idea of 'conjectural terms' as a logical category was introduced into the history of logic by Nicholas of Cusa (see Nikolaus von Kues, 1964–67, 2: 3 ff.). By integrating the inevitable uncertainties of understanding as an essential principle of self-consciousness into the logical process (*cf.* also footnote 14), Nicholas of Cusa outlined a new logic reflecting in the modes of its constitution the differentiations of world and knowledge. According to its construction principle this logic becomes conjectural when it deals with the final condition or truth of man and world. It does not define by negation – an approach which, when strictly handled, can only lead to the well-known night where all cows become dark – but by pointing from various angles to the structural centers of the envisaged reality. Negation is no end in itself, but a means of affirmation. Instead of pigeonholing the world, conjectural logic finds its *raison d'être* in discovering the structure of the world in and through a movement in which the logical and ontological idea of totality is always in the making.

factor of language, the other that of space and time. While language withdraws into the inwardness of man and the experience of consciousness, time and space retract to the world of visible and tangible things. Yet the factor of space and time also belongs to language in its external manifestation and thus gives us a positive indication that both factors are to be connected. The inwardness of man as a constitutive factor of the concrete human situation appeared already in the inter-cultural circle of hermeneutics as the prerequisite minimum of personal experiences as a condition of the possibility of cultural studies in general. However, since it partakes in the fundamental structure of the given, it cannot be treated as an isolated problem. Instead, we have to see it in connection with the quest for the methodological and cognitive value of the visible and tangible objects as the temporal and spatial facet of a situation where persons speak with one another. Consequently, our first problem is not the autonomy of the inward but the question of how we can find a reliable way to its structure within and through the context of the visible and tangible.

As shown by the extension of knowledge through inventions such as script, paper, telephone, tape recorder, and many others, the dimensions of space and time have to be considered primary necessities in the cultural process. Therefore we may ask, is time, or better is history as the fulfillment of time, a means for structuring the actual connection of the hermeneutical circles? Does the historical method offer genuine access to the particular reality of anything cultural, especially if it is combined with a method concerned with the spatial conditions of culture? These methods which describe the emergence of various phenomena according to their genesis in space and time certainly offer many objective facts. But the facts alone are not culture, just as the appearance of religion in written dogmas is not religion. On the contrary, the study of history realizes the idea of comprehension as the anticipation of its meaning only when it understands itself as culture-history and, thus, becomes a study of culture. The same can be said about a predominantly functional or functionalistic approach, which, different from the proximity of history to time, shows a definite proneness to the spatial dimension. Nevertheless, the categories of space and time remain necessary conditions for the cultural process as well as for its understanding (in space and time). We can neither separate them from the cultural data nor from the methodology by which we try to determine our approach to these data. We therefore must not look for time and space in their most complex syntheses of culture-time and space, but in their most direct and objective manifestation.

This synthesis is neither the biological, the social, nor the strictly intentional articulation of a given culture, where the interrelation of these aspects accounts for what they are in particular, but is rather the practical or economic dimension of the cultural process. Since work is an immediate datum of practical consciousness, we can describe it as the first synthesis of the world with the human mind or logos, presupposing that the context of this description is marked by the idea of initial cultural completion. Within this situation an independent environment is turned into a living space, in which the instrumental process of survival (work) concretizes and reflects the primary conditions of its origination. We thus can say that work may serve as a gateway to elementary units of the cultural process and, insofar as these units are operative in either circle of hermeneutics, as introduction into and as a bridge between these circles. For the fact that work is connected with the survival of speaking beings enables us to interpret it as a sign of basic completion and therefore of truth as far as the idea of primitive culture is concerned.

It is important to resume here the reflections on the concept of an independent environment (as a criterion of primitivity), because the whole argument depends on it. A general feature of our technological culture is its relative independence from the natural environment. Equipped with the appropriate instruments, modern man is able to live even in an environment like the Arctic Zone. Unlike the Eskimo, however, he does not rely upon natural resources, but on his technological world. Although the instruments of this world are manufactured on this earth (that is, in connection with an originally independent environment), they nevertheless shape a kind of second or culturized nature with respect to the Arctic environment. For the Eskimo, on the contrary, environment and culture are so interrelated that work not only forces the environment to release its scanty means for survival but forms an integral aspect of what we call Eskimo culture. For people belong to the technological culture, work has lost this character of immediacy. It is the company, the union, the interests of peace and war, and finally the whole technological civilization that enables him to survive under conditions set forth to a good extent by this whole. The objects of freedom and slavery are not so much the facts of nature but the complex realities of the cultural environment. In a word, there is a basic difference in the meaning of work in these two types of culture. While the fundamental character of work gets more or less lost in the complexity of a technological civilization – we do all kinds of jobs to make a living by buying things with the money we earn –

it exercises an exceptional function in a culture that is built up by optimal adaptation to an independent environment. This difference in the character of work shows indeed a relation that points clearly to the primary interaction of elementary units when measured against the criterion of primitivity. As such it justifies the concept of *primitive cultures* as a typological title for those empirical realities that are marked by this sort of work.

Because the economic situation of a culture is generally accessible, and because the optimal adaptation to an independent environment can be unequivocally determined, the analysis of work becomes particularly significant for the meaning and the study of the protocultural conditions and, thus, as we have already indicated, for the study of culture in general. In this sense we can also say that the investigation of the economic situation can no longer be considered as a by-product of cultural studies. On the contrary, we must see it as the key that opens for us the door to a genuine understanding of the cultural whole and the preconditions of its development in space and time. In other words, it is essential for a theory of culture as the necessary presupposition of the description and interpretation of cultural data. The optimal adaptation to different and independent environments is specified by variable economic systems. The natural and objectively verifiable differentiations that accompany these systems can thus be used as an indirect parameter in our search for elementary units in other cultural fields.

As we know from the data provided by cultural anthropology work will mainly be absorbed by survival and cultural continuation when seen within an independent environment. As such it gives access to the whole of culture and not just to the one or other aspect of cultural reality. If we contrast this general observation with the fact of variation both with regard to the economical systems and the independent environments we have to conclude that the interrelation between the cultural whole and this respective type of work must be of an order that cannot be reduced to a unilineal scheme of dependence (as K. Marx has tried to do). We thus can expect that an understanding of work as a cultural phenomenon may serve as a device that enables us to sift fundamental- or elementary units from the context of their own effects, presupposing again that we remain within the framework of protocultural conditions. As such the analysis leads us straight to the idea and reality of primitive culture in particular and cultural dynamics and constitution in general. It provides the formal framework in which we can recognize the philosophical premises as well as the empirical data that are to be confirmed and interpreted.

There can be no doubt that this result answers the question about the herme-neutical circles of culture and the cultural studies, even though it must be granted that no *a priori* constructions can be given. On the contrary, the quest for the *a priori* has been made the subject of our reflections in correlation with the mean-ing and reality of culture as such. In addition we become aware that the question about primitive culture is more than an historical and ideological problem. It is indeed a fundamental problem that has to be treated a such, and which, sooner or later, has to come forth in the analysis of cultural data. Moreover, since we are dealing here with the whole of culture, none of its many facets including religion as a particular articulation of man can be excluded from this process nor must they be excluded methodologically speaking.

Before we close these deliberations there still should be a word on primitive religion as a problem of its own. So far we proceeded from the premise that truth is neither a superstructure nor a kind of gnoseological net that can be spread over the cultural reality. In the light of what has been said, we can add that it is the original and primary meaning of cultural reality itself. In this sense it may even be added that the protoculture is indeed identical with the truth of the beginning in each cultural activity, however deficient or complete. All the factors and constitutive units of the cultural process depend on the reciprocal interrelation between the beginning and the end, between the phenomena and their truth. Accordingly we can say that primitive religion has to be understood as the truth of religion with respect to its initial integration into the cultural process. It is a theoretical postulate for which we have to search in any cultural situation. At the same time we have to add, however, that the methodological organization of this search must look for situations that permit us to do so in an optimal manner. Where these situations are to be found cannot be determined *a priori*, although it may be expected that in the event of cultures whose typo-logical structure reflects the conditions of primitivity, these cultures may indeed comply with this methodological request. At any rate we have here the reason why this study turns to the analysis of primitive cultures. Whether the religious data of the cultures we are going to study will shed light upon the meaning of primitive religion, or whether we can also talk of primitive religions in a typolog-ical sense has to be seen. What matters is the theoretical assumption that each cultural situation is fundamentally open to this question. In this sense we have to see that the study of primitive religion can adequately be defined only if we conceptualize it within a larger horizon of reality and truth. Or, if we integrate the significance of the cultural situation into its human and historical background, we can also say that a practical (and not a theoretical) functionalism has to be adopted for the study of the empirical data, including those of primitive cultures, while a universal (and not an empirical) humanism has to be outlined through and for their interpretation. If one of these two poles is ignored, the goal to outline the meaning of primitive religion turns either into a constructive or an ideological systematization; it ends either by arrogantly twisting the phenomena, or by abusing them for political and ideological purposes.

Practical functionalism, on the one hand, indicates a pre-theoretical attitude rather than a well-established method and theory. It implies the acceptance of each phenomenon, and in particular of each religious situation, as a cultural phenomenon bearing an original meaning of its own. This does not mean that the social and historical background and context of such situations is not to be investigated or ignored. It signifies only that the theory or the interpretaton of facts and data must be developed primarily from the cultural situation, to which one has access through work as an objective manifestation of meaning and truth within the categories of space and time. As such, however, work must be understood as a phenomenon that permits us to consider such symbols as language, cult and play as autonomous and concomitant modalities of its coming into being.

Universal humanism, on the other hand, is an expression of the fundamental human truth, which dwells within man's existence as a natural being. Thus, each culture has enough values of its own to be taken seriously on the level of theoretical constitution.[17] Actual and fictitious deficiencies, especially in the religious field, are finally capable of explanation only in the light of a certain philosophy, whose presupposition are in themselves factors in the making of a cultural situation, and thus, already more than a matter of abstract knowledge and theory.

17. To take a culture seriously is an ethical principle that is needed for the constitution of the human person as ethical center and horizon. In addition, it has epistemological or methodological implications. This is obvious if we consider the disdain and discrimination that result from a failure to take culture seriously, for when this happens prejudices to alien cultures raise basic obstacles for entering into and coordinating the hermeneutical circles of cultural studies. 'As long as one does not take other people seriously, one considers patronization to be justified, and that means to colonize them in a spiritual and mental sense' (P. Schebesta, 1967, p. 52.). While one rejects the ethical implication of discourse, the latter unawares turns into an issue of ethics. See also G. W. Allport (1958, pp. 3 ff., 161 ff.).

The consequences of these reflections for the present study on religion in primitive cultures can be seen in two ways. First there is the need for describing a sufficient series of religious situations, whose cultural set-up permits us to speak of primitive cultures. The second is the necessity for reducing inter-cultural presuppositions to a minimum by a process of comparison, while simultaneously describing the inner-cultural horizon to a maximum degree. The idea of protocultural conditions may thereby serve as both the principle that provides the condition for the possibility of this analysis and the aim for which we ultimately reach. Both these paths of thought remain, of course, a tentative and circular enterprise, since their truth and verification depend on the stringency they possess in clarifying the phenomena as well as the comprehension they achieve with regard to the universal meaning of man and reality.

According to the preceding considerations we can summarize the present stage of this study as follows: Because of the cultural significance of work in general and that of work in an independent environment in particular we are justified in speaking of primitive cultures, presupposing we do not lose sight of the theoretical character of the concept of primitive culture. Accordingly, if we study religion in these cultures, we cannot do so without the search for primitive religion in order to comply with the particular situation of primitive cultures and their phenomena. We thus are expecting that the ethnoreligious data provided by these cultures are methodologically significant in particular with regard to the philosophical postulate of primitive religion. In other words, by relating the analysis of the empirical data to their constitutive genesis in the horizon of culture in general, the interpretation should try to include the required verification of an objective description as a principle of its procedure. Consequently the ethnoreligious data have to be examined in accordance with the general rules of cultural studies, which are focused by the inter- and inner-cultural circle of hermeneutics. However, before entering on further preliminary questions such as the typology of primitive cultures and the interpretation of the religious reality, it is appropriate to give greater concreteness to the preceding considerations by sketching the history of theories on primitive religion and the study of religion in primitive cultures. This takes on all the more importance, since the consciousness of religion in one's own culture is not only unavoidable but also indispensable for a universal understanding. The tendency to objectify this consciousness in actual theories at least points to what they were in their existential and culture constituting significance. Since the history of these studies is generally marked by a misapprehension of primitive religion which resulted from disregarding the difference between culture and cultures, and which, in consequence, identified the protocultural conditions with the empirical data of particular cultures, it seems to be reasonable to speak at once of primitive religion and religions, i.e., of primitive religion(s).

2. HISTORICAL SKETCH OF THE STUDY ON PRIMITIVE RELIGION(S)

Ever since the Scholastic theologians introduced the idea of a natural and a super-natural world in order to preserve the cultural identity of the Christian universe, 'natural man' has been a topic of special interest for generations of philosophers and theologians. Especially during the Enlightenment, when new stress was laid upon the meaning of reason and nature, the expression 'natural religion' turned into a kind of magic spell. We need mention only such titles as J. Toland's *Christianity Not Mysterious* (1696) and M. Tyndal's *Christianity As Old As Creation, or The Gospel, A Republication of the Religion of Nature* (1730). As a consequence of such interests, the study of primitive peoples received a definite impetus. Largely rationalistic and a-historical in outlook and intention, however, it did not stimulate an unprejudiced interpretation of primitive cultures but was concerned rather with the ideal image of the beginning (Montaigne, Rousseau, Chateaubriand, and others), or with the horror of uncivilized forms of behavior (Bodin, Hobbes, Vico, Kant, and others) as has been indicated above. In any case, 'primitive', or better non-Western, cultures became a theoretical hunting ground for allegedly empirical theories concerning man's condition and religion. As a result, the comparative study of religion which started about the beginning of the nineteenth century[18] dealt with religion in 'primitive cultures' for two reasons. In the first place, data concerning the newly discovered cultures de-manded a response from scholars. In the second place, however, there were the ideological interests of the age. Accordingly, the study of non-Western cultures was seen to be both an extension of knowledge of mankind (comparable with

18. See W. Hurd, *A New Universal History of the Religious Rites, Ceremonies, and Customs of the Whole World: A Complete and Impartial View of all the Religions in the Various Nations of the Universe. Both Antient (sic) and Modern*, London 1788. (The Dutch translation 'Oude en Tegenwoordige Staat en Geschiedenis van oude Godsdiensten van de Schepping af tot op den teegenwoordigen Tijd' dates of 1781 ff.). Also, C. Meiners, *Allgemeine kritische Geschichte der Religionen*, 1806/07.

that of the earth) and a way to 'prove' what was actually a cultural evidence, that is, the superiority of Western culture in the development of man. Especially after Darwin expounded his theory of evolution, these tendencies received a new impetus. Consequently, the history of the study of primitive religion has been from the very beginning also a history of ideologies – a kind of mythological narrative that came into being as the result of the joint efforts of Western scholars. Philosophical questions about the beginning are combined and mixed with empirical problems concerning the actual state of affairs. The theoretical impulse concurs with the mythological need for cultural self-identity in the apparent neutrality of 'scientific' language. Significantly enough, the theories concerning primitive religion did not begin with the analysis of nonliterate cultures but with the newly discovered documents of India and the Near East. This fact alone would not have mattered much, of course, if a strict distinction had been made between the speculative and the empirical question. But that there is such a non-distinction is part of the problem.

2.1 *Nature Mythology and Pan-Babylonism*

The pioneer scholars of the Indo-European languages, and later those of the Babylonian and Assyrian traditions, did not deal with primitive cultures as we understand them today. Nevertheless, by referring to these cultures, they developed theories that were intended to cover the entire picture of the beginning and development of religion. This attitude becomes understandable when we take into consideration that the age attributed to mankind did not exceed a few thousand years. Today we know more about these matters. If we take the figures provided by paleontology, the theories that were built upon the assumption of a very limited extension of history become necessarily obsolete. On the other hand, if we want to understand the questions about primitive religion, we have to know something of the mental climate in which the respective questions were raised. Hence, at least some of the main traits of these theories must be mentioned.

According to the scholars of the Indian traditions (Vedas), the origin of religion was to be sought in the impressions that natural phenomena made upon man. The mythological figures were thought to be personifications of natural objects. The impressive manifestations of nature stimulated the personifying fantasy of man. The primary stage of religion was not due to the religious nature of man, or to the 'need of the human heart', as O. Müller expressed it in his *Prolegomena zu einer wissenschaftlichen Mythologie* (1825), but to man's elementary capability of seeing personal figures in the impersonal phenomena of his surroundings. What finally led to the formation of religion was, thus, the elaboration of a nature mythology and the veneration of the respective figures. The beginning of religion was an anthropomorphic polytheism, with a predominance of such phenomena as the sun (M. Müller), the sky (Ch. Ploix), thunderstorm, lightning, rain (A. Kuhn), and fire (Regnaud).

According to Max Müller,[19] who worked indefatigably in developing the new discipline of comparative religion, mythologies were due to a 'disease of thought', that is, to the inability of early man to distinguish between concrete and abstract meanings. By thinking in language he thus fell victim to the seduction of his very language. Though the mythologies were first concentrated on the sun (solar myth), they became distorted through the course of history when language forgot itself. Due to the infantile 'disease of language' the original meaning of words was lost. What was first only a name, *nomen*, turned into a godhead, *numen*, and the mythology that had been associated with them became corrupted.

Max Müller was, however, too much of a scholar and a romanticist that he should not have tried other ways to approach the origin of religion. Perhaps inspired by the philosophy of Kant (see his translation of Kant's *Critique of Pure Reason*, 1881, available today from Doubleday), he accepted a more theosophical and psychological form of religion. In this respect the mythological figures should be understood as the expression of a deep longing for infinity which enables man to apprehend the infinite under different names and under various disguises. In the beginning there was, strictly speaking, no polytheism, but only henotheism. When people turned to one of the mythological deities (theism), this deity or godhead became the only (*hen, henos*) God during the moment and act of worship.

In opposition to the Indo-European specialists, but without offering truly new ideas, the scholars of the religions of the Near East emphasized, as F. Dupuis had already done in *The Origin of All Cults* (1794), sidereal phenomena, and among

---

19. See *Chips from a German Workshop* (1876); *Introduction to the Science of Religion* (1873); *Hibbert Lectures on the Origin and Growth of Religion as Illustrated by the Religions of India* (1878); *Natural Religion* (1889); *Contributions to the Science of Mythology* (1897). It seems to me that M. Müller's view of mythology is strongly dependent on G. Hermann, *Über das Wesen und die Behandlung der Mythologie*, Leipzig 1819.

them especially the moon, in the early formation of religion (E. Siecke). In addition to their pan-lunar assumptions, such men as H. Winkler, A. Jeremias, E. Stucken, and G. Hüsing also maintained that all mythologies originated from Babylon (Pan-Babylonism).

There is no need to insist that ethnologists were opposed to such theories from the beginning. If we take, for instance, H. Winckler's *Himmels- und Weltbild der Babylonier als Grundlage der Weltanschauung und Mythologie aller Völker*, which he published in 1901, and confront it with the ethnological data as they were known about that time, we could get the impression of dealing here with an anachronism. At any rate, when P. Ehrenreich published *Die allgemeine Mythologie und ihre ethnologischen Grundlagen* in 1910, such theories were no longer defensible. Since the peoples and cultures upon which they based their analysis were all but primitive, the theories developed from such materials had to fall short with respect to the data of non-literate cultures. But as we already indicated, this fact alone does not diminish the general significance of these theories for the study of religion and the kind of questions that have been asked in the nineteenth and early twentieth century.

2.2 *Early Ethnological Theories Concerning the Origin of Religion*

The ethnological theories concerning 'primitive religion' began more or less with the work of Ch. de Brosses, who, in 1760, published his famous work *Du culte des dieux fétiches ou parallèle de l'ancienne religion de l'Egypte avec la religion actuelle de la nigritie*. In this work he argued for fetishism and sabaism or astrolatry as the original and primitive forms of religion. Departing from the promise that 'savages' are like children who live in an uninterrupted state of childhood, he came to the conclusion that fetishism[20] was born of fear, while sabaism, or astrolatry, arose out of a feeling of admiration.

De Brosses' theory, which was strongly inspired by D. Hume and, somewhat contradictorily, by J. Lafitau's argument that the originally pure idea of God degenerated through the centuries, was taken up by A. Comte in the sixth lesson of his *Cours de philosophie positive* (1830) and turned into a philosophical system. For Comte, religion is typical of the stage in the development of man that pre-

---

20. The word derives from the Portuguese *feitico*, charm, amulet, sacred object. It was used by Portuguese sailors to describe the various cult objects of West African peoples.

cedes the metaphysical stage, which is subsequently replaced by the positive or scientific stage in which man understands himself in accordance with the positive sciences. The religious stage begins with fetishism, in which physical objects are taken for supernatural beings and then develops through polytheism into monotheism.

According to J. Lubbock, who published *The Origin of Civilization and the Primitive Condition of Man* in 1870, such a system of development was still too inaccurate. In his opinion, man began at a stage where he knew nothing about religion. After successive periods of fetishism, nature worhsip or totemism, shamanism, idolatry or anthropomorphism, and belief in the idea of God as the creator of the world, religion finally arrived at its present form as a system of morality.

With the acquisition of new and more comprehensive data concerning primitive cultures, it became gradually clear that fetishism could not be taken as an autonomous form of religion or as a specific state in human development. Even in such cultures as those of West Africa where fetishes or sacred objects play a very important role in symbolic life, they do not exhaust this symbolism, nor can they be isolated from such ideas as 'vital force', 'ancestor worship' and 'God'. There had to be an opposition to a total reduction of religion to fetishism, particularly when the theories in question tried to cover a broader spectrum of empirical reality. Since such attempts are dependent on the limitations of the known and the selection of the available materials, as well as on the philosophical outlook of the authors, a change in one or both complexes of reference necessarily results in a change of theory. There was and still is no limitation in gaining new insights and forming more comprehensive hypotheses as long as there are shifts in the available materials and the conscious or unconscious philosophies of their interpreters.

From the viewpoint of historical development it is important to see that the ideology of progression enriched by an evolutionistic outlook, continues to be the basic philosophy for the classical theories on the origin of religion. It is a legacy that enjoys epochal evidence. Manism, animism and preanimism, though divergent in the empirical aspects they emphasize, are basically variations of the same theoretical conception. They try to reduce religious phenomena to one common and empirically observable form, without taking into consideration the speculative component of the image they contribute to 'early man' and his history.

2.3 *Manism, Animism, Preanimism: The Classical Theories*

Manism, or the cult of the dead, of ancestors and/or chieftains and heroes, can be found in a large number of preliterate cultures. According to H. Spencer who developed this theory in his *Principles of Sociology* (3 vols, 1876-96), manism must be considered as the root and primary form of religious development. His reasoning, eagerly accepted by the philosophers and sociologists of his time, began with an analysis of changing nature and man's death. The experience of day and night, sunshine and rain, summer and winter, suggested to early man the existence of a basic dualism, which he extended to cover and explain the nature of death. Consequently, nearly all peoples came to believe that a part of man that we call 'soul' survives the decay of the body, at least temporarily. As a result of this belief, which was supported by the experience of dreams, primitive man began to worship the surviving 'souls'. As the practices of embalming and the provision of food show, at first he hoped for reanimation. But since it turned out that such hope was vain, primitive people began to form definite ideas about the hereafter, the soul and its destiny. The cult of the dead turned into the cult of ancestors or of heroes (that is, of persons who showed special gifts and powers during their lifetime). Gradually such heroes became deified. Manism developed into polytheism, which through henotheism finally turned into monotheism.

Whereas Spencer used the ethnological data in a more or less sporadic way, E. B. Tylor tried to base his interpretation upon a methodological collection and comparison of available data. With his work on *Primitive Culture* (1871) he not only gave the status of an autonomous discipline to cultural anthropology, but also became the leading anthropologist of his time. His theory became 'classical' in the sense that it was generally accepted by anthropologists at the turn of the century. As a result, he influenced practically all scholars who dealt with the problem of religion. If we call Spencer's theory and those of his opponents classical, it is because of him.

Like Spencer, Tylor believed in the principle of progress, that is, that mankind advanced from a childlike stage to the present situation, and that primitive cultures of today should be considered survivals of the early periods of human history. By reducing the religious ideas of the 'lower races' to a common denominator, Tylor arrived at a 'rudimentary' or 'minimum definition of religion, a belief in Spiritual Beings' (1958, II, p. 8) which he called animism. He explained this theory, which can be traced to B. de Fontenelle's *De l'origine des fables* (1724) and N. S. Bergier's *L'origine des dieux du paganisme* (1767), by analyzing the empirical data in the light of a speculative interpretation of dreams and a related concept of the soul.

Impressed and challenged by such phenomena as waking and sleeping, hallucination and dreaming, illness and death, early man began to distinguish between the material body and its life, and the phantom or the second self. By combining life and the phantom he arrived at the conception of the ghost-soul. In his attempt to explain biological events and natural phenomena, primitive man applied this concept of the ghost-soul to the various problems that puzzled him. He explained the world by an uncritical analogy to himself. The dead continued to live as ghost-souls, became *manes*, and finally turned into deities. Furthermore, the idea of the ghost-soul was extended to animals, plants, and even to inanimate objects such as water and stones. Since the ghost-soul was superior to the body, man tried to influence it by turning his beliefs into action. Human and animal sacrifices, for instance, were thought to be a way to free souls from the body and thus to influence the world of the deceased (ancestor worship) and the guardian and nature spirits (nature worship). Within a framework of various 'doctrines' Tylor then tried to understand the development of beliefs as well as of rituals. As man progressed from the savage to the barbaric and finally to the civilized stage animism evolved into polydemonism, polytheism, and eventually, into monotheism. But within these various forms animism shows an unbroken continuity from first to last into the midst of 'high modern culture'. In addition, there has been a development of morality from a stage where the distinction between the useful and harmful functioned as the basic principle of the ethical code up to the present understanding of good and evil.

Tylor held that the simplest forms of religious life as they survived among the 'lower races' were in principle those found at the beginning. But in accordance with this principle his animistic theory was soon opposed by different interpretations. Since all of these explanations attempted to prove a less complex and nonanimistic beginning of religion, they can be formally described in opposition to Tylor's animism, as preanimism. With respect to the content, however, preanimism evolved in two directions. On the one hand, there were the so-called dynamistic theories (magism), which identified the beginning of religion more or less with magic. On the other hand, there were the monotheistic theories, which presumed that, whenever man emerged, he had a more or less monotheistic religion from the very beginning.

According to R. R. Marett, who published in 1909 and with major revisions in 1914 *The Threshold of Religion*, animism was already too differentiated to be acceptable as the simplest form of religion. Therefore, he postulated a pre-animistic stage, which he believed prevailed in the Polynesian concept of *mana*, a kind of universal power that penetrates all things and that may be concentrated in certain objects and persons. Early man experienced the presence of unspecified powers in the surrounding world to which he reacted with emotions such as fear, awe, wonder and admiration. In analogy to himself, he thought that all nature was animated. He began to objectify and to personify the supernatural and the mysterious something, upon which he built a system of religious beliefs and rituals. Instead of animism we better should speak of animatism as far as the beginning of religion is concerned.

About twenty years before Marett, J. H. King, an American anthropologist, had argued along similar lines in *The Supernatural: Its Origin, Nature and Evolution* (1892). There are two kinds of power in the world, King claimed, the mental powers, which belong to man and animals, and the impersonal forces, which can be felt in physical phenomena. Both attract the human mind and instigate it to draw natural as well as 'supernatural' conclusions. The mental powers suggest the presence of supernatural beings (spirits), while the impersonal powers lead to thoughts and ideas about good luck and bad luck, and, so far as we can say, to the beginning of religion. Thus the universal emotions of happiness and unhappiness are to be regarded as the root of all religion, and their magic transformations were probably the first forms of its realization.

The idea that religion originated in dynamistic conceptions and magical rituals found many followers, although the explanations of the origin of magic differed considerably. The same holds true with respect to the question concerning the transition from magic to religion. One group of scholars (J. G. Frazer, A. Vierkandt, R. Otto, and others) presumed that religion simply evolved from magic. Another group (E. S. Hartland, K. Beth, Th. Preuss, G. Wobbermin, N. Söderblom, and others) accepted, as did King, a more or less diffuse coexistence of both forms, in which magic prevailed.[21] A brief exposition of the reasoning of Frazer and Preuss will illustrate this point.

As indicated by scholars such as Otto, Wobbermin, and Söderblom, the dynamistic theory on the origin of religion was not restricted to anthropologists,

21. See also C. H. Ratschow's (1947) concept of the *unio magica*, which has been accepted by G. Mensching (1959).

but also won the approval of the theory-oriented historians of religion, who were primarily concerned with primitive religion (and not so much with primitive religions) from the viewpoint of the basic forms of religious life. We should keep this in mind when dealing with Frazer and Preuss.

Sir James G. Frazer, whose voluminous works *The Golden Bough* (13 vols., 1890–1915), *Totemism and Exogamy* (5 vols., 1910–1937), *The Belief in Immortality and the Worship of the Dead* (3 vols., 1913–1924), and others, established his influence far beyond the boundaries of cultural anthropology, held that man passed through three stages of intellectual development: From magic he came to religion, and from religion to science. In and during the first period man believed that personal and impersonal powers were responsible for the events of life. Consequently, he responded to the world in a rather irrational and superstitious way. Instead of distinguishing between reality and idea, he mixed both these realms and thus based his actions on erroneous interpretations of the cause-effect relationship. Magical rituals became a kind of pseudoscience by which primitive man tried to influence and to manipulate nature in accordance with the laws of similarity (like produces like) and contagion (the part affects the whole). After he discovered, however, that magical actions were not always efficient, he began to approach the personal powers by invocations and offerings. The magical stage turned into the religious stage through the application of correct reasoning to the human situation.

To do justice to Frazer and his tireless efforts to collect ethnological data and to interpret them through comprehensive comparison, it should be added that he was very much aware of the hypothetical character of his theoretical framework. More important than his speculations on the origin of religion were his attempts – stimulated by J. Mannhardt's *Wald und Feldkulte* (2 vols., 1875–79) – to establish the interrelations between religion, society, and political organization and to clarify such religious complexes as burial customs, totemism and taboos, and, particularly, the sacred kingship.

According to K. Th. Preuss it is difficult to see how the theory of animism should be reconciled with most of the primitive cult patterns. As he explains in his *Der Ursprung von Religion und Kunst* (1905) and in *Die geistige Kultur der Naturvölker* (1914), the religious problem evolved when man passed beyond the animal stage. As soon as the emerging human being was no longer guided by instincts, a chain of errors was unavoidable. Nevertheless, it was at this stage of proto- or arch-stupidity (*Urdummheit*) where magical and reasonable actions merged with one another that religion and art were born. The undifferentiated 'something' of the beginning, which in its enchanting power connected the natural with the supernatural, and impersonal power-objects with personal power, eventually turned into specified ideas. Through a process of inclusion religion and magic developed into pantheism, and through a process of subordination they developed into monotheism. In either case we are referred to a situation where magic and religion share one common root. They were, as E. S. Hartland put it (1914, p. 29), two sides of one coin.

The monotheistic version of the preanimistic theory was initiated by A. Lang, who like R. Marett, was a former student of Tylor. According to Lang, who presented this critique in his study on *The Making of Religion* (1898), animism could not give an adequate answer to the ethnological fact that a number of very simple tribes worshipped and knew of a moral, all-powerful and supreme being whom they addressed in personal terms. For that reason Lang considered it very unlikely that the monotheistic God had evolved from the conception of the ghost-soul or from manistic traditions. Rather, one should take into consideration that lower, or mythological, elements can be connected with higher, or religious, elements in any situation without being genetically related to one another. If this is true, why should we not assume that it was only at a later stage, when religion had become more complex, that mythology began to distort religious symbolism. In the beginning mankind arrived at the conception of a creator God and All-Father by rational deliberation. In analogy to the work of man, this God was thought of as the maker of all things. The curious and strange forms of religion and magic (as we find them apparently in more differentiated cultures) were the results of later developments, which had deviated from the original belief in a cultless high God.

At first Lang's ideas were generally rejected by his contemporaries, although they were developed by the same ethnological methods and thus as good as hypotheses as the others, in that they too shed light upon certain data. But whereas his colleagues approached 'primitive man' alternately as a nineteenth century rationalist and as a four-year-old child, he tried to be more consistent. At any rate, his ideas found soon a very determined advocate in W. Schmidt. With the help of the highly diffusionist methodology of the *Kulturkreislehre*, he tried first of all to reconstruct a historical sequence of world cultures. Since such an attempt required reducing speculative explanations as much as possible and making full use of the empirical methods of historical investigation, Schmidt tried to base his analysis on all available ethnoreligious data and stimulated the study of those peoples who were then only very imperfectly known as well. In this sense there was a definite turn to the empirically given, although it has to be added that it was more than squared up by a kind of theological constructionism. In any case, the fruits of this approach, which on the practical level resulted in the foundation of the Anthropos Institute, were Schmidt's monumental work *Der Ursprung der Gottesideee* (12 vols., 1912–1955), his *Handbuch der vergleichenden Religionsgeschichte* (1930), and many other publications.

By singling out the so-called *Urkulturen* (protocultures), Schmidt believed that he had found an empirical basis for reconstructing the conditions of the beginning, which he outlined as '... belief in a highest being, creater of the world, often called father, moral and social legislator and judge. Formless, spontaneous prayers, and primitial sacrifices, but no others. No polytheism, no images of the godhead, no temples, no priests. Magic only rudimentarily developed, few or no amulets, either no worship or only incomplete worship of nature spirits (animism) and of ancestors (manism), no totemism, and no fetishism' (1964, 20, p. 4). Thus religion began with a kind of protomonotheistic stage, which, as Lang had pointed out, degenerated during the course of history by being surfeited with, or even replaced by, symbolic forms such as magic, animism, fetishism, and polytheism. But the *Urkulturen* still bear witness of these primeval conditions.

The somewhat polarized opposition to Schmidt's ideas underlined in a more polemic way a need that had been present all along, that is, the acquisition of cultural data, their confirmation and interpretation and the corresponding methodology. As it cannot be otherwise, we have here one of the sources for the factual development and the eventual changes in the various theories on culture and religion. Of special note among these theories are the sociological and functionalistic or, as they are called today, the social-anthropological, and psychological interpretations. Although these theories and respective methodologies did not develop independently from the ideological premises of the age, they brought about a fundamental shift in the interest in the nature of religion that finally stimulated a basic reorientation in the study of culture.

2.4 *Social-anthropological and Psychological Approaches to Religion*

Though Marx and Engels were no cultural anthropologists they nevertheless influenced both the study of culture and the interpretation of primitive religion.

It was a form of influence which worked mainly by contrast. Both Marx and Engels differed from the anthropologists in two ways. First, they had a strongly eschatological interest when they spoke about religion. For them, the study of the beginning of religion implies the projection of its future, and vice versa. Second, they looked at religion no longer as a distinct phenomenon among others but related it to the whole of man and culture in such a way that the reality of religion became an epiphenomenon of the historical process. Like other evolutionists, Marx and Engels, who were strongly influenced by L. H. Morgan, find the beginnings of religion in the powers of nature, which are fantastically mirrored in the minds of people. The real basis for such reflections, that is, their meaning, is not thinking or emotion but the economic situation, inasmuch as through the social process it creates the spiritual superstructure that includes religion. Religion is thus the result of a fundamental conflict situation or, as Marx said, of cultural self-alienation, which permeates the process of history. Consequently, if we understand the study of religion correctly, it should not be a study of its ideas and content primarily but a study of cultural, that is, economical, involvements. When the 'last alienating power, which is still mirrored in religion, disappears, the religious reflection will also disappear, for the simple reason that there is nothing else to reflect upon (Marx/Engels, 1958, p. 120). But at this point we have to know what religion is, and, in particular, what it has been in its beginning or first emergence. Marx and Engels are convinced that the data of cultural anthropology substantiate this view.

Unlike Marx, who studied religion in a framework that gave absolute priority to economic processes, E. Durkheim emphasized the priority of society as such. He arrived at this conclusion partly because he rejected all 'speculation about the fundamental nature of beings', and partly because of the universality of the religious phenomena. From the perspective of a positive conception of society, religion could not be erroneous because, as indicated by its universality, it was fundamentally related to society. In consequence of this view, the primary object of religion must be seen in society itself, which created religion and rituals as a means to maintain and to rejuvenate itself spiritually or symbolically. The idea and practice of the sacred, by which thought and action are set apart from the profane – and which for this reason is the key concept of Durkheim's definition of religion – give rise to religion as the particular expression of societal presence. God, religion, and worship are nothing but the symbol and emblem of the society 'because the idea of society is the soul of religion' (Durkheim, 1967, p. 466).

Therefore, religion necessarily precedes magic, which is understood as the attempt to take advantage of religious beliefs for individual rather than communal purposes. But with the exception of this significant difference, magic and religion are the same.

To prove this theory, Durkheim analyzed the religious ideas and practices of the Australian aborigines, whose social organization he considered 'the most primitive and simple that is actually known' (1967, p. 115). By doing so he accepted in a very decisive point Tylor's principles of cultural survivals, although he was clearly opposed to the evolutionistic attempt to seek the empirico-historical beginning of religion by evaluating primitive cultures with the yardstick of nineteenth-century rationalism. Moreover, while he did this analysis he came to the conclusion that the root from which all religion originated had to be seen in the phenomena of totemism,[22] or, as he said also, in the conception of a 'mana totémique'. Like J. F. McLennan, who had discovered totemistic exogamy (1869/70), and W. Robertson Smith, who emphasized the communal and sacramental character of religion,[23] Durkheim considered totemism the original form of religion.

Although the idea that totemism should be viewed as the beginning of religion proved untenable when it was examined in the light of all the available ethno-religious data (see Goldenweiser, 1931), the new direction in religious studies initiated by Durkheim's questions gained more and more ground among anthropologists. His thought especially influenced the so-called French sociological school (H. Hubert, M. Mauss; in America, W. Lloyd Warner). But it had also a strong influence on functionalists or social anthropologists like B. Malinowski and A. R. Radcliffe-Brown, who more than ever before emphasized the significance of the cultural context for the meaning and interpretation of cultural data (Malinowski, 1925, 1926; Radcliff-Brown, 1952). Because of this interest and view the question of primitive religion and the historical origin of religion became second-

22. The term was brought to Europe in 1791 by J. Long. It is taken from the Cree Indian word 'ototema' (Ojibway: 'ototeman') and means 'his relations'. An animal is addressed, which is believed to be the ancestor of the clan. The clan, in turn, is called by the name of the animal. For a general orientation, see J. Haekel (1952). Also C. Lévi-Strauss (1967b).

23. For Robertson Smith (*Lectures on the Religion of the Semites*, 1889) totemism was the starting point of all religion. He arrived at this conclusion by analyzing the sacrifice of the Semites in the light of the totem communal mean and under the premise that ritual preceded myth. See also F. B. Jevons (1896); S. Reinach (1905). Durkheim (1967) acknowledges the theory of Robertson Smith on p. 109.

ary if not irrelevant. What matters within this theoretical framework is the functional emergence of religion in crisis situations, and, in general, its function and accomplishments in a given culture.

While the previous positions are characterized by an approach to religion that emphasizes the context of society, the psychological interpretations try to put more emphasis on the individual. After all, it is not society that actually feels, thinks and speaks, but the individual, even though it must be granted that no individual can exist without reference to his life community. On the other hand, we may look at the society as the result and product of psychic atoms. The phenomenon of the society is thus no contradiction to this sort of psychological reductionism.

The spectrum of psychological approaches ranges from Freud's psychoanalytical explanation of religion in the context of the Oedipus complex, promiscuity,and the totemistic sacrifice (1913), to C. G. Jung's archetypal theory of the collective unconscious (1912, 1940). Anthropologists who relied heavily upon psychological methods in their approach to religion were J. H. Leuba (1912), A. Kroeber (1920), G. Roheim (1932), B. Bettelheim (1954), R. H. Lowie (1927), and others. Also to be mentioned here is W. Wundt's *Völkerpsychologie* (10 vols., 1900–1920), in which he tried to connect the psychology of the individual with that of the group.

2.5 *Phenomenology of Religion*

The emergence of various interests in and approaches to religion not only brought new insights but also exercised a strong influence upon the further development of religious studies. Schools and scholars modified their position in the light both of new data and of their mutual criticism. New aspects necessitated the development of more adequate methods and vice versa. Examples of this trend are the proposed synthesis of functional and psychoanalytic approaches as favored by anthropologists such as A. Irving Hallowell (1955), Clyde Kluckhohn (1942) and others, or the attempts to integrate meaning and ritual as developed in the work of Evans-Pritchard (1967). The same can be said of the morphologica school and its main representatives, L. Frobenius (1898) and A. Jensen (1960), who tried to approach religion from within the worldview of a given people, or of such anthropologists as Franz Boas (1938), Radin (1927), and L. Lévy-Bruhl (1921, 1949), but also of a philosopher like E. Cassirer (1953), who paid special attention to the particular features in the thinking of primitive peoples as a necessary foundation for the interpretation of their religion.

In the midst of conflicting and inspirational theories on the origin of religion scholars began to become sensitive to the need for a closer attention to the meaning of the empirically given. The movement began at the turn of the century and was not restricted to any particular discipline. It gained ground during the crisis situations brought about by both World Wars. Among philosophers this trend was most strongly expressed in the phenomenological movement inspired by the work of Dilthey, Husserl, Scheler, Tillich, Heidegger, Merleau-Ponty, and others. According to these philosophers, an analysis of everyday life shows that the highly acclaimed objectivity of positivism and rationalism is really only a form of prejudice and self-deception. To avoid this subtle pitfall in which we are prone to stumble because of the historical and cultural situation of man, it will be necessary to recognize the correlation between life-world (*Lebenswelt*), society, and culture. As a result philosophical and theoretical evidence cannot be sought on the surface of a historically grown interpretation of man and world. Rather we must tie our judgments to the concomitant discovery of these principles and conditions that work together in the constitution of meaning and culture. Husserl's call 'to the things themselves!' was not only a demand to look upon the world as it is but also a summons to think of it as it appears to us and how reflection interferes with this appearance both when it originates from the life-world and when it attempts to interpret this world.

Since phenomenology is in a certain sense an ideational force, an original impetus, and imperative of consciousness which is at work whenever and wherever man tries to discover the foundations of his existence, that is, to break out of the world of the familiar and of mythological praxis and to return to it in the consciousness of theoretical mediation, it is very difficult to say exactly where and how it emerges in an age like ours, which has begun to recognize the destructive forces of cultural and national self-complacency and myopia. For this reason we consider it legitimate to use the word phenomenology in a rather broad sense, presupposing that the phenomenological imperative is followed. It seems, for instance, that the goal of a phenomenological intention has been realized when the analysis of history and religion attempted to retrieve the qualitative character of the process of history in the language of its interpretation. Even instances such as W. Schmidt's rejection of the identification of 'primitive' with 'childlike', or Pettazzoni's criticism (1967, p. 4 ff) of Schmidt's use of the term 'monotheism' in the contxet of primitive cultures could serve as examples of a phenomenological intention. The same holds true with respect to the reevaluation of the relationships among myth, symbol, and ritual by such scholars as Lévi-Strauss, C. Geertz, E. R. Leach, R. Firth, J. v. Baal, and others, or with regard to the preference for intensive studies of various religious situations or of newly emerging religious movements over speculative theories on religion in general. These are indications of a growing recognition of the phenomenological principle even though the respective scholars cannot be said to be phenomenologists when judged by mere historical standards.

Besides these symptomatic signs of a phenomenological consciousness there have been several attempts to develop a definite phenomenology of religion. These attempts are partially independent from the respective traditions in philosophy; partially they are inspired by them. In either case they respond to the same intellectual need that gave birth to phenomenological philosophy. Here the most notable efforts can be found among the Dutch historians of religion such as P. D. Chantepie de la Saussaye, W. B. Kristensen, G. van der Leeuw, Jan de Vries, C. J. Bleeker, K. A. H. Hidding, Th. P. v. Baaren, E. Cornélis and others (see Waardenburg 1926b, pp. 128–203). Other names are J. Heiler (1962), J. Wach (1969), K. Goldhammer (1960), G. Mensching (1959), W. L. King (1954) and, in particular, M. Eliade (1965). Despite all the particular differences, their goal is an understanding of religion that is based on an interpretation of man as a cultural and historical being, and, in consequence, on the attempt to synthesize the principles of interpretation with those that account for the phenomenality of the phenomena. This implies that each human situation, including that of primitive cultures, has to be understood in its specific sense before it can be submitted to general comparisons and conclusions. The phenomenology of religion is therefore not in opposition to the history or the function of religion, but, presupposing it follows the logic of its beginning, integrates the discoveries of the evolutionistic and social-anthropological approaches with its own interpretation of the present and vice versa. The difference that does exist between the present and the past, between society and meaning, accounts for different interests, methods and aspects, but not for a difference in the philosophical impetus that is presupposed by the phenomenological concern for reality. Since the philosophy in question is realized concretely only in the description and interpretation of the phenomenal world, it is necessarily open and unfinished, participating in totality and definiteness only to the extent that it shares in the totality of man and culture as the background for the representative concretion of the human situation. The phenomenological study of religion is a part of the study of culture as the totality of man's emergence in world and history. As such, it deals with fundamental problems as well as with the structural coordination of phenomena and their genesis. This holds also true with respect to the problem of primitive religion, particularly if we understand, as Husserl did, phenomenology as philosophical archeology, that is, as a theoretical concern for the beginnings (*archai*). As far as the analysis of the studies on primitive religion(s) is concerned we have reached here the point where the historical perspective of this problem becomes an issue of present efforts.

In retrospect we may say that the question about primitive religion has been one of the most significant issues of the history of religious studies.[24] And it has also been a topic that has attracted all sorts of interests and confusing treatment. From this point of view its conception did not contribute too much to the clarification of religion. However, if we take into consideration the impact 'primitive religion' has had on the interpreters, we may expect that a reconsideration of this question can only be advantageous, particularly if we combine it with the coordination of the confirmation of religious data and the theoretical interest of their interpretation. 'Primitive religion' is primarily a theoretical issue. But it is practically significant, if we consider the religious data from the viewpoint of cultural dynamics. As a result there can be no adequate treatment of the theoretical problem without the empirical data, nor can we expect to bring these data into an adequate perspective without dealing with the theoretical question accordingly. We shall try to realize this task in the following chapters.

---

24. As for further studies on the subject of 'primitive religion' see: H. Berndt (1960), J. Campbell (1968), S. Diamond (1964), E. P. Dozier (1961), O. Eberle (1955), M. Eliade (1973), V. Ferm (1950), W. J. Goode (1951, 1955), F. Herrmann (1961), W. Koppers (1951), G. v. d. Leeuw (1937), H. Lommel (1965), R. R. Marett (1932), A. Montagu (1968), M. Nilsson (1934). E. Norbeck (1961), R. Redfield (1963), R. F. Spencer (1963), W. D. Wallis (1939) and G. Widengren (1945).

2

Geographical Survey and Description of Primitive Cultures and Their Religion

Since there are no written and canonized traditions in primitive cultures, the study of their religion has to be focused on typical phenomena. The societies themselves and their respective cultures have to be considered from the vantage point of a structural and morphological analysis of the conditions that brought them into and maintained them in their being. Before we can start with a general survey of primitive cultures and their respective religion we thus have to resume the question about their typological character and its significance for the evaluation and morphological identification of cultural complexities.

1. THE TYPOLOGY OF PRIMITIVE CULTURES

As we know from the history of cultural anthropology primitive cultures have been classified on the basis of evolutionistic, racial, social and sometimes even on psychological ideas. Also the presence of certain cultural instances such as the possession of script has been used as a means of distinction. But as the deliberations of the previous chapter show, neither one of these aspects provides sufficient evidence to grasp the meaning of primitivity. This holds true also with regard to the perhaps most comprehensive typology of primitive cultures as outlined by W. Schmidt's *Kulturkreislehre*. There are too many heterogeneous elements that have been worked into this theory and that prevent it from serving as a flexible and transformable tool in the morphological presentation of cultural genesis.

Within the methodological framework set forth by this study, we are at once referred to the mediating position of work both as a possible index for the type of culture under investigation and the interpretation of the respective data. As we have already seen, it is, however, not work as such[1] which may serve as a criterion

---

1. In the aftermath of the *Kulturkreislehre* many attempts have been made to overcome its

of primitivity but work in connection with the idea of optimal adaptation to an independent environment. In order to shed light upon the extension of primitive cultures and their typological differentiation, we thus have to resume our reflections on work within an independent environment.

According to the inherent possibilities of work in an independent environment, four types of economies, and in consequence of cultures, can be distinguished which describe the range of primitive cultures. These are the cultures of gatherers hunters, planters and animal-breeders. In the *first* instance the natural resources are more or less evenly used and exploited. A local nomadism is the result because the recovery of natural resources is not controlled by man. For the same reason groups have to remain small, and within their own cultural setting, more or less isolated. Since an environment that does not change too much throughout the year is especially favorable for this kind of economy, it is found mainly in the equatorial zone and above all in the rain forest. In the *second* case the unspecified exploitation of the natural resources turns into the exploitation of specified objects, in this instance of animal life. These cultures require, of course, the presence of sufficient game or animal life and thus can be found wherever nature supplies it. Groups may be bigger and mutual contacts more frequent. But again, sooner or later the environment will set its limitation to this sort of development. In the *third* instance the dependence on natural resources is modified by the passive or selective cultivation of plants and/or tubers. Since these cultures require an ample amount of vegetable life, they can be found especially in the tropic and subtropic zones. It goes without saying that the environmental limitations of the accumulation of people and on the extension and intensity of intercourse between the various groups are lifted, though not entirely. The same holds true for the next type of economy. In the *fourth* case man is making his living by cultivating the resources of animal life. Since the domestication is only a passive one – if it were active we could no longer speak of an independent environment – these cultures have to be nomadic. Depending on the animals involved – reindeer,

---

shortcomings. One of them is a typology of culture which is mainly based on the nature and function of work, even though work is not interpreted as it has been done here. As outlined by H. Ringgren and A. V. Ström (1967, chap. V) this typology distinguishes between the cultures of hunters, planters and animal breeders, which in turn are subdivided according to particular traits of their economy and working methods. Though valid on the basis of descriptive inventory, it seems to me that, in view of the questions we have raised, too much emphasis on details would obfuscate the issue.

horse, cattle – animal breeding nomads can be found wherever the environment is favorable for the respective species.[2]

If we consider these economical systems in their concrete realizations, we become easily aware that the transitions are fluid and that the respective cultures frequently overlap when speaking from a typological point of view. Hunting for instance, is an essential, although not predominant, element in all gathering cultures. On the other hand, hunters and animal breeders make frequent use of the resources provided by the vegetable environment. There is, however, a very important difference between the first two types of primitive cultures and the following ones. While man is exploiting the environment as it actually presents itself in the former cultures, he is somehow interferring with the natural environment in the latter ones, thus leaving the primary conditions of cultural behavior behind him. Since these changes modify the environment rather than alter it – we spoke of passive or selective cultivation – these types of culture may be included as forms of transition as far as primitive cultures are concerned. Nevertheless, a good deal of methodological precaution must be maintained. We have to pay constant attention to the fact that the cultures of planters and animal breeding nomads represent the first step in the process of cultural estrangement. The development of social systems, for instance, which is made possible by a relatively independent economy, may permeate the whole cultural process and, in effect, destroy the environmental immediacy. The exploitation of plants can turn through a new social stratification toward specialized agricultural systems and develop as a part of archaic urban civilizations. Or the exploitation of animals may be the beginning of a social system that succeeds in making full use of nomadic independence and ends in the erection of an archaic empire. In these cases we no longer have an optimal realization of cultural life with regard to an independent environment. The cultural estrangement as seen in the context of primitivity is accompanied by an exogenic development (typological change), which in its turn characterizes primitive cultures as the result of endogenic developments. Although such a development is not necessarily restricted to cultural situations that exist in an independent environment, it is nevertheless a typical feature and thus a criterion for the constitution of primitive cultures when approached from a historical point of view.

2. This statement is morphological, not chronological. Thus nothing is said about the actual beginning of animal-breeding nomadism. In this context we can leave this question open.

By referring to the dialectics of the inner- and intercultural circle of hermeneutics, we may interpret this break within the typology of primitive cultures as
follows: From the viewpoint of gatherers and hunters, the cultures of planters
and animal breeding nomads are already part of the neolithic metamorphosis
which took place when man began to detach himself from the conditions of an
independent environment. In this sense they belong to the tradition of the so-
called high-cultures. If we approach them, however, from the viewpoint of our
own situation, i.e., from the viewpoint of complex societies with more or less
distinct class structures, then the break in man's tradition is not so much a matter
of economics but of organization and orientation. It begins when leadership
becomes autonomous in and for the sustenance of society, i.e., when the acquisition of food becomes a matter of societal planning and the function of distinct
entities within the social body. Here the passive interference with the environment
becomes an active one and thus has to be distinguished as such. As a result the type
'primitive cultures' shifts from those of gatherers and hunters to those of planters
and animal-breeding nomads.

It is quite obvious that the meaning and function of religion in primitive cultures will not remain uninfluenced in such a metamorphosis of cultural dialectics
and that it may lose many of its primary qualities, or at least undergo change with
respect to them. Thus the cultures and religions of planters and animal-breeding
nomads are not expressly covered in this study, although they are not excluded.
Their presence will be considered as a transitional 'field' in which the borderlines
between 'religion in primitive cultures' and 'religion in incipient high cultures'
are very fluid.

The typological horizon of primitive cultures, which has been developed in
accordance with the functional and constitutive significance of their economical
system, offers general guidelines and a selective principle for a study of cultures or
religions in the world today and as they have been recorded in the last centuries.
Since there are so many, it is necessary to select typical examples. To make this
selection we shall first draw up a general inventory of religion in the world's
primitive cultures to obtain a general survey.[3] By conducting this survey we will

3. We exclude here the treatmen of prehistoric primiiv cultures because of the analo gous
character of the conclusions that we are forced to make about their religion. As for the sources of
this survey we refer to a bibliographical appendix at the end of this chapter.

try to clarify, as our methodology requires, our preconceived idea of religion and at the same time prepare for the general guidelines of a phenomenological approach to primitive religion.

2. TOWARD A DEFINITION OF RELIGION

To grasp the fundamentals of religion in primitive cultures through a general survey, we need at the outset a description of what we would like to talk about. Or to express the same in methodological terms: We need a comprehensive definition. Yet, in attempting a general survey we are in some way already presuming later results. In order to define what is, we have somehow to know 'what is' and thus are presupposing what we would like to define.

To overcome this paradox of not-yet and yet, of ignorance and knowledge, we have to take into consideration that it is quite a different thing if we try to order, to outline, to define the world of our senses and of sense experience, or if we refer to the reality of history, culture and meaning. From the definition that talks about something (in the sense of an objective totality) we are transferred to the definition that speaks into a certain direction, and by doing so, is entering its own reality (in the sense of an objectifying totality), i.e., the reality that subsists in words and as articulation and culture. The definition no longer is neutral from what it defines. It becomes a part of that about which we talk. In a situation where we have a certain idea, an habitualized opinion and a more or less 'definite' view the definition becomes functional inasmuch as it brings us into a certain direction. It guides our eye. Within the tension of description, explanation and comprehension the definition becomes the mediating principle of thought and thinking as culture-receiving and culture-forming activity and enterprise. When we speak and talk we are not just designating a given world, but the world itself is in the making in and through the process of articulation. It is its function to mediate, i.e., to connect the one with the other and to see it in its unity. As such it is not truth, but a matter of truth as it comes into being in and through culture history.

By defining man and the history of his articulations and expressions we thus enter the intercultural circle of hermeneutics, which, in its turn, is already functional – thereby giving us a solution to our paradox – because each human being necessarily shares a definite cultural context. The fact that man has culture, and that he is man by virtue of having it, confirms the working hypothesis that there is a thorough-going and universal similarity between different cultures and between fundamental human experiences. Thus it can reasonably be expected that the descriptive conceptions covering specific phenomena in one culture will also do so, at least to some extent, in others. Because of the implicit cross-culturality of an articulating and of articulated being an attempt may be made at defining religion out of one's own cultural context in order to grasp the phenomena properly belonging to other peoples' cultures.

The history of religious studies offers nearly as many definitions of religion as there are scholars, or even more (see Klostermeier, 1960, p. 38 ff). But this is a necessary development, for man cannot abandon the elements of his *Weltanschauung*, which is involved in all cultural studies. Nevertheless, there are some general indications that must be considered for an introductory definition and description. Above all it has to be a definition that confronts us with the reality of *religion* and not such a one that, no matter how distinct and clear, deters us from realizing the reality we are looking for.

The purpose of an introductory definition is a collective one. It must be broad and, at the same time, an open definition, embracing authentic and inauthentic or derivative phenomena alike. In addition it should be a definition implying only a minimum of theory. When religion is defined, for instance, as 'belief in spiritual beings' (E. B. Tylor), or as 'social precipitates of fear' (P. Radin), the definition is highly theoretical and presumes either the sophisticated language of the Western world or a previously adopted system of philosophy. Such definitions might be right, but what they lack is sufficient openness for the yet unknown extent of phenomena that are to be discovered with their help. Moreover, they fail to do justice to their own cultural environment, which at least pretends to see the essence of religion elsewhere than in the patterns mentioned.

According to the situation and outlook of the Western world, religion can be described in many ways. We presume a religious behavior if people go to church, if they observe special calender days, if they follow certain rites and rituals, if they pray. On the theoretical level, this behavior can be described as being accompanied by belief in God or gods or in a certain sacred history. If we stress belief as a dynamic factor in such phenomena, we can also say that this behavior is often connected with attitudes which can be described as belief in magic, in idols, the future (the coming paradise), the past (the ideal of ultraconservatism), democarcy, founders, money, power, work and even science. The meaning of 'belief' however, becomes more confused the more we try to trace it in its concrete context. The range of possible interpretations is so wide that a definition specifying the contents of belief encounters many insoluble questions and problems. The same holds true when we use words such as God, precipitates, sublimation, projection, etc. Thus it may be convenient here to concentrate more on the existential and genetic aspects of religion in the dynamics of culture than on its theoretical content(s), neither describing it with such terms as God or spiritual being, nor using such concepts as belief, precipitate, sublimation, and superstructure, but emphasizing the common attitude behind and in all these phenomena. In other words, since all that has been mentioned points in one way or another to symbols, we should not try to interpret these symbols, but understand them in their making.

Symbols are used when we try to grasp the world in which we live, or even more generally, since our actions are in one way or another connected with consciousness, when we do something.[4] We need them to maintain the rationality of our action as something that is connected with the past and directed toward a future accomplishment. Because of this condition of ours we are capable of identifying the world in signs and of representing ourselves in a variety of modes. As such symbols permeate the whole of our life. In them our consciousness discovers the efficacy of its own awareness and realizes the urge for meaning because they are the matrix of its life In this sense they are neither isolated entities nor abstract essences but coincide with what we are, do and think. They are in the making, and thus, must be seen as a process for which differences are an integral aspect of its unity and innermost similarity. Consequently, since symbols relate always to something other than themselves, we may not only speak of a process of symbolization but may look at it as a symbol of its own, and thus, can ask for its basic features, and, if these features allow us to distinguish various dimensions, how they in turn could give us access to the 'content' of those 'elements' that 'fill' them 'up'.

We speak of symbols in the making or of symbolization. This gives us the idea

---

4. We interpret there the word symbol not as an abstract sign but as the result of man's ability and effort to articulate. In doing so he brings the pieces of the world together (Gr.: *symballein*: to throw together) and thus creates a configuration of instances in which he recognizes his own work and presence as well as that of others including world and reality as a basis and background of meaningful activities. In other words we use here the term symbol in a similar way as presented by E. Cassirer (1953b), S. K. Langer (1951), and others. See also the following chapter.

of symbolization as a symbol of its own, which, if we consider it as comprehending all and everything, is absolute. But if we look at it as our symbol, i.e., as a symbol of which we are thinking here and now, we cannot call it absolute but have to consider it as a symbol among symbols. Within the symbol of symbolization, we encounter the paradox that the absolute is relative and the relative absolute.

To repeat this idea in a slightly modified manner we can also say, because there are symbols, because we live in and through symbols, we are capable of conceiving the symbol of symbolization. Since we are departing from the idea of looking at symbols in the making, we can ask for the beginning and end of this symbol of symbolization. But if we do so, we have to take into consideration that this very question points to beginning and end of symbolization as such, i.e., to a borderline where the conceptualization of beginning and end meets its own end and beginning and thus becomes absolute. We touch the borderline of sense and non-sense. We reach a point where it does not make sense any more to ask for meaning, and yet, where it becomes obvious that this must be the origin of meaning, in which things are related to one another and which is grasped through the interrelation of instances that characterize the cultural situation. In other words we have to postulate the coincidence of meaning and reality, of nothing and something, thinking and being, freedom and necessity, multiplicity and unity, beginning and end, silence and sound, will and intellect, etc. The symbol of symbolization presents itself as the concept of a process of reversal within the horizon of ultimacy. It begins and ends in (leads to) what is given and yet leads far away from everything.

What conclusions can we draw from this analysis? First and foremost we must say that, if this analysis is correct, we are pointing here to a fundamental condition of consciousness. Thus, it should be traceable whenever and wherever consciousness appears, no matter if it is reflective or unreflective consciousness. This seems to be the case when we observe how the rationalization of life and culture is encountered by symbols of derationalization (which, as M. Weber, 1963, has shown, may initiate new modes of rationalization) but only to be encountered again by further symbols of derationalization, e.g., when eating becomes a banquet, work a play, life a celebration, thinking poetry, etc., or to be quite general, when values as interrelated centers of orientation become absolute. Within and through the symbol of symbolization we thus discover the 'quality' of absoluteness as an unsurmountable condition of articulating consciousness.

Secondly, since culture must be understood as the total concretion of consciousness in, through, and as the process of articulation, this analysis enables us to 'identify' the symbolic reversal within the horizon of ultimacy as a dimension of culture itself. And thus we may ask, is this dimension the source and initial completion of religion, the dimension out of which symbols emerge, thereby recalling this origin in particular modes and – in their particularity – on different levels with different intensity? Whatever the answer may be, it is a legitimate procedure to introduce here the hypothesis (or even better, to try the hypothesis) that this dimension is indeed the place where we have to search for religion, wheref religion has its reality. The truth of such a hypothesis, its confirmation, is of course its workability. We are dependent on what it explains and how it enables us to grasp the meaning of culture-history and of consciousness, i.e., the particular as well as the universal.

Religion understood in this manner is definitely both an implication and a presupposition of consciousness and culture. It is an implication insofar as culture and consciousness are there; a presupposition insofar as they are in the making. If the hypothesis is correct, religion is born with man and thus intimately connected with the process of hominization. Moreover, since it is approached in the limit[5] of culture and consciousness, it will be necessary to distinguish between religion as ultimate dimension of culture and consciousness and the religious symbols, re-calling and unfolding this dimension in clusters of functional units and concepts of varying coherence. In other words, we have to approach religion under the premise of symbolic transformation and its symbols with the intention of total integration. What is at stake in such an attempt is not less than the totality of man in his personal and cultural reality.

If we apply these deliberations to the meaning and function of an introductory definition – i.e., a definition that is aimed at discovering and finding a way to reality – we can well agree with R. N. Bellah (1969, p. 263), who speaks of religion 'as a set of symbolic forms and acts which relate man to the ultimate conditions of his existence'. Or, if we want to emphasize the unifying function

---

5. We use here the word 'limit' analogously to the use of this term in mathematics. We are, of course, not concerned with numbers but with qualitative differences. Accordingly we cannot functionalize the referential terms. This does not mean, however, that the mode of thinking that leads to the conception of the calculus must be restricted to this conception. On the contrary thinking has to be recognized for what it is, i.e., the successful and necessary attempt of consciousness to encounter reality in the dialectics of presence and absence on the terms of its innermost possibilities.

of the dimension of ultimacy, we can describe religion as the comprehensive reality of man's attempt to integrate himself, his consciousness, the world, and society in a prescientific and metascientific system of absolute symbols.

Although this definition is not intended to be perfect, it at least has the advantage of being applicable in every kind of cultural behavior inasmuch as it is based on man as a questioning being who is conscious of himself. Man raises the question of meaningfulness either on a prescientific (that is, unreflected and even subconscious) level by the fact of his conduct or he does it in the metascientific dimension. Science and reflection, as methodological processes, do not deal with ultimates, but presuppose them. Consequently if reflection tries to grasp the ultimate, it is, strictly speaking, no longer scientific, but, since it is not simply submerged into the subconscious, metascientific. Thus, human consciousness itself as a total dimension of being aware of oneself plays the essential role in man's quest for meaning and not the one or other component of the reflected particularizations of this consciousness. The result of this quest is neither exclusively theoretical nor practical but embraces both aspects. It is symbolic. And finally, because of the ultimate character of this quest, the symbols themselves are, though finite in appearance, ultimate and absolute in function and significance. Thus, whatever can be considered as forming an inner part of this process of absolute symbolization can be analyzed as a potential element of religion. We cannot say *a priori* what religion is as far as the concrete situation is concerned. Rather, it is the context of the cultural situation, its structure and dynamics which decide if this or that phenomenon should be considered a religious phenomenon. For this reason we are not simply speaking of absolute symbols but of a 'set' or 'system' of absolute symbols. They are interrelated to one another by the cultural situation out of which they grow and which they determine by way of cultural integration. These elements may belong to the subjective or habitual aspect of religion as well as to its objectification in dogmas, rites, sacrifices, laws and prayers. They may be magically manipulated or faithfully witnessed and celebrated.

Perhaps one might ask here, what happened to the minimum of theory as asked for by an introductory definition. If we understand this request literally, it does not mean that this is tantamount to a minimum of words because words may easily encapsulate highly theoretical decisions. Instead, we should try to hold the theoretical predecisions at a minimum level. This at least is what we tried to accomplish by the previous remarks.

3. RELIGION IN AFRICAN CULTURES

Although the cultural and tribal map of Africa resembles a many-colored mosaic, it nevertheless shows some specific features that are direct consequences of the environmental and historical conditions of this continent. They can probably be reduced to three factors that constituted, by their mutual dependence, the pre-colonial situation of Africa.

The first factor is Africa's connection with Eurasian history. Cultural diffusions, as they are reflected in the early Mediterranean and Egyptian relations, racial mixtures as represented in the Nilo-Hamitic peoples of the East, and martial clashes throughout the last two thousand years, were contributing factors in the formation of the technological, social and symbolic structure of Africa. To give only one example: When in 350 AD the Christian empire of northern Abyssinia (Aksum) destroyed the millenial kingdom of Nubia, the latter continued to exist in sacred kingdoms as far away as Guinea in the west and Zimbabue in the east (Southern Rhodesia).

The most important contribution of this historical link, on the religious level, is the recent Islamization of the whole of northern and Sudanese Africa which has overlapped even the relatively primitive cultural survivals.

The second factor in the process of cultural stratification in Africa is the continous desiccation of the Sahara. An abundant living space for hunters, agricultural and pastoral nomads alike during the neolithic period, it gradually became a hostile environment, which forced the different populations to search for new places in which to live. Thus, the permanent pressure from the North caused a continuous mass migration that, until the final extension of the desert had been reached, kept the entire continent south of the Sahara in an almost permanent motion.

The third factor is the geographical and climatic situation of Africa. The rain forest region, surrounded by moist and arid savannas, offered favorable conditions for a variety of cultural types yet was sometimes highly definitive in excluding one or another of them. The entire intertropical region of Africa, for instance, did not permit cattle-raising societies because of the tsetse fly, and the rain forest, though favorable for gatherers and hunters, is absolutely hostile for planters and agriculturists. They had, so to speak, to change the environment, as they actually did, in order to survive.

If we add these three points together, many characteristics of African culture and religion become understandable. The permanent migrations led to a lively exchange of cultural elements, and this simultaneously brought unity and diversity. This can be seen not only in the African languages but also in the range of religious ideas.

Because migrations brought into contact different peoples of differing cultures with varying specialization, they furnished the background for the development of non-primitive cultures. This was especially the case when pastoral nomads as in eastern and southern Africa and the Sudan came into contact with planters and agriculturists. The religious type resulting from such conditions is inseparable from the institution of the sacred kingship.

The fact that there are survivals of pre-negroid populations (such as the Bushmen in the south or some hunting tribes in the east) bestows high probability to the assumption that the population in the rain forest, commonly known as the African Pygmies, was at least until modern times protected and isolated from all the events mentioned above and has preserved a very archaic, if not the most archaic, culture of the world. It even offers good reasons for the hypothesis that their culture can be considered typical of the stratum that formed the general base of the later cultures in Africa. For this and other reasons special attention will be paid to the religion of the African Pygmies. We thus can exclude them in this general description of African religious ideas.

Apart from this hunter (gatherer) stratum, Africa shows a variety of cultural types. In the forest region and in southeastern Africa the relatively unspecialized forms of the cultivation of bananas and tubers are found. In the north, east and south they are surrounded by often highly organized agricultural societies with cattle and small livestock and by pastoral nomads. Being dependent primarily on cattle breeding, these nomads can be found in the south (Hottentots), the lake region and the northeast (Nilotic and East Hamitic peoples).

There is no African tribe whose life is not surrounded and penetrated by rites and rituals. Such events as birth and death, initiation and marriage, planting and harvesting, drought and rain, are freighted with symbolism, finding visible expression in the accompanying cults and customs. The invisible background of this symbolism consists of the different myths that connect the particularities of life with the totality of being. Heaven and earth, life and death, weakness and power are put into perspective by the recollection and affirmation of a meaningful world that unifies the scattered pieces of common experience. Against this background people live and act and orient themselves. Thus it is necessary to note the major traits of African mythology to get a concrete idea of African religions.

African myths are deeply concerned with the creation of man (and the world) and the origin of death. Creation is not an event that took place once upon a time, but an everlasting presence. It is the truth and the reality of all beings as they exist today. It continues in the life of nature and the growth of man, plants, and animals. *Mulungu*, the word for God among the Bantu tribes of southeast Africa, means creation and the power to create – a power that sustains all things now and forever. The world is not a matter of static essences but is in the making, centered on man as the most important force among all created and visible forces. Existence is thus of variable intensity, capable of being diminished or of being strengthened by the creative and responsible behavior of man.

The myths express this idea of a continued creation and of man as its foremost realization or as the measure of all things when they identify the mythological godhead with the culture hero, the great mother, the first ancestor, the chieftain, the eldest, or with the first smith, whose representatives still hold a sacred position throughout the entire continent. The same idea underlies the office of the 'master (priest) of the forest' (*gao-tu* among the Gurunsi of west Africa) and the 'master (priest) of the earth' (*kuaar muon* among the Nuer in northeast Africa). When man interferes with the forest (hunting or clearing), or with the earth (settlement or planting) he actually enters the process of creation and thus becomes responsible for its meaning and harmonious continuation. To resume and to fulfill this responsibility, the masters of the forest and of the earth are needed.

Analogous to the mythological identification of God and man, the mythic godhead is also associated with atmospheric phenomena. If we take the mythological process as an event that develops almost on its own, we may say that the godhead incorporates itself – as the name *dzingbe*, *njame*, *nzambe* (west and central Africa) tells us – in celestial or luminous phenomena. God and the sky (western and southern Africa), or God and the sun (Ethiopia), or God and the moon or the stars (Bushmen, Rhodesian astral-mythology) are symbolically identical. At times it is impossible to determine whether the name for God means the sun or the sky or both, as for instance *ruwa* among the Dschagga tribes at the Kilimandsharo. But whether this be so or not, what matters here is the semantic thrust of African mythology, namely, that God is presence, continuing providence, mysterious power in all things, the one because of whom man is capable of acting and is morally responsible for what he is doing.

There are different mythological explanations for the origin of death. Nearly all of them culminate in the idea that God withdrew because man did not follow his demands and that this withdrawal was the beginning of all evil in the present world.

The fundamental awareness of continued creation and divine providence, of a universe of interacting forces in which man makes his decisions in personal terms and with regard to a personalized world, undergoes a process of reversal within mythology. God was active during primordial times. What remains are the graves of *heitsi-eibib* (the God of the Hottentots), which can be found everywhere, and death. The appearance and manifestation of death in a world interpreted according to the creative and ethical patterns of personal behavior entails such a contradiction that only the mythic withdrawal of the God-person can explain this fundamental distortion of meaning. On the other hand, is this withdrawal truly sufficient to explain the contradiction of death? In some instances the mythologies speak of chance events, where some unfortunate accident happened. An animal trusted with man's eternal life was not careful enough, was beguiled by others, etc.

The mythological necessity to connect death with God entails what may be called the dualism of the African religions. God and the figures of his mythic representation are either good, bad or both. The mythology speaks about good and bad sons and attributes favorable circumstances such as the day sky to the good god, and menacing realities such as the night sky to the evil god. Often this dualism is expressed in the figure of a trickster-godhead, sometimes the 'bad' god of the neighbor tribe.

The major effect of this mythological structure on the theoretical level is the conception of a so-called *Deus otiosus*, of an almost cultless God or godhead, whose impact is above all on consciousness. People know that he is there beyond the worries of everyday life – a consciousness which is mainly transmitted in all kinds of proverbs and sayings. On the practical level he is more or less 'replaced' by the worship of ancestors or other deified symbols or natural spirits. God is so powerful and infinitely great that, as the Lundu in Angola say, everyone who dares to portray *zambi-kalunga* will die. To fulfill the needs for rites and rituals they thus have to recur to other instances of the mythological universe. Consequently, the most important godhead among the different hunting groups throughout Africa is the forest god or the master of the game. Tribes dependent on rain substitute or reidentify him with the rain god. The same can be said about the atmospheric phenomena such as thunderstorm or rainbow, which are associated with the godhead and identified as god in various ways. The earth, as the mythic wife of the high god and represented in myths describing world parents or the world egg, is predominant in the religious consciousness of the agriculturist tribes in the Sudan and west-coast and central Africa and is often accompanied by a dual organization of society. In east Africa sacred crocodiles and snakes also fall within this process of mythological identification, association and replacement. The most common feature is, however, the symbolic identification with man himself.

In keeping with the idea that God is the origin of life and death, the living and the dead are not absolutely separate but form one large unity. Present life is possible only because of the support of man's ancestors. They are responsible for the growing of fruits, for the health of the community, for the fertility of women and other things. Sacrifices and prayers must be offered to keep the ancestors in a good mood or to reconciliate them if they have been insulted by offenses against customs. Sometimes even human sacrifices were necessary to accomplish these goals.

The relationship between the living and the dead is ambivalent. The ancestors are loved and feared, depending on the circumstances of the individual or the tribe. This relationship, with its accompanying substitution of ancestor worship for the cult of the creator God, has already been indicated by the mythological identification of God, the bringer of blessings, as the first ancestor. *Unkulunkulu,* the God of the Zulus, appears in all these different colors. In the mythology of the Nguni of south Africa, who actually worship a heavenly queen, the first ancestor called and created man and beast out of a swamp. The Herero of South Africa, who believe in a more or less cultless sky god, tell us that the first ancestor called man and cattle out of a (sacred) tree. He brought all cultural blessings, among them fire. He continues to live in this fire.

This substitution of the 'highest being' with its symbolizations can also be noticed in the identification of God and the dead. This happens when the spirit of the deceased is summoned by the name of God, for example, *mulungu* in eastern Africa. The metempsychosis of the dead into snakes in eastern Africa and the Sudan can be interpreted as a kind of two-fold substitution: The association of the deceased with God is recognized in the mythological instances of the godhead.

Ancestor worship is also connected with a general belief in reincarnation, which becomes functional in the socially significant ideology of the African chieftainship. As a representative of the ancestors, the chieftain is not only physically responsible for the prosperity of his community, but often he is also worshipped as a demigod. Many rituals (among them ritual murder or human sacrifice) were connected with the idea of the chieftain, especially when it developed into the idea of the sacred kingship, where the position of the king was surrounded by endless rules and taboos and an institutional priesthood.

Another feature of African religions, which might be seen in the horizon of ancestor-ideology, are the initiation rituals for boys and, very often, also for girls, and at least some of the secret societies. The connection of initiation with the social institution of age classes in eastern Africa is a good example to show the interdependence of religious traditions and social development.

The use of masks, such as those found on the west coast and in central Africa, points more to the general basic mythology (the celebration of primordial events and contact with invisible powers) than to ancestor-ideology, which however may play an important role in individual cases.

Typical cults, which belong mainly to the complex of hierophanies in natural phenomena, are the rites and rituals centered on the sacred fire (from southern to eastern Africa) and the fertility rites centered on the snake, especially among the Bantu tribes in the southwest. The widespread totemistic aspects of African religions, the reverential awe for certain animals or other objects, occasionally connected with the search for a guardian spirit or individual totem, can be seen as a synthesis of both kinds of hierophanies, the symbolization of the divine in natural and social signs. Clan-totemism (*oruzo* among the Herero) is an all-African socioreligious phenomenon.

While the African mythology has been discussed so far in its human and natural symbols (ancestor-ideology and nature symbolism), it also should be examined from the viewpoint of its more or less unspecified side that appears in the idea of power. According to African myths, divine power can be interpreted as the creative force of the whole universe. *Njama*, as it is called on the west coast, or *imana* as it is called in Ruanda, or *modimo* as the Sotho in southern Africa designate it, is difficult to define. It is the all-powerful presence of God himself, which can be understood in personal as well as in impersonal terms. As such it interplays with all that is important. This theory of divine power becomes obvious in the interpretation of man, who is thought of as being composed of different principles of life. Only as long as man is gifted with divine power can he be said to be alive. If this power diminishes, man dies, and the different principles or souls pass away.

The African interpretation of the human soul or of man usually distinguishes between two principles that interact in the constitution of the human being. These are the body-soul, or power of life, and the image- or shadow-soul, which may be interpreted as spiritual body, or as free soul. In addition to this interpretation, we have more complicated ones. Man is understood, for instance, as the result of three or four and even more principles. The Nuer, for instance, speak of *ring* (flesh), *yiegh* (breath or life) and *tie* (intellect or soul). Occasionally we also hear about a female soul and a male soul, or about a little thing which will be transformed into a spiritual body when man dies. According to this interpretation of man, the problem of reincarnation is therefore not just that of an individual principle but that of the universal creation, or, so to speak, of the meta-individual aspects of the human being. But whatever the ideas about the particular make-up of man might be, they are integrated by the mythological consciousness of all-pervasive power. The preservation and augmentation of this power in its particular appearances, i.e., in man, becomes an absolute demand of his well-being. It is achieved by prayers, sacrifices, customs, rituals, wisdom and conduct, sometimes even by eating corpses. Specific illustrations of these ideas concerning divine power are the cult of the dead, of the underworld, the metamorphosis of powerful persons into certain animals (a leopard, for example), ritual cannibalism (mainly in the west), and the veneration of skulls (in central Africa).

There are still other forms in which the mythic power becomes manifest. Fetishes mainly used on the west coast, are little bundles of stones, hair, teeth, rings, and the like, that are believed to be powerful and to protect a house and its owner. To understand these objects and their cultural and religious significance, we must presuppose the mythology or ideology of power. Within this context they become symbols of orientation, consecrated objects, in which the person who lives with them recognizes important features of world and life, while the outside observer has his particular difficulties to grasp the sense and/or non-sense of instances that are apparently alien to him. In combination with the ancestor worship, the fetishes are believed sometimes to be inhabited by an ancestor's ghost. To the extent that ideas, cult and customs connected with certain trees or shrines or other objects show the same patterns, they can be subsumed under the category of the divine power mythology.

Also to be mentioned in the context are various sacrifices, which rely, by their very nature, on the symbolism of the sustenance and completion of life. They are especially cultivated among pastoral tribes such as the Shilluk, Galla, Nuer, and others, where they are centered on the symbolic identity between the soul (blood) of the animal and the soul (life) of man, in which the power of the universe (God) becomes manifest. As a consequence, cattle symbolize power and greatness, equally attributable to God, the first ancestor (first mother), and the chieftain, and are thus an integral part of social and religious interactions. Within this process of transformation they lose their empirical and economical significance in order to become mythological figures themselves. As a result it becomes possible that among the Nuer a cucumber may be substituted for the animal if there is no ox because people are too poor.

Various hunting rituals, intended to prevent the release of dangerous forces that may result from the killing of animals, also mirror the divine-power mythology; so do various forms of sexual symbolism, which range from the use of nakedness as part of hunting rituals and initiation ceremonies to cultic cohabitation (especially among the more specialized planters).

Within the process of symbolization we can distinguish between various attitudes toward this process itself; for instance, between an attitude of 'persuasion, petition or propitiation and the attitude of coercion, constraint or compulsion' (see Cooper, 1929, p. 33 and Marwick, 1970). Consequently we may hypothetically preserve the use of the term 'religion' for those instances, which relate to 'activities that are characterized by a persuasive or propitiatory attitude toward the supernatural world' (*ibid.*), or as we may also say, within the world of absolute symbols, while the term magic could be applied to those phenomena, which are accompanied by the attitude of coercion, constraint or compulsion. As such, both attitudes are part of the general process of symbolization and its emergence in absolute symbols and thus belong in some way together.

Magic, which generally plays an important role in religion, is spread throughout the continent, sometimes becoming the sole concern and replacing almost all other kinds of religious customs. The purpose of magic is to gain prosperity and power. To achieve this, certain rituals and ceremonies (for example, rock painting among the Bushmen) must be performed. Rules and supporting objects (colorstones, powerful substances, and the like) must be known. The performer must also have special powers and gifts. We have here an indication of shamanism, which exists in Africa, but in a less-developed form than it does in other areas. As long as such rites and actions are performed for the good of the community, they can be called white magic because they do not necessarily lack a positive relationship to religion and to the actualization of the symbolic gifts of man. The moment they are used for destruction and egotistic purposes, however, the African peoples consider them absolutely evil. Such practices can be called black magic, or *bulozi*, the common name given to them among the Bantu peoples.

The development of magic has a tremendous impact on religious practices in general, as is obvious if we consider only such phenomena as the interpretation of dreams and their significance for ancestor worship, or the observation of omens. But magic contributes very strongly to a sociologically relevant institution too, the office of the priest or medicine man, the official magician.

Normally, priestly functions are exercised by the eldest member of the group (family) or the chieftain. They represent the first ancestor and do what he did, for instance, tasting milk among the Herero. It ought also be mentioned here that cattle-breeding very often serves solely religious purposes because the animals used in sacrifices have meaning only when they are regarded from the viewpoint of the ancestor cult and its mythology. In cultural areas, however, where magical rites supplanted religious rites, as in western Africa, 'specialists' are needed. Here we find the beginning of an autonomous profession and class. These specialists, who can be either male or female, should not be confused with persons who receive prophetic messages. As it is apparent today, such messages and the respective movements are numerous. But here we reach the point where the context with primitive cultures is lost, while a new chapter of history is in the process of being written.

4. RELIGIONS OF ASIAN PRIMITIVES

Asia not only gave birth to the leading literate cultures, but also to the great universal religions. Buddhism, Taoism, Confucianism, Judaism, Christianity, and Islam, all originated within the continent and have permeated and penetrated nearly all cultural areas. There are, of course, many features and traits of primitive religions in these areas which have been preserved or spared by the world religions. Their inclusion into the general configuration of the Asian high cultures, however, makes it doubtful if an attempt to outline these instances of primitive religions would contribute to a clarification of the issue. Because of this complexity their methodological significance for the study of primitive religions is reduced considerably. Moreover, they raise additional problems that can be meaningfully approached only when the empirico-philosophical phenomenon of primitive religion has been sufficiently elucidated. Accordingly they do not form a point of departure but an object that is to become investigated after an analysis of primitive religion has been completed. For this reason we will restrict ourselves to those ethnoreligious data which show a significant contrast between their own cultural tradition and that of the bordering high cultures.

Six different areas in Asia can be distinguished that show a certain degree of cultural uniformity. They are southwest Asia, the Indian subcontinent, southeast Asia (including Indonesia), east Asia, interior Asia, and northern Siberia (with northern Europe). For reasons just mentioned southwest Asia (which includes the Arab states, Afghanistan, Iran, and Turkey) can be excluded from our survey. And this is also the case with east Asia, which covers China, Japan and Korea. Both these areas are either dominated by universal religions such as Islam, Taoism, Buddhism or Confucianism or by typical non-primitive cultures.

4.1 *The Indian Subcontinent*

The Indian subcontinent, including India, Pakistan, Nepal, Bhutan, Kashmir and Ceylon, is dominated by the Indic high culture. The leading religions are Hinduism and Islam. Buddhism, Jainism and Parseeism were and are further influential traditions. As a response to Islam the Sikhs formed their own monotheistic religion. Judaism and Christianity also have long traditions in various parts of India. Among these different religious denominations, some primitive cultures survived with their own religious traditions, but they are often in a stage of acute atrophy. The tribal population in the plains, for instance, which has been isolated from the Hindu society and socially degraded, has preserved some of its old rituals, particularly those associated with the preparation for raids. Sacrifices to the tribal divinity and the observation of omens are used as protecting spells. During a raid no word is spoken lest the spell be broken. In earlier times there were even (as elsewhere in India) human sacrifices, until the English outlawed them.

The culture of the inland tribes ranges from that of food gatherers to highly developed farming cultures. Sometimes, like the Vedda in Ceylon, one people belongs to different culture types.

Although all the primitive tribes can be linguistically assigned to the Dravidian, Indo-Aryan, Munda or Sino-Tibetan groups, it is not possible to follow similar patterns in the description of their religions. This is due to the specific history of the subcontinent and also partly to a general lack of information about Indian primitives. As a result, this survey will resemble a mosaic rather than a well-sketched picture. Moreover, because of this lack of adequate information as well as of the universal influence of Hinduism, no Indian religion will be selected as a paradigmatic or representative example of primitive religion.

One of the most primitive tribes of India are the Chenchus in Hyderabad (Andhra Pradesh). Because of their life as gatherers and hunters, elaborate institutions had no chance to develop and to complicate the religious situation. Every adult may function as priest. There is a general unity between the world of man and the world of the divine, which is centered around a forest goddess and a sky god. *Garelamaisama*, the goddess of the forest, is responsible for the growth of plants and animal life. She is called upon in the morning, when the hunters or the fruit gatherers begin their work. She is also invoked when the work has been successfully ended. A small piece of the game or fruit is thrown into the forest informally, or some drops of an intoxicating liquid are poured out before drinking begins. Primitial offerings are also usual, as elsewhere in India.

A second divinity who takes a major position in the cult and life of the Chenchus is *bhagavantaru*, a sky god (with a Vedic name) who is responsible for thunder and rain. His protection is sought in dangerous situations. The soul or the power of life (*jiv*) originates from him. To him it also returns, if he does not reject it. In case he does, the soul becomes an evil ghost (*dayam*). Both divinities are responsible for the maintenance of the tribal customs. *Bhagavantaru* may punish their transgression by a penalty as severe as death. Besides *garelamaisama* and *bhagavantaru*, there are many minor gods and goddesses. Their benevolence can be obtained by a great variety of sacrifices.

A creation myth is known among the Kadar, a primitive planting tribe of Kerala. The mountains, the forest, and all things were made by a couple that came out of the earth. *Melavay* and *melakuratti* created man, who had a paradise-like life. All man needed was there abundantly. But the human beings began digging up roots and tubers without any reason, and finally they were forced to do so. From that time, the paradise condition ceased. The Kadar still worship this creator god, together with a goddess, who is descended from the same creator god. Whatever the full and adequate interpretation of the myth may be, it shows that an experience based on growing vegetation and the consciousness of cultural alienation was one of the major features in their religion.

When we contrast the religion of primitive hunters and gatherers with the religion of primitive planters, the religious life of the planters is generally marked by a sort of increasing complexification. The number of important gods and ghosts becomes augmented. Ancestors begin to become predominant. The performance of priestly functions needs special training and knowledge. The enlarged role of the ghosts and spirits favors the profession of seers and shamans. Some examples will serve as illustration.

Belief in one almighty and highest God is attested to by the Bhils, a tribe with a long tradition that lives in the mountains (Satpura, Vindhya and Aravalli) north of Bombay. *Bhagwan*, or *iswar*, is the good king, the true master, the giver of bread, the father, the creator. He dwells in the heights. In addition, there are many gods and goddesses who administer the different events and significant situations of daily life. The dead go to *bhagwan*. But many and complicated ceremonies are necessary before the soul finally attains peace. However, not all of the dead find it; only the good. The worship of souls is also a part of the worship of *bhagwan*. There is no doubt that the influence of Hinduism penetrated not only the social structure of these tribes, but also their whole religious outlook.

Among the Kurumba, south of Mysore, whose economy shows a wide range of agricultural types, sacrifices and prayers are directed toward the first ancestor of the tribe, who also is their highest God (*hetaya*). The village chief inaugurates the rituals surrounding farming customs. He also erects the main post of each house, which has, as elsewhere in India, a special symbolic significance as the place where the supporting and protecting gods dwell. Related groups are centered on a common cultic ground where they have meetings to worship their kin god.

Ancestor worship can also be found among the Gond, who live southeast of Nagpur and whose economy shows similar patterns to that of the Kurumba. Planting and harvesting are accompanied by sacrifices of goats, pigs and hogs. They are presented to the spirits of the hamlet, to the mother Earth, and to the ancestors. New fruits may be eaten only after thanksgiving rituals have been performed. Like the Kurumba, the Gond tribes also have their cult centers for the kin. The god of the kin is thought to dwell in a sacred tree. When a member of the kin has died he is brought to this place where a *menhir* will be erected in his honor. All these events are accompanied by sacrifices and rituals. The stones are considered signs and sources of blessing for the descendants. The ancestors who are on guard over the *gotul*-house where the boys and girls of the hamlet live together, or over marriage, whose stability they guarantee, are especially present in a huge earthenware pot. The wife is mainly responsible for the care of this ancestor-pot.

The division of kins is generally marked by the name of an animal mythologically connected with the history of the kin (totemism) and which must not be eaten by its members.

Besides these deities, there is also a highest being called *bhagavan*, or *maha-puruh*, the great East. His wife is *parvati*, the earth. Both play their cultic and religious role as *auwal*, the mother of the hamlet, and *aki pen*, the guardian of the hamlet. The principle of life (also called *jiv* here) comes from *bhagavan*. Life will be brought back to *bhagavan* by his messenger. Reincarnation is possible. The personality of the deceased continues to exist as a *sanal* or ancestor divinity.

It is understandable that a world with so many powers needs special functionaries to be kept in order. This is the purpose of the priests and the seers. An example from the Saora of Orissa will make this clear.

The Saora tribes, whose language belongs to the Munda stock (which, in turn, points to the Austro-Asiatic Mon-Khmer languages), are greatly concerned with the underworld in their religion. The ordinary world cannot exist without the underworld, and the dead need the living. Therefore, it is necessary to have a shaman.[6] Like other people, he has two souls, a big soul and a small soul. The small soul is identical with the principle of life. Its separation from the body would cause death. The big soul, however, has the ability to walk through the earth and the underworld, while a shaman spirit takes its place. When that occurs, that is, when the shaman falls into trance, his soul is able to communicate with the other world and to help the living and the dead, healing the living from their sickness and restoring a full death-life to the dead. The shaman himself is elected by a ghost of the underworld (*ildasum*), who wants to contract a marriage. The ghost wife or husband will support the human husband or wife in all the duties

---

6. The term 'shaman' is of Tungusic origin. It is used for all those individuals who possess (special) faculties with regard to man's relationship to the symbolic that distinguish them from others. These faculties might stem from 'vocation', but they might also be acquired by training, or both. If the distinction between shaman and other people becomes the basis of religious orientation and ritual, one can speak of shamanism as a religious system. On the other hand and depending on the context, the word shaman may be translated by such words as priest, minister, medicine man, bard and wise man. In this sense it is not possible to restrict the use of the word shaman to situations that represent shamanistic religions.

as priest, seer, and physician. There also exists a sun god among the Saora divinities, who takes the highest position and reigns over the deities of the stars (angels). Sometimes he is thought to be the creator God and bringer of blessings (*kittung*). At other times, he appears as an expression of a collective godhead. At any rate, more important for daily life are the ghosts and the dead who are contacted by the (male or female) shaman.

Although the primitive tribes in Bhutan, Sikkim, Nepal and Kashmir are strongly influenced by Hindu culture, they have preserved their own 'animistic' religion, or at least parts of it. The highest peaks are considered the seats of the gods, who are often bisexual figures. Tribal priests and shamans are responsible for maintaining communication between man and the ghosts or gods. Unlike the shamans of the Saora and other primitive tribes in the Deccan, they do not consider themselves the medium of a divinity or as having been selected by a ghost.

The concept of the soul, or the principle(s) of life, plays a very important role in these religions. The Konyak Naga in Assam, for instance, conceive of three souls that survive man's death. *Yaha*, the first soul, wanders through the land of the dead, to which the shamans also have access. The second soul, *mio*, adheres to the skull, from which it distributes power and fertility. (This belief seems to have been a strong motive for the cannibalism of these tribes.) The third soul, *hiba*, is a ghost that flies around the home.

Most important for these tribes is the power of the dead. The erection of *menhirs* and posts, which can be found throughout India and southeast Asia as the survival of a once widespread and powerful megalith culture, is the most expressive symbol of the belief in the power of the soul and its interrelation with the world of the living.

The Tibetan version of these 'animistic' traditions is the so-called *bon* religion, whose followers (*bon-po*) practice a mixture of pre-Buddhistic and Buddhistic traditions.

4.2 Southeast Asia

According to its cultural traditions, Southeast Asia includes not only the states and nations of Indochina but also the Indonesian Islands. The languages spoken here belong to the Mon-Khmer, the Sino-Burman-Tai, or the Malayo-Polynesian stock. Although many civilizations originated in this area and despite the fact that the universal religions became influential among the different peoples, many primitive cultures survived in inaccessible jungles and in the interior of many islands.

The Moi in Vietnam, the Pong in Cambodia, the Kha in Laos are primitive groups inhabiting the forests. They live by hunting and gathering, but they have adopted the plow in many places as well. The social systems dominant among them vary from the matriarchate to the patriarchate. Religion is of special importance because it not only penetrates the whole tribal life (as in all primitive cultures) but it has also put its stamp on their view of the world, which otherwise shows many features of a high culture. The entire world is understood as a manifestation and field of action of invisible powers. Man encounters them constantly in all possible situations. He tries to master them, but, at the same time, is forced to be subject to them. By means of sacrifices he may even become part of them.

A special representative of the divinity is the buffalo, which takes a foremost position in religious ceremonies. The ghosts receive its soul, men eat its meat and use its blood as a sacramental sign. The blood of a buffalo is put on an equal basis with that of a human being.

The priest, who is sometimes also the chief, is responsible for good relations with the ghosts. He must conquer the bad influence of evil ghosts, whose power is shown in sickness and death. Many rituals surround death and burial. The spirits of the hamlet, who live in the houses of men, are called upon for the success of the hunt and the harvest. Ancestors, however, are often more important and are honored during their own feasts each year. The ghosts of the ancestors dwell in the skull of a buffalo, which is exposed on the altar of the ancestors in the house.

An interesting feature of the religion of the Lamet in northern Laos is their belief that only man and rice have a soul. Therefore, it is necessary to take care of the rice soul with sacrifices and prayers, which provide the rice field with a protective shield against the influence of evil ghosts. At the same time, they please the ancestors and gain the support of the spirits of the hamlet. During harvest time, the rice soul flees from field to field until it finds peace and rest on a sacred place near the field cottage.

Perhaps the oldest and most primitive culture in this area, and the least influenced by others, is that of the Negritos who can be found on the mainland in Malaya (Semang), the Philippines (Aeta) and the Andaman Islands (Andamans), although they once had wider distribution. Because of their simple economy and social organization, they will be treated separately.

A further group of primitive cultures is represented by the Veddoids, already mentioned as inhabitants of Ceylon. They are also found in Malaya, southern Celebes, eastern Indonesia and eastern Sumatra. On Ceylon their religion centers on *kande yaka*, the lord of animals. In the interior of Malaya, where they live as gatherers and planters (Sakai, Senoi), they worship a thunder god and a female creator. Other groups strongly influenced by the Paleo-Indonesians are the Sakai and Kubu of Sumatra, the Tokea, Toala, and Tomuna of Celebes, and others. Together with the so-called primitive Indonesians, who began migrating into the archipelago 4,000 years ago and whose remains can be found among the Djakudn and Mantra in Malaya, the Punan, Bukitan, Tagbanua, and others in Borneo and the Philippines, the Lubu and Mamek in Sumatra, the Orang Laut or Sea Gypsies on the coast of Malaya and Sumatra, they believe in a supreme sky god, who often has the earth as his wife. Sometimes both are considered two aspects of one being. They represent the universe. Personal and impersonal features intercross. The tense and polar togetherness of the divinity is the principle underlying the general order of the world which is reflected in the rituals. They also have many ghosts, that is, beings endowed with power. The ancestors are part of these beings. Their support is sought by shaman priests.

The same ideas are found in a more sophisticated manner among the Paleo-Indonesians, who have adopted a sedentary and agricultural mode of life. The most important of these populations (who occasionally number more than one million) are the Batak in Sumatra, the Dayak in Borneo, the Igorots in Luzon and others. They usually have one or several higher gods, who do not always have a special cult. Nevertheless, they are considered to be the creators and guardians of order and helpers in utmost danger. The Dayak, for instance, consider *batara* the highest being, who is above all things and who is responsible for them. But there are two *batara*: One is the higher region, the other the lower. All spirits and ghosts obey the latter. The *batara* below, however, obeys the upper. Both are equal in knowledge and in all other properties. They are, in a certain way, their own completion in one another.

Mythology explains this character of the divine by using the motive of a holy struggle between the upperworld and the underworld, which led to the present structure of the world and the cosmos. Mythological variants of this theme are the sacred wedding of heaven and earth (the myth of the cosmic parents) and the separation of heaven and earth. Here, the gods appear as birds or snakes, or (seen in their unity) as the tree of life, which gave birth to all the gods and to man. Often, one among them is considered the bringer of blessings. As the myth of Hainuwele (among the Wemale of Ceram) tells us, the mythic divinity is sometimes killed. But after the corpse has been cut into pieces and buried, it sprouts again as domesticated plants, by which the people are now able to live. In the mythologies of the Marian in New Guinea, these gods or goddesses are usually called by the name *dema*; a name, which has reached widespread use in the description of similar patterns.[7] Sometimes the explanation of the domesticated plants is less dramatic but uses the same motive: A semi-divine girl dies seven days after she has been born and becomes the rice plant (among the Paleo-Indonesians of Celebes).

Among these peoples, mythology not only hints to an epoch that explains the existence of the present world and cosmos, but it also understands this epoch as the beginning of a solid and necessary order, of a heavenly or sacred body of custom (called *oroisa langi* among the tribes of Nias, or *kadanyan* in northern Luzon). To follow these traditions gives power and wisdom. Their celebration is an ideo-religious necessity. The great festival of the Ngadyu-Dayak, the *tiwah* feast, is in this sense believed to renew and restore the divine order by representing the myth of creation, which is narrated in an archaic language.

Closely connected with these ideas is the worship of ancestors. Man is composed of three or more principles: The body, the power of life (called *tondi* among the Batak and *hambaruan* among the Dayak), and the shadow-image being, which survives and continues to live on mountains, small islands, or in the far distance. The 'shadows' are honored by megaliths, which were already mentioned in connection with Indic traditions. The contact between the spirits and people is established by the shaman.

7. Since the theme of a dying godhead can be found among religions the world over, A. E. Jensen (1966, p. 10) has suggested that the term 'dema' should be used to designate this universal motif. In contrast to Jensen, J. v. Baal (1971, p. 176) argues against such an application of the word 'dema': 'Its application as a generic term in the wide sense given to it by Jensen seems hardly warranted.' As in similar cases, there is without a doubt a point in this argument. On the other hand it is difficult to deny a certain historical precedence in coining generic terms. For this reason we do not plea for an abolishment of the term, even though the cultural context might have been (at least partially) misapprehended by Jensen. At any rate, when we refer to a dema-godhead, we are alluding to the idea that the godhead or divine being becomes creative, usually as a culture hero, through its death, that is, through a transformation in which death reveals its meaning as rebirth and new beginning.

Closely interrelated with the idea of power, the over-emphasis on which occasionally dominates or replaces other religious traditions, is the practice of cannibalism and of running amuck among the Paleo-Indonesians. The mythological tree of life or the world-egg, which are seen as source of life and which are often represented in cult objects, point in the same direction.

One should mention also the different taboos[8] that, like the divine order itself, permeate all important events, such as the construction of houses and boats, birth, marriage, death, war and planting. The word-taboos developed at times into so-called taboo-languages because speaking the common words would be calamitous.

Beside the shamans, there are also well-trained priests. But it is not always possible to separate these two functions.

In summary, it can be said that there are considerable differences among the various cultures in Southeast Asia. Because of their geographical position, many areas, including islands of the archipelago such as Celebes and eastern Indonesia, became a crucible of the different cultures. There are, however, two cultural types that can be clearly distinguished: The gatherers and hunters, best represented by the Negritos, and the agricultural type, which extends in many points into an archaic high-culture and which is mainly represented by the Paleo-Indonesian cultures of Sumatra and Borneo. There can be no doubt that their religious traditions show a degree of compexity that settles them at the borderline of primitive culture typologically speaking.

4.3 *Inner Asia*

With its wide steppe zones and steppe forests, inner Asia offered a highly favorable environment for the development of animal breeding and nomadic pastoralism. The nomadic tribes, which can be found from the Pacific in the northeast to the Balkans in the west and from the Altai Mountains in the south to the

---

8. The etymology of the Polynesian word *taboo* (*tabu*, *tapu*) is not clear. It is thought to be composed of *ta* (to designate, to mark) and *pu* (extraordinary, exceedingly). See F. R. Lehmann (1930, p. 65). From a functional perspective a taboo is any kind of prohibition; it is that which is forbidden, which must not be touched, which has to be avoided for its sacredness, or because it is (factually or by interpretation) dangerous or powerful, or because of custom. The concept of taboo emphasizes not so much the ought-character of a commandment but the irrational side of the genesis and consequences of 'law'. In other words, taboo stresses the element of fear in man's self-awareness and his respective acting.

taiga and occasionally even to the Arctic Ocean in the north, are for linguistic reasons collectively called the Altaic peoples. They comprise the Turkic peoples, the Mongols and the Tungus. Their culture ranges from a type of primitive pastoralism to a well-specialized type of pastoral imperialism. The main sources of livelihood are (or better, were) herds of sheep, goats, cattle and horses. In the steppe-desert they also breed camels, and, in the highlands, the yak and a yak-hybrid. Pastoralism in the north, which slowly shifts to a hunting economy, relies upon the reindeer. Enclaves of agriculture, which developed in some areas, depending mainly on water, are rather a supplementary than a main source for livelihood.

The original religion of these peoples, which is generally called shamanism because of the dominant role of the shaman, has been preserved among the Turkic tribes of the Altai Mountains, among the Yakuts, the Mongolic Buryats and the northern Tungus. The Mongols have been influenced by Buddhism since the days of their great empire in the thirteenth century. Manicheism, Nestorianism, Islam, and Orthodox Christianity are other sources of a long-term influence that overlapped the indigenous traditions.

Common to these cultures and at the root of their religion is a cosmic mythology. The earth is thought to be a circular disk surrounded by an immense ocean. The idea that the earth has also a ring of mountains is found sporadically. Because the earth is placed in the primeval ocean, it needs a support. This is symbolized by either a pillar or an animal (a turtle, waterbird, fish, an ox, or in the northern regions, a mammoth). The sky is the roof of a big tent, which is pierced by holes, the stars. In the midst of the sky stands the world-pillar, which ends in the lodestar, the nail of the sky. The cultic ceremony of erecting a post is a symbol for this world-pillar, which is at the same time the world-axle. The sky or heaven is subdivided into many layers, whose number ranges from 3 to 7, to 9, or more. The same can be said about the structure of the underworld. When the shaman ascends into heaven, he has to pass these different layers. A birch tree with 7 or 9 notches supports him symbolically. The cosmic pillar is also thought to be an evergreen world-tree, from which the world-streams originate. When these flow into the Arctic Ocean, they form a deep ravine, which provides the entrance to the underworld for souls. A beautiful poetic imagery is frequently associated with the idea of the cosmic pillar.

The origin of the earth is explained in various ways. The Mongols believe that fire was created to separate heaven and earth. Other tribes understand the earth as the thickened surface of the primeval sea. Others know a divine motif. The earth was brought out of the depths of the primeval sea. Also known is the myth of a primeval giant or monster, out of whom the earth was formed.

Man was made by God, who collected the human subtances from the four directions. Earth became flesh and bone, iron turned into the heart and water into blood. The warmth of the body finally was due to fire.

Above all gods and other divine beings there is the Sky God. He has no image like the others and is called by various names. The Turkic peoples use the name *jajacy* (Mongolian: *zajagan*), meaning archer, governor, creator. Another name, which stems probably from the Chinese *tien-li*, Lord of Heaven, is *tengri*. The blue *tengri* is a God of fate, the giver of life, the creater. His absolute power is reflected in the *patria potestas* of the patriarch, while his love is mirrored in the affection between father and son. According to some tribes, *tengri* was supported by other gods when he made all things. Among them was a goddess with the poetic name of 'Mother of the vivifying milk-lake'.

The interpretation of *tengri* is not necessarily consistent. The Buryats, for example, know 99 *tengere* and worship the sun as the highest being. Generally speaking, however, *ülgän*, the great, is predominant. Especially the end of the times will be his. Then he will send *maidere* (bringer of blessings; divine son) to the earth in order to teach and to convert men in the fear of God. When *maidere* is killed by *erlik*, his adversary, a great fire emerges from his blood, which burns toward the sky. At this point, *ülgän* will come to the earth and resuscitate the dead. *Erlik* and all evil men will perish and disappear once and for all.

The lines and shadows on the moon, and the eclipse of the sun and moon, were signs causing many speculations. Together with the constellations of the stars, they play a significant role in the explanation of various earthly phenomena.

Besides the gods of heaven and the underworld we find many lower divinities. Thunder, for instance, symbolized by a bird, hunts the evil ghosts. The rainbow sucks water from the streams and the lakes. The best protection against thunder and ghosts is making noise and occasionally sacrificing a white horse.

The Turkic peoples worship earth and water, the Mongols fire. If fire is produced by lightning or rubbing, it is especially powerful.

As in the case of houses, the forest, water, streams and springs, each human being has his special guardian spirit, who forms a further object of veneration.

Most important for the religion of these peoples is the conception of the human soul. Actually there are two different souls. One is an independent being, able to leave the body during sleep or during sneezing and illness; the other is the conscious ego. Death means that the soul, in the form of a bird, quits the body through the mouth and nostrils. The deceased enters the other world which is a mirror image of the present one.

Since man is composed of two souls, shamanism found a very fertile soul among these peoples – or vice versa. In any case, when the shaman falls into a trance, his soul visits remote areas or the world of gods and ghosts. He is priest, prophet, seer and medicine man. It is his responsibility to determine which sacrifices are most fitting in a given situation and which ceremonies are to be performed to keep the world intact. In the case of illness he heals the sick and drives away the evil spirits. During such performances he wears clothing decorated with symbols, above all with the sign of a bird, which is his special mark. The profession of the shaman is often hereditary, though it needs a certain psychosomatic disposition. In any case, long training is necessary before a person becomes capable of self-hypnosis, achieved with the aid of the magic drum and various dances.

The Asian pastoral peoples also know the Lord of Animals, who is called upon during the hunt and in whose honor special hunting rituals are enacted. Together with the ceremonies surrounding the bear, these customs point to the religious traditions of the Arctic tribes, which developed them extensively.

4.4 Northern Siberia

Northern Siberia comprises the treeless tundra of the northern coasts and lowlands of the continent and the forest zone, or taiga. The economies that have been developed are fishing, the hunting of land and sea mammals and reindeer breeding. The indigenous social organization and technology have been relatively simple.

From a linguistic point of view, three groups of peoples can be dinstinguished: The Paleo-Siberian peoples who occupied the east, the Finno-Ugric peoples who extended as far as northern Europe in the West and the Tungus (Evenki) and Yakuts (Dolgan), mentioned previously, who pushed their way into the region between the Yenisei and Lena rivers. Although the history of these peoples and cultures is a very complex one, the present situation shows a certain degree of uniformity, the result of longterm mutual exchange and diffusion of cultural ideas and of the marked influence of a relatively homogeneous environment.

The peoples of the Paleo-Siberian group are the Asiatic Eskimos on the Bering Strait, the Chukchi around Chaunskaya Bay (the largest and least influenced group), the Koryak sout of Anadyr, the Itelmeni in Kamchatka, the Gilyak on Sakhalm Island and (in some respects) the Ainu on the Japanese island of Hokkaido. Recently the Yukaghirs of northeast Siberia have been assigned to the Uralic-speaking peoples. Since the general features of these cultures are simple, a more detailed account of this type of religion will be given in treating the religious life of the Eskimos as a representative example.

The Finno-Ugric group can be subdivided into three sections: The Samoyed, Ostyak, Vogul and Selkup in and around the Ural Mountains; the Finns around the Baltic Sea; and the Lapps in Lapland. Because of the various influences on these cultures and their subsequent integration into the higher cultures, their religion will be treated only in a general way.

Although the religions of these circumpolar peoples have many similarities in common with the Altaic peoples, especially as regards the institution and function of the shaman, their general view of the world is usually much simpler. The immediate experiences and questions of ordinary life affected and molded their religions and speculations in a more direct way.

The first and most impressive experience of the Arctic hunters is connected with the existence of animal life. Animals are not merely objects among others; rather, they are the most important manifestation of the divine, for man's own existence is entirely dependent on them. This manifestation is, however, not singularized in individual animals but embedded in the whole complex of nature which, in turn, is attuned to the ideas connected with animal life. Like man, the animal too has a soul. It is protected by an individual guardian spirit, who helps the hunter to catch the animal. To say that man has *pe'jul* (that is, the guardian spirit of the individual animal among the Yukaghirs) is the same as saying man is favored by the guardian spirit. Besides this guardian spirit we often find a guardian of the species, who is at the same time its owner.

The extension of this idea to nature in general accounts for the widespread feature of the so-called owner-divinities. Every natural object (tree, place, stone, water, stream) has its owner, who has to be respected by man in his conduct and cult (sacrifices). The common source of these and similar manifestations of the divine is the owner or God of the forest, or of the water, or the sea in areas where fishing has been the main support of life, or of the reindeer where reindeer-breeding became the predominant economy. The God of the forest, sometimes identified with the forest, water, or reindeer itself, is generally a benevolent deity. Occasionally he has been transformed into a trickster and evil god or goddess, who misleads peoples and tries to ruin them.

The religious significance of animals found its most touching expression in the rites and rituals connected with the bear. According to the belief of the Ainus, the bear represents an imprisoned divinity who can only be liberated by the killing of the animal. Freed from the body and pleased by prayers and ceremonies, he will protect the settlement. For that reason they catch young bears and raise them. When bears are killed, the women bemoan them. Their skin and heads are hung up in a room, and thus the divinity is enabled to watch the festivities and to enjoy them.

The Ostyaks, like other tribes, are said to awaken the sleeping bear before they kill it. Afterwards they ask forgiveness of the bear by dancing around its skin and head with masks made of birch bark.

The Lapps, who probably were familiar with the most intrinsic bear-rituals, began their ceremonies by walking in a procession to the lair of the sleeping animal. After the bear had been killed, they gave thanks that the animal had done no harm to the hunters. Arriving in the hamlet they told the animal that foreigners had slain it. Many taboos were imposed while the meat was being prepared. The whole animal had to be eaten in three days. Dances and dialogues conveyed the idea that the bear was satisfied with its treatment. Finally, the bones, the head with the snout, the genitals, and the tip of the tail were buried.

A further feature of the Arctic religions is the concept of a supreme being who dwells in the sky or heaven. His role and position vary. While the farmers and raisers of cattle worshipped him with various cults and assigned him special functions, the hunters considered him either a cultless deity, called upon only in utmost danger, or identified him with the master of the forest. Sometimes he is even all that is, the highest being, the reality of the world, hunting, success and his idol.

The God in heaven, called *ilmarinen* by the Finns, *inmar* by the Ostyaks, and *num-turem* by the Samoyeds, all meaning sky-heaven, lives 'above'. He is symbolically identified with the sky, sometimes also with the sun or certain atmospheric phenomena. The sky itself and everything bright is *inmar*. At the same time, he is the God of fertility, the completion of mother earth.

A whole chain of agricultural and pastoral deities has developed out of this sky-god conception, and there is a parallel in the manifestations or hierophanies of the forest god. The Ostyaks, for instance, speak of the soul of the field (*busi-urt*) and the grain (*du-urt*). They worship a guardian spirit of the field (*du-kiltsin*). Similarly, pastoral nomads believe in the Lord of the Meadow. Mother Earth appears as a good or evil deity, who is sometimes thought of as fluid. Her luck (*musud*), for instance, can be stolen.

A further net of ideas and rituals, which probably has its place between the sky, forest and water complex, is centered on the house. Each house or family has its own special spirits and protectors, represented in various idols but especially in the sacred hearth-fire. They are not identical with the ancestors, who generally play only a negative role in these religions. Except for some mythic ancestors, who are worshipped as gods, the souls of the dead are feared as causing illness and death.

The conception of the soul is generally dualistic. A soul that is identical with the life of the body (*lili* among the Voguls) and a so-called shadow-soul (*is, ijs*) are believed to constitute man. The latter (man's alter ego) appears also as the soul of a dream, as a lost soul, as the soul of the shaman. The shadow goes into the underworld, where it continues to live under similar conditions. It is the symbol of a counter-reality that mirrors the given while it forms part of it. Perhaps we may also say that the shadow symbolizes a contradiction that is present. As such it offers the materials to build up a world in man's fantasy which at the same time is real and not. It is a matter of realization which apart from ritual and cult loses all meaning, while nothing could be more real and meaningful when experienced within the world of cult performances.

Besides these (from a descriptive point) simple ideas, there are also very complex ones, which appear, for instance, when the relationship between the shadow-soul and the corpse has to be explained, or when several souls are enumerated, which may even undergo reincarnation wandering from plants to animals and finally to man again.

A last feature that may be mentioned in this survey is the symbolism of idols (called *seida* among the Lapps) which has cultic as well as magic implications. The general tendency to associate the world of ghosts, spirits and the high gods with figures and symbols leads to their use for mythological or sacramental and practical purposes; for instance, when the souls of the animals are first caught by a soul or shadow-catching idol – a figure of the animal in question – or when troublesome spirits are driven into an idol. The idols – or, as we may also translate (interpret) them, the sacramental objects – are an essential part of all cult performances. They belong to the reality of man and express it. The performances as such actualize this presence and its meaning. They may be conducted by the eldest member of the family but more often need the expert knowledge of a shaman or priest.

5. Religions of Oceania and Australia

While the settlement of the Australian continent was discontinued when the Sahul Shelf was flooded at the end of the last glacial epoch and the present Torres Strait was formed between Australia and New Guinea, the islands of Oceania witnessed continuous waves of immigrants from the west. The last and most extensive immigration was carried out by the Polynesians, who experienced their golden age between the seventh and twelfth centuries A. D. Apart from the more or less complete cultural isolation of Australia, resulting from geological conditions, the outcome of the various waves of migration into Oceania was the formation of a huge cultural area, including the islands from New Guinea in the west to Easter Island in the east, and from New Zealand in the south to Hawaii in the north. Taking into consideration that there are numerous local variations of cultural development, this area can be subdivided into three sections, which should be distinguished in a general treatment of Oceania. The first of these sections is usually known as Melanesia, consisting of the islands from New Guinea to the New Hebrides. Micronesia includes the islands north of Melanesia, mainly the Caroline Islands, the Marshall Islands and the Mariana Islands. Polynesia finally embraces all the islands between Hawaii, Easter Island and New Zealand. The Fiji Islands form a transitional link between Polynesia and Melanesia.

5.1 *Oceania*

Because of its geography and climate, Oceania has always favored the culture type of planters and fishers. Sago, the coco-palm and various kinds of tubers were cultivated. An abundance of leisure time made possible by this economical background provided ample opportunity for the development of a highly complex structure of socio-religious life.

The experience of witnessing the growth and death of vegetation probably produced the deepest influence on the religious consciousness of these peoples. The idea of the dying god or goddess (*dema*), and the interpretation of nature and the environment as populated by an infinite number of invisible powers and powerful entities, are expressions of this experience, or must at least be seen in connection with it. The indigenous peoples themselves conceived the category of *mana* (power, also *ingal*, voice, or *apir*, word, speech, tradition) in order to signify the genuine core and idea of life and religion.

Mana invisibly penetrates all things but becomes manifest only in extraordinary events, forms (things) and persons. Ancestors, the souls and the bones of the deceased, the sacred (soul-) bird and the deities (spirits) possess it originally. The effective word, the skilled craftsman or warrior, individuals with a strong personality, are further manifestations of the *mana*-power. 'It essentially belongs to personal beings to originate it, though it may act through the medium of water, or a stone, or a bone' (Codrington, 1891, p. 119, footnotes). *Mana* and reality belong together. Its presence therefore can be ascertained by proof. Through the observation of this presence, through prayers and sacrifices (for instance, through a piece of food for a departed friend) man is concerned with its augmentation and realization. Thus, while the power is said to be impersonal, 'it is always connected with some person who directs it' (Codrington, 1891, p. 119, footnote). Like the word of man, which is the sign of his creativity, and yet, when spoken, is no longer his, *mana* seems to be the power of creation. Though it is not always regarded in connection with a creator godhead, where this relationship exists such an interpretation can be sufficiently justified, for example, when it is said that the highest being created the world by saying all things. The power of the word may thus be considered as a link between the idea of a creator god and reality when seen in the light of *mana*.

Closely connected with the conception of *mana* is that of *taboo*, which is expressed in the observation of the sacredness of places, persons and customs. Such places are not always inherently sacred but may have been set apart by a person who has the power, for example, in order to protect his property. When they are duly observed, taboos are not harmful. Otherwise, of course, they are supposed to impose a curse upon those who violate them. For that reason, women and children (the non-initiated; those who do not share the power; who are not fully created) are very often excluded from religious rites, from man's dealing with the powers of the universe.

While the idea of *mana* may serve as an introduction into the symbolic world of Oceania, it will now be necessary to discuss the more specific data along the lines indicated above.

5.1.1 *Melanesia*

Melanesia, generally speaking, is settled by the oldest peoples in Oceania. As may be expected it exhibits a great variety of local developments. Nevertheless, there are some general features in the religious life of these peoples that are typical of the islands in the Melanesian group.

The experience of the universal meaning of growing life gave rise to the mythological conception of a world whose fractional structure is counterbalanced by the consciousness of a deep-rooted unity between all things and events. Thus, there is no functional necessity for a supreme God, although such traditions emerged now and then in esoteric circles. The gods described by mythology are transitory figures in the cultic and sacred events of the beginning. Their range of action is large and fluid. They mediate as *dema* between the divine and the vegetative life, especially that of the domesticated plants.

In a similar way the distance between man and the life of nature is bridged by totemic ideas, cults and social customs. Birth and death are not final events. Like adolescence, they manifest the beginning of a new stage, and thus are surrounded by various 'rites of passage'. Sacrifices, even in the forms of cannibalistic rituals and human sacrifices, are a symbolic expression of a cosmomorphic togetherness and transition of all life, which includes the dead no less than the living and ultimately identifies body and soul, life and death.

For the same reason, no strict distinction is made between the living and their ancestors, who are commemorated by various sacrifices and cults. Like the living they can hate and love, destroy and support. Generally, the cult of ancestors in Melanesia is centered on the cult of the skull. After the deceased has been buried for some time, the skull is excavated, and a layer of clay is laid over it. The head, painted with the colors that the deceased used to wear, is connected with a statue, or put into it. This ancestor figure (*corware*) is then either set up in the communal house or in a special skull house.

The impression made by growth and death and their eternal return in the fertility of field and man finds expression in the view that sexuality is a highly religious and symbolic sign. Thus, a rich system of sexual symbols and cults, usually grouped around initiation, has been established.

A final pattern to be regarded as emanating from this vision of unity is the socioreligious function of secrecy. Secret societies, secret initiation and death rituals, accompanied by dramatic performances with masks at secret places or in the tabooed communal house, the burial of the *uli* (chieftain) figures and of the masks, which were made in secret, and the use of secret languages are all elements of this complex phenomenon. The secret societies, for instance, are the representations of the hereafter or the divine order, which gives and justifies their special position in the society. They hold power, because they are initiated into the mysteries of the divine, especially into the mysteries of magic (ritual know-how) and taboo, which play an all-important role in the cultures of Oceania.

A recent expression of the Melanesian attitude toward life and culture, which tries to integrate modern events with traditional conceptions, is the cargo-cult, the belief that the goods that the white people bring to the islands are in reality gifts from their ancestors.

5.1.2 *Micronesia*

Among the common features of the Oceanian religions, ancestor worship is the most important in Micronesia. Although the totemistic complex (with secret cults and societies, fertility rites, masks and initiation rites) can also be found in Micronesia, its overall importance is diminished. Worship is centered on the ancestors, who have lost much of their cosmic mystique and have gained a status of their own.

Ancestors, the donors of food and shelter, continue to support their families or kin, provided they are pleased by sacrifices and rituals. Among them, the first ancestors or persons, who possessed more *mana* than the others, are deified and considered as gods (hero-cult). Such persons are especially associated with events connected with the boat, its construction, its achievements and its general symbolism. Sacred stones, which are the seats of the souls, paintings of the deceased, and various forms of burials, take precedence over rituals connected with the skull and figures of mystic unity.

While the dead of the kin are benevolent, the deceased of other groups are hostile and feared. They bring about illness and death. Protection against them is sought by a large variety of magic procedures, for instance, by the wearing of an armlet, which is braided with the hair of thedec eased. Contact with the ancestors is made by the eldest, who can be a man or a woman, depending on the social structure. Traits known from shamanistic traditions can be found occasionally.

5.1.3 *Polynesia*

Although the Polynesians are planters and fishers, who never used metal tools, their culture has left behind, by and large, all characteristic features of primitivity. Since they migrated, probably from India, and started the settlement of the Polynesian Islands 2,000 years ago, they not only became excellent navigators but also developed an historical consciousness. The establishment of a sacred and cultural center on Raiatea (Tahiti), with schools for the aristocracy, as well as an aristocracy itself, are typical features of a high culture despite the lack of written documents. (The development of the mysterious *rongo-rongo* hieroglyphs on Rapanui [Easter Island] was a local phenomenon, which does not affect the general picture). Similarly, the secret teaching about the most holy *io* (or *kiho*), who created the world through his word of wisdom and who was praised by the *tohungas* (priests, specialists) in highly speculative hymns must be considered a typical trait of a non-primitive religion. Nevertheless, there are still several religious traditions that must be mentioned in this survey of primitive religions.

While the Polynesians share the *mana-taboo* conception with the other peoples of Oceania, their view of the world itself is much more complex. On the socio-religious level, the taboos become highly complex, with a tendency to the extreme. They lead to a basic separation between common people and aristocrats (including the priests), between the world of the sacred (*tapu*) and the profane (*noa*). The same can be said about ancestor worship, which is replaced by the cult of heros, as indicated in Micronesia. The priests and kings considered themselves the representatives and descendants of the gods. The graves of the chiefs very often became the cultic and political centers (*marae*) of the community. They were marked by pyramids decorated with various symbols and idols.

On the conceptual level the world of the divine is much more stratified. There are higher and lower gods. The latter (*tua*) are everywhere. They appear as animals, especially as birds. The higher gods, whose number does not exceed a dozen, are responsible for certain domains. *Tane*, identified with the sun, is responsible for fertility. He is the god of the forest and of all things made of wood. Particularly boats are seen in connection with *tane*. Sometimes he is also the first man; in fact, the word *tane* can be translated as 'man'. *Tu*, the god of war, was worshipped in special temples and by human sacrifices. The domain of *rongo* was the fertility and vegetation of the field. In Central Polynesia the higher gods were headed by *tangaloa*, the god of the sea. Occasionally, the motif of the cosmic lovers was used to explain the creation of the world: *Atea*, the goddess of space and the infinite sky, united with *tangaloa*. The result of this divine union is the present world.

Although a well-established realm of action is attributed to the gods, their names are not always consistent. *Rongo*, for instance, generally the god of the field, became the god of war on the Cook Islands.

Despite this conception of higher gods, ordinary cult was much more concerned with the *atua*-deities and with magic. The latter becomes particularly clear in the integration of invocations into the working process. An invocation was necessary in order to render things and tools efficacious. Thus, it was not enough to build a boat; its construction became effective only when accompanied by the right rituals and taboos, sometimes even by human sacrifices. The interpretation of the taboo could go so far that even cannibalistic rituals needed special instruments, although many chieftains exercised strong opposition to such customs. The painting of the body, tattooing, and ornamentation were further means for protection against the evil forces of the universe. In this respect, the Polynesian religions do not differ greatly from the Melanesian and Micronesian traditions.

5.2 *Australia*

Even after its cultural dissociation from the Oceanic Islands, Australia remained a continent of perennial, if limited, migrations. Its culture, based on hunting and gathering, underwent a development that resulted in what may be called the final stratification of primitive cultures. An intertribal trading system, using a gesture language as means of communication, distributed not only goods and objects throughout the continent but also disseminated ideas, cults and social institutions. A surprisingly poor economy – a sophisticated invention like the boomerang, which was used among some tribes, does not change the general situation – was no impediment to the evolution of a well-developed social and religious system that covered the whole continent. Yet, apart from sporadic chieftainships, no real political system emerged. Within the societal structure the life-community remained of primary importance. Perhaps it should be said that it was precisely the spellbound symbolism of the society and its religion (or vice versa), that tended to spread and to maintain universal patterns in a cultural and economic situation where the concrete circumstances were usually more important than lore and tradition.

The core of the Australian religions seems to be connected with an extreme experience of the mythic dimension. The time and the world of today were understood as the expression of a time and world real only in mythology and dreams. Though all-pervasive (as in any functional mythology), this world of the mythic was also a separate entity to be reckoned with in the affairs of the day. Although ordinary occurrences were linked by temporal succession, the single stages of this temporal continuum did not present a sufficient reason for the mystery of their existence, nor was it the indefinite totality of the mythic which accounted for the equally indefinite totality of the *hic et nunc*. The mystery of man, for instance, was in this sense not to be understood through the act of begetting and its setting within the mythological tradition but as the formal participation of mythological beings in the present situation.

Mythological time, known as *lalan* among the Ungarinyin or *alcheringa* among the Aranda, is the time of creation and creativity. The conception of this time is comprehensive but at the same time concentrated in personal figures. *Mungan ngana* (our father) was for the Kurnai the creator of all things; he bestowed culture on man and authorized rites and ceremonies. By being mythologically interrelated with the visible phenomena of the present time, however, *bajame*, *bundjil, daramulun, nurrundere, walanganda*, or however the mythological figures may be called, can be identified with the sky, the sun, the moon, the galaxy or also with the first ancestor. What matters is the creation itself, the operational structures of the beginning, which still determine the world of the present. They are recalled in the mythological ancestors or progenitors, who are real in what they left behind: The landscape, vegetative and animal life and man with his customs and traditions. The medicine man (or shaman) and the eldest member of the group still share the power of the *lalan*-beings. Thus, limited changes of the primordial conditions can also be authorized by them in the present situation, for example, legalization of illegitimate connections and relations.

By virtue of his *ya-yari* or dream-soul, each human being is basically capable of becoming aware of the mythic world through dreams and visions. However, to achieve this awareness, complicated and secret initiation rituals, which occasionally cover several years, are necessary. They usually culminate in a circumcision ceremony. At this time, the initiate will hear the buzz of the bull-roarer, the voice of his ancestors. Being reborn in the sacred ceremony, he also will receive a new name, the name of a mythological being, who now inhabitates his body, and whose name his father heard before he was born.

The conception of these mythological beings and their function had far-reaching consequences. Being connected with them in a specific manner, man is also related to their creational origins, to the landscape, and to special plants and animals. The particular way by which this totemic connection with plants and animals was handled – the number and species differ from individual to individual and from sex to sex – led to a continent-wide totemistic system, which consisted of very complicated (two-, four- and eight-class) marriage and relation systems, not limited to tribal boundaries. The cultic implications are the regard for or avoidance of the totem (called *kobong* among the Aranda) and its ritual killing and communion from time to time. The purpose of such ceremonies was to augment the *kobong* and to signify that a mythological being had become available for reincarnation. Its effect was the recognition of the manifold identity of the individual and the transformation of this identity into societal structures.

The relationship to the land and the landscape as specified by mythology – man does not possess the land, but the land owns him – forms the general horizon of the cultic and ideational customs. The *kobong*-ancestors shaped the present land, in which they continue as sleeping and hidden powers. Sacred stones or trees or the rainbow-snake and mother of fertility, who dwells as creative power in the interior of the earth, are concrete manifestations of these ideas. Though the *kobong*-progenitors are sleeping, they have the power to send illness and death, rain and drought, and especially 'spirit children'. When a father finds such a child in his dream or vision, he gives it to his wife or sister-in-law or saves it for a later time, since no human child can be born without the existence of this 'spirit child'.

Cultic dances and dramas recall the primordial conditions but also increase the creative power of the *kobong*-beings, which are symbolized in sacred sticks (called *tjurunga* among the Aranda) during the ceremonies. In order to inaugurate the rain period, it is necessary to recolor the paintings of the mythological beings on the sacred rocks, where they are represented as anthropomorphic or animal-like figures without a mouth – a circumstance that made the present aborigines believe that for this reason the Europeans could conquer their country. To be effective, all these ceremonies had to be accompanied by songs.

More details on these religious features will be given later when Australian totemism will be treated as one of the facets of primitive religions.

6. Religion in North and South American Cultures

Present archeological and anthropological studies indicate that the settlement of America did not begin earlier than about 40,000 years ago. Probably during the last glacial epoch Proto-Mongoloid big-game hunters pushed into America when the Bering Strait was still a land bridge between Asia and North America. According to archeological evidence, some of these hunters had reached the southern tip of the double continent as early as 8,000 years ago. The cultural development of the American tribes took different forms. While the Meso-american and Andean populations created high cultures, the other tribes contin-ued to live either as gatherers and hunters with various degrees of specialization or adopted the economy of planters and agriculturists.

Since a study of primitive religion excludes, for methodological reasons, the analysis of high-culture religions, the religions of the Aztecs, the Mayas and the Incas will not be treated here. At the same time, the existence of these high cultures furnishes a sufficient reason to consider the North American tribes separately from the South American, although many morphological similarities can be noted in both.

6.1 *North America*

Apart from the area occupied by the Eskimo groups, which range from the Ale-utian Islands along the northern coasts to Greenland and whose religion will be examined as a representative example for the subarctic hunters, the following regions can be distinguished for the purpose of describing the general religious features of the North American Indians: The area of the hunters, who lived in the Canadian woodlands and around the Great Lakes, consisting mainly of Athapascan and Algonkian tribes; the area of the Californian gatherers (Yokuts, Maidu, Wintun, and others); the agricultural province of the Pueblo Indians and assimilated tribes (such as the Athapascan Apaches and Navahos) of the

Southwest; the area of the former agricultural Mound Builders or, perhaps better, the Hopewell-Adena culture in the Middle West and the Southeast, including the Muskogean, Sioux, Iroquois, Delaware and other peoples. The well-known type of the Plains Indians has been a recent development, which began with the introduction of the horse after 1680. The fundamental traits of their religion will be covered in the description of the religions of the northern and southeastern areas.

There has always been a tendency among the American Indians toward migration and tribal isolation, especially among the nomadic hunters. The result was a general splintering of the Indian languages and the formation of various transitions in their symbolic culture. At the same time we can observe how the attempt at realizing an optimal response to the basic needs of human life led to a morphological integration of various and even heterogenous religious ideas, where fundamental patterns prevail even though the symbols in which they are expressed originated elsewhere.

Although the environment of the northern area presents the general background for the formation of the religious concepts of the peoples, the religion that emerged here can be approached only by tracing it toward and from the core of deeply personal experiences. Nothing is more important than the reality of dreams and words. While the dream opens the door to the world of the mystique, the word offers the key to its contents. Therefore the northern Indians attempted to reach by fasting and silence the basic dream of their life, in which they became aware of their guardian spirit. Without his support, man has no chance to survive. He needs his help in all situations and actions. Unlike animals, which usually have only a species guardian, man has a personal guardian spirit. The shaman, or medicine man, has the strongest guardian spirit – an idea that suggested a gradation among the shamans and an institutionalization of shamanism. Classes of shamans and the shamanistic hierarchy were gauged by the strength of the respective guardian spirits.

Since mythology speaks of various guardian and owner spirits, the idea of the strongest owner spirit of mankind and the universe suggested itself. This great owner and highest God is usually symbolized by light (for example, the Athapascan *yakista*). But like the sun, the moon, the stars, and the soul, he is also *manitu*. Though it is extremely difficult to say what is meant by *manitu*, it is nevertheless such that it can be addressed by personal terms, above all by prayers, which range from the simple rhythmical invocation ho, ho, ho, to carefully formulated supplications and thanks. There are also instances where the meaning of *manitu* and the divine developed into a purely magical interpretation of the religious world. Hence, an Indian from the Great Bear Lake region could say: 'There are no gods, there is only medicine.'

Man is aware of the presence of his personal guardian spirit by the medicine bundle, which contains symbolic objects that recall his first vision. These objects are either parts of an animal or a plant, if the guardian spirit appeared in connection with them, or artificial symbols, if noncorporeal pictures formed the the vision. Occasionally medicine men with the same totem formed their own secret or esoteric societies with special rituals. They were celebrated when a new member was initiated. The center of such ceremonies was the medicine house that symbolized the order of the world and the events that had taken place, especially that of the creation of the present world by the Great Rabbit.

To please the elements, to heal illness and to ward off the evil powers are the main functions of the medicine man and/or shaman. He achieves these goals by magical operations, ceremonies and prayers. Most important, however, is the shaman's journey into the twelvefold heaven, which his soul completes while the body lies motionless on the earth. In making this trip he is supported by the sacred voice of the shaman drum, which may even serve by its own power the needs of man. As *medeolinu* (drum-sound-person), it is a part of the world of visions, of the sacred and mythic pictures and figures, which the shaman encounters but which are first of all known by the mythological narratives, the completion of the visionary experience.

A general frame of reference for the mythological tales is the narration of world history. During the first epoch the earth was dominated by animals. Man was more asleep than awake, living between dream and reality if he existed at all. The second epoch is marked by the emergence of a culture hero, who defeats the primordial monsters and restores the world after a great flood or catastrophe. Through him, the great bringer of change who gave the blessing of culture, man became man. When he disappeared, the third and present period began. Some day the culture hero will return. Then the earth will turn into flames, and this third epoch will come to an end. The concern of the present time, however, is not the future but the recovery of the contact with the mythic animals which generally has been lost. Therefore the shaman is needed, for he still participates in the mythic world of the beginning.

The most important figure in this mythological context is the culture hero or bringer of blessings. Since he formed the world through his thought and word, the spoken myth, the only true word that exists, not only repeats what he did but also represents him as myth. Although the context may be different in several respects, we still can hear this importance of myth when a Navaho informant tells us that 'knowing a good story will protect your home and children and property. A myth is just like a big stone foundation – it lasts a long time' (Kluckhohn, 1942, p. 163). But then we may ask, what is more important than the story of the beginning of man and his culture?

While the general and central idea of the culture hero is the same throughout all American mythologies, the manner of his appearance differs widely. The Great Rabbit, the Liar who does the contrary of what he says, the First Brother, the Great Shaman, and others, are his identifications in the North. In the Rockies he is identified with the Coyote, who brought order into the chaotic world. The Pacific Indians consider the Crow as the Great Demiurge and, at the same time, as Trickster. In the Southeast he appears in a dualistic way, twin brothers opposing each other and thus, in a dramatic way, performing the creative play of the beginnings.

Besides the story of the bringing of blessings, mythology introduces and explains the various invisible beings. Cannibalistic giants, benevolent dwarfs, legions of spirits, ghosts and demons people the earth, while evil itself lurks in the murky depths. Among the various ghosts are the deceased. They are thought to be transformations of the blood-soul. The image-soul, which dwells in the heart, usually is admitted to the Island of the Blessed or to the Happy Hunting Grounds. But reincarnation is also possible.

Although the relationship between myth and ritual is not of a unilineal kind, they are both in their own way modes of the mythic becoming functional and concrete. Accordingly rituals and cults were developed as means to deepen the mythological experiences and to correlate them with the significant instances of life, even though this correlation had not to be verbalized as such. They either followed the major events of the economical life or were connected with the seasonal calendar or with other instances of societal or individual import. The main purpose of the cultic rituals was the repetition of the sacred history by means of dances, masks, and prayers or songs. The experience of ecstasy, in which reason ceases and *manitu* overwhelms while reality is encountered in its truth, was the climax of the cultic event. The figures of the primordial times became alive: Animals, heaven, earth, the sun, the moon, the stars. For that reason many festivities were connected and designated by the name of an animal, especially the Bear and the Beaver.

One of the major ceremonies in the north was the New Year feast, which continued with dances and prayers for twelve days. The main figure was the Celestial Bear, who sacrificed his life on the world pillar that connects the earth with the twelvefold heaven. When the Lenape (Delaware Indians) came to the southeast and adopted an agricultural economy, the same cultic event was turned into the so-called Big House Ceremony, a thanksgiving ritual that continued for twelve days. The bear ritual was replaced by a ritual stag hunt that lasted for three days. The rest of the ceremony focused on *gischelemukaong*, the creator and his creation, as indicated by the symbolism of the Big House. Especially the middle pole was most important because it represented the structural center of the world. The repetition of this ceremony was necessary for the order of time, whose continued existence in man's being was most precarious and thus had to be created anew every day. The human response to this experience of the beginning was first of all an attitude of devout prayer.

Although historically the Pacific fishers and hunters belong to the woodland Indians, the basic conceptions of their religious life differ from the latter in many respects. The richness of sea and forest found genuine expression in the large and powerful structures of houses and totem poles, and also in the *potlatch* banquets, where by dances and ritual dramas the entire property of the host could be destroyed.

The general style of this megaxylic culture (as it has been called after the analogy of the megalithic cultures)[9] becomes paradigmatically clear in the initiation ritual of the *hamatsa* club. Its symbolism referred to the Great Cannibal at the northern brink of the earth, the first and noblest of all gods. Unless the candidate's family was rich enough, he could not apply for admission to the club. Since the ceremony was also a national festival, sumptuous means were needed to perform it.

After a time spent in the solitude of the woods, where the candidate learned by fasting and various rituals the mysteries of the Great Cannibal, he returned to the cult house with a readied corpse. The new *hamatsa* was possessed by the god and his wild desire for flesh; he was even the god himself. Symbolic per-

9. See W. Müller (1961, p. 243). The word 'megaxylic' derives from *megas* (Gr.: great, mighty) and *xylon* (Gr.: wood).

formances of death and resurrection, accompanied by an imitative cannibalistic ritual, led to a general ecstasy on the part of participants, who finally were healed (returned to normal) by a water ceremony. A procession of lights ended the ritual. The candidate himself, since he was now born anew by the god, had to learn everything over again. He thus recalled in his very behavior that the meaning of his being as well as that of tradition could not be thought and conceived of without the god(s) and the things that happened in the beginning.

A further feature of the Pacific religion was the sociocultic distinction of summer and winter. While the winter season was the time of the gods and the religious communities (as social units), the summertime was structured around other symbols. The social units were the clans which centered around the totem poles erected in front of their dwellings. The carved and painted totems symbolized the mythological history of the clan and the totem ancestor (clan-totemism). The mythology itself followed the usual patterns.

The American culture that came perhaps closest to the conditions of an independent environment was that of the acorn-gathering tribes in central California. Except for the Pumo and Yuki, who show a more differentiated culture pattern than the Wintun, Maidu, Kato, Yokuti and others, these groups all belong linguistically to the Penuti-speaking family. Like other Indian tribes, they knew the office of a medicine man (shaman), who gained his power from his fathers or the spiritual world. Other similarities were the search for a guardian spirit and the use of the medicine bundle. Like the Eskimos, they also used a semi-subterranean sweat house for communal and ceremonial purposes.

More than any other group, the Californian Indians emphasized the spoken word as a medium of their religious performances. Since all things share life, nothing was more important for them than the recitation of the *tilasinii*, the legends or stories of past ages. To say prayers is equivalent to sharing the harmony of the world, where things speak to one another. Consequently they were said not only in critical situations but also in connection with ordinary events such as eating, hunting and gathering.

According to the Achomavi tribe, there was only water in the beginning. Silver Fox, the highest being, spoke to himself. He thought and in doing so he laid a clod of earth in his hand. He sang and threw it into the universe, where it turned into the earth. Through the intervention of Coyote, many things come into being, finally also death.

Since there was no orthodox norm for these stories, we have many versions about the beginning of things. For instance, Silver Fox and Coyote are together in a boat that floats on the primeval ocean. They think of and create the trees, rocks, the world, the sweat-house and other things. Man and the animals are made from sticks. Silver Fox, who holds the primary position, wants to stop the tricks of Coyote and thus finally kills him. But though Coyote is killed in the one story, others point out that he, too, is immortal.

The Yuki knew about *taikomol* (he who comes alone), who swims as a feather on the primeval ocean. He sings and becomes a human being. By opening his body he creates the earth and everything that exists on it. Coyote helps him, but through his intervention death enters the world.

The Wintun called their creator *olelbis* (he who dwells above). He is benevolent, but again Coyote disturbs his creation and brings death into the world.

The Maidu begin their world history with *wonomi* (without death) or *kodoyanpe* (earth-caller). Again *wonomi*, who is as bright as the sun, is in the same boat with Coyote. He sings and thus creates the earth. But whatever good he does is counteracted by Coyote. Without Coyote's interference mankind would have been immortal.

Among the Pomo the position of the creator is occasionally held by Coyote. The ceremonies of the Californian Indians combine features that are focused on the person with traits that are of more cosmic significance. The breath of a newborn is a gift of Taikomol, and thus it entails a personal relationship between man and God. Consequently each individual searches for his own religious way of life. Thus, while the foundation of one's being is general, its realization is such that the individual plays the essential role. The same pattern can be seen in the *kuksu* ceremony, which was held among the Kato, Yuki, Pomo and others. It proceeded in two stages. The first was a general initiation of the whole group (settlement or village). It was followed by a ceremony in which the death-rebirth idea was symbolized, and the creation myth was repeated. This second part of the ceremony was realized in such a way that the individual candidates became the momentary centers of the cult. An example of a cosmic ceremony was the *hesi* ritual, which was intended to bring rain for the earth, good harvest, protection from sickness and finally the salvation and renovation of the whole world.

Unlike these religions, which emphasized individual and visionary experiences, those of the planters in the south and southwest were more inclined toward universal and cosmic patterns. Instead of the situational sacred word they emphasized ritual and formalized prayer, while the general orientation within a universe of divine dynamics shifted to an orientation within a well-structured universe of divine order. We can best observe these differences when we contrast the religious ideas of the northern regions with those of the Pueblo area.

The order that prevails in the world of the gods is sharply mirrored in the world of man. As such it is the absolute measure for the deeds and acts of human beings. The village as the final stage in the genesis of the people, who settled here after a long journey from the fourfold interior of the earth, is the cultic and social representation of the divine order. Its very existence is the continuous myth of the universe. Like the symbols of mound or shrine, it is identical with the center of the world. The same holds true for the *kivas*, i.e., cultic places beneath the surface of the ground, where most of the cults have been performed.

The divine hierarchy is headed by the Father Sun. His first vassals are the rain-makers at the brink of the world. They are followed by the animal deities from the four points of the compass, and below and above, which are the patrons of the medicine men. The *koko* masks represent the divine, which includes also the deceased, in its public appearance. The lowest group of the divine beings are the war gods, the twin sons of the Father Sun. Each group has its priests or priestesses, who are presided over by the *pekwin*, the priest of the sun.

The priests and primarily the pekwin are responsible for the right interpretation of the sacred calendar. The welfare of the community can be guaranteed only if the course of the year is accompanied by the right ceremonies and sacrifices. Most important is the implanting of the prayer sticks, since they bring prayers to the gods. The preparation of sand pictures, the strewing of flour and the sacrifice of the first morsel of a meal are other means to please the gods and the deceased, who live in a world not unlike that of the living. Thus when, for instance, the members of the rain-god society died, they arrived at the villages of the rain-makers at the brink of the world.

The sociocultic complexity is intensified by a rich mythology. Day and night, wind, clouds, trees, and other objects are *hoi*, persons. The prayers call upon *awonawilona* the all-embracing heavenly father and the fourfold mother-earth-container. If a supreme being appears, its creative powers turn almost immediately into different figures. The sisters *jatiki* and *nautsiti* (among the Acoma), the mothers *utset* and *nowutset*, East and West (among the Sia), are modes of the creative power. Only the Navahos and Apaches who came to live here much later consider the highest being (the highest sacred wind of the Navahos, or the Lord of Life of the Apaches) as a power of its own.

Although the southeastern tribes also worshipped the sun as the highest divinity and built mounds, their religion seems far less structured than the religion of the Pueblo Indians. Like the mythology, the ritual also expressed a deep-rooted experience and sense of the polarity in man and the world. The union of heaven (sun) and earth (the sex of both is inconsistent) as the origin and renewal of all life was the great mystery of their cults which often culminated in human sacrifices. The ear of corn, the sun dances that played such an important role among the Plains Indians, and the sacred fire were further symbols of the new life. Also the *calumet*, the well-known pipe of peace, expressed this polar symbolism, when one pipe represented the (masculine) earth and the other the (feminine) heaven.

An outline of the Iroquoian creation myth may illustrate the extension and depth of this polarity. Each phenomenon that appears on the earth has its older brother (*ongwe*), who is noncreated, immortal, and lives on the opposite side of the sky. It all began when the girl *awenhai* married the chieftain, who lived beneath a light-tree (*onodsha*), which illuminated the whole sky. She became pregnant through his breath, but nobody knew how this happened. The chief became angry and uprooted *onodsha*. He pushed his wife and the protobeings (corn, beans, tobacco, bear, deer) through the hole that resulted from the uprooting. Only the older brothers of these beings remained in the sky-world. The woman fell upon an endless sea. The animals saw what was going on, and the big turtle rose from the depths of the ocean to the surface in order to carry *awenhai*. The other animals brought mud from the ocean floor and built a huge shield around the turtle. It was the earth which grew very fast. *Awenhai*, who was brought down upon this newly created island by birds, gave birth to a daughter, who grew extraordinarily fast. One day the mother gave her to a young man, who made her pregnant by laying an arrow on her side. The girl gave birth to twins. While the older twin takes the normal way, the younger one comes through the armpit and kills his mother. *Awenhai* turns the body of her dead daughter into the sun and the moon. When she asks the twins who had killed her, *tawiskaron* (Firestone) deceives his grandmother by telling her that it was his brother, who looks like a human being and who was born first. She exiles him, but his father, the big turtle, takes care of his son, giving him a bow and two ears of corn, one for his meal, the other for sowing.

Wata oterongtongnia (young maple tree), as he wanted to be called by man, strolls over the earth and makes it grow until it gains the same shape it has today.

Tawiskaron tries to imitate his brother but in all instances creates evil forms instead of good ones. The two brothers fight against each other. Many things emerge during this struggle. Finally *oterongtongnia* overcomes his adversary by lighting such a strong fire that Firestone bursts into many pieces. The Rocky Mountains are the remains of *tawiskaron*.

The deeply experienced polarity of man and world, man and god, god and god, which appears here in many forms and associations, is actually synthesized in an idea, which comprises the mythical world and that of fantasy as well as the present situation and its rational endeavors. This idea is known as the *orenda* among the Iroquois and *wakan* (*wakonda*) among the Sioux Indians. Like *manitu*, it stands for the mysterious power of life. It penetrates all beings and forms and shapes all phases of man's conscious and unconscious life. *Wakonda* brings everything into existence, but certain things are closer to their source than others. A tree is *wakonda* because it has a residence for it. No living man will ever see *wakonda* but that does not exclude the knowledge about its (his) all-presence. *Wakonda* teaches man to be truthful and to show pity toward others. To find a guardian means to become reconciled with *wakonda*. And a person is *wakonda*, if he has special knowledge and is capable of communicating with the deceased. The wind is *wakonda* because it gives life to the newborn child. Thus, while *wakonda* shows many traits that suggest the idea of an impersonal and, in opposition to *manitu*, an occasionally essentialized power, there is nevertheless a personal quality from which its dynamism originates. By creating the world in a variety of appearances the divine person (that is, the divine as the personal otherness of man) unites the oneness of personal presence with the plurality of things and thus can be thought of only when addressed in personal as well as in impersonal terms. So far as this is done, *wakonda* gives meaning to the polarity of the creation myth by showing that the world is nevertheless truly one in and through his and its presence.

6.2 *South America*

Despite a nearly limitless fracturing of tribes and languages, the cultural map of the peoples who stayed more or less outside the sphere of influence of the Meso- and South American high-cultures shows relatively homogeneous patterns. For the purpose of a general orientation, four areas can be distinguished: The Circum-Carribean and Sub-Andean regions with intensive agriculture, largely influenced by the high cultures; the already extinct Patagonian hunters and gatherers, including the tribes on Tierra del Fuego; the hunter-planter stratum of the Gran Chaco and the eastern Brazilian Highlands, comprising the Guaranian and Ge peoples; and finally the most important area of the Tropical Forest, including the Guiana Highlands, with the Cariban and the Tupian peoples. The Tupians are usually planters but have also strong tendencies toward hunting.

Since the typological value of this classification is highly limited, an informative description strictly along these lines would lead only to unnecessary repetition. Therefore it seems appropriate to filter out the main religious conceptions, although their combination in the individual cultures differs greatly from tribe to tribe. A more detailed description of the religion of the Ge-speaking peoples in the Brazilian Highlands might compensate, at least to a certain degree, for the following generalizations. It may be added that the sources on the indigenous religions are with a few exceptions scanty and incomplete.

If we approach the South American religions from their practical side, the shaman or medicine man appears as the center of the tribe's religious life. His contact with the invisible world, his ability to go to the underworld and to heaven, while the body lies in trance, to send his soul away to places where it can counsel with the gods, to change into the jaguar or other animals, confers on him a central position. His very being is a symbol of orientation and a source of continuous revelation as far as ultimate meaning is concerned. The shaman is usually a man. But sometimes women, for example, the *machi* of the Araucanians, also have access to this office. The prerequisites for being selected differ among various tribes. In the northern regions the older shamans normally take care of the novices, while in the south candidates are recruited by the spirits themselves or even by the highest god. At any rate, long training is required to prepare the candidates for their profession of healing, recovering lost souls, using the right spell, heading the rites of passage, augmenting fertility, preparing the hunt and other practices. The shamanistic ministry is usually distinguished from that of the chieftain. But there are enough cases where chiefs were powerful shamans and vice versa. In the regions influenced by the high cultures, shamanism tended to develop into a professional priesthood.

With the one exception of the Araucanian shamans in northern Chile, who, like their colleagues in North America and Siberia, use a drum, a rattle is generally regarded as the symbol of their vocation. Its noise symbolizes the voices of the spirits and ghosts who are associated with the little stones of the rattle. In Guiana a bench with the emblems of the Cayman, the Lord of all life in the water, was needed in order to realize the contact with the other world. But more important than these widely varying aspects of the shaman's office is the achievement of trance, often supported by excessive smoking, drinking tobacco juice, and other stimulants. The power of the shaman is based on a mysterious fluid, whose positive form he possesses. In a negative way the same mysterious element produces illness and death, when it exists as a thorn or crystal in the body.

As these remarks on the shaman indicate, the world behind this office is complex. Above all it is the world of South American mythology, where an endless chain of unreflected speculations connects the highest god(s) with the world of spirits and vegetation gods, the culture hero with the first ancestor, the souls with the ghosts, the divine with dances, masks, and musical instruments.

Although a long period of Christian influence makes it difficult to trace the exact features, it seems certain that nearly all tribes knew of a supreme god or goddess (the goddess mainly among tribes with a matriarchate) who created the earth, who is the father or mother of all things. Depending on the mythology, this creator god may become identified with the sun, the moon, the stars, with the Lord of animals and of plants, and with the Master of the underworld. His impact on the daily life and its problems differs. A general pattern seems to be that the religions of planters acknowledge him in an almost cultless way, while the hunting tribes usually call upon him in prayers. If it is a goddess who stands at the beginning, the character of these instances changes accordingly.

The Yamana on Tierra del Fuego considered *watauinewa* the highest, almighty being. They called upon him in ritualized prayers, but also spontaneously, addressing him as 'father'. Occasionally, when disaster and illness did not end, he was named the 'killer in heaven' and plants and animals were destroyed in order to 'hurt' him. As the authority for law and order *watauinewa* also sponsored the initiation ceremonies for boys and girls.

The creator of all things is usually thought to be accompanied by different serving spirits. But we know also of instances where the highest divinity, e.g., *puru* among the Orinoco-Indians, is identical with the creative power that permeates all things. As the bringer of blessings and as culture hero (often thought of as twins or brothers who authorized the widespread dual organization of the society), or as first ancestor, the highest god (goddess) is in one way or another present in all religious phenomena. To give only one example, for the Caribbean Galibi *amana*, the virginal and navelless mother, is the source of all things. She is a beautiful woman whose body ends in that of a snake. Being the core of time, she gave birth to all things and is able to appear in all forms. Her dwelling place is the water of the sky, believed to be situated beyond the Pleiades. She is also known as *wala-yumu*, the spirit of the species and the mistress of all water ghosts. She gave birth to the twin brothers *tamusi* and *yolikan-tamulu*, i.e., to the ancestor of the Galibi, who lives in the moon, the realm of the good souls, and to the grandfather (*tamulu*) of the nature spirits (*yolikan*). The shamans are able to contact *amana*. *Tamusi* and *yolikan-tamulu* are associated with one of the shaman's rattle-stones.

Although the mythology allows such a universal interconnection of the divine, from the viewpoint of the ordinary life it functions more as a sort of general background than as a context of immediate determination and qualification. What really matters in this respect are the demons and spirits of nature. Invisible and powerful beings settle everywhere. Among them the spirit of the forest, and the deities of field and vegetation (comparable to the dema-goddesses in Oceania) take the first place. They are worshipped by complex hunting rituals, fertility and mask dances, often including a flagellation ceremony, by ball games, human sacrifices, and cannibalistic ceremonies, accompanied by the worship of idols and the magic sound of various musical instruments. Fertility (phallic) rites are especially cultivated among secret societies. The cannibalistic rituals, a reason for endless warfare between the individual villages, are necessary for the maintenance of fertility. Instead of anthropophagy some tribes practiced head hunting, a custom that was intended to accomplish the same goals as cannibalism. The Jivaro Indians of Ecuador, for instance, believed that the magic power *tsarutama*, which connects the much-feared ghosts of the dead with the fertility of the field, could be gained from the shrunken head (*tsantsa*) of an enemy.

This complexity of the invisible world is shared by man himself. Several souls with different destinies are necessary to complete the human being, not to mention the second or alter-ego conception, in which many tribes believed. Accordingly the ideology and worship of the deceased and of ancestors differed greatly in the various regions. While ancestor worship was important for the tribes in eastern Brazil, the Patagonian Indians did not practice it. In the Amazonian area it was part of the fertility cults.

Since a more detailed description of these phenomena would exceed the frame of this survey, the collection of informative data can be discontinued here. So far as these data are concerned, the survey shows sufficiently how complex the world of primitive cultures and their respective religions can be, although many apparent similarities do exist. Before we continue with the description of empirical situations, it thus makes sense to reflect upon some of the speculative and conceptual implications of these data and the way we are dealing with them. According to the circular patterns of cultural studies, such a step is necessary in order to avoid the viciousness of an unreflected circularity. At the same time we shall try to find workable guidelines for a typological approach to specified situations and their respective analysis.

7. BIBLIOGRAPHICAL APPENDIX

7.1 *Africa*

ABRAHAMSSON, H. (1951), *The Origin of Death: Studies in African Mythology*. Studia Ethnographica Upsaliensia III. Uppsala.
ANKERMANN, B. (1918), 'Totenkult und Seelenglauben bei afrikanischen Völkern', *Zeitschrift für Ethnologie*, 50: 89–153.
ARINZE, F. A. (1970), *Sacrifice in Ibo Religion*. Ibadan, University Press.
BAUMANN, H. (1936), *Schöpfung und Urzeit des Menschen im Mythus der afrikanischen Völker* Berlin, Reimer, Andrews and Steiner.
— (1938), 'Afrikanische Wild- und Buschgeister', *Zeitschrift für Ethnologie*, 70: 208–239.
— (1955), 'Die Sonne in Mythus und Religion der Afrikaner', pp. 252–294 in S. Lukas (ed.), *Afrikanistische Studien*. Berlin, Akademie-Verlag.
BEIER, U., ed. (1968), *The Origin of Life and Death: African Myth*. London, Heinemann.
DAMMANN, E. (1963), *Die Religionen Afrikas*. Vol. 6 of *Die Religionen der Menschheit*, ed. by C. M. Schröder. Stuttgart, W. Kohlhammer.
DESCHAMPS, H. (1954), *Les religions de l'Afrique noire*. Paris, Presses Universitaires de France.
DIETERLEN, G. (1951), *Essai sur la religion bambara*. Paris, Presses Universitaires de France.
DOUTRELOUX, A. (1967), *L'ombre des fétiches: société et culture yombe*. Louvain, Nauwelaerts.
EVANS-PRITCHARD, E. E. (1937), *Witchcraft, Oracles and Magic Among the Azande*. Oxford, Clarendon.
— (1956), *Nuer Religion*. Oxford, Clarendon.
FORDE, D., ed. (1965), *African Worlds: Studies in the Cosmological Ideas and Social Values of African Peoples*. London–New York, Oxford University Press.
FROBENIUS, L. (1931), *Erythräa. Länder und Zeiten des heiligen Königsmordes*. Berlin–Zürich, Atlantis.
GARNIER, C. and J. FRALON (1951), *Le fétichisme en Afrique noire*. Paris, Payot.
GRIAULE, M. and G. DIETERLEN (1965), *Le Renard Pâle*. Vol. 1 of *Le Mythe Cosmogonique*. Paris, Institut d'ethnologie.

GUSINDE, M. (1966), *Von Gelben und Schwarzen Buschmännern: Eine untergehende Altkultur im Süden Afrikas*. Graz, Akademische Druck.

HAMBLY, W. D. (1937), *Serpent Worship in Afrika*. London.

JUNOD, H. (1927), *The Life of a South African Tribe* (second ed.). London, D. Nutt.

LIENHARDT, G. (1961), *Divinity and Experience: The Religion of the Dinka*. Oxford, Oxford University Press.

MBITI, J. S. (1970), *Concepts of God in Africa*. London.

— (1970), *African Religions and Philosophy*. New York, Doubleday.

MEEK, C. K. (1923), *The Northern Tribes of Nigeria*. Oxford.

NADEL, S. F. (1954), *Nupe Religion*. London, Oxford University Press.

PARRINDER, C. (1954), *African Traditional Religion*. London, S.P.C.K.

— (1967), *African Mythology*. London, P. Hamlyn.

— and E. W. SMITH, eds. (1966), *African Ideas of God: A Symposium*. London, Edinburgh House Press.

PETTERSON, O. (1953), *Chiefs and Gods*. Lund, Gleerup.

RANGER, T. O. and J. KIMANBO (1972), *The Historical Study of African Religion*. Berkeley, University of California Press.

SPIETH, J. (1911), *Die Religion der Eweer in Süd-Togo*. Leipzig, Hinrichs.

TALBOT, P. A. (1932), *Tribes of the Niger Delta*. London, Sheldon.

TEMPELS, P. (1959), *Bantu Philosophy* (Tr. by Colin King). Paris, Présence africaine: Eureux.

WERNER, A. (1933), *Myths and Legends of the Bantu*. London, Harrap.

ZAHAN, D., ed. (1965), *Réincarnation et vie mystique en Afrique Noire*. Paris.

7.2 Asia

ARNDT, P. (1951), *Religion auf Ostflores*. Freiburg, Switzerland, Paulus-Verlag (Studia Inst. Anthropos, No. 1).

BARTON, R. F. (1946), *The Religion of the Ifugaos*. Menasha, Wisc., American Anthropological Assn. (Memoir series of the American Anthropological Association, No. 1)

BOGORAS, W. (1904–07), *The Chukchee*. New York, Stechert.

EVANS, I. H. N. (1923), *Studies in Religion, Folk-lore and Custom in British North Borneo and the Malay Peninsula*. Cambridge, Eng., University Press.

— (1953), *The Religion of the Tempassuk Dusuns of North Borneo*. Cambridge, Eng., University Press.

FÜRER-HAIMENDORF, C. VON (1962), 'Primitivvölker', pp. 243–293 in *Die Religionen Indiens III*, vol. 13 of *Die Religionen der Menschheit*, edited by C. M. Schröder. Stuttgart, Kohlhammer.

GAHS, A. (1928), 'Kopf-, Schädel- und Langknochenopfer bei Rentiervölkern', pp. 231–268 in Koppers (ed.), *Festschrift P. W. Schmidt*. Vienna, Mechitharisten-congregations.

HARPER, E. B., ed. (1964), *Religion in South Asia*. Seattle, University of Washington Press.

HARVA, U. (1938), *Die religiöse Vorstellungen der altaischen Völker*. Helsinki, Soumalainen Tiedeakatemia.

JOCHELSON, W. (1905), *The Koryak; Religion and Myths*. New York, Stechert.

KRADER, L. (1966), *Peoples of Central Asia*. Bloomington, Indiana Univ. and The Hague, Mouton.

PAULSON, I., A. HULTKRANTZ and K. JETTMAR (1962), *Die Religionen Nordeurasiens and der amerikanischen Arktis*. Vol. 3 of *Die Religionen der Menschheit*, ed. by C. M. Schröder. Stuttgart, Kohlhammer.
STÖHR, W. and P. ZOETMULDER (1965), *Die Religionen Indonesiens*. Vol. 5, pt. 1 of *Die Religionen der Menschheit*, ed. by C. M. Schröder. Stuttgart, Kohlhammer.
WARNECK, J. (1909), *Die Religion der Batak*. Leipzig, Hinrichs.

7.3 Oceania and Australia

BAAL, J. VAN (1966), *Dema. Description and Analysis of Marind-anim Culture (South New Guinea)*. The Hague, Nijhoff.
BERNDT, R. M. and C. H. BERNDT (1964), *The World of the First Australians: An Introduction to the Traditional Life of the Australian Aborigines*. Chicago, University of Chicago Press.
CODRINGTON, R. H. (1891), *The Melanesians: Studies in their Anthropology and Folk-lore*. Oxford, Clarendon Press. Reprinted: New Haven, H.R.A.F. Press, 1957.
FIRTH, R. (1967), *The Work of the Gods in Tikopia*. New York, Humanities.
FISCHER, H. (1965) *Studien über Seelenvorstellungen in Ozeanien*. Munich, Renner.
HANDY, E. S. C. (1927), *Polynesian Religion*. London.
LANDTMAN, G. (1927), *The Kiwai Papuans of British New Guinea*. London, Macmillan.
LAWRENCE, P. and M. J. MEGGITT, eds. (1965), *Gods, Ghosts and Man in Melanesia: Some Religions of Australian New Guinea and the New Hebrides*. Melbourne – New York, Oxford University Press.
LEENHARDT, M. (1947), *Do Kamo: La Personne et le mythe dans le monde mélanésien*. Paris, Gallimard.
LEHMANN, F. R. (1930), *Mana*. Leipzig, Spamer.
— (1930), *Die polynesischen Tabusitten*. Leipzig, Voigtländer.
LOMMEL, A. (1952), *Die Unambal: Ein Stamm in Nordwest-Australien*. Hamburg.
REED, A. W. (1965), *Myths and Legends of Australia*. Sydney, Reed.
SCHLESIER, E. (1958), *Die melanesischen Geheimkulte*. Göttingen, Musterschmidt-Verlag.
STREHLOW, C. (1907–20), *Die Aranda- und Loritja-Stämme in Zentral-Australien*, 5 vols. Frankfurt a. M., Baer.
WILLIAMSON, R. W. (1933), *Religions and Cosmic Beliefs in Central Polynesia*, 2 vols. Cambridge, Eng., University Press.
WIRZ, P. (1922), *Die Marind-anim von Holländisch Sud-Neu-Guinea*. Vol. 1, pt. 2 of *Religion und Mythen*. Hamburg.

7.4 North America and South America

ALEXANDER, H. B. (1967), *The World's Rim: Great Mysteries of the North American Indians*. Lincoln, University of Nebraska Press.
BALDUS, H. (1958), *Die Jaguarzwillinge*. Kassel – Eisenach.
BOAS, F. (1930), *The Religion of the Kwakiutl Indians*. New York, Columbia University Press.
BÖDIGER, U. (1965), *Die Religion der Tukano im nordwestlichen Amazonas*. Dissertation. Cologne.
COOPER, J. M. (1934), *The Northern Algonquian Supreme Being*. Washington, Catholic University of America Press.

— (1956), *The Gros Ventres of Montana: Religion and Ritual.* Washington, Catholic University of America Press (Anthropology Series, Vol. 16).

COVARRUBIAS, M. (1945), *The Eagle, the Jaguar, and the Serpent.* New York, Knopf.

EHRENREICH, P. (1905), *Die Mythen und Legenden der Südamerikanischen Urvölker und ihre Beziehungen zu denen Nordamerikas und der alten Welt,* Supplement of *Zeitschrift für Ethnologie* (Berlin), Vol. 37.

FLETCHER, A. and F. LA FLESCHE (1911), 'The Omaha Tribe', pp. 15–672 in *37th Annual Report of the Bureau of American Ethnology.* Washington, Government Printing Office.

GOEJE, C. H. DE (1943), *Philosophy, Initiation and Myths of the Indians in Guiana and Adjacent Countries.* Leyden, Brill.

GUSINDE, M. (1937), *Die Feuerland Indianer,* 3 vols. Mödling-Vienna, Internationale Zeitschrift 'Anthropos'.

HAEKEL, J. (1958), 'Purá und Hochgott, Probleme der Südamerikanischen Religionsethnologie'. *Archiv für Völkerkunde,* 83: 25–50.

HARRINGTON, M. R. (1921), *Religion and Ceremonies of the Lenape.* New York, Museum of American Indian, Heye Foundation.

HEIZER, R. F. and M. A. WIPPLE, eds. (1971), *The Californian Indians: A Sourcebook* (second rev. and enlarged ed.). Berkeley – Los Angeles, University of Californi Press.

HULTKRANTZ, A. (1953), *Conceptions of the Soul among the North American Indians.* Stockholm.

KARSTEN, R. (1964), *Studies in the Religion of South American Indians East of the Andes.* Ed. by A. Runeberg and M. Webster. Helsinki.

KRICKEBERG, W., H. TRIMBORN, W. MÜLLER and O. ZERRIES (1967), *Die Religionen des alten Amerika.* Vol. 7 of *Die Religionen der Menschheit,* ed. by C. M. Schröder. Stuttgart, W. Kohlhammer.

KROEBER, A. L. (1906–07), 'The Religion of the Indians of California', *Journal of American Archaeology and Ethnology,* 4: 319–356.

MÉTRAUX, A. (1967), *Religions et magies indiennes d'Amérique du Sud.* Paris.

MURPHY, R. F. (1958), *Mundurucu Religion.* Los Angeles.

OWEN, R. C. (1967), *The North American Indians: A Sourcebook.* New York.

PARSONS, E. C. (1939), *Pueblo Indian Religion,* 2 vols. Chicago, University Press.

PREUSS, K. (1921–23), *Religion und Mythologie der Uitoto,* 2 vols. Göttingen, Ruprecht.

RADIN, P. (1972), *The Trickster: A Study in American Indian Mythology.* New York, Schorbeen (Reprint; originally published in 1956).

REICHARD, G. A. (1950), *Navaho Religion: A Study of Symbolism,* 2 vols. New York, Pantheon.

SCHMIDT, W. (1933), *High Gods in North America.* Oxford, Clarendon.

SPENCER, R. F., *et al.* (1965), *The Native Americans: Prehistory and Ethnology of the North American Indians.* New York, Harper.

STEWARD, J. H., ed. (1946–59), *Handbook of South American Indians,* 7 vols. Washington G.P.O. For Series or Collections: U. S. Bureau of Amer. Ethnology, Bulletin 143. Reprinted: New York, Cooper Square Pub. 1963.

THOMPSON, S. (1929), *Tales of the North American Indians.* Cambridge. Harvard University Press. Reprinted: Bloomington, Indiana University Press, 1966.

WOLF, M. (1919), *Ironquois Religion.* New York, Columbia University Press.

ZERRIES, O. (1954), *Wild und Buschgeister in Südamerika.* Wiesbaden, Steiner.

7.5 Handbooks

BIANCHI, U. (1967), *Introduzione alle religioni dei primitive*. Rome, Atenco.

BLEEKER, C. J. and G. WIDENGREN, eds. (1971), *Historia Religionum. Handbook for the History of Religions*, vol. 2. Leyden, E. J. Brill.

CASTELLANI, G. ed. (1970), *Storia delle Religioni* (sixth ed.). Torino, Unione.

CHANTEPIE DE LA SAUSSAYE, P. D. (1924–25), *Lehrbuch der Religionsgeschichte* (fourth ed., rev by A. Bertholet and E. Lehmann, 2 vols.). Tübingen.

CLEMEN, C., *et al.* (1927), *Die Religionen der Erde*. Munich.

ELIADE, M. (1967), *From Primitives to Zen: A Thematic Sourcebook on the History of Religions*. New York – Evanston, Harper.

FRAZER, J. G. (1911–15), *The Golden Bough. A Study in Comparative Religion* (third ed.), 12 vols. London, MacMillan and Co.

GENNEP, A. VAN (1908–21), *Religions, mœurs et légendes*, 5 vols. Paris, Mercure de France.

— (1960), *The Rites of Passage*. Translated by M.B. Vizedom. Chicago, University of Chicago Press; London, Routledge.

GORCE, M., R. Mortier, *et al.* (1944–51), *Histoire générale des religions*, 4 vols. Paris.

HEILER, F., *et al.* (1932), *Die Religionen der Menschenheit in Vergangenheit und Gegenwart* (second ed.) Stuttgart, Kohlhammer.

HERRMANN, F. (1961), *Symbolik in den Religionen der Naturvölker*. Stuttgart, Hiersemann.

JENSEN, A. E. (1963), *Myth and Cult among Primitive Peoples*, (tr. by M. T. Choldin and W. Weissleder). Chicago, University of Chicago Press.

JOCKEL, R. (1953), *Götter und Dämonen*. Darmstadt.

MIDDLETON, J., ed. (1967), *American Museum Sourcebooks in Anthopology*, Vols. 5–7. Garden City, Doubleday.

PETTAZZONI, R. (1948–53), *Miti e Leggende*, 4 vols. Turin, Unione.

POIRIER, J., ed. (1958), *Ethnologie générale*. Paris, Gallimard (Encyclopédie de la Pléjade).

SCHMIDT, W. (1926–55), *Der Ursprung der Gottesidee*, 12 vols. Münster, Aschendorff.

SCHRÖDER, C. M., ed. (1961, ff), *Die Religionen der Menscheit*. Stuttgart.

VROKLAGE, B. A. G. (1949), *De godsdienst der primitiven*.

See also the literature quoted in the References at the end of the book.

3

Constitutive Analysis:
A Methodological Interlude

The interpretation of man as a cultural being makes it necessary to look upon religion not merely as an artifact and intentional object but as a phenomenon. By trying to grasp the reality and meaning of religion within the process of articulation and symbolization, or, in brief, of culture-genesis, we have to attune our methodology to the implicit logic of this process and to the modality of its being. This does not imply that the truths of religions such as the existence of God, the need for salvation, the significance of history, etc., must be denied, even if the theoretical affirmation of these truths has to be suspended momentarily. Prior to these questions there is the phenomenon of man that manifests the reality of religion and that initiates the theoretical search for its meaning. Accordingly, there is neither need nor possibility to search for a reality outside of man in order to find a measure for human behavior and understanding. If we need such a measure we have to find it in the context of man, world, and history.

Since there is no knowledge as such but only man's knowledge, the content and meaning of what man knows depends always on his involvement in the genesis and recollection of his understanding. While this relationship may be kept in abeyance as long as we are dealing with the cybernetical and technological aspects of our world, i.e., with the world as subject of the natural sciences and technology, it becomes imperative to take it into consideration the moment we try to understand the various forms of behavioral and theoretical self-interpretation. It is at this point that objects and actions, ideas and, most of all, man himself, turn into phenomena and manifest themselves as symbols. As for man who distinguishes between truth and falsity, reality and appearance, the familiar and the unfamiliar or alien, the within and the without, the mode of being as presented by perception and sense-experience can be only one aspect of the larger spectrum of reality. What he sees, hears, feels, does and thinks is, although with varying intensity, integrated into a functional texture of meaning and importance. As exemplified by the halves of the coin which are brought together and thus permit people to find their identity in that of the sym-bolon (see above Ch. 2; also, Schlesinger, 1912; Muri, 1931; Looff, 1955; Vergote, 1959; Wisse, 1963; Foster, 1967; Boelen, 1968; Duran, 1968; Munson, 1968; Ricœur, 1968; Wellek and Warren, 1970; Fortmann, 1961; and many others) man is capable of releasing a world of symbols as well as of interpreting the world symbolically. Any instance where experience and articulation serve as a means of identification is symbolically significant. Consequently we cannot consider the respective instances as entities that exist in the abstract, but we must look at them as phenomena whose being as symbols refers to both the principles and the results of cultural dynamics. Moreover, if we are not sure about the content and meaning of religion, there can be no doubt that we have to deal with this problem in the context of man's symbolic existence. If the message conveyed by words points beyond these words it does not do so without the context in which words speak. We should thus know something about this context before we analyze its messages.

As the introductory chapter indicated, man's relationship to culture cannot be reduced to a mechanism of parts and causal relations. Since culture implies totality, the particulars by which we grasp culture are qualified by a relationship that has been characterized as participation. Whatever cultural reality may be, we cannot detach its concept from the dialectics between part and whole. In view of this dialectics we begin to see how the apparent autonomy of natural entities is transformed into a situational whole that reveals its cultural status by being centered on the meta-natural pole of consciousness and meaning. The describable and objectifiable aspects of man's behavior as well as the various modifications of his precultural appearance as a biological, social and psychological being become the indications of a morphological process through which the human being gains and achieves self-realization while culture becomes real in these indications. As a result man is not just a being among others. Instead, he is a being faced with the problem of truth as a problem of his existence. His identity is dependent on the degree with which he, as a part of the world, represents and relates to this world as a totality. Accordingly, if we are to deal with the human phenomenon, it is not enough to identify the causal conditions of man's existence. In addition, there has to be an attempt to interrelate these conditions with the process of human self-realization and cultural reality. For this reason the phenomenology of man cannot be less empirical than it is speculative, and vice versa.

In order to understand man we cannot content ourselves with accumulating data the world over and analyzing them along the lines of causal connections.

Since the data that concern man are cultural, we have to understand them as instances, which are not only constitutively dependent on the idea of culture that is real in them, but whose understanding equally implies and presupposes the reality of culture as it becomes ideational in them. The 'part' requests the 'whole', and the 'whole' is represented by the 'part'. What is needed under these circumstances is neither an exclusively 'verificational' nor 'functional' analysis,[1] but an analysis of the particulars that receives its logic from the whole which bears them in their particularity. Since this problem is indicated by the word constitution, we may speak here of a *constitutive analysis*.

Again, if we take into consideration that man and culture, culture and totality, describe the reality that we would like to grasp and to understand, we need a method that proceeds within the framework of practical functionalism and universal humanism (as characterized in the first chapter) uniting the emiprical as well as the speculative aspects of reality. This method which we introduce here as constitutive analysis is not merely an option that can be realized or not (as for instance in the sciences; there we might philosophize but do not have to do so expressly in order to get results; on the contrary, if scientists on both sides would have philosophized about the atomic bomb they probably would never have built it) but, as far as cultural reality is concerned, a methodological requirement that becomes necessary because man himself forms part of the subject-matter that is to be studied.

Whereas the possibility of a constitutive analysis is anticipated by the experience that we as parts of the cultural process are factually capable of asking for it, its actualization and realization is based on the assumption that despite and because of the variety of cultural appearances, mankind is truly one in its quest for meaning (the universality of consciousness) and its encounter with the most inexplicable, yet most obvious: Birth, existence, death. Since the response to these questions comes forth in and as the process of symbolization, thereby giving us the idea of culture in general and of symbolic culture in particular, it will be necessary to inquire into the meaning of symbolization as such and to ask for the characteristic features that mark the various transitions of this process. Should it prove possible to show a transitional unity between *homo existens* (as the mediating presupposition of symbolization), *homo symbolicus* (as its realization) and *homo*

---

1. These two expressions have been used by F. Ferré (1969, p. 8 ff) in order to 'christen' the two major movements of contemporary language analysis, which can roughly be coordinated with the work of the early and the later L. Wittgenstein. See also B. R. Gross (1970).

religiosus (perhaps as its immanent tendency), such an analysis would not only provide a perspective for dealing with the empirical data but would also give us a horizon for evaluating these data and a basis for focusing on the pivotal points of the philosophical system implicit to both the phenomena and their interpretation.

The program set forth by the title of constitutive analysis thus concurs with the very description of this method. If we recall the conditions of its possibility constitutive analysis not only gains structure by and through its application (as any other method does) but turns out to be a method whose elaboration stands under the principle of its application. Even the attempt to outline its meaning in a mere descriptive way has to set out with the insight that constitutive analysis implies its application as the very logic of this description.

Since 'part' and 'whole' are not related with one another on the basis of quantitative summation but of qualitative integration, we can also say that such investigations entail a permanent oscillation between the within of our own situation and that of the other situation, and vice versa. In line with the conception of the inter- and inner-cultural circles of hermeneutics they are held to recognize the hermeneutical and reflective necessity of working with the conceptual means as offered by 'our' language and culture history, while the awareness of the unavoidable and necessary distance that stays between the interpreter and the phenomena in question becomes something like an inbuilt safeguard against deviation and premature repose.[2]

To find the truth of his own and to interpret that of those with whom he communicates, man has to become aware of the hermeneutical situation as a fundamental principle of practical and theoretical existence and vice versa. There can be understanding to the extent only that we subject its development to the demands of reality and truth, by which logic becomes logical and methods conclusive. To recall these conditions when processing the data of culture history is the purpose of constitutive analysis. But while we understand this goal we should not miss the fact that the process of processing the data of culture history

2. In order to effectuate this awareness it is appropriate to use the indigenous terminology. Although these terms must be translated and interpreted in some way – otherwise we do not know what we are talking about – they may nevertheless serve as a symbol reminding us of the hermeneutic situation. They provide us with an actual experience of the phenomenological suspension (*epoché*) which achieves certainty by making the interrogative character of man's knowledge an integral part of its answers.

has already begun when we speak about man, his language and culture, and the things that he is supposed to do. The following remarks on *homo existens, homo symbolicus* and *homo religiosus* may serve as an example of the workings of constitutive analysis (see also Ch. 1. part 1.2, and Ch. 8, where we discuss the interpretative value of primitive religion).

1. THE SYMBOLIC IMPLICATION OF HOMO EXISTENS

Like all other living beings, man is dependent on space and time and on the integration of individual and psychic conditions throughout the sequence of generations (see Bidney, 1967, p. 3 ff). But in distinction to all other beings we know of, he is also aware of himself in such a way that he knows about himself in and through his articulations. By the very fact of language (which we consider the decisive criterium in the various questions about *homo sapiens*), he expresses the consciousness of his existence. He knows that he exists. But while he knows that he exists, he also recognizes birth as the beginning of a life that is faced with death as the final break of this life. In the 'prequestionable' certainty of such self-awareness man thus begins to 'understand' that the uncertainty of events and circumstances must be mastered and overcome in order to realize a truly 'human' mode of life. And, while he begins to 'understand' this problem he 'knows' by the same token that it can be done and that there is a logic upon which he can rely, even if it has not been articulated as such. It is the primary simplicity of this demand and the universality of such an answer that unifies mankind as an evolving existence, no matter what the actual 'standard' of a given culture may be. Thus, whenever we ask for the fundamental conditions and elementary units of cultural reality, we must do so in the horizon of man's experience as *homo existens*. By doing this we implicitly postulate a minimum of experience and cultural reality that is presupposed whenever there are human beings and wherever we – as human beings – try to understand them and their articulations. In its expressive form, we have to address this minimum of experience and the corresponding cultural reality as the fundamental presupposition both of homogenesis and universal understanding (see Jensen's remarks on the human character of early man and the consequences it has for the study of man, 1960, p. 16 ff).

Without claiming completeness we shall try now to set off some aspects of this minimum of experience which we deem fundamental. Since they describe the context wherein constitution takes place, their analysis becomes essential for any analytical treatment of reality that is aimed at comprehending reality in its parts and not at loosing it because of them. It may be worth mentioning that such an attempt confronts us with issues that run like an unbroken thread through the centuries of philosophical investigation.[3] This fact alone corroborates their importance. But it shows also that answers given in these matters are likely to be fragmentary in one way or another. Nevertheless this is no sufficient reason to exempt oneself from this task, nor could we call it absurd if we see any meaning in articulation at all. The fact is that we have made our presuppositions in these matters anyhow and that it can only be useful to know by reflection what we have come to know by articulation.

The basic experience of *homo existens* of which we know because of the implicit correlation between self-awareness and speech can be specified in at least two directions. On the one hand there is the experience of things, events, and of various feelings and emotions that are observable and registrable. On the other hand there is the experience of human presence and action. Both kinds of experiences are so interrelated that one is not possible without the other. Even though many attempts have been made in this direction, they cannot be reduced to either one kind of experience.[4] It is unity in polar diversity we encounter here. The variety of object experiences (beings) is mediated by the presence of man. In the unlimited comprehension of his presence things become substances that refer to being as the universal foundation of whatever might be identified by knowledge. The manifold instances of the so given are thus transformed into a conception of the world as the unified sum total of solid things with which and by which we live. They become the world of economic struggles and technological devices, of sociophysical conditions, of laws and interacting constants, of traditions and cultures, and finally, of meaningful or absurd encounter. Even if we discover that all the substances can be analyzed in one way or another as though they were mere imagination, we do not only need substantiality in order to realize such an analysis in the first place, but it also returns in the results by which we recognize its achievement, no matter how tentative it might be.

If we distinguish between the pre-human and the post-human component in

3. A fine analysis of these problems in the light of substance and freedom has been given by E. Heintel (1968).

4. As for the critique of analytic philosophy which has shown a tendency to skip the transcendental pole (human presence), see E. Gellner (1959).

the process of existential mediation, we may also say that the variety of object experiences is transformed into the conception of the world as nature, where the meaning of phenomenality reaches the outer limit of the given, and as culture, where phenomenality culminates in the 'here and now' as a beginning that anticipates whatever might be reached for. The experience of man's presence, which by its very 'nature' is not objectifiable although all objectivity is mediated by it, is thus modified by the world and its own mode of mediating this world. As a result, man is not only an empirical reality, but a transcendental reality too, thereby proving in his own existence the transcendental character of the empirical as an unmistakable dimension of its appearance (Heintel, 1968, p. 178 ff, and Boelen, 1968, p. 177 ff). A reciprocal relationship between man and world comes into focus, where it is not only the 'object' that specifies the 'subject' but also the 'subject' that specifies the 'object'. We affirm what is and imagine what is not, what could have been, what might be, and so forth. While I see the top of the tree in front of the window I 'know' that there is 'more'. Past, present and future merge with one another in order to reappear again as the distinct steps that have to be taken in the course of actions by which we live with others and through which we understand and change the world. In the spontaneous concretion of our thinking here and now we experience ourselves not as things among others but as unique instances and centers of the world, no matter how limited and contingent we may be as far as our understanding and actions are concerned. On the other hand, while we come to conceive of ourselves as presence that rests upon itself in the momentary here and now, it is the recollection of previous experiences and the anticipation of events to come that bestows duration upon this presence by keeping it short of ultimate fulfillment. We recognize ourselves in what we have been before and thus experience ourselves as presence that lasts with varying intensity together with the more or less permanent 'presence' of the world around us. Landscapes, stones, buildings, become the firm centers of the world in which we live. But that they are centers is not their merit but the expression of man's presence.

Depending on how we live in this world of ours there are marked differences between a 'world' that is mediated by the conscious experience of recollection and expectation, and a 'world' that is mediated by semiconscious presence in dream and ecstatic vision (see above Ch. 2 or between a 'world' that is envisaged in the metaconscious experience of spontaneous intuitions. It is a somewhat different 'world' if we look at it from the viewpoint of a presence experience that concurs with our individuality and a presence that merges with that of others in the various forms of communal existence, of fashion, ideological evidence, and epochal style. In any case, man living within this world of his has many faces. His identity is not that of a biological individual but of a person who is as identical with himself as he lives in the various dimensions of the world. The meaning of substantiality as mediated by language gains a new perspective if we turn it back upon man himself. What appeared as a world of solid things turns out to be one aspect only of what we ought to call reality, if we want to understand what we are talking about.[5]

The human awareness of 'being there' is an indefinite experience that becomes definite through the particular situation in which we live, and that defines the same situation by the modality of its presence. Since this presence is total and universal in outlook, human existence can be adequately characterized as total and universal existence. But since it achieves this totality and universality only in company and union with definite and particular beings, it is equally a hetero-thetic existence, an existence that is real by 'positing' (Gr: *thesis*) the 'other' (Gr: *heteron*) against itself as the limitation of an otherwise undetermined modality.[6] Thus, in order to be and to find his identity, man has to become one

---

5. It should be noted that it would be incongruous with the 'presence of man' to conceive of it only in terms of individual being. The experience of human presence includes equally the human 'thou' and all that is accomplished by words. If we ask for the elementary unit of cultural being in terms of the individual and the presence of man, we arrive at the life-community as the most basic element. As such it is that minimal unit of societal instances, which is needed to constitute culture in relation to man as a person, a unit, which continues throughout the social processes of differentiation, even though the concrete aspects may change from situation to situation. To the extent that the concept of the life-community presupposes the idea of totality we cannot call it an empirically given. However, it is a transcendental postulate which can be recognized in every appearance of man. As such it is that *real* field of space, time, and thought which exists between the individual and the community as the sum total of societal entities. As far as the empirical meaning of the life-community is concerned it can be best recognized in the group communities of gatherers and hunters. In this respect one need not emphasize that the concept of the life-community is particularly relevant for a study such as this. As for the history of this term and its philosophical significance see M. Scheler (1954, 1960). Also M. S. Frings (1971).

6. As for the philosophical evaluation of the term heterothesis, which has been developed within those philosophical traditions which were, as exemplified by Augustine, primarily concerned with the personal, see J. Mader (1965, p. 62 ff). This interpretation of man enables us also to understand culture as a heterothetic reality, that is, as the goal of all intellectual endeavor, as well as its foundation. Together with the idea of the life-community as it grows out of the analysis of man's presence, culture becomes thus the strongest contradiction to the nominalistic world view that has held and still holds Western history in its grip.

with the otherness of being and world (as he understands them) according to the logos of his very presence. But since this presence is analogical, he is not simply identical with himself, as already indicated, but the same in analogous universality and universal analogy. In contrast to the biological world as we know it, man cannot be fitted into the scheme of species and genus without destroying his peculiarity as man. We have to take him as person whose universality is founded in the total significance of his uniqueness, and who begins anew wherever and whenever he emerges.

If we understand the heterothetic character of man's existence as an expression of his descendance from earth and universe, we have also to see that this is only one side of the coin. Whereas it is true that man finds himself in the many instances of the world, including his body, it is also true that the same instances are assimilated by man's presence. By being integrated in and with this presence they no longer are what they have been in the correlational field that described their being. Because man is present to himself, he not only discovers the world, but he becomes equally an element of dissolution in the structure of the world. When assimilated by man things no longer rest upon themselves and within their correlational texture but are turned into identities that are absolute. As such they mark man's presence. Accordingly, while man lives in this world, he has to dissolve himself and the many instances that mark his presence from this world, i.e., he has to exist as a cultural and symbolic being, in order to be himself. Man has to absolutize the world in which he lives through the ordered identity of distinct concepts. He has to realize himself as a broken (estranged) existence that encounters the 'end' of his identity as a necessary condition of its growing synthesis and substantiality. He is not only capable of speech, but he must speak. He is not only capable of completion but asked for it. The absolute that we discover in such an analysis is not just an abstraction of our thinking, but an indication that anticipates the possibility of thought and spontaneity as necessities of man's existence. Because of the absolute character of cultural life, we cannot only speak of a because, but we become equally free to believe, to hope, to encounter, and, finally, to be. As *homo existens* man is by dint of his very existence *homo symbolicus*. He points beyond the immediate situation and at the same time concentrates this 'beyond' in the concreteness of this very situation. He is himself the most symbolic symbol, rendering symbolic as we have indicated above whatever he 'touches' and whatever touches him. Economy, work, play, society, the psychic background, and whatever else counts in the human situation are penetrated by 'man' and qualified accordingly. They are integrated with and as the hetero-thetic reality of culture, which explains that culture is not only the goal of all intellectual endeavor and action but its ground as well.

If we try to interpret the meaning of man along these lines we are referred to his culture and the mutual interdependence of the cultural instances. We have to deal with reality as symbol – and with the instances of reality as symbols – of the human presence, which in its totality merges with the presence of culture as such. Conversely, whatever is looked at as a symbol has to be interpreted and evaluated with respect to this background. The circle of hermeneutics as it becomes obvious in this context is the circle of culture and man. In order to overcome the possible viciousness of this circle we have to transpose its problems into the correlation of man and culture. *Homo existens* refers to *homo symbolicus* as the meaning of his being-there. The fact that we speak and think is absolute. But as we are doing it, we not only begin to 'see' what we 'knew' all along but become also aware of the possibility of ever shifting and growing insights that take their dwelling in the intervals spared by the dialectics of the absolute as the result of a heterothetic existence.

It does not need emphasizing that it is not only highly desirable but ultimate-ly necessary to pay attention to these conditions of existence and understanding both when confirming and when interpreting the data of culture history. But before we turn to this task it will be appropriate to continue the analysis of *homo existens* whom we have come to know as *homo symbolicus*. As regards the religious implication of *homo symbolicus* the previous deliberations are part of the argu-ment.

2. The Religious Implication of Homo Symbolicus

In his existence man necessarily points beyond the immediate impressions of his situation. By being dependent on a plurality of objects and events, but also by dealing with them in terms of his own presence, he refers to the world as both the basis and the unlimited horizon of all his activities. Things, and still more the figures and signs that are abbreviations of this world in the context of actions and reactions, of space and time, become symbols of a reality that is basically in-telligible and thoroughly accessible to language. Even the world itself becomes, as we have already indicated, a symbol of its own and of man's existence, thereby mirroring the synthesizing as well as the disruptive impact of his presence. Ascent and descent, movements on and through different levels, begin to take place and to shape the total dimension of the symbolic, while the basic unity, and thus, substantiality of this dimension is confirmed inasmuch as the experience of the human existence is absolutely irrevocable. We cannot reach beyond the 'yonder' of this experience, nor can we shorten it without bringing absurdity upon the world both in a sense that life as a whole becomes meaningless and that the apparent absurdities of this life begin to disappear. If we want to find the specific place that religion holds in a reality of which man is both result and principle, i.e., if we want to understand religious phenomena we have to trace the symbolic structure of the human situation and to turn it into a concept that enables us to bring the cultural data into perspective. While speaking about culture we have to affirm the thrust of language and to search for those transformations that turn phenomena from symbols that are to be said into symbols that speak.

Through the processes of learning and interaction we are quite familiar with informative symbols: The word that makes a thing present, the formula that represents a functional relationship of several objects, the sentence or picture that presents a situation – all inform us because in being perceived they point to something other than themselves. But while the enlargement of such symbols expands the sum total of facts and functions, the process itself through which this expansion and even the informative symbols themselves become possible remains in the 'dark'. It is not exhausted by the many symbols but maintains a life of its own. The without of man is played off against his within. The mediating meaning of his presence is retained in the self-evidence with which the results of this mediation refer to 'their' objects. In short, informative symbols are based on and presuppose revealing symbols through which man's inwardness achieves recognition while being transformed into the outwardness of language, world, and action. Articulation encounters the problem of articulating the articulated, i.e., of 'working' with a given language, as well as of articulating articulation as such. In the first instance we refer to the fact that we need an established language and culture in order to communicate with one another and to understand the world in the light of communication. In the second case we refer to the experience that we have to begin anew whenever we want to understand what we are doing and talking about. We have to be present to ourselves and to others. Dead letters remain meaningless configurations within the time-space continuum unless they are synthesized with the generative presence of attentive beings. Thus, to understand what it means that we understand, we have to focus on the very conditions under which this presence becomes operative. We have to turn to revealing symbols.

Revealing symbols which work, of course, also with perceptible signs and thus have to appear and to share in the informative surface, not only point to something other than themselves – for instance, the world – but to something that originates in the unfathomable presence or depths of man from which they emerge and which is measured by the world at a point where the multitude of objects and events recalls the unity of thinking and being alike. If we depart from the factual articulation as an experience that substantiates the correlation between possibility and potency as well as the transition from possibility to actuality through potency, we may also say: Confronted with the distinct results of man's symbolic potency, this potency begins to come forth in symbols that relate these results with the conditions of their possibility and vice versa. As such, revealing symbols initiate the process of learning and knowledge. But they equally permit us to gain insight in the meaning of this process. Because of them we can speak of 'recalling' things we have never seen before, that is, we can speak of our own consciousness and how it 'creates' the world from its own 'stuff'.[7]

Like the words of a poem, revealing symbols point to dispositions and insights. They express the values and not merely the rules of work and play, of scientific discovery and esthetic encounter. Ideas such as democracy, equality, justice, names of men such as Moses, Confucius, Buddha, Jesus, or cities such as Rome, Moscow, Peking, which have become the common good of a culture's history are such revealing symbols. Since they come into being under the conditions of the dialectical synthesis of man's presence, they unite those who share the same normative insights as is the case, for instance, with the community forming reality of a religious creed or symbolon.

In contrast to the informative symbols that relate to the cybernetical and technical aspects of the world and the respective modality of man's presence, the revealing symbols are deeply involved in the process of their own genesis. It is not the objective world in its functional and abstract composition of imaginable entities upon which they have to shed light, but the meaning of this world in its existence in which it coincides with that of man which they have to purport.

---

7. We refer here to the problem of the origin of ideas as it has been introduced by Plato's anamnesis myth. See Heintel (1968, p. 214).

Although revealing symbols share the indeterminate character of existence-experience, by virtue of being symbols and concretions of the dialectical self-encounter of time and reality in man's presence they transform the indefiniteness of this experience into the particular modality of actual culture and living consciousness. They are the words in which culture becomes substantial and man human. Even if we should try to uproot these symbols, we have to assure ourselves of their help, i.e., we need revealing symbols that are such that they hide behind the vacuity of all too much 'matter of course' while and inasmuch as they give this illusion.

If we interpret the human situation in the light of revealing symbols we can do this along two tracks. First, we can concentrate upon their correlation with the modality of human existence, its presence and the various ways it is realized. Accordingly revealing symbols may be spontaneous, creative, absolute, but also semi-conscious and paideumatic, the results of upbringing, tradition and personal decisions. They point to existence and reality by emerging from the culture-producing and culture-maintaining presence of man himself. In the second place we may focus on the 'materials' that are needed to make revealing symbols perceptible. Generally speaking they are those materials that are offered by the human situation. We can think here of the variety of perceptions and what has been done with them throughout history, of emotions and emotive instances that determine individuals and societies alike, and above all, of the complexity of custom and language and its interferential results. These materials are not an amorphous mass, but in one way or another already specified. Accordingly we have to take into account that there are factors that contribute to the specification of revealing symbols because of the selective impact thay have on the human situation. We may think here particularly on the forces that qualify the make-up of the subconscious, on the facts and feelings of early childhood, on the motivations that structure social life, on activities that please the individual. But we have also to see that these factors alone never account for the symbolic dimension itself. Their effectiveness presupposes the presence of man and whatever it implies.[8]

8. See P. Tillich (1961, pp. 301–321, p. 306): 'When psychoanalysis, for example, interprets the use of the father symbol in reference to God as an expression of the analytical father-complex (just as sociology on its part interprets it as an indication of the dominance of the male), we must raise the question as to how far the significance of this explanation extends. Obviously no further than its next assertion: That the *selection* of this symbol is to be explained by the father-complex. But the interpretation that in general the setting-up of religious symbols is determined by complexes

In either case, the discovery of depth and modality, but also the insight into the 'material' character of revealing symbols and their generative function as far as the human situation is concerned, makes it possible and necessary to confirm and to distinguish again among various levels of the symbolic. This, of course, raises the question about the proper structuralization of the symbolic. What are the dimensions of the symbolic? Especially, in what sense can or must we speak of religion in this context?

If we take here a hint that comes from the generative character of presence and symbolization, we may say that even though there exists considerable doubt about the proper structuralization of the symbolic, there can be no doubt about a basic dimension in which the process originates and (presupposing we look upon it from a reflective point of view) where it ends. This is not the dimension of philosophy, which by its essence as a reflective enterprise is bound to retract from semi-conscious and meta-conscious symbols, although it cannot eliminate them or renounce them. Nor is it any other more specific form of articulate behavior. For this reason we may tentatively describe this basic dimension as religion, which, according to common understanding, stretches from that of pious devotion to the highly speculative idea of God. In doing this we refer to an understanding of religion as it is alive in common talk. But it should also be emphasized that this alone proves nothing. Its value is heuristical and, unless we integrate ordinary language into a theory of language and culture, not hermeneutical.

In a certain sense we repeat here our previous approach toward a definition of religion (see above Ch. 2). Whereas we proceeded there on an abstract and formalized plane, we do it here on the plane of concrete differentiation insofar as we are referring to presence experience and cultural dynamics. The question

is not valid. In other words, a theory of the religious symbol is not given but rather a theory as to how religious symbols are selected. Nor is anything more than this possible, for the positing of an unconditioned transcendent can by no means be explained on the basis of the conditioned and immanent impulses of the unconscious. But the final thing has not yet been said on the question of the selection of religious symbols; the possibility has not been taken into account that the vital impulses which induce the selection of the father symbol are themselves the operation of a primordial shaping of life, and therefore the intuition of the Unconditioned in this symbol expresses a truth which, though limited, is yet an ultimate, and therefore a religious truth. The same thing would hold also for the sociological theory of the selection of symbols. Psychological and social impulses control the selection; but they can themselves be viewed as symbols for an ultimate metaphysical structure of existence. This consideration deprives these theories of their negative implications even when they are correct, namely, in their explanation of the *selection* of symbols.'

about the symbol of symbolization is thus extended by the analysis of symbol and reality as mediated by the presence of man. But both approaches seem to corroborate one another.

In case this identification of the religious dimension is adequate – a presupposition that will be corroborated by the perspective it gives – we can thus say that it is *homo existens* who gives rise to *homo symbolicus* whereas *homo symbolicus* gains the impetus toward completion in being and becoming *homo religiosus*. The idea of *homo religiosus* is not alien to that of *homo existens* but forms an integral aspect of his manifestation and symbolic realization. Whenever the thrust of this process comes to rest upon its very achievement, whenever man asks and lives the question about the meaning of world and being including that of culture and meaning alike, we face the issue of religion. As a result we thus come to an understanding of religion that takes it as the implicit presence of depth and cultural beginning in revealing symbols as well as the result of any effort to make this presence explicit. Since religion originates in the depth of man it may appear everywhere.

As we just mentioned, this analysis of man and culture which gives us religion both as implicit and as explicit quality of revealing symbols is under the present circumstances still a tentative one. It refers us to more questions than answers. What, for instance, does depth mean in the various contexts of person and community? How is the problem of truth related to that of religious symbolization? What is the truth of religion? What is that of the 'basic' dimension of cultural existence? In either case we face the problem of transformation. Within the depth of man's cultural being there originate symbols which in their particular make-up point to this depth and dimension either directly or indirectly, either implicitly or explicitly. Are the respective symbols, as our thesis suggests, religious symbols? Or are the symbols of religion something else? How do we have to understand the transition from the implicit to the explicit? Is it a process that leads 'automatically' to religion, or do we have to differentiate here, let us say, between religion and magic?

These are some of the questions that might be asked in this context. But no matter how we intend to answer them, if they can be answered at all we have to test these and similar questions by confronting them with those symbols that either in fact or by pretension make religion explicit and thus, when adequately understood, objective.

3. SYMBOLS OF RELIGION

So far we have looked at religion as a dimension that precedes the particularity and perceptibility of appearance. We came to this conclusion on theoretical grounds. But since this dimension turned out to be a necessary condition of the possibility of appearance, religion cannot be said to be alien to the world of appearance. On the contrary, it belongs to this world. From a practical point of view we therefore may speak of religion as an intensive dimension. As a result we may expect religion in practically all instances of cultural life. But how do we know that we are dealing with religion?

Above we introduced the idea of absolute symbols or instances where it does not make sense any longer to look for further relations. Since it is the work of reason to separate things in order to bring them together in new combinations, we can easily identify such instances in situations where this work of reason is no longer in process. Instead of rationalization, as we might also describe this work of reason, we encounter a process of de-rationalization. As we have already indicated, this does not imply that we are dealing here with the absurd and the irrational. This may be so. But it is equally possible that we face the premises and their enactment upon which rationality and rationalization rest.

By accepting the idea of de-rationalization as an indication of the absolute in the generative dynamics of the symbolic, we can distinguish between two forms of religious symbolism. The one refers to rites, rituals[9] and human behavior in the widest sense of the word, the other to verbal expressions, ideas and customs.

In the first instance we are referring to a process of de-rationalization which stands in particular proximity to the rationality of actions. If an event such as birth is celebrated by dances and processions, such acts can be described as a simple expression of joy. But since this joy is at least to a certain extent without a further purpose, it begins to collect what life stands for. The dances and processions point in one way or another to basic problems of life and world and to their integration into the whole of culture. They become absolute. There is no further meaning of dance and song except dancing and singing. If cattle are bred not for the purpose of sustenance but for sacrifices only, the human behavior expressed

---

9. Though 'rites' and 'rituals' are often used synonymously, in this study we are using the word 'rite' for each kind of symbolic, non-purposive (at least as far as the immanent effect is concerned) gesture, while the 'ritual' is used to express complexes of rites which are, at least in principle, aimed at repetition.

therein exceeds the economic rationale of cattle breeding. It refers to a symbolic dimension that, together with the sacrifice, points to the genesis and generation of meaning in this culture. It is its own purpose and thus, without purpose, if we ask for a because. Although it is true that every articulated act of life that is not immediately determined by the goal it reaches must be interpreted as a symbol, it does not follow that such symbols recall and represent this very detachment. Not all the symbols are absolute, but they may become absolute. When they do so we should speak of religious symbols. In this sense we can also say that the meaning of symbolism, and the specific character of religious symbols depend on the mind behind and in it; it depends on the cultural context. This is all the more true when acts with an immediate determination such as eating or sexual cohabitation are integrated into a ritual.

In the second instance we are referring to those processes of de-rationalization that concern the manifestation of reason itself. As a being that speaks, man not only uses language to convey facts and informations on conveying these facts (convention), but he lives through and in language. He appeals, he questions, he answers, he narrates, he prays and he sings. He synthesizes the reality as he encounters it with the consciousness of verbal expression for no other purpose than of encountering reality again. What has been said about the de-rationalizing effect of certain actions has to be extended to the realm of language and thought as the dimension of the cultural process where this process is turned and turns back upon itself. Accordingly, man is not only free to use his language in order to speak about the ultimate conditions of his being, but language will enforce him to do so in any case. If dogmas are not articulated as such, they withdraw behind the 'lines'. In either case it is up to man to turn whatever knowledge he acquires into a symbol of world and being that does not exhaust itself by what it explains, but that gains its very significance in the orientation it gives to life in its totality. If we take, for instance, the idea of God, we can look at this idea as an expression of certain philosophical problems. To the extent that this idea is tied up with these problems, it would not make sense to speak here of a symbol of religion. On the other hand, if we find that this idea is primarily not a speculative conception but a practical reality that structures life in its totality, or if the same holds true for the respective problems of philosophy, then we may, indeed, speak of a religious symbol. Moreover, if the enactment of such a synthesis between consciousness (knowledge) and life is demanded by custom and tradition, we are able to speak on the one hand of religion-in-the-making, and, on

the other hand, when we consider the results of this synthesis, of cult performances and cult systems. Words and acts which according to the workings of
reason and rationalization should remain separate become one as instances that
perpetuate culture for no other than its own purpose. When judged from the
viewpoint of rational enactment, i.e., that a definite goal is to be reached by a
minimum of expenditure, they are without purpose. At any rate it depends on
the symbolic circumstances and not on the particular content, that a symbolic
act, for instance, a ball game, is turned into a part or aspect of the cult system
of a culture,[10] so that we may speak either of religion-in-the-making, or of a
factual religion, or of both these possibilities. Also, there is no reason why it
should not be possible that the conduct of life and the cult system become at
least in principle symbolically identical. In this case culture itself has to be
addressed as its respective religion.

The symbolism of expressions, ideas and customs concurs in principle with
the concretization of meaning itself. On the other hand we can speak of meaning
as the culmination of life in general. Consequently the process of symbolization
is not restricted to verbalized ideas and conceptions or their artful abbreviations,
but comprises unreflected values, patterns of behavior, and their respective
objects, alike. Divergent phenomena like animals, trees, water, blood (biological
symbols), stones, places, artificial objects or fetishes, medicine bundles, the sky
with all its aspects such as sun, moon, rainbow (cosmic symbols), but also man
himself and what he knows or believes to know, can be integrated in this category of forthcoming meaning and thus may become functional in the making
of religion and find their place in the cultural whole and its respective religion.
What we observe here is the emergence of symbolic culture. The symbols
themselves are united by sharing in and pointing toward something that is final
and ultimate, and both, exhausted because represented and inexhaustable because un-represented, by them. 'It' is represented, because this is what the symbols stand for, and un-represented, because of their contingency and limitation.
If we focus on the making of religion within the process of cultural dynamics, as
it has been suggested by the de-rationalizing effect of the absolute, we now
can ask ourselves whether an analysis of 'ultimate' reality could not bring about
a further clarification of the symbols of religion. But then, what is ultimate reality?

10. An example would be the ball games of the Mesoamerican and southwestern Indians. But
one can also think of our modern ball games. *Cf.* V. Gardavský (1969).

Perhaps we may speak of ultimate reality as the mysterious, i.e., fearful and marvelous, beginning and end of all things; a beginning and end where reason ceases, and yet, where it knows that it has to take off again if something reasonable is to be accomplished. Since this reality is so different from all that is visible, we may look at it as having a quality of its own. As such it would be the other, the sacred, the one that is set apart, and that can be recognized in the reality of things and words when and to the extent that they are touched by the immediacy of the inexplicable beginning and end.[11]

If we think along this line we could say that religious symbols are marked by a relation in which they manifest in their visibility the unspecifiable depth of man, his beginning and end, and that of all other existence. They are, in the words of Mircea Eliade, hierophanies, i.e., manifestations of the sacred (1967d. Introduction, in particular p. 7 ff.). Depending on how the sacred is experienced, such hierophanies may be characterized either as kratophanies (Gr.: *kratos*, power; the sacred appears as mana, orenda, and whatever the name we want to use in order to indicate the power of being and creation) or as theophanies (Gr.: *theos*, godhead, and god).

If we take this analysis of the symbols of religion for granted, we cannot deny one obvious advantage: It enables us to bring order into the manifoldness of religious phenomena. The ambivalent character of beginning and end, of *kratos* and *theos*, explains the ambivalence of religion in general. What beginning and end bring forth is visible, while the process or the power that does it, remains invisible; what has been set forth is removed by passing away in time and decay. Religion belongs to man and, in being shaped by him, shapes his behavior in a variety of modes. Yet in its true reality religion refers to the invisible and the disappearing, the 'super'-natural, where all that can be thought and done reaches the borderline of understanding and the limit of action. The invisible and thus dreadful (tremendous) otherness of the sacred opens the gap between life and death, between the reality of the world and its beginning and end. But while it opens this gap, it also fills it by touching and fascinating the human mind as its only true center (see Otto, 1964, p. 8 ff).

Again, if we follow the logic of this conception, the sacred as the proper object of religious behavior is given to us through a process of *manifestation*

---

11. For a further elaboration of this more psychological excursion see F. Schleiermacher (1965). Also for a recapitulation of the development of this approach since Schleiermacher: L. Dupré (1972).

(see Goldhammer, 1960, p. 51 ff.). Since the meaning of this term can be understood in accordance with the consciousness and experience of the within and the without, we can 'define' the sacred accordingly, i.e., by classifying the respective phenomena in accordance with the structure of this model. If the sacred comes forth in its absolute power, traces remain in miraculous objects, places and events. If things, and especially man or the soul, disappear, they may continue in the invisible 'presence' of the sacred – an idea that recommends itself when we remember that, strictly speaking, our own presence is not visible either. If personal relations do exist between visible realities they may also exits between invisible realities: The ghosts of the deceased, spiritual beings, and, if the latter share a status of absoluteness, the gods. If the invisible inwardness of man communicates by turning to the outwardness of gestures, actions, and words, the same outwardness may contact and influence the inward beginning and end together with their representative forms. Invocations, prayers, sacrifices, cannibalistic rituals (in which the vital power of other beings is consumed), become possible modes of response. The selection of men with special faculties (shamans, medicine men) or knowledge (priests), the formation of society in accordance with conditions of various hierophanies (cult groups, socio-religious stratification, caste, secret societies – but also the legitimation of an established society by projecting it into the 'realm' of the sacred and by protecting it both with the fear of and the admiration for the sacred), the initiation of the unexperienced and, later on, of the deceased into the mysterious truth of the sacred (rites de passage), the adherence to the ghost-souls (ancestor worship), to spirits (nature worship), and to gods during the changing modes of life – all are further possibilities to realize the cult of the sacred. Also, the observance of taboos, the avoidance of dangerous situations or contacts, the acceptance and socio-cultic interpretation of mystic unities (totemism), of sacred order (sacred kingship), all these phenomena and attitudes become classifiable, provided the ultimate reality of beginning and its end is grasped in the rational entity of the sacred.

The haunting question that keeps this approach in suspense, even though it does not deny its classificatory value, is that of the adequacy of this interpretation with regard to the lived symbolism. Is the sacred indeed a theoretical and *a priori* category, as Otto maintains? Can we indeed recognize the intensive quality of religion in the reality of the sacred and in sacred reality? What is the significance of the personal relation as it is used or referred to in the interaction between the spheres of the visible and the invisible? What is the impact of God as ultimate reality and as coincidence of beginning and end on the conception of the sacred? And finally, how do we have to interpret the sacred with respect to its own and to the meaning of man as a person? Is it accidental that we should ask for the meaning of the sacred?

Considering the dialectics of the sacred and the profane as it has been discovered by E. Durkheim (1967, p. 51 ff; also Caillois, 1939), it should be difficult if not impossible to eliminate idea and reality of the sacred from the making of religion and religious symbols. Since this process is necessarily dialectical, as the analysis of revealing symbols has shown, the dialectics of the sacred and the profane must have to do with it in one way or another. On the other hand we may also ask ourselves if the identification of religion and the sacred is not caused by, and is causing, a form of dialectics that has lost its meaning. If this is true, the resulting dichotomy between the sacred and the profane that is marked by a form of 'integration' which in truth is the tyranny of power no longer refers to the end of religion as the fulfillment of its dynamics and meaning but as its cessation. In this case we could also say that the presence of religion is negative, and its absence the principle that (dis)qualifies life in its ultimate meaning.

In fact, this view will actually be supported if we try to bring the identification of religion and the sacred in line with the conditions of culture and the symbolic. It seems to me that the motive at the bottom of this interpretation is the wish to establish the autonomy of religion as an objective and separate reality. If, however, religion must be seen as a reality that originates in the depth of man and culture, such an attempt will be confronted with the problem of introducing totality through the particular without transforming the particular into the whole of cultural reality. The result we may expect under these circumstances is indeed that of a negative dialectics: The reality of culture becomes parasitical, and in consequence, illusionary and destructive. The theocracy that has been aimed at keeping man sacred will end up by sacrificing man's dignity and freedom, whereas the entirely secularized society that has been aimed at providing a place where man is free to be himself will end up in deifying its very profanity. In either case, when looking at religion from the viewpoint of the sacred as a rational entity, we come to understand why religion has been interpreted as self-deception, as the 'heart of a heartless world'(Marx), and the illusionary projection of secret wishes and longings (Feuerbach, Freud). Although these interpretations as such are no argument against the

sacred as the stuff that generates religion (a metaphor that seems to be justified when we think of the homological use of holy and sacred), or, for the
same reason, an argument against Otto's introduction of the term numen as a
substitute for sacred, they should be accepted nevertheless as a critical shock,
presupposing we do not agree with them in the first place.

As an alternative to this interpretation of ultimate reality I suggest we do
not lose sight of the problem of meaning and of existing consciousness. In the
lived situation we always encounter phenomena of particular significance. If we
describe them with the word 'sacred' it is not because we perceive some special
quality but because they come to us within certain patterns of expectation
and narration, or quite in general, within the context of a 'mythology' that
'explains' the circumstances which make it necessary to pay attention to a
particular phenomenon, to 'remember' a cult action, or which gives an account
for the existence of invisible beings, of 'sacred' objects such as trees and animals,
and of rules and customs. When we introduce here the word mythology, we do
not understand it as a discipline that analyzes myths, but as the 'saying of myths'
in a given culture or cultural situation. Such myths may be narratives about
gods and special events connected with them. But they include also statements
about the beginning, the significance of history, the origin and destiny of man
and world. In addition we may distinguish between myths that are said in more
or less definite articulations and others that speak only in the attitudes with which
people take a position in and to the particular situation in which they live.
What connects these various instances and what permits us to bring them together by the one term mythology is their common function. In one way or another
they partake in the enactment of tradition and the realization of orientation and
meaning. If we consider the psychogenetic fact that there is a one-word stage
of language, we may also say that mythology refers us to the one word that
speaks in and through the many words of a tradition. We thus resume the idea
of the concretization of meaning as the proper medium for the question about
religion and, in consequence, the sacred.

It is not the place here to go into a more detailed analysis of the meaning and
significance of mythology. We shall return to this problem when more data
have been collected. But whatever the specific meaning of mythology may be,
we cannot detach the sacred from it, whatever it means. If there is a correlation
between meaning and the sacred, the sacred must be correlated with the world
or language of man. Everything we said above about the two forms of religious

symbolism can be said again, presupposing we connect the classificatory comp-lexes of the sacred with their emergence in life and culture. Moreover, like the word itself, the sacred can neither be separated from the person, i.e., the one who speaks, nor from the mythological context, i.e., the depth-dimensions out of which he and others speak, and the directional frame of reference according to which they speak. If there is substantiality in the sacred, it cannot be sought apart and outside the many dimensions of the personal. In line with the previous analysis of man we may therefore say that person and meaning affect one another in such a way that the heterothetic syntheses of the mythological reports, i.e., the mythological figures and what they are doing, become signposts for the person on his way toward a completion whose medium or value is that of the sacred, or better, of the holy (see M. Scheler's philosophy of values as presented in the works cited. Also, M. Frings, 1969, p. 27 ff; Dupré, 1972, p. 19 ff). Primary and apart from rationalistic fixations, the sacred is not a rational entity or a category upon which religion rests but the mythology-related medium in which man as a person originates and continues to grow. It comes forth as the meaning of personal being, and thus, has to be taken as such. If one of these two poles – the sacred in its mythology relation (that is, the sacred in conno-tation with holy and whole) or the personal task (that is, the sacred in conno-tation with well-being and personal health) – is suppressed, it can be expected that the human response to the demands of beginning and end deteriorates either into meaningless though rational and socially effective manipulation of mythological associations, or into the equally meaningless attitude of agnostic mysticism and self-complacent rationalism.

The interpretation of the sacred as meaningful quality and as mythology-related medium of personal completion permits an open response to the many symbols of religion. It permits us to see religion primarily as an intensive quality of the process of symbolization in general. This quality might be expressed as such, and thus, brought forth as 'positive' religion. But if it is done it works again through the process of symbolization. As a result, religion appears indeed as the free expression of insight and belief,[12] but it is also tied up with the dyna-

12. Here again we touch upon the relationship between philosophy and religion (see Introduc-tion) which has been one of the central issues of transcendental philosophy. According to Schelling (no date, p. 250) we have to distinguish between religion as it 'takes place' in history, and philo-sophical religion. The latter includes the factors of actual religion on the basis and by mode of understanding and comprehension. Its goal is to hold in freedom what as a real relation characterizes consciousness and history with regard to God. Philosophy itself appears as a sort of cult, but within

mics of culture genesis. In this sense it is present where there are living symbols no matter if it is realized in them or not. Religion and culture are dialectically correlated. Man is free to create his religion, but he is not free to exist without it. If we ask for the conditions of the possibility of this dialectics, we are referred to the idea of the personal as immanent and yet transcendent center of reality. Within this context we may refer to the sacred as that particular quality which enables us to connect religion as necessity with religion as freedom. But it must be 'handled' accordingly.

Religion in its concrete manifestation cannot be defined *a priori*, nor can we identify it as the sum total of all those symbols that 'intend' to make it explicit. Like man and culture it is simultaneously one and many. It depends on situations and their intensive structure even if attempts have been made to give expression to this structure. Nevertheless if we try to define religion – as we have to if we would like to speak about it at all – we have to take this into consideration. Accordingly, we may well speak of religion as the totality of man's 'encounter with the sacred' as Mensching sees it. But then we have to emphasize that the sacred, though objectified by language, must not be understood as an object. We may avoid doing this by adding that it is such an encounter that the ultimate of consciousness, or, in the language of P. Tillich, that man's 'ultimate concern' is shaped and symbolized in accordance with the various situations of life, world and history, and vice versa. And whenever situations show traces of such an encounter they can be treated as religious phenomena. In short, if we speak about religion it is not enough to look for a logic that structures (or ought to structure) the expressions of the respective symbols and the context wherein they subsist, but we must also ask ourselves about the logic by which we have to treat these symbols. As in case of the well-known symbol '0' we have to know that imagination is one thing and thinking another.

From a methodological point of view we may add here that the study of religion above all must evolve out of an analysis of culture and man. Only an approach that takes the human situation unconditionally into consideration can be expected to do justice to a culture and the respective religion. The methodological ideal of an unconditioned functionalism as it has been indicated in the

---

a 'community' which, by the force of thought, is prevented from being turned into a 'church'. It seems to me that the recognition of this dialectics that is consistent with the 'movement' of learned ignorance would add very much to the 'objectivity' of research and interpretation, both on the part of the apologist and of the agnostic.

first chapter becomes thus the basic guideline of an analysis of religion. However, this analysis too must be aware of the constitutive demands and implications of cultural data. The situation and the problem to which we refer in such an analysis is not a 'natural' or an 'objective' one as is largely the case with natural sciences but a human problem and situation. This explains why there is no other condition such as a special sensorium but only the minimum of experience as it is presupposed where and when there is language, in order to get access to religious phenomena. But it also indicates the need and the task to anticipate a universal humanism as the final horizon of cultural existence and understanding in which existing consciousness recognizes its own significance and possibilities. Both aspects must be brought together if we are to come to grips with religion as it is. If we speak in this context of constitutive analysis we understand it as the realization of an unconditioned functionalism that establishes its respective theory as a universal humanism. Their mutual togetherness thus becomes the criterion of truth and adequacy. As such it is founded in the symbolic character of man's existence or, put differently, of existing consciousness. But if existing consciousness is to realize this possibility we should add that we also need the confrontation with concrete symbols in order to accomplish our task.

4. RELIGION AND MAGIC

Like man himself and his symbolic mode of existence, religion is a complementary tot ity whose becoming is its being. It does not subsist like things do, but is re i in man and culture. It may be set forth as such but only in order to follow the same rules and principles that are valid for the symbolic in general. We thus can speak about religion as we speak about things, but if we want to know what we are talking about we have to 'correct' our speaking. To say in this sense that man is a religious being is not to be mistaken as a strict predication even though the sentence has a predicative structure. Instead we have to understand this statement as a dialectical proposition which is true as long as we use it in and with the ease of unreflected speaking, that becomes wrong if we press it into the artificial universe of reason, and that becomes true again if we comprehend it on the level of theoretical reflection, i.e., on a level where reason recalls the conditions of its possibility by meeting the borders of its world and by remembering what it has forgottten in order to be successful in its abstractions. Moreover, since religion is brought forth by the symbolic both by implication and as the realization of its potentials, the dialectics to which we have to subject our speaking about religion concerns the process of religion too. As dialectical reality religion is tied up with the process of personalization and of personal achievement, with the problem of receiving and giving meaning as well as with realizing it. Accordingly the phenomena of religion must not be taken as mere facts that are what they are in the same sense as the facts of perception. To the extent that they are moments of a dialectical process their 'is' is correlated with an 'ought' that has to be taken into account if we want to comprehend the respective phenomena in what they are.[13] The negativity or positivity of the respective phenomena is not merely a matter of emotion and subjective evaluation but part of their being.

If we look at the dialectics of 'is' and 'ought' in the constitution of religious phenomena from the viewpoint of constitutive analysis, we can expect something like the problem of disconstitution. Because of the correlation between religion, the personal and their respective dialectics as indicated by the idea of the sacred, the analysis of religion has to take into consideration the possibility of phenomena that structurally belong to the complex of religion whereas constitutively they contradict both the reality and the meaning of religion. Thus, if we do not want to miss the point we must not lose sight of this difference.

Again, if we admit that there is a relationship between religion and personalization we can expect that religion, like the personal, refers to and remains bound up with a heterothetic reality that belongs to it as theoretical and practical presupposition of its realization. Because of the particular character of man's presence, the resulting synthesis cannot be understood as the outcome of mere computation. On the contrary, if there is any synthesis at all it will be a dialectical one that includes the dynamics of its genesis as an orientation giving impulse to consciousness and understanding on the basis of necessity and freedom. On the other hand, since this process is necessarily in the making we have to take into consideration that the dialectics of personal becoming might be and factually will be superseded by patterns that disrupt the consistency of this process. To bring things into perspective we thus have to take this possibility into consideration.

13. This view is exemplified to a certain extent by Max Weber's (1920–21) approach to religion in general and Calvinist protestantism in particular (as the source of capitalism).

It seems that phenomena commonly labeled as magic comply with this expectation. Accordingly, if we recognize in magic a possible, though disarranged, trait of man's dialectical unfolding, we must not look at it as an exceptional form of cultural and mental insufficiency but as an unavoidable and to a certain degree complementary aspect of culture history. Wherever magic plays a role in man's life it cannot be completely devoid of religion, nor can we ever expect to find a religion that has eliminated magic successfully. In either case no study of religion can or should be indifferent to the problem of magic.

In the previous chapter we applied the concept of magic to those phenomena where a coercive or compulsive attitude toward the world of the symbolic could be noted. We can add now that from the perspective of the symbolic and the logic of its constitution magic attempts to reverse the unconditioned presence of the ultimate beginning and end into the availability of objects, formulae, rituals and institutions. This is indeed contrary to the logic of symbolization and the meaning of the symbolic, but it is also understandable when we consider the fact that any symbol relates in one way or another to the perceptible and that, for better and for worse, man is a being that forgets. By turning the invisibility of the symbolic into a manipulative set of fixed symbols, i.e., by reifying revealing symbols,[14] magic reveres and forgets, so to speak, the ground upon which *homo symbolicus* stands. It falls prey to the temptation to take face values for real. Despite the social effectiveness which may result from this manipulation, from the viewpoint of the constitution of culture, magic not only turns the symbolic against itself but depersonalizes the person by using it as a means instead of a goal. In either case man will be caught by illusion whereas culture becomes illusionary, an existing illusion whose thrust will sooner or later be destructive.

There are many ways to relate to the symbolic in such a manner that the resulting practice contradicts the logic on which the respective symbols are based. In a certain sense each symbol and situation faces this problem in its own particular way. On the other hand there are certain patterns that return again and again. Depending on the symbols and the principles that are deployed, we can

14. In the language of Austin (1962, p. 99 ff) we could add that religious phenomena are real inasmuch as they are 'illocutionary' activities. In a similar way as he does with reference to ordinary speaking we thus may ask about the conditions that are necessary to achieve complete performances of the religious act. Conversely, we have also to inquire into the typology of deficiencies as far as the ontological status of these acts is concerned.

distinguish between various types of magic with more or less distinct boundaries. Without claiming completeness we can mention here at least five forms of magic.

In a first instance we could speak of *substitute magic*. Man seizes power over someone else by taking possession of parts of the other being, for instance, hair, nails, or even a footprint. Since these parts are at his disposal without resistance, he gains through them full power over the other. What actually happens is thus a reversal of the transcendental principle that the part may represent the whole into the assumption that the part becomes (is) the whole. If this assumption would be correct there could be no complaints about the adequacy of the respective actions as far as efficiency is concerned.

In a second instance we may speak of *contagious magic*. This type of magic is given when the substitution of the whole by the part is only partially realized because it remains integrated into a scheme of causal connections. By touching or wearing power-laden objects such as relics, fetishes, amulets, or even by assimilating them, for instance, in form of living tissues as is the case in cannibalistic rituals, man integrates himself and his deeds into the efficacy of an invisible reality and power structure. Also the observation of taboos might be added to this type of magic. Under the premise that there are invisible-visible powers it is only reasonable to attune to their demands. For the same reason we may also speak of superstititon as a form of contagious magic.

In the third instance we could refer to *sympathetic magic*. This type of magic results from an application of analogy that replaces the sequential unity of causal interrelations by that of sympathetic feelings and ideas. It operates within a framework that consists of picture-like settings – J. G. Frazer speaks also of the magic of similarity – as well as of fixed symbol structures. We may think here of the anticipation of a successful hunt by striking a picture of the animal; or of the manipulation of pictures and figures in general; or of the use of formulae both in connection with pictures and statues and independent from them. Also the practice of subjecting the godhead, a ghost, or an other human being by means of the name, may be mentioned here. We recognize in such attitudes the principle of substitute magic. On the other hand there is a difference because of the ideational character of the substitution, which under certain conditions may permit a more positive interpretation.

In the fourth place we may refer to a type of magic which has to do with the particular character of knowledge. As a moment of the process of symbolization knowledge is equally subject to the temptation of the symbolic and to be misapprehended in its meaning and efficacy, especially when the instrumental function of knowledge and reason becomes an end in itself. The knowledge of the 'right' time, the 'right' setting, the proper godhead (*deus certus*), ascertains the desired goal as if cult and ritual were only one more form of technology. The world of the sacred as an instance of orientation and expression of personal growth and meaning turns into a state of impersonal anonymity. While it loses thereby more and more its transcendental character, it becomes dangerous and mechanically effective – but also manageable when encountered by sufficient and adequate 'knowledge'. Ascetic techniques as a know-how of virtuous life become their own end under these circumstances, thus working by their very deployment. This *gnoseological type of magic* which ranges from the teachings and practices of the ritual-conscious shaman to modern theosophy can also be found in the many forms of so-called secular ideology, particularly when revolutions begin to devour their own children.

As an impetus that keeps reason busy with itself gnoseological magic gained importance not only for the elaboration of magical techniques such as divination and astrology, but also in the development of law and science; a heritage that is still effective in our age, presupposing we do not consider the content of law and science, but their functional integration into the social processes of evaluating and setting objectives.

The last form of magic we would like to mention here is that of *societal magic*. This form of magic does not concur with the distinction between private and official magic, which in turn depends on the private or public circumstances under which magical acts and attitudes are realized. On the contrary it concerns the manipulation of man by both religion and magic. When we said above that magic depersonalizes the person the previous forms of magic corroborate this view by revealing a sort of misapprehension of the symbolic that falls back upon the integration and in consequences the integrity of the most symbolic symbol. But as such they remain indefinite as far as the social status of the individual person was concerned.[15] This changes, however, when we consider man within

15. Many of the African tribes have been particularly sensitive to this problem. Among the Bantu the word *bulozi* was coined in order to indicate the kind of magic which absolutizes the interest of the individual practitioner. Ritual and knowledge become a device that works at the expense of others. Since bulozi destroys the fundamental integrity of other human beings, it is considered the crime that exceeds all hideousness. See p. 75.

a societal context that is marked by various forms of tensions and by the need to integrate a variety of life-communities. Since this integration cannot be achieved by reason alone, which in this sense is primarily a matter of the individual and not of the life-community, it will be necessary to take refuge in the process of symbolization and the symbolic in its cultural significance. As a result a new sphere of influence will be opened for magic and religion alike where they will be subjected to, and have their impact on, the forces that determine the societal processes. Within this context we encounter the polarity of state and church and the problem of their mutual relation which confronts us in its own way with various forms of magic and religion. But what matters most here is, on the one hand, the fact that the depersonalizing effect of magic will be more comprehensive and direct than in any other form of magic, and, on the other hand, that the relationship between magic and religion becomes more complex. For what must be considered as a form of magic in the one instance might well concur with religion in the other. If an established system of religious symbols is used by those who dominate to perpetuate their domination, and thus, a form of magic, it is quite possible that the same symbols, though differently understood, liberate indeed those who are the victim of this magical manipulation. In addition, matters become even more complicated when we take into consideration that the will to power and domination might be synthesized with the idea of responsibility, which might set a limit to the deviations of power, but which also may conceal the true motives both to those who hold offices and to those who are integrated by these offices.

It is not the place here to continue this analysis of possible forms of magic. They are complex and lurking wherever and whenever we speak of and encounter religion. In this sense we may say that the awareness of magic becomes significant in many respects. Because of the particular complexity of the issue, it becomes a self-evident request to search for the elementary units and conditions that bring about these results. Since magic concerns the whole of life and culture history, it becomes hermeneutically significant inasmuch as it forces us to be critical both with respect to possible magical implications of our own intellectual efforts and to the phenomena in question, and to distinguish accordingly (see Schillebeeckx, 1972, p. 190 ff). Nevertheless, the borderlines of the magical reversal where man is turned and turns himself, his history, and his ideas, into parts of the world instead of maintaining their creative openness in which they participate as symbolic reality, are always fluid. In case of public magic (a rain ceremony or a fertility ritual) it may be impossible to decide whether such performances are symbolizations of the mythological conditions that recognize 'divine revelation', i.e., where things are done for their own purpose within the total integration of life and world, or a compulsive attempt to master a particular situation by means of the sacred or of an objectified illusion. We can even assume that some of the participants are religiously oriented, whereas others perform a magic ritual. It is true, if we look at such ceremonies from a mere descriptive point of view, there is no difference in the faces of those who can be said to be religious and those who do a magical performance. But in this case or to the extent that we do not see 'more' we should not, unless we want to take the risk of performing a magical ritual by means of a 'description', claim to deal with religious phenomena.[16]

The actual relationship between magic and religion, especially when it is considered in connection with the idea of a highest being, remains an open question for further discussion. We have to come back to this problem in the evaluation of the respective data. However, to consider magic as a preliminary stage leading to religion or even as a source of religion is not only opposed to the data of culture history but an ideological dogma that misapprehends the dialectics of culture history and that tells reality how it has to look like.[17] Religion and magic are embedded in the texture and dynamics of culture and symbolization both as expression and as limitation of dialectical existence.

5. CONCLUSION

Constitutive analysis rejects an anti-empirical attitude. As analysis it is concerned with the empirical as the proper object of questions and investigations. We want to know what is and to be as complete as possible in exploring the grounds. On the other hand, constitutive analysis is well aware that the data under investigation are those of cultural reality. For this reason it rejects equally an anti-speculative attitude. The data of culture history have to be taken for what

16. It should be noted that from this viewpoint the program of a mere descriptive phenomenology of religion cannot be maintained. Or better, if we accept it, we should not regard it as a particular method but as an expression of ideological interests.

17. Though we owe to Hegel the insight into the problem of history and dialectics, he also serves as an example for the misapprehension of which I speak. See (no date, vol. I, p. 278 ff).

they are. Since this is not possible without recurring to the conditions that turn the natural into the cultural thereby sustaining the latter, we should realize the empirical analysis by synthesizing it with the speculative anticipation of these very conditions and thus to render expressive what is already operative in the practice of perceiving the world and of speaking about it. In this sense we may also say that constitutive analysis becomes the method of cultural studies insofar as and to the extent that we comprehend that speaking about culture is in itself a realization of culture. So much for the method and methodology of this study.

Before we can attempt to give a final synthesis and evaluation of the basic conditions under which religion begins to appear both in culture in general and in primitive culture in particular, some cultural situations have to be examined more closely. It would be ideal to do this for all those situations for which reliable information is available. But since neither time nor space allow an enterprise of this scope, we must confine ourselves to a few selections from the cultures of gatherers and hunters which are, since they can be typologized as primitive cultures, of special interest for this study.

Among the representatives of this cultural type we will concentrate on the Bambuti Pygmies in the Ituri Region of the Congo forest (Africa). We shall put emphasis on them not only because of their 'ethnological age', but also because of the unique relationship of their culture in respect to an independent environment. Because of sufficient food supply that can be acquired with relatively simple means and of the isolating character of the rain forest that keeps the groups small enough to interdict the social perpetuation of interpersonal differences, their culture is one of the least rationalized ones known today. Therefore, it can be expected that the primary conditions of human life, which in our own situation are subject to very complex mechanisms of selection, sublimation, and other transformations, are less hidden and less complicated here than anywhere else, presupposing we maintain the principle of man's analogous universality and universal analogy.[18]

This more detailed approach to several cultural situations is not only intended to furnish additional data of religious symbolism but also to provide test cases where an attempt will be made to synthesize the principle of an unconditioned functionalism with that of a universal humanism. In this context it is not our

---

18. In this context the sociology of knowledge speaks also of a transcultural being of man. See K. H. Wolff (1968, p. 142). See also Th. P. v. Baaren (1960) p. 9 ff.

intention to attempt a reconstruction of the historical and chronological genesis of cultures. The historical aspects are taken into consideration where possible and necessary. But they are not our primary concern, nor are they goals in themselves. It would be desirable, of course, to have a reliable analysis of the genesis of the world's cultures, but in this respect much is still to be done despite many ingenious attempts to shed light on these problems. For that reason we emphasize the taking of various situations as units of cultural dynamics rather then as building stones of a comparative system of the history of religions, even though we do not deny the legitimacy of this objective. Any comparisons made are intended to serve the morphological understanding of culture and religion. Their significance is determined by their possible contribution to an understanding of cultural dynamics. Within this context we may look at them as cross-cultural indications of a universal humanism.

4

The Religion of the African Pygmies

Pygmy and Pygmoid groups can be found today in the territories northwest and east of the Congo River, i.e., in the tropical rain forest from the west coast of Central Africa to the lake region in the east. There are indications that formerly they occupied a much larger territory. We do not know when the Pygmies actually entered the rain forest. They were already living there when Herkhuf, a high official of Pharaoh Pepi II Neferkere (2275–2185 B.C.) brought a 'dancer of God' from the land of Imam (see Schebesta, 1938, p. 9).

More important than this early historical reference for the evaluation of the present status of the Pygmy populations were the migrations throughout Africa. Their impact on the Pygmy stratum ranges from extermination and assimilation to a symbiosis that varies between serfdom and a more or less free coexistence, depending mainly on the environmental conditions and the density of the Negro population. Since these historical changes developed only gradually, the influence of the Pygmy culture in respect to the symbolic patterns of the African forest cultures can be felt in many ways. Although none of the known Pygmy groups now speaks a language entirely of its own, there are indications that their original languages deeply influenced the formation of the idioms spoken in the forest regions (see Schebesta, 1952, 426 ff, esp. 451; 1953, p. 63 ff).

Even though the historical development of the Pygmy stratum apparently did not dissolve the basic patterns of its culture (see Dupré, 1962–63, p. 9 ff, esp. 166 ff), it is necessary to discover authentic groups among the various forms of the Pygmy cultures. Neither the Babinga (Beki, Akoa, and others) in the west, nor the Batwa in Ruanda, nor the Bachwa southeast of Lake Leopold satisfy our methodological requirements. Only the Bambuti of the Ituri Forest do so. Hence it is a fortunate coincidence that precisely these groups have been more thoroughly investigated than any other of the Pygmy groups.[1]

1. This holds true in contrast to the information on the western populations, especially since it became obvious that H. Trille's (1932) publications must be considered by and large as fake

The main share in the investigation of the Bambuti culture belongs to Paul Schebesta, who arrived at the Ituri Forest in January 1929, some time before roads opened this area to the influence of civilization.[2] After extensive inquiries throughout the entire region, which were finished in September 1930, Schebesta returned for three additional and more thorough explorations in 1934/35, 1949/50, and 1954/55.[3]

In the second instance we have to mention here the work of Colin M. Turnbull. In addition to two shorter trips in 1951 and 1954, Turnbull spent some fourteen months as a member of a group at the Epulu River in 1957/58. Despite the fact that this group had been deeply affected by recent developments in this area and had lost some of the traits of the traditional way of Pygmy life, Turnbull's insights are of special value in the overall picture presented by Shebesta.[4]

1. The Forest World of the Bambuti Pygmies

For the Pygmies the forest is not just one environment among others, it is the home in which they live. It is both their territory and hunting ground. There is no need to establish a body of special institutions to insure the continuance of human life, since the forest is the permanent guarantee for man's duration, providing only that man is willing to accept the terms of the forest. This means that man must adapt himself to the economic possibilitites of the forest and that he has to adopt a social organization in harmony with the economic conditions of forest life.

(K. Piskaty, 1957, p. 52). See also W. Dupré (1963–63); on the investigations of the Bachwa and Batwa, see P. Schebesta (1934), P. Schumacher (1950), and G. Hulstaert (1963).

2. The first information on the Pygmies in the Ituri Forest comes from G. Schweinfurth, H. Stanley, Emin Pascha and F. Stuhlmann. See also W. Schmidt (1910), M. Gusinde (1942, 1948), P. Julien (1954), A. Vorbichler (1965), P. E. Joset (1948). Insofar as these sources are relevant for the religious life of the Pygmies, they are quoted in Schebesta (1950, II).

3. On the following pages we are mainly referring to Schebesta (1950, II, Part 3). Other works by Schebesta are (1932; 1936; 1941, II, 1 and 2). Since I had the opportunity of studying P. Schebesta's unpublished notes and of discussing them with him during spring and summer of 1967, I have used them also.

4. The main works of C. M. Turnbull used here are (1961; 1965). In respect to the situation of these groups covered by Turnbull's study, see Turnbull, 1961, p. 11 ff; Turnbull, 1965, p. 7 ff; and Schebesta (1963, esp. p. 214 f).

The Bambuti never developed a tribal or political system. The vastness of the forest, combined with a relative scarcity of food in any one location, did not allow for a social organization larger than the totemistic clan, which has only a temporary significance (Schebesta, 1941, II, 289 ff., 304 ff. and 428 ff.). The social community is thus identical with the economically optimal unit, the (patrilineal) group or 'band' (Turnbull, 1965, p. 24). Consisting of several nuclear families, such a group is large enough to give mutual support and small enough for its members to live effectively a nomadic form of life in a given area.

Man's ability to create and use tools, and the continued daily work he does to support himself, are no substitute for the search and striving for absolute symbols. In fact the unreflected, although not unconscious, awareness of 'yesterday' and 'tomorrow', of beginning and end, permeates and penetrates the life and the world of the Forest People. This becomes clear when we examine the basic features of their ordinary day.

When the sun is shining, life in the camp[5] starts early. If it is raining, people take their time in coming out of their huts. Their mood is low and no one really desires to hunt or gather. The women take their children and go searching for bulbs, roots, mushrooms, fruits. When they leave the camp and while working, they sing. They ask *asobe*, *tore* or *epilipili* to give them the things they are looking for (Schebesta, 1950, II, p. 68). The phrases they use are adjusted to the situation: '*Epilipili*, let me find a snake' (Schebesta, 1950, II, p. 69). Or: 'Morning is here. *Asobe* shall protect us against suffering, troubles and disaster. *Asobe* shall be with us on the way home' (Schebesta, 1950, II, p. 68). When they discover newly ripened fruits, *Tore* will get a symbolic share. *Tore* take it and eat' (Schebesta, 1950, II, p. 76). After a successful return and when the work of cooking and eating is done, little pieces of food are laid aside on a leaf for *mungu* (or *mbali*, *kalisia*, etc.[6]). It is a part of the preparation for the next day's gathering (Schebesta, 1950, II, p. 78).

5. The camp averages between 4 to 12 huts, built by the women. On special occasions (religious festivals) a camp may comprise 50 to 60 huts. But there may be also very small camps, especially during the termite season, when each family builds its hut close to the termite burrow (Schebesta, 1941, II).

6. The various Pygmy groups know and use different names in the addresses of their prayers and rituals. The names are not confined to one group, but reoccur throughout the entire region, though one or the other may be prevalent in certain areas. Since it is our intention to describe the situational character of the religious life before an interpretation is given, the various names are reported without arranging them systematically. That they do not lack a certain systematic aspect will be shown later.

While the women prepare for gathering, the men depart for hunting. They too call upon *tore* or *kalisia* or simply upon their father(s): 'Father, give me game. *Mbali*, tell (ask) my father that he should give me game to kill. *Kalisia*, eh! Grandfather give us the game of the forest, be with me when I kill the game. *Tore*, go ahead of us, then we shall kill the game of the forest' (Schebesta, 1950, II, p. 67 f., and unpubl.; the texts are situational and informal).

When an animal has been killed, it is brought into the camp to be divided among the families by the eldest. By this action the eldest and the community obey a law of *mungu*. At the same time, a piece of the animal's heart (or of another organ) is cast into the forest or put aside on a leaf, which is laid upon the ground or in the fork of a tree. Such a ceremony is accompanied by the words: '*Muema* (or *mungu, epilipili, tore, befe*), that is for you' (Schebesta, 1950, II, p. 75). There is no need to repeat the same ceremony with each animal that is killed. The expression of a basic gratitude to *mungu* and the beings of the forest is considered sufficient. 'Only stupid people forget this ritual' (Schebesta, 1950, II, p. 74, and unpubl.).

When night falls, the hunter, with an invocation for the next day's hunt, puts his spear beside the fork of the tree where he exposed the gift for *tore* (*kalisia, mungu*). He may also put an arrow under his head. When he dreams about a successful hunt, he knows that *kalisia* is with him (Schebesta, 1950, II, p. 68).

Similarily, the eldest realizes that it is time to change the camp's location when *kalisia* tells him to do so in a dream. The entire community will respect such a dream even if the eldest in question has not too much to say otherwise (Schebesta, 1950, II, p. 23).

When a hunter finds a honey tree, he first knocks against the bark with the words: 'Father, let me find honey'. Afterward, before taking his own share, he casts some honeycombs into the forest. To neglect this ritual would entail illness (Schebesta, 1950, II, p. 79). The same is done with termites and caterpillars. Some of the prey is put into a hollow tree for *tore* (Schebesta, 1950, II, p. 76).

Schebesta observed the wives of the hunters performing a libation ceremony. Early one morning, before the hunters departed for an elephant hunt, their wives filled their mouths with water and squirted it over the husbands. They then asked *tore* to help and protect the hunters (Schebesta, 1950, II, p. 76).

Considering the overall picture of a typical Pygmy day, we can say that man's work and behavior begins with and ends in an absolute symbolism. Even in the most primitive (or unsophisticated) Pygmy culture, where the fulfillment of essential needs exhausts almost all time available, man is highly aware of something that expresses clearly that there is no human act for its own sake. Since a system of well-established social or psychological transformations and sublimations of the ways and means of production does not yet exist in this culture, work is factually bound into a hypostatic situation, which practically refers to an irreducible dimension that cannot be identified with what we see and observe with our eyes. This situation is clearly distinguished from the rational hypostasis that turns organic efforts and instincts into human work and play. But is the hypostasis in question therefore a matter of the irrational? Since it does not destroy the rationale in man's work, this conclusion would be at least very improbable. Perhaps we should consider it as an indication of what we must call the religious dimension. If names like *mungu, epilipili,* and *tore,* can be translated by our term 'god', this theory would certainly gain force. Before we can decide this question, it is necessary to analyze the anthropological picture the Bambuti formed about themselves.

2. BAMBUTI ANTHROPOLOGY

Like other primitive peoples, the Bambuti have never developed a doctrinal theory about man. This, however, does not imply that they have no understanding at all on this point. An implicit understanding of man and various states of consciousness are clearly revealed in connection with the decisive events of human life. There is without a doubt what we may call the spontaneity of consciousness that expresses itself in the cultural situation. We must analyze, therefore, the accounts given of events such as birth, death, suffering, joy and survival in order to find their communicable implications. This is the more important in a situation such as that of the Bambuti because for them tradition – understood as an institutionalized set of rules and interpretations – is very loosely woven. There is, of course, the usual 'My father told me so' as a reason for certain customs. Its meaning, however, is that of a situational revival rather than of the received word applied by institutionalized patterns. The office of the eldest, for instance, though given by tradition and sanctioned by mythological accounts (*epilipili* gave the commandment: 'I left them behind me, you shall not mistreat them'; Schebesta, 1941, II, p. 222 f.), depends largely on the ability of the person to expect the cooperation of the group. The final criterion for this cooperation, which Turnbull calls the key to Pygmy society (1961, p. 124), is a mutual equilibrium of interests, which is optimal for survival. The eldest himself is only *primus inter pares* (Schebesta, 1941, II, p. 290). For the same reason, the equality of man and woman is a practical expression of the general Bambuti anthropology. Because the groups are small and the cooperation of every individual is a necessity of survival, its members maintain a degree of autonomy which forbids a permanent suppression of man by man. The meaning of the culture exhausts itself almost entirely in the existence of man. Its purpose coincides with that of the life-community wherein the person can be said to be itself in cooperative dependence on and freedom from others.

Since death is the most decisive of all human events, we are likely to find in connection with it some of the essential features concerning the Bambuti's self-understanding of man. Among the Bambuti, the attitude toward death is to a certain degree ambivalent. Schebesta was told that there is nothing beyond the present life. Death is the end of everything. But then he discovered that such a statement concerns only one aspect of man's life. Man is not just bodily existence. Rather, he is 'composed' of different principles. When they speak of man the Bambuti distinguish between the following aspects: *ela* or body, *tedi* (*muri*) or shadow, and *borupi* (also *boru-e'i*) or 'moon fruit' (with the connotation of heart, fire and eye). The difference between the living and the dead consists of the pulse and breath, *tukutuku* and *ekeu* (*ekuma*). The heart is kept alive by *borupi*, which is also present in the eyes. *Borupi* goes to *tore* (or *mungu, epilipili*), who is either above or in the forest, when *ekeu* ceases. The dead man becomes a *mbefe* (or *lodi, keti, balimo*), or *tore*, but may also live as *boru-e'i* (as a star, with *epilipili* in the sky, where he has his forest and game) (Schebesta, 1950, II, p. 86 ff.; unpubl.).

Though the further interpretation of these principles or aspects may vary from group to group, there is one underlying 'reality' (and practical theory) that unites the divergent opinions, namely, *megbe*, or the vital force (also called *elima, bongisu, mara*). *Megbe* is the ground from which the person emerges and by which man lives as his own purpose. It gives the power to act, to speak, and to think; in a word, to be successful as a human being. When *megbe* fades and leaves the body together with *boru-e'i*, man ceases to exist, even if the body may show traces of life for some hours.

Since *megbe* permeates the different aspects of life (and life in nature), there is no unequivocal function that can be attributed to it. The vital force is at the same time a total force (Schebesta, 1941, II, p. 444 ff.; unpubl.). Like all other living things, man possesses this power by virtue of his birth. *Songe abongisi,*[7] the moon, has created and still is creating all things; that is, *songe* empowers all things to be. Man especially has been made by 'him' in the menstrual blood, also called *songe.* This force can be developed – and even inherited – by the individual, an idea that occasionally led to a strict distinction between the force given by birth (*mota*) and the force acquired by special circumstances (*bongisu*) The eldest, successful hunters, and wise people have an abundance of *megbe.* Without this force nothing endures and succeeds. As such this force is imperishable.[8] It returns as *buka-mema (boru-e'i)* to the moon, while the shadow escapes into the forest.[9] The forest, however, according to the Bambuti mentality, is finally identical with the realm of the moon, or, and this is the usual interpretation, changes into the 'totem'. Before discussing this so-called megbe-totemism (Schebesta, 1968, p. 311) and its anthropological implications, some further indications of the general conception of man may serve to complete the anthropological picture. The polar end of man's death is his beginning. From a purely factual point of view, the Pygmies are well aware of the connection between begetting and birth, as they are also aware of the interrelation between bad days and a bad mood, or suffering, aging, and death. Their approach to the factual circumstances, so far as the survival of the individual and the group is concerned, is quite rational. But if the Bambuti are asked for their personal opinion, we find that all answers point to a mythic dimension: the events of the beginning, the maintenance of the present by the all-embracing power of life, the self-sufficiency of this power, the undiscussable end, the total coherence of the texture of life and world. Social conditions, although affected by these mythic assumptions, are not (yet) ideologized by them. Rather, they reveal a 'superstructural' minimum as far as their legitimation and maintenance is concerned. In other words, limited by the environment and the material culture, the economic and social complex shows a high degree of self-sufficiency. Thus, instead of 'producing' myths in order to obtain and to secure its own continuation, the socioeconomic complex

7. The suffix – *si* – indicates the agent character of a word, but also a present tense, which indicates an unlimited (continuing) time (Schebesta).

8. For the *megbe*-complex see also Turnbull (1965, p. 246 ff). Since at least three of the keywords are originally Kingwana (i.e. *pepo, roho,* and *satani*), this report does not add to the general picture except in the sense that it underlines the basic idea.

9. Since the villagers substituted their manistic underworld for the forest – *tore* is the God of the deceased – this interpretation might be the result of the cultural contact situation.

corroborates by its own token the originality of the mythic as a dimension of its own. Mythology as total complex becomes, thereby, the final content of the Bambuti anthropology and of all that goes beyond the situational rationale in its universal meaning. On this basis, it is sufficiently clear that all further questions concerning man and religion have to be seen in and through this context, at least hypothetically.

3. IDEA AND FUNCTION OF MEGBE-TOTEMISM

The most striking aspect of the *megbe* conception is the general conviction that the deceased turns into his *giniso* (also *betoli, o'u*) or totem. Though this part of the Bambuti world and anthropology also points to a mythic explanation, there are some psychological, or better paideumatic,[10] and social factors that can be treated as a kind of introduction to their mythology.

The young Bambuti inherit their *giniso* from the father. The *giniso* is usually an animal: Leopard, chimpanzee, buffalo, or certain snakes or birds. Plants are seldom included. Atmospheric phenomena, which occasionally have also been mentioned, are always associated with certain animals and thus belong to the first category.

The first consequence of the *giniso* idea is the prohibition against eating the respective animal, and this is usually connected with the prohibition against killing it. If people do not observe this prohibition, illness or death of the individual or even the whole group will follow. They also try not to meet or to touch the eerie animal. If several neighboring groups have the same *giniso* or *betoli*, clan exogamy is observed. If the women has a totem different from that of her husband, she respects the husband's totem only in his presence and vice versa (Schebesta, 1941, II, p. 433 ff).

The totem entails a mystic relationship between all persons in question, whether they are related to it by birth, marriage, or even initiation. In this sense the totem becomes an informal or nonstructural principle of societal connection and

---

10. The term *paideuma* (Gr.: training, teaching, habit) has been used by Leo Frobenius to indicate basic and long-lasting affections as a constitutive part in the formation of cultures. Paideuma symbolizes something like a 'cultural soul' (or thrust), which forms man by being rooted in specific world-emotions and affections, perpetuated by the patterns of growth and social integration.

communication, which is not only feared but is also revered and invoked together with *tore*, *mungu*, and others (Schebesta, 1941, II, p. 431, 439).

The Bambuti have different explanations for their belief in the 'mystic' bond between man and his *giniso*. We may hear an explanation such as this: Someone killed and ate an animal. Soon he became ill and died. His fellow men connected the two events and drew the conclusion : 'This animal is our brother, we must not kill or touch it' (Schebesta, 1941, II, p. 439). However, this kind of an explanation presupposes the idea of the totem-union, whose circumstances it only sets forth. It underlines an evidence that is out of question. Another explanation finds the reason for the totem-relation in the common ancestor. Two days after a man's death, his blood becomes a chimpanzee, his ancestor, who retired into the forest after the fire had been stolen (Schebesta, 1941, II, p. 443 f).

More light can be shed on the problem than these pseudo-rational and semi-mythological explanations can provide if we examine related behavior or ideas. Dreams are the principal means of communicating with the dead. One dreams about the death of a human being, about *kalisia*, the *keti*. In dreams the deceased come back (Schebesta, 1950, II, p. 88; unpubl.). As linguistics suggests, dreaming (*edotsi*) might well be interpreted as being with the dead (*ode*), or with *tore* himself. Thus, the *betoli* (*giniso*) may be reasonably interpreted as the trace of the dream world that remains when man awakes again, being the undetermined-determined presence of this world in everyday life: Ancestor, *megbe*, and 'God' at once.

This explanation is strongly supported by the fact that the hunters call upon the totem when they ask for a successful hunt. Both *mungu*, *tore*, etc., and the totem are addressed as father and helper (Schebesta, 1941, II, p. 447 ff). A further indication that this interpretation is valid is given by the attitude that the Bambuti have toward various animals, birds, and a small number of plants, which are *tuniso* (*ovovi*), that is taboo. They are headed by *ame-uri*, the chameleon. *Aru-mei*, as it is also called, is a very old animal, 'which whistles first in the forest'. When one meets the chameleon, one spits in 'his' direction (saliva is a symbol for the vital force) or gives him a bit of tabacco. Bambuti mythology relates that *aru-mei* opened the forest (*ti'i* tree) and set man free from the interior of the tree (Schebesta, 1950, II, p. 188 f.). Thus *aru-mei* is no other than the Lord (or Moon Lord) of the Forest (*aru*, moon; *me'i*, forest), he is the creative power of the moon (*ame-uri*, force of the moon). At the same time the *ti'i* tree is the origin of all trees and was planted by *ame-uri*. Considering the whole complex of totem and taboo, we can also say that it is the permanent reminder of the creative present (*megbe*) of the dream world (moon forest) that 'personalizes' itself into the various objects between man and its own ineffability.

In addition to such organo-psychic manifestations of the *megbe*-conception, there are cultic and social articulations of this 'idea'. The position of the eldest especially cannot be understood outside this mythic-'mystic' *megbe* context (Fabian, 1963, p. 35 ff., esp. 51 ff. and 69 f.). But cultic performances such as the *tore* celebration and the *elima* festival, the feast of the Forest and that of Life, can be properly understood only in the general context of the *megbe*-conception. The connecting link in these cases, which shall be described later, is the sound of the *lusomba*, the sacred trumpet or horn of *tore*, and of the songs men and women sing. Since sound and song (but not noise) signify symbolic participation in the *megbe*-force, the festival of *tore*'s voice, which is also present in the sound of atmospheric phenomena, is a celebration of creative power. This power is especially needed in time of crisis (Turnbull, 1965, p. 265) and is also present in times of great joy (Schebesta, unpubl.). As the Epulu Pygmies say, 'Song is good, song is strong' (Turnbull, 1965, p. 255). The *elima* festival, celebrating the creative blood of the woman's first menstruation, is a *megbe* festival, since *elima* is another name for *megbe*.

The eldest of the group relies upon his *megbe* when he acts in the interest of the community. If he identifies group interest with his own, he sooner or later encounters resistance. He is, as noted, the first among equals, all of whom share the same power of life and man. To enjoy one's own life and interests this power has to be maintained. All that makes it grow is good, all that destroys it is evil. The eldest, who usually 'fixes' things, such as quarrels or misconduct, during the night by a 'big discourse' (Schebesta, 1936, p. 97; 1941, II, p. 48), – perhaps another reference to the sound-*megbe* equation – acts in the name of *kalisia*, who speaks through the eldest's *megbe* (Schebesta, 1950, II, p. 120).

The total aspect of the *megbe*-conception, together with the special living conditions of this culture, reflects a good functioning substitute for a structuralized tradition. As such it bestows permanence upon a tradition which under the circumstances of forest nomadism must find its self-identity almost always anew, i.e., a tradition that is marked by the generative character of its continuation. The eldest, and sometimes also an old woman,[11] seems to be the social response

11. The Pygmies do not have female elders, although old ladies are very much respected. The interests of the women are maintained and protected by the band from which they come.

and answer to the invisible-visible totem world, whose truth reveals itself to the degree that it enables man to live a truly human life. In its origin, however, the *megbe* world withdraws from all practical rationalizations and returns to the mythic as a sign of man that gains objectivity through the manifestations of his culture.

4. BAMBUTI MYTHOLOGY

Since the linguistic situation in the Ituri Forest is a complex one,[12] it might seem at first practically impossible to give a satisfactory account of the mythology of its nomadic inhabitants. Names such as *mungu, tore, muri-muri, mupere, muere, muaba, keti, lodi, asobe(li), epilipili, kalisia,* and many others, which seem to point toward the same reality (namely, the forest-moon-godhead) give a kind of fore-taste of the problems at issue. On the other hand, there is a striking similarity between many of the mythological words, although the terms themselves are used by linguistically different groups of Pygmies. The word *tore* (t-ore), for example, points to *mu-ere, m-uri, ep-ili-p-ili (r – l), asob-eli.* Since the cultural structure of these different groups is situational, forming and recreating itself through the stability of the environment and the balanced economy adapted to

12. Generalizing as much as possible, we can distinguish among three 'Bambuti-languages': The *kimbuti,* spoken by the Sua-Kango Pygmies, who live among the Bantu-speaking Bira tribes (and others); the *asua-ti,* which is spoken by the Asua or Aka, who live among the Mangbetu-tribes; and the *efe,* spoken by the Efe Pygmies, who live mainly among the Balese. The language of the latter groups seems to belong to the 'Sudanic' stem. Though this is not the place to give a detail-ed and comprehensive account of Schebesta's view of the Pygmy language, the basic meaning of his hypothesis concerning the formation of mythological terms should at least be outlined for the non-specialist to the extent that it can be considered as a well-established, i.e., actually working and explanatory theory. Since each mythology is deeply rooted in the language from which it originated, the difficulties of all the terms and various myths of Bambuti-mythology should be faced in the attempt to present a significant example for the general discussion of the mythic mind, especially if the mythology in question shows all the signs of being a mythology in the making. For the study itself some indications of the linguistic background are the more desirable as they reveal a good deal of its method, i.e., its approach to the various Pygmy groups of the Ituri region irrespec-tive of their linguistic peculiarities. Such a procedure is justifiable (and thus necessary) to the degree as basic similarities of (quasi-) subcultural complexes become evident, thereby completing each other throughout the study. Since language offers, although the most difficult and sophisti-cated, but nevertheless also most decisive criterium for the meaning of these problems, a short glance at its 'working', or should we say, at the 'working' of the mythological mind with respect to language, can only promote the issue.

its conditions, it may be possible that the language reflects somehow such primary conditions; that the linguistic findings in the forest region are much more uniformly structured than seems to be the case if we approach them in the usual way; or that the Pygmy mentality prevailed despite the different Negro migrations and their *ad hoc* influence on the actual languages, especially so far as mythology and mythological speech are concerned.

When these and similar observations were joined to a comparative and functional study of several hundred terms, they suggested to Schebesta the working hypothesis that the Pygmy mythology in its various linguistic expressions is reducible to a few key words (stems), which in their mutual flection and combination entail the richness and variety of actual ideas and attitudes (Schebesta, 1950, II, p. 124 ff.). The linguistic findings go so far in their suggestions that it seems appropriate to say that formative principles of the language coincide with basic principles of the actual mythology and the mythological world; that language is a sort of heterothesis into which myth has molded its form and wherein it is kept alive by language while giving its particular style to the meaning of language for man.

According to Schebesta's linguistic analysis, four stems with two affixes became mainly formative for mythological conceptions. These stems are formally reducible to the roots *aga, ada, ara,* and *aba.* Since the vowel before the consonant and that following it may run through the whole scale of given sounds, it is possible to form new combinations that can be abbreviated as $V_{1-n}CV_{1-n}$. Hence by changing the sound value of the vowels, the basic meaning of these roots, which is usually preceded by a consonant, will be modified. We thus arrive at the word structure $/C/-V_{1-n}CV_{1-n}$. (Though the interpretation of the preceding consonant $/C/$ is still to be achieved, there are many indications that at least in some cases this consonant must be seen as the stripped remnant of a word of the type vowel-consonant-vowel. As such this consonant becomes a further variable of the semantic determination of the four stems.) *T-e(m)ba,* for instance, means moon, but *s-umbu* or *s-umba* means wind or storm, and *l-emba* means song, while *s-amba* is the boy who is initiated (Schebesta, 1950, II, p. 130). *Uri* (also *alu*) is moon. As *oru,* however, it means fire, as *elu* thunder, while *k-uru* is used for tortoise, *l-ele* for rattle, *b-ili* for a musical instrument (Schebesta, 1950, II, p. 134 ff.). By a process of synthesis, through the simplification of such compositions, the possible variations become increasingly complicated. For instance, *s-omba* and *eli* may be combined into *(a)sobeli* (God), but may be simplified to *a-sobe'i, a-sobé* (*a* or *e*, being a kind of reverential particle). *Mbali* (God) may well be the result of *amba-ali*, which is synthesized into *mbali* or *bali*.

The two affixes mentioned above are *mo-* and *ma-*; *mo-* indicates personal life, spirit, and also ghost, while *ma-* has much to do with power and vital force (Schebesta, 1950, II, p. 127). Accordingly *ambelema* (rainbow), for instance, means the power (ma) of *amba-eli* (*bali*); however, *molimo* (forest ghost) indicates the *eli*-person (*mo-li-mo*), the ghost(s) in the forest. In addition, concrete terms such as *ambelema* (rainbow) or *meli* (forest) are not explained by the coordination of sound pattern and concrete objects, but, if this theory is adequate, have to be understood as the expression of a consciousness that lives in its own world out of which it points to the empirically given. To understand this 'pointing to' (signification) it thus is necessary to deal with a complex *a priori* of consciousness which has its own thrust with respect to the empirically given.

The meaning of the *aga* (*agwa, aka*) stem refers mainly to man: To be human and to be strong, to make strong. Its secondary meaning points to fire, to burning and shining (Schebesta, 1950, II, p. 142 ff., 169 ff.). *Ada* also refers to man, stressing his ability to know and the power connected with knowledge and intelligence. Power, vital force, knowledge, magical power and also death and blood describe the field of possible meanings (Schebesta, 1950, II, p. 145 ff., 176 ff.). The primary meaning of *ara* is to be bright or white, to shine, to burn. It refers chiefly to the moon, but also to the principles of life such as the heart, soul, woman and to be (Schebesta, 1950, II, p. 134 ff., 172 ff.). The *aba* stem in its etymological meaning is close to the *ara* stem. To illuminate, to burn is its basic meaning, but it also has the connotation of good, to make good, to sing, to roar and to create (Schebesta, 1950, II, p. 128 ff., 175 ff.).

The impact of this linguistic situation on the actual mythology appears in two ways, which are both decisive for the understanding of the Bambuti mythos and the mythic dimension in general. On the one hand there is a basic unity that connects the mythological figures in their functional variations. As such it integrates them into a mytho-linguistic structure. On the other hand, this linguistic situation indicates that there is a difference separating the actual mythology from its mythic foundation, which actually governs and shapes the various stories and articulations, but remains hidden and inexpressible as regards their objective forms. The mythic foundation qualifies, and even forms expression but is not expressed as such.

Before it is possible to evaluate these ideas in their overall significance, it will be necessary to see how they work and how they are shaped in the actual mythology.

4.1 *The Mythic Beginning*

Although mythology in its very nature as an etiological account reveals a permanent quest for the beginning, the origin of things and of man in their present form it is at the same time something like an absolute evidence. After all, it is *epilipili, kalisia* or *songe*, who has made all that is and that continues to exist. In this sense each problem and puzzle is penultimate, but apart from this basic certainty and awareness there are many ways to ask for and to speak about the beginning.[13]

In the beginning *arebati*, the moon, left the earth and went to heaven, but his representative, the chameleon, remains (Schebesta, 1941, II, p. 399). When *ame-uri* (the chameleon) strolls through the forest, he hears a rustling sound in the *ti'i* tree. With the help of his hatchet (the crescent moon) he opens the tree. Water flows out and becomes a huge stream that gushes forth over the earth. In the water are *mupa* and his wife *otu* (blood), to whom a son with the name *magiti* (*magidi*) is born, the ancestor of all men (Schebesta, 1950, II, p. 52).

Another version tells us that *magidi* survives a terrible war by climbing up the *ti'i* tree in which he hides. Nearby lives a couple, together with a daughter called *otu*. *Otu* is thirsty and wants water. Her father comes to the *ti'i* tree and opens it. *Magidi*, hidden in the water, returns with the father and becomes the husband of *otu*. At this point the story changes. Instead of *magidi*, the lightning (*gbara*) comes and takes *otu* as wife. Both live as brother and sister together. The moon (*arebati*) however, does not like this. He instructs *gbara* to have intercourse with *otu*, but *gbara* does not consent. The moon in his turn sends the menses to the wife and instigates a boy (probably *magidi*) to sleep with *otu*, who is, this time, his mother. *Otu* gives birth to a Pygmy boy. Now *gbara* changes his mind and unites with *otu*. Their son is *mupe*, and later they have many other children. When *otu* dies, *arebati* orders *gbara* back, who returns with all his children (the stars) to the sky (Schebesta, 1950, II, p. 53).

The motif of a great war in the beginning is also expressed in the myths around

---

13. The myths which will be reported on the following pages are of course only abstracts of the stories, which in real life are told with much flavor and detailed description, interrupted by songs and accompanied by vivid gestures.

ba'atsi. Ba'atsi, from whom all men descend, finds human beings whom he does not know. He starts killing them one after another. Finally, he decides it would not be good to destroy all of them, because then he would be all alone. When he strolls through the forest he finds bananas. Leaving them to his *bambuti*, he returns to heaven, where he lives in his celestial forest. With him are the sun and the moon. However the sun is not that significant for the Bambuti mythology. In the evening *ba'atsi* can be heard, when the chameleon (*ame-uri*) raises his voice (Schebesta, 1950, II, p. 49).

Other names that are mentioned in the stories about the beginning are *tambanea* and *pucho-pucho*. *Tambanea* was the first man created by *mengo* or *mungu*. He came at sunrise and brought fire with him (Schebesta, 1950, II, p. 18). *Pucho-pucho* emerged from a rock with his brother *befe* – in another myth they are *bali* and *bigi* (Schebesta, 1950, II, p. 189). Both take *matu* (*cf. otu*) as their wife. *Pucho-pucho* and *matu* beget *tore* and become the progenitors of the Pygmies.

Motivated by the mystery of begetting, another myth tells us that in the beginning all human beings were female. One day a son of *epilipili* comes down and sleeps with one of the women. She asks him to give her a penis for her husband so they may be able to sleep together and beget children. *Epilipili* agrees and gives her a basket full of virilia. She gives one to her husband and the rest to her relatives (Schebesta, 1941, II, p. 401).

By changing the poles, another myth reports that *alu* (the moon) saw how mankind, consisting only of male beings, lived without purpose and in sorrow. He decided to change this situation and gave them wives. Since that time the stars are astonished at the number of their descendants on earth (Joset; Schebesta, 1950, II, p. 185).

If birth gives us the opportunity to experience an actual beginning, nevertheless it is death that turns this experience into the idea of and the quest for the beginning. This is true for the Pygmies as well. Accordingly, there is more about the beginning in the mythological accounts concerning the origin of death.

In the beginning, *mugasa* created two men and one woman, who became the progenitors of the Bambuti and the Negroes. *Mangietu* was the father of the Pygmies and *bali* of the Negroes. The name of the woman is not known. At this time *mugasa* lived among his people. He took care of all they needed. The only

14. Concerning the cry of the chameleon, which is also heard as an omen for a successful honey season, see Turnbull (1965, p. 170).

commandment he had given to them was a prohibition against any attempt to see him. He worked in a huge hut and hammered on the anvil. But as time passed by, the woman who used to bring water and firewood to his cottage became very curious. She hid herself in the bushes and waited until *mugasa* came to take what she had brought. She saw the beautiful arm adorned with many rings. Her joy, however, did not last long. *Mugasa* knew instantly what had happened. He called his children together and told them that he would leave them forever and that death would be with them. All repentance was in vain. Before he left, he gave them cultural blessings and instructions, the knowledge of which would help them to overcome all obstacles. The woman was cursed and damned to give birth with great pain. Soon after *mugasa* left, the woman became pregnant and gave birth to a child. But two days later the child died. Since then everyone has had to die (Schebesta, 1950, II, p. 19 f.).

In another version it is said that *mungu* made the first man, *ba'atsi*. He tells him that he will beget many children, who are to live in the forest and be happy there. The only commandment imposed on him was the prohibition of the *tahu* fruit. *Ba'atsi* goes to heaven. One day a pregnant woman is plagued by desire for the fruit. She presses her husband hard, and he finally submits to her wish and gets a piece of the fruit. It was no sooner done than the moon saw the transgression and told it to *mungu*. As punishment, *mungu* sends death (Schebesta, 1950, II, p. 49).

The prohibition of the *tahu* fruit may be replaced by another commandment for instance in the myth of *kodzapilipili*, the first man. When he, whose wife is *akerede*, leaves for a long trip, he asks his children not to follow him. At his return he learns that no one except his eldest son obeyed his command. He blows the so-called *segbe* pipe and the guilty have to pay with their lives (Schebesta, 1950, II, p. 106). The same story is also reported with *pucho-pucho*. In this case it is merely said that people die because of this disobedience. The *segbe* pipe is not mentioned.

A second chain of motifs expresses this basic incomprehensibility of death by the contingency of mythological events. *Mbali* asks a toad to transport a corpse to a certain place to be brought back to life. On the way, a frog wants to relieve the toad of the burden. After some dispute, the toad finally gives in. The frog takes the corpse but drops it. Since that time men must die (Schebesta, 1950, II, p. 25). Names mentioned in this context are *amasede*, *amenge*, *agbogbu*, *egbe*, and others. The pot is probably a symbol for the moon, or even the moon itself (Schebesta, 1950, II, p. 200). It may be that social conflict also plays a significant role in the various stories about the animals, just as the association of death and taboo recalls the possibility that death might have been avoided if man had known and done better.

A myth that belongs to the disobedience motif, but points to a third group of motifs, that of totem-transformation, is the story of a woman who wanted to eat her totem animal. All her children die. That is how death entered the world (Schebesta, unpubl.). But the death of the totem does not necessarily result in disaster. The event of death is the beginning of a new (cultural) life. A Pygmy kills his totem (*aporu*). As a result all cultural products and goods fly toward him. However, he does not keep them for himself, but turns them over to the villagers (Schebesta, unpubl.). In another story, we hear that death came into the world through a general slaughter. Finally *apagoi*, the main figure in this event, drowns himself and takes all things with him. At the lower course of the *Ituri*, however, they appear again (Schebesta, unpubl.). Similarly, the fight with *kalisia*, or with *matu*, or *befe*, ends in the death of these figures, but not until they have been forced to revive their victims. The blood – in the case of *matu* the removal of the clitoris is the only way to kill her – flows over the whole earth (Schebesta, 1950, II, p. 37; unpubl.).

4.2 *The Culture Hero and Bringer of Blessings*

Although the number of their cultural objects is relatively small the Pygmies are nevertheless well aware of their importance. Asked why the chimpanzee is not human, they answer that it is because he does not know fire (Schebesta, 1932, p. 30; 1941, II, p. 160), or because he does not live in a camp (Schebesta, 1932, p. 59). The acquisition of cultural goods completes, therefore, the cycles of the beginning of man and welds them together with the amythic-mythic figures and instances of the present time.

Apart from the apodictic statement that *mungu* taught his children how to live before he left the world, the mythic mind also knows separate persons and stories accounting for the origin of culture. *Aparofandza*, for instance, had many children. He taught them the use of bow and arrow. When he strolled through the forest one day, he met a crocodile and saw many tools lying about. He took them and brought them to his children. *Aparofandza* (*cf.* the totem *aporu* that gives the goods of culture by being killed) taught them everything, hunting as well as procreation (Schebesta, 1950, II, p. 56).

Another hero of the beginning is *pa geregere*, who possessed such power (*megbe*) that he could turn himself into the miraculous dog *girimiso*. One day his adversary, also called *geregere*, killed all his people. *Geregere* changed into *girimiso* (elsewhere *epilipili*'s or *tore*'s dog) and retaliated. With the surviving women and children he becomes the progenitor of a new mankind (Schebesta, 1950, II, p. 59). In a modified version the culture hero is not *geregese* but his bitch, who gives birth to four male and two female Pygmies. Their father is *asamu*, a forest animal. The bitch gets all tools for them and introduces them into hunting and the search for honey (Schebesta, 1950, II, p. 199).

The origin of *geregere* is ambivalent. One time he is said to stem from the *modi utu* shrub, but again it is he who lets man emerge from the *modi utu* and who guarantees the continuity of the world. As an Efe put it: '*Geregere* (also *gerengese*) will never die. If he did, the whole world would disintegrate' (Schebesta, 1950, II, p. 33, 192).

The antagonistic ambivalence of the culture hero also appears in stories about *aparofandza* and *emengoro*. *Emengoro*, who is *aparofandza*'s wife in this myth, did not serve *kisobi* roots to her husband. *Aparofandza* becomes sad at this behavior and retires to heaven. *Emengoro* follows her husband and sees all the things he has there. They make peace with each other and return to earth (Schebesta, 1950, II, p. 56). In other circumstances *emengoro* is a (male) hypostasis of *epilipili*, who falls in love with the daughter of *gbara*, the lightning (Schebesta, 1950, II, p. 57).

Not all the themes of the origin of culture or the gain of special blessings formally refer to the beginning. They take place in a nonspecified time, although the names themselves show a clear interrelation with the whole mythological texture. First there is the acquisition of fire. Its owners are the forest-moon-godhead under many different names (*oru ogbi, tore, muri-muri, mungu, pucho-pucho, bali, matu, lodi, befe, bechiri*), but also the chimpanzee, or another animal. While *muri-muri*, for instance, is rocking on his swing made of lianas, *matu* sits beside the fire (*bolu*). An Efe (Pygmy) steals the fire and *matu* begins to freeze. *Muri-muri* sees this, swings down on his liana, and takes the fire back to her. The same thing happens a second time. The third time, however, it is *doru* who tries to catch the fire. In addition to the strong forces (*megbe*) he already has, he wears the feathers of the crow, the sacred bird of *bali*. He steals the fire like the others. But *muri-muri* cannot seize him; his swing is not powerful enough. He can only acknowledge that there is someone equal to him. 'Both of us have the same mother.' In his desperation *muri-muri* embraces the *ugbu* tree and returns to his mother, *matu*, who has died of the cold. As punishment, men must also die from now on. *Doru* distributes the fire as recompensation (Schebesta, 1941, II, p. 166; 1950, II, p. 29).

In other versions the successful fire raid, sometimes accomplished by help of a bird or a dog, results in a rejection of the fire by its former possessors: The chimpanzee or the *befe* (forest ghost) throws it away, and since that time both of them prefer to live in the forest without fire (Schebesta, 1941, II, p. 163 f.).

Although the myths concerning the origin of the banana are not so dramatic, nevertheless they connect this blessing with *tore* (represented by the chimpanzee) and *pucho-pucho* (Schebesta, 1950, II, p. 28 ff.).

Also to be mentioned in the context of miraculous events that account for the present situation of the Pygmy world and its meaning are the stories about various adventures in the heavenly world and the struggles against a monster or a villain. In some cases the border between myth and fairy tale is often fluid.

Evadu, a very powerful Pygmy, climbs on a liana to *epilipili*'s domain. He falls in love with his daughter *mengoro*, who becomes pregnant. Since *epilipili* does not know of this secret love, both believe that it will be better if *evadu* goes back to earth. Meanwhile *mengoro* gives birth to a son, called *aparofandza*. When she sees *evadu* again she asks him to see their son. *Evadu* is very proud of him, but does not dare to take him back to the earth. Later, *evadu* meets some heavenly maidens. One of them is *endzimane*, daughter of the rain. She falls in love with *evadu* and persuades him to come with her. *Evadu* agrees and goes to the camp of the rain, where *endzimane* hides him in a cottage made of ore or of rock. *Evadu* goes on a hunt with *endzimane*'s younger brother. Her mother notices the alien smell and becomes very upset. But when her daughter gives her some of *evadu's* game, she is appeased. She is delighted and wants to know her daughter's secret. However, she is only permitted to see *evadu*'s arm (*cf. mungu*'s arm). When *evadu* finally kills some additional elephants, *endzimane* reveals her love. All are proud of this great hunter. *Evadu* and *endzimane* go down to earth and beget many children (Schebesta, 1941, II, p. 352 f.).

Another time it is *ba'atsi* (known already as the first man, who was made by the moon), who remembers the Pygmy he has put on earth. He orders him to his place. Everyone is astonished to see this great hunter. The next day the Pygmy brings back a huge elephant as prey. This happens several times. A meeting with the lightning shows the incredible strength of the hunter and establishes a friendly relation between *gbara* and the Pygmy. After some time *ba'atsi* gives the Pygmy many good things and lets him down to earth again. But the Pygmy is caught in the top of a *boru* tree. *Ba'atsi* tries again. This time he is successful. The Pygmy returns home; no one recognizes him except his eldest son and his brother. They ask him what happened: 'The father, who made me, brought me to heaven to hunt for him', is his answer. 'Lo: this is what he gave me.' The Negroes also heard about this event. They asked the Pygmy: 'How? Is our father still alive?' The Pygmy replied: 'Certainly, for I was with him' (Schebesta, 1950, II, 47 f., 98).

The patterns of man's encounter with a monster (*lulu*, *piombo*, *okalai*, and others) usually run as follows: The Pygmies attempt in vain to overcome a terrible and monstrous being, which swallows all of them. Only one woman survives, but she gives birth to a child (occasionally also to as many as ten children) in an unusual way; through the knee, the big toe, etc. The boy, who is a grownup from the beginning, wants to know where his father is. At first his mother does not want to tell the truth, but finally she gives in. The boy defeats the monster and frees his father and all others, who are still alive inside the monster. In gratitude everyone gives a girl to the hero, who restored mankind by his deed (Schebesta, 1950, II, p. 99 ff.).

As examples of the encounter of a hero with a villain (usually a *befe* or *keti*, sometimes the snakedog *oa*), we may cite the stories of *mamelife* and *amoane*. *Mamelife* falls in love with a girl whose relatives do not like him. When he plays the flute, they mock him. When he goes for a hunt, they cut the string of his bow. One of the rogues changes into a buffalo (totem) and wounds him, when the broken string makes the hunter defenseless. The next day *mamelife* meets an ill and lonely fellow, who asks him to clean his face. When he does so the cripple tells him of the bad intentions of these people. He also gives him an invisible string for his bow. When *mamelife* returns, nobody plays the *tsei* flute better than he. The next time before they go hunting, he changes the string before the buffalo attacks him. This time he hits the beast immediately and all the relatives fall dead. Before he leaves the camp with his bride, he revives them with medicine (Schebesta, 1941, II, p. 436 f.).

Like his brothers, *amoane* has heard of the most beautiful daughter of *apangulu*. Many wanted to marry her, but *apangulu* killed all of them in their sleep and ate them. When *amoane* tries his luck he meets a poor and ill man who asks for his help. The boy does as the stranger wants him to do. In return he gives him a chameleon and two birds. During the night, when *apangulu* is waiting for *amoane* to fall asleep, the animals answer his testing questions, thus deceiving him about *amoane*. The next day, *amoane* defeats *apangulu*, and frees his brothers whom he brings back to life by boiling their bones (Schebesta, unpubl.).

Although the last two stories bear many traits of fairyland with its magic, the main motif of the myth is still present: The defeat of death and the beginning of a new life, obtained through the figure of the forest man (*avi melia*, forest man), no other than *tore* himself (Schebesta, 1950, II, p. 104). It is the same reality that stands behind the motif of the totem death mentioned above: The symbol and total concept of man's meaning as a moral being. Mythology thus brings the struggle for survival against the polar forces of life (*cf.* also the social tensions present in these narrations) into the midst of everyday affairs. It is therefore necessary to trace the mythological texture to its basic, elementary meaning, as indicated in the discussion of the relationship between language and myth. One of the basic features shown there, and one that has been sufficiently illustrated by the examples cited here, is the permanent interpenetration and metamorphosis of the various mythological figures. As we have seen, *ba'atsi*, for instance, is the first man, the culture hero, and the creator. To understand this fluidity we must consider the comprehensive meaning of the different mythological figures, their independence, and mutual interrelation.

4.3 *The Mythic A-mythic Origin*

Who are *tore*, *mungu*, *arembati*? In analogy to the Biblical statement that God created heaven and earth in the beginning (Gen 1.1), the conclusion is justified to see in these figures none other than the God of the Bambuti.[15] The knowledge and consciousness of this God is mythic. It is momentaneous and associative, absolute and relative at the same time. God is the moon, but also its creator (Schebesta, 1950, II, p. 57). He is identified in the moon, but not personified in the concept

15. Although this comparison is not intended to go beyond the functional and morphological similarity between two creative 'beings' in the beginning, nonetheless it offers the foundation for identifying *tore*, *mungu*, etc., with the Western *god* and to connect the two fields of experience and articulation in some way. In addition, we should not exclude the possibility that the concept of God is co-original with the connection of beginning, heaven and earth, and creation. In this case none of the single elements is self-sufficient. Their meaning results from this particular context and even *is* it. But if this is true the theological history of God (in the West) can only be of minor import with regard to the message that is articulated through the consciousness of the beginning.

of its appearance. Perhaps we can also say, the divine and the worldly are distinguished from one another, but in praxis they are associated without intermediary relations. Within and for the consciousness of origin and creation they belong intimately together. They are the world in which man lives. God is *tore, mungu, epilipili, kalisia, ambelema,* who made the world, the trees the animals. But at the same time no one knows 'his' name (Schebesta, 1950, II, p. 45). Or there is still someone in heaven, whose name is not known (Schebesta, 1950, II, p. 55), or there is only one who has made everything (Schebesta, 1950, II, p. 55). As all-embracing as the mythology may be, ultimately it reveals that the most mythic is also the least mythic: The ineffable that gains its specific structure only to the degree that mythological propositions are able to recall this silent origin of spontaneous consciousness – a recollection that in the case of the Bambuti mythology finds its 'propositional' or 'logical' form in the rational inconsistencies of the mytho-logical accounts. *Tore* is God and the son of *matu*; the first man, but also his creator; the world is present before it is created. Mythology provides the idea of totality as and in the praxis of personal becoming and cultural being.

To set into relief this mythic-amythic dimension of the Bambuti godhead and the respective consciousness, it will be useful to complete the various data concerning the mythological figures. These data largely reflect the situation of the interview rather than the context of the mythological story. As such they are primarily related to the practical life and the cult behavior of their reporters. Their integration into the mythology is thus a practical matter. But if we are to understand this integration, we cannot do so without a reflective interpretation.

4.3.1 *The God of the Forest*

Although the names of the godhead vary from place to place, there are not only linguistic similarities, but also functional identities that permit us to bring the various beings under one headline. The first general feature is that of the 'Forest God'.

The Forest God owns the forest and the life in it. He strolls through the forest whipping the trees from time to time. He follows the hunter and guides his arrow but may also close the forest when men do not obey his commandments (Schebesta, 1950, II, p. 25 f.). He is *afa*, father, or *odu*, grandfather, but he may also be an evil force, punishing man by death through the glance of his eyes and the lightning flash. Both successful and futile hunts are a result of the will of God

(Schebesta, 1950, II, p. 34). He is almighty. Everything was made by him. Therefore, the animals are his property (Schebesta, 1950, II, p. 23). When people do not behave properly, when they commit adultery, are quarrelsome and noisy, or do not distribute the game, and do not respect the eldest and the old people, he will punish them, for he sees everything (Schebesta, 1941, II, p. 323; 1950, II, p. 57). He is man's destiny. His messenger is the lightning flash (*gbara*), the thunder is his voice (Schebesta, 1950, II, p. 22 f.). He communicates with man in dreams but also by slight incidents such as a slap on the upper arm.

Apart from these basic similarities there are divergent features, indicated in the mythological motif of the exchange between heaven and earth, between the Forest God and the Sky God, and the various modifications of this motif: When the Pygmies became hungry, they called upon *tore*, who sent the earth down to them (Schebesta, 1950, II, p. 28); In the beginning, the earth was above the heaven, but dirt fell down into *tore*'s meals. He became angry and turned the locations upside down (Schebesta, 1950, II, p. 28); Another reason for the divine removal was the jealousy of the earth. The earth (male) thought that *epilipili* had fallen in love with (the earth's) wife, because he looked upon her (Schebesta, 1950, II, p. 57; apparently God is already above the earth); Or the toad spoiled the concept of the godhead; Finally there is the motif of black magic. A wife killed two children by black magic. This destructive act ended in the withdrawal of God and death for all (Schebesta, 1950, II, p. 57).

This combination and synthesis of rational inconsistency and mythic firmness not only accounts for the tension within the godhead (good-evil), but also reveals its hypostatic character. As was said about *ba'atsi* (who created the world by circumcising his penis and turning it into a uterus), the godhead dwells in the sky, but has its alter ego on the earth (Schebesta, unpubl.; 1950, II, p 27 f., 217 ff.). Thus, the Forest God is not conceivable without an immanent polarity that renders him a Sky God as well, while revealing his nature in the symbol of fire and light. The myths describe God or his representative as the warden and owner of the fire. *Tore*, the highest being, is the Lord of the Forest and the Sky. His father is *ogbi oro* the fire (*ogbi*) of the moon (*oro*). When he moves his beard, wind, storm, and rain are the result. As *tore-mo-ichü* he is the one who dwells above the abyss. To hear his call is a favorable sign, for the man of the forest (*avi melia*) is present (Schebesta, 1950, II, p. 32 f., 42 f.).

Mbali, the great and the good, strolls and flies through the forest but dwells in the sky, whence he orders the moon to take the life of a child. He is above *mungu* and the forest, though *mungu* (*akuli, muketi*) also dwells in the sky, depending on the context (Schebesta, 1950, II, p, 31, 41). Similarly, *epilipili* (*bapele, asobeli, abeli, mupe*) looks upon the moon, who creates man, while he determines his sex (Schebesta, 1950, II, p. 57). *Aparofandza*, the first man (and the bird who kills him), lives in a heavenly forest after leaving the earth for the sky (Schebesta, 1950, II, p. 57). *Borumbi*, who made the water, the trees and the animals, dwells in the sky and speaks through the thunder (Schebesta, 1950, II, p. 22 f.).

A second polarity that can be found in the godhead is that between the personal and its pre- and metapersonal foundation, between man and the life (blood) from which he originates. The manifold and universal (impersonal) power of heaven and earth on the one hand, and the singularity and uniqueness of a personal being constitute a permanent tension in the divine.

Tore made everything, including *pucho-pucho* (*geregere*, and others), the first man. In another context, *pucho-pucho* is greater than *tore*, who was his father (Schebesta, 1950, II, p. 32). *Tore* is accompanied by *bi'i*, the brother of *bali* (Schebesta, 1950, II, p. 43, 54). But then we hear: '*Mbali* is above the *mungu* and the forest (*tore* and his spirits)' (Schebesta, 1950, II, p. 41). The same can be said about *epilipili* and *aparofandza* (Schebesta, 1950, II, p. 79), *ba'atsi*, and *mungu* (Schebesta, 1950, II, p. 48). There usually is only one *tore*, but in his concretizations as *muri-muri, tore-mo-ichü, befe, balimo, matu*, there are as many *tores* as there are *ame-uris* (chamaleons) and deceased (Schebesta, 1950, II, p. 25, 43). *Matu* is also known as *tore*'s mother or even *tore* himself (Schebesta, 1950, II, p. 27 f, 32, 210). We thus cannot separate the god-consciousness from the experience of a variety of personal beings as manifestations of the ineffable (a-mythic) and all-embracing totality of life.

The conviction that the Pygmies are the children of *mbali* (Schebesta, 1950, II, p. 34) is also in the same line of thought. The linguistic analysis emphasizes this view so far as the names the Pygmies use to designate themselves are formed of the same roots by which the names of the godhead are composed.[16] *Bambuti*, for instance, means etymologically the beings (*ti*, personal being) of *ambu* (God, the moon, the sacred fire; *mu-amba* is the name of God among some groups, Schebesta, 1950, II, p. 131). It also confirms the mythological transition between the first man and the godhead, since the identity of the etymological root (especi-

16. See W. Dupré (1962–63, p. 33 ff), where an analysis of not less than 95 Pygmy names has been attempted.

ally *aga, agwa, ekwe, efe*) in both names reveals and justifies at least a basic affinity between God and man.

Extending this etymological consideration to the complex of mythological names and the interpretative theory at the beginning of this section, the polarity becomes structurally visible. There are not only the basic roots (*aga, ada, ara, aba*), which generally speaking became formative but also the structural preference for certain combinations (Schebesta, 1950, II, p. 129 ff). *Aba* seems to prefer a combination with *ara*, while *aga* shows a certain preference for *ada: aba-ara – aga-ada*. If the first combination substitutes one component with that of the second, *aba* prefers *aga* and *ada* favors *ara*. Such correlations strongly suggest the conclusion (see also W. Dupré, 1963, p. 85 ff) that an ambivalence between *aba-ara* and *aga-ada*, on the one hand and *aga/ara* and *aba/ada* on the other, is basic for the structure and the respective consciousness of the Bambuti mythology; that sky and earth, *aba-ara* and *ada-aga*, oppose and demand one another in a similar way as the personal (*aga/ara*) and the universal (*ada/aba*) do; that the celestial force (*aba*) seeks the celestial or earthly person (*ara/aga*), while the earthly power (*ada*) turns toward the earthly or celestial person (*aga/ara*).[17]

This linguistic interpretation is supported by the assertions of the Pygmy 'theologians' concerning the moon, the chameleon, the rainbow and *matu*. At the same time it sheds light upon this whole complex and its relationship to mythology and the mythic in general and the conception of God in particular, which will be discussed in the systematic part of this study.

4.3.2 God and the Moon

Like the God of the Forest, the Moon (*alu, arebati, teba, songe*) is also the Lord of all men and of divine beings. He has created man and the world and continues to create through blood (menstruation). He forms the child in the womb and, like *epilipili*, limits his lifetime. He incarnates the *boru-e'i* and takes it back. The stars are the children of the Moon (Schebesta, 1941, II, p. 400; 1950, II, p. 55, 155 ff, 180 ff).

The Bambuti are well aware of a difference between the visible moon (*temba*) and the godhead (*arembati*; reverend Moon person); a difference of which they

---

17. This basic tension appears also in the linguistic significance of the categories 'animated' and 'non-animated', which seem to be typical for the Bambuti languages and which have not yet been replaced by the Bantu classes. *Cf.* A. Vorbichler (1963).

become permanently aware through their contact with the Forest. The mythology expresses this difference by its rational inconsistency when it notes that the moon is created by the Moon (Schebesta, 1950, II, p. 180 f). Thus it might be more correct to describe this difference as a hypostatic one. Or if we look at this difference in terms of the respective unity, we can also say that it is a hypostatic or heterothetic unity. As such it mirrors the character of the mythic in relation to mythos and mythology. From this point of view it is a logical development of the same conception, when the Moon (*alu, ali, ere*) becomes *t-ore* (*muri-muri, p-ili-p-ili*), the God of the Forest. Indeed, like the Forest God the Moon closes the forest and punishes man, when man unnecessarily destroys his fruits (Schebesta, 1950, II, p. 54).

The symbols (symbolic identifications) of the Moon are *ame-uri*, the chameleon, and *ambelema*, the rainbow. The chameleon (occasionally also called *muri-muri*) lives in the top of the trees, because there it is closest to the moon. Its throaty cry is known as the voice of the Forest God (Schebesta, 1950, II, p. 53). The meaning of its name has already been mentioned. We noted also that *ame-uri* freed man from the *ti'i* tree. Another myth tells us that *ame-uri*, eldest brother of *mangbe* (frog) planted the fruits of the *ti'i* tree. Each fruit became a new species that got its name from the chameleon. Similarly the moon sent a goat (or elephant) to the earth, which gave birth to different animals. Again, *ame-uri* names them. When the goat (probably identical with the lightning) brings forth a kid, it returns to the moon (Schebesta, 1950, II, p. 51 gg). The *ti'i* tree (*ati-igi;* also *taku* tree) is the tree of knowledge (*ata*) and life. Its 'water of life' (*otu*, blood) gives birth to *magidi* (*ama-agi-edi*), the powerful and knowing (*edi*) man (*ama-igi*). The tension indicated in *ame-uri*'s relationship to the *ti'i* tree returns in *mataligeda*, the celestial force that fights with *marubogeda*, the celestial power (Schebesta, 1950, II, p. 55, 188). *Mataligeda* and *marubogeda* the evening star and the morning star (also called *akambele* and *akupe*), are the wives of the moon, or his creative forces or brothers which build and destroy at once (Schebesta, 1950, II, p. 115, 183). When man dies, the *boru-e'i* (the fire of the moon-person) returns to its origin and becomes a *b-efe* (*b-igi*), a child of the moon (the star understood as 'forest' ghost; Schebesta, 1950, II, p. 190). The same myth is also immanent to figures such as *mugasa* and *ba'atsi*. *Muga-asa* is like *baga-atsi* the Fire Man (*asa, atsi*, fire; *muga, baga*, man), who is close to the earth as well as to the sky, depending on the circumstantial emphasis (Schebesta, 1950, II, p. 170 f).

The chameleon's character as a culture hero is also expressed in a myth about *aru-mei* and *gbara* (the chameleon and the lightning). In the beginning *gbara* lived at the foot of a mountain. He wanted to transfer to the mountain top and promised his daughter to anyone who could bring his anvil to the peak. Many animals try, but none succeeds. Finally, *aru-mei* tries his luck. The anvil sings that he will not be dropped. When *aru-mei* arrives at the top, *gbara* shakes hands with him and gives him his daughter. On his way home, the animals laugh at the chameleon and try to take his bride away (*cf.* the Forest Man who appears as regrettable figure; but also the social circumstances concerning the relationship Bambuti-Negroes). But he is stronger than all of them. He orders his bride to collect all the cultural products the animals possess. That is how *aru-mei* became the Lord and Owner of all things (Schebesta, unpubl.).

Ambelema the rainbow is a further concretization of the moon-mythology. (Names such as *alumei, mugu, ugumu, egbiti, abu, raba-raba* are also recorded, Schebesta, 1950, II, p. 205). *Ambelema* is called upon as father but is also feared because like *tore* and *arembati* the rainbow kills man (Schebesta, 1950, II, p. 15 f). He is even the *odi avie*, the man-killer (Schebesta, 1950, II, p. 205). On the other hand, he causes the eclipse of the moon to stop the killing of his people (Schebesta, 1950, II, p. 55). His counterpart on earth is the snake, especially the python, which plays a ceremonial role in the *mambelema* initiation (as a phallic symbol; Schebesta, 1950, II, p. 20) and the myths of the monster. *Ambelema* can also be seen around the moon as a halo.

The ambivalent character of the godhead finds expression in the belief that the rainbow in the west (*ambelema; tomba*) is good, while the rainbow in the east (*akelima: tidi*) is dangerous. As the names show, the rainbow belongs to the same mythological complex of vital force (*eli-ma; egbi-ti*), light and sky (*ambe; eli*), as the godhead (Schebesta, 1950, II, p. 206). *Ambelema* is the master of the lightning flash, which in turn is related to such figures as *tore, kalisia*, the mythic monster (Schebesta, 1950, II, p. 206).

4.3.3 *Matu*

Matu has already been mentioned as the mother of *tore* or *muri-muri*. She sits at the fire – apparently her husband *ogbi oro*, the celestial (oro) fire (ogbi) – and dies when a Pygmy steals it (Schebesta, 1950, II, p. 34 f). Despite the many similarities with *muri-muri* and the other mythic figures, there is a strong tendency to reduce these functional transitions to a predominant trait of hers – the mysterious and the sinister, the awesome and eerie magical aspects of the godhead. As the mythological symbol for the origin of life in the featureless universality of the bood, *matu* becomes a magic principle of destruction (Schebesta, 1932, 146 f). Perhaps this development is largely the result of the symbiosis with the Negro tribes, among which black magic (*bulozi*) is a predominant aspect of the 'religious' life. Nonetheless, together with the concept of *ambelema* it reveals an inherent principle of the Bambuti mythology and its respective mentality. Such an interpretation is also supported in that there are many *matus* and that the features incorporated in her are likewise present, though not so predominantly, in the *keti* (forest ghosts; also *befe, balimo, lodi; tore-mo-ichü* is said to live with the *balimo* in mountain dens; each deceased becomes a *tore*), the totem and even in *tore* himself.

Matu looks like a small animal that lives in caves, mountains, and the *bvolu*-tree (*cf.* the uterus motif). She is very clever and powerful. Her eyes are dangerous and even deadly. She seduces children by her arts, then kills them or bestows upon them special powers. If one loses the way or the game it is through her trickery (Schebesta, 1950, II, 43 f).

4.3.4 *Bambuti Mythology and Social Conflict*

If it is correct to consider the mythology of a culture as the pictorial and associative expression of paideumatic experiences and their respective style of life,[18] it is only to be expected that it mirrors the social situation too. This is the case with such institutions as the eldest, the totem relation, and the moral code, although the mythology is much more concerned with meta-institutional implications. This changes, however, as soon as we encounter the conflict between the gathering culture and the economically stronger planting culture.

When *mbali* and *mbigi* emerged from the same rock, one became the progenitor of the Pygmies, the other of the Negroes. This happened when *mbigi* tricked *mbali* by asking him to go into the forest to seek people. When he could not find them he stayed there, and since that time the Pygmies have lived in the forest (Sche-

---

18. Speaking about the paideumatic significance of the forest, its life and its sounds, Turnbull expresses it this way: 'Even the silence is a myth. If you have ears for them, the forest is full of sounds – exciting, mysterious, mournful, joyful' (Turnbull, 1961, p. 2).

besta, 1950, II, p. 55). In another version *mbigi* and *mbali* beget many children. Since one group laughed at the other, they parted and started to speak different languages (Schebesta, 1950, II, p. 55). In another instance an elephant devastated the planting of a villager. His wife, a Pygmy girl, offered the help of her brother. When the Efe killed the elephant it was clear that it was the Negro himself who had changed into the animal. The Negro thus intruded into the world of the forest, since the Pygmies were originally the owners of the banana and other fruits. This was the beginning of the quarrels between the two groups (Schebesta, unpubl.).

Apart from these myths, which state the difference between the two cultures more or less by the mere fact of a division in the beginning, there are others that express the primacy of the Pygmies over the intruding planters, while acknowledging the latter's superior position. The Pygmy teaches the Negro the mystery of procreation. But when he has been taught, the Negro takes the Pygmy's wife and begets many children (Schebesta, 1941, II, p. 453; 1950, II, p. 51). The Pygmy acquires all cultural products by killing *aporu*, but he gives them to the Negro (*cf.* above). In the mythological account of the origin of the banana we hear that the Bambuti found (or got) it first, but gave it to the Negro (Schebesta, 1936, p. 132 f), or the Negro stole it. Since then, the Pygmies steal it back (Schebesta, 1932, p. 43 ff). Sometimes the Negro was more clever than the Pygmy, who originally found the fruit. The Negro did not plant the fruit as the Pygmy did, but planted the banana shoots. The Pygmy, who returns to the Negro after some time, discovers the new trees and is astonished. Then he remarks, 'I prefer hunting, you may stay with your bananas. However, I will also eat them, for you got them through me' (Schebesta, 1932, p. 42 f).

In a legend that Turnbull reports (1965, p. 239, 308 f), the Bambuti possessed bananas before the people of the village had them, but the villagers tricked them and destroyed their plantation. At this point the report changes, obviously substituting the forest for the plantation and the elephants for the villagers. It narrates further that an old Pygmy tricks the elephants by inspiring them with the fear of spirits. Since that time no one has bothered the Pygmies.

Another legend tells how wild boars devastated a Negro plantation. The Negro tried to catch them (the Pygmies), but each time the Pygmies wounded him. Finally he came to the Old Boar – perhaps the Forest God. He gives as many boars to the Negro as he had wounds (thus sanctioning the serfdom of the Pygmies; Schebesta, 1932, p. 98 f.).

More impressive is a story of a Negro who lived among rocks. An old woman, obviously *matu*, was his accomplice. Through magic she tricks the dwarfs, who are killed by the Negro. The last dwarf, however, saw through her tricks. With the help of a hidden string (*cf.* above) he killed the Negro. He then went to the wailing Pygmy women and moved far away with them (Schebesta, 1932, p. 196 f).

Another motif relates a punishment imposed by *mungu*. In the beginning all people lived with *mungu*, who asked them to hunt boars. The Negroes tried it first, but were not successful. When the Bambuti went on the hunt, they immediately succeeded, since they were the people of the forest; but, contrary to the order of *mungu*, they ate the game in the forest (instead of in the camp?). Since that time *mungu* has restricted them to forest life. Although *mungu* was very angry, he was not cruel but gave them various fruits. *Mbera*, the hunter who was banned to the forest, became the ancestor of all Pygmies (Schebesta, 1932, p. 149).

Instructive in this context is a Balese (Negro) legend that recognizes the law of the forest but also overcomes its consequences by replacing it with an institution of their own. A villager caught game in a trap. When he started to bring it home, a *lodi* stopped him and demanded the heart and the liver. The Negro's wife was upset by this and followed the *lodi* secretly, though this was forbidden to her. The *lodi* took both of them to task and sentenced them to death. He brought them to his camp. On the way they met *apopo*, the rabbit. He stopped them and changed the sentence, for it is he who owns the forest and the game. Finally, he released husband and wife. The wife promised not to send her husband to the forest any more (Schebesta, unpubl.).

In the face and on the verge of cultural and social destruction, even a remodeling of the whole mythological and religious consciousness may take place. As Turnbull points out, the conflict between the Pygmy culture and that of the village turns into a negative, though interdependent, or as we may say, dialectical, distinction between forest and non-forest, between the sacred and the profane (1961, p. 1 ff; 1965, p. 14, 229, 248 ff; also, 1959, 1960). In this new situation *kalisia* (*mungu*, etc.) becomes identical with the forest; he even *is* the forest. What remains is a reduced or leveled mythology and religious world as the only survival of a once well-structured life. In other words, the Pygmies' dialectical response to the Negro culture (which regards *tore* and the other figures of Pygmy mythology and cult as the manifestation and incorporation of evil and trickery because of their closeness to the forest) is a structureless identification of all that is divine with their own forest world.[19]

This examination of the mythological dimension of the Bambuti culture, which has been understood as the theoretical, though largely unreflective, response to the various affections of life, provides a basis for interpreting the practical expressions of the absolute in the light of and within their own and inherent context. We thus may turn now to the analysis of the cult of the Bambuti.

5. BAMBUTI CULT

If we anticipate the general picture of the ways in which the Bambuti culture expressed the dialectics of absolute symbols we can outline the following structural and functional features. The mythology is ambivalent not only in its own inner texture but also in its practical assimilations. Either it may be adopted as the inner meaning of – when viewed from the effectiveness of work – rationally meaningless acts, such as prayer, sacrifice, or festivals, which in their turn can be interpreted as recalled and reactualized mythology, or it presents the background for an apparently rational and non-mythological attitude. In the latter case the mythology becomes the tacit presupposition for pseudo- or semirational behavior, which we usually call magic . Since the boundaries between these two possibilities are fluid (provided that magic does not turn into black magic and sorcery), magic is largely interwoven with the cultic and symbolic patterns, and therefore cannot be separated from the description of religious life and culture.

5.1 *The Bambuti Cult as Recalled Mythology*

The informality of cultic acts such as the throwing of bits of game into the forest, with the firm conviction that the omission of this act would disturb the integrity of the world, is sufficiently explained by the mythic consciousness

19. The situation described above is extreme. It is, so to speak, the end of a cultural development, which reveals paradigmatically the impact of religion (mythology) on the society, especially in a critical situation and vice versa. For the overall picture it is important to see that the various degrees of cultural transition as well as the abundance of names for the godhead qualify the respective 'synthesis' accordingly from place to place. *Cf.* also H. Loiskandl (1966, p. 154 ff).

of this culture. In its hypostatic or heterothetic character it permeates everyday life: Work, play and custom. Since everything *is* basically a part of the mythological world, the contact between the *now* of today and the everlasting *was* of the beginning is given (constituted) as a permanent possibility, to which man has usually only to point in order to experience its actual presence. Such contacts with the mythic origin and presence are made over and over again and are not confined to the examples that have been given. A women calls upon *mbali* for children while she goes for water (Schebesta, 1950, II, p. 69). The eldest tells his people during the ritual of a burial that they should stop crying, since the deceased has gone to God (Schebesta, 1932, p. 148). When a honey-seeker whips the honey-tree like *tore*, or when someone knocks against the hut with the word: '*Mungu*, go away', while the rainbow appears in the sky (Schebesta, 1950, II, p. 70 f), the references to myth are obvious. Another frequent occasion to recall the conditions told by mythology is provided by thunderstorms. At such times the eldest kindles a strongly smoking fire (or covers it; Schebesta, unpubl.; Turnbull, 1965, p. 58) while saying; 'My father, your children die with fear. Please, go away' (Schebesta, 1950, II, p. 71). He may also use the *segbe* pipe, which *ba'atsi* taught them to blow in such a situation (Schebesta, 1936, p. 125, 127).

How deep the impact of the mythology on cultic reactions can be is shown by the behavior of a group who reported the story of a friendly encounter with the lightning flash. Since they are on friendly terms, they do not fear a thunderstorm. If lightning occurs, *gbara* only means to frighten them; he will not kill them (Schebesta, 1932, p. 223).

If somebody walks through the forest and meets a *keti* (*befe*, *matu*), – recognizing such an encounter by a sudden shiver – he makes a fire as soon as he returns to the camp. Apparently this may be understood as the recollection of the mythological fight between the Forest-Spirit and man, for the fire was first owned by the Forest God (Schebesta, 1932, p. 152). Similarly, they respond with reverent acts when they see the chameleon or a taboo animal (Schebesta, unpubl.).

Another occasion for recalling the mythological conditions is given when *kalisia* closes the forest. The Pygmies respond by prayers, by the sacrifice of a chicken, or by offering gifts for the *lodi*. If they are accepted, there will be great joy (Schebesta, 1950, II, p. 80 ff). Such ceremonies (which Turnbull calls 'the lesser Molimo', 1965, p. 260) may continue for some days. In this case, they point to what can be interpreted as a mythic reactualization or reintegration.

It is not merely a single action that recalls the mythic present but a quasi-dramatic repetition of the events, which reactualize the meaning of the beginning.

5.2 *The Bambuti Cult as Mythic Reactualization*

Rituals that can be interpreted as mythic reactualizations are events such as the beat-hunt, which takes place only occasionally[20] and in which the whole community is involved (men and women); the ceremony that precedes the honey season; or the *tore* (*molimo*) festival, which is celebrated if someone of special importance dies (Turnbull, 1961, p. 43 ff; 1965, p. 261 ff), or at an event of special joy (Schebesta, unpubl.). The puberty feast of the girls (*elima*) also seems to belong to this sort of cultic ritual.

The leaders of the *begbe* (beat) hunt (Schebesta, 1936, p. 115 f; 1941, II, p. 99; 1950, II, p. 71 and unpubl.) are an old man and an old woman (*cf. tore* and *matu*). At the beginning of the hunt they build and rake the fire (*borue* or *mota e'ba*) with branches of the *boru* or *ato* tree under a *matega* tree. They put various leaves into the fire. The hunting group starts from this fire, which symbolizes man's call upon *kalisia* not to send a thunderstorm, or, in another version, to look at his children and to remember them. The ashes of the leaves are smeared over the temples and the eyes to strengthen man's knowledge and eyesight. When resting on their way, the fire ceremony is repeated. The hunters hold their bows, on which various herbs are bound, over the fire. If the hunt is successful, the band returns with much joy to the camp. The old woman claims special right to the game.

The first *begbe* hunt Schebesta experienced was a failure. A thunderstorm brought the hunt to a halt. Allegedly the reason for this failure was intercourse which some of the hunters had had the night before, though this was forbidden.

The honey ritual that Turnbull reports (1965, p. 171, 231 f) is also centered on a fire and its smoke, accompanied by a libation ceremony, the whistling of honey whistles (*singbe*), and a dance, which symbolizes the reversal of the sexes (and, we may add, the creative conflict immanent to the mythology). This

---

20. The net hunt, which has become in some areas the rule rather than the exception today, seems to have preserved the *begbe-* ritual as a more or less institutionalized ceremony (Schebesta, 1932, p. 250, 1941, II, p. 101, unpub; Turnbull, 1965, p. 162).

dance is also said to be the dance of the *keti*[21] (i.e., of the life of the dead and the godhead) who are supposed to hear the Pygmies call for honey. The tug-of-war play, which Schebesta (unpubl.) describes as a joyful entertainment after the successful collection of honey, is probably the continuation of the honey ritual.

Both these ceremonies point toward what Turnball calls the 'greater Molimo' (1965, p. 261), and it seems that they are simply different aspects of the same 'institution': The so-called *tore* or *molimo* association (Schebesta, 1941, II, p. 492 ff).

According to Turnbull the *molimo* was celebrated on the occasion of the death of a well-beloved old lady. The festival, whose meaning was the 'reaffirmation of life' (1965, p. 262), continued for several weeks. For the band concerned it actually became the framework of a temporal return to the forest, for death is 'a matter for the forest' (Turnbull, 1961, p. 43); 'a time to get back to the forest' (p. 45); to 'wake the forest up with the *molimo*' (p. 90), and to 'make the forest happy' (p. 43). It 'reaffirms', as Turnbull puts it, 'the unity of the Mbuti in opposition to the village' (1965, p. 281). In other words, the *molimo* Turnbull experienced was something like a cultural memorial service, a nostalgic ritual that reveals some of the fundamental and basic features of the Bambuti mentality and religiosity. The festival itself centered on the fire and the sound of the trumpet (Turnbull, 1961, p. 73 ff), around life (Turnbull, 1965, p. 262), and the power of life (Turnbull, 1965, p. 254 f). The real work of the *molimo* is to sing[22] although the dance of the 'reversal of the sexes' also plays an important role (Turnbull, 1961, p. 76; 1965, p. 171 f). This singing was first done by the hunters when the voice of the trumpet,[23] the great animal of the forest,[24]

21. It seems that this dance is identical or very similar to the *bebele-* performance, the dance of the chimpanzee (Schebesta, unpubl.).

22. Turnbull (1961, p. 79) mentions in this context a story about a singing bird. One day this bird was killed and with it the song and with the song the killer himself. Apart from the custom of singing before and during gatherings, the importance of song and sound is also underlined by the fact that singing is not only a motif that returns very often in the mythology but that the myths themselves are always interrupted by songs when they are told.

23. The trumpet that was actually used was a metal tube, which indicates on the one hand the cultural deterioration of this band, for the Pygmies originally had their own wooden trumpets. On the other hand, however, it emphasizes all the more the importance of the sound and the generative character of this cultural tradition (*cf.* Turnbull, 1961, p. 73 ff).

24. This idea shows clearly the relationship with *ambelema* and with the accounts on the mythological monster (*matu*). Indeed, there were many ceremonies connected with the trumpet itself. It was kept in water during the festival – a ritual that shows its connection with life, sex, and the origin of man. Moreover it was rubbed with ashes and live coals were put into the far end (Turn-

roared through the night (Turnbull, 1961, p. 78 f). 'The men sang their songs of praise to the forest' and the '*molimo* answered them' (Turnbull, 1961, p. 16). Such songs were sung in the evening mainly by the elders, while the younger men sang chiefly in the morning. The festival culminated and ended with the appearance of an old woman and a fire dance[25] (Turnbull, 1965, p. 264). While the woman tried to stamp out the fire, the men gathered the embers again, performing an erotic dance. On this occasion, the whole camp was involved (Turnbull, 1961, p. 152 ff). Turnbull mentions 'that once it was the women who "owned" the Molimo, but then men stole it from them and ever since the women have been forbidden to see it' (1961, p. 156). It seems justifiable to interpret this ceremony as the reactualization of the fire myth, when a Pygmy stole the fire from *matu*, and *matu* finally died.

Schebesta's inquiries and information concerning the *tore* association (1932, p. 95; 237 ff; 1941, II, p. 492 ff; 1950, II, p. 96; p. 219 and the unpubl. notes) can be summarized as follows. Names for the festivals of the *tore* association (hereafter referred to as Tore) and for its representatives among the Bambuti are *tore*, *molimo* (probably identical with *moli-moli*, *muri-muri*), and *mpa* (the owner of the camp). The songs and ceremonies (dances) of Tore (also called *mpa-ma*) are concerned with the Forest God, upon whom they call and pray and are rooted in the whole of the Bambuti mythology. Although many villagers have their Tore too, there is a basic difference between the Bambuti and Negro association and festival,[26] a difference which becomes particularly apparent in the function of the trumpet. The hut of Tore is near the camp. Many things are kept secret from the women and children, especially the *lusomba* (trumpet). However, they may watch the Tore activities from some distance. Old women have access to the Tore. There is even a Tore dance in which both sexes participate. One of the oldest men and a widow are allegedly the leaders of the Tore. The Tore trumpet

bull, 1961, p. 78) – a ceremony that connects it with all the implications of the fire. Finally, its 'sleeping place' is considered taboo, and to see it would entail death (Turnbull, 1961, pp. 68, 79) – again a sign of its relationship to *ambelema* and *tore*.

25. Schebesta saw a similar dance when he left one of the camps (1932, p. 93; 1950, II, p. 72 f), and when, in another camp, the birth of a child was celebrated (1950, II, p. 73), but he did not understand the context and the meaning of those rituals at that time.

26. Since these Negro tribes assimilated much Pygmy blood, it is very probable that the core of their Tore association is a survival of the Bambuti culture. The *molimo* festival of the Epulu Pygmies as Turnbull saw it, and the name *mpa-ma* (songs of the camp-owner), at least point in this direction.

and the bull-roarer, which is also used, represent the voice of God or the first ancestor. As a myth says (Schebesta, 1941, II, p. 439), the first *apefa* (Pygmy) was the child of the leopard (*molí*). When the leopard had more children, he told them to go the village (probably the life in the camp), while he stayed (like *tore* himself) in the forest. He gave them the *lusomba* trumpet (also called *amangole, apadia, pandia, asaragba, amengutu,* etc.), which repeats his voice. Together with pipes and pots, the *lusomba* and the bullroarer represent the various mythological figures: *tore, keti, mati, avi melia, ambelema,* the respective totem. Important ceremonies such as the *sulia*-ritual (the opening of the forest) are related to the Tore. The fire, which plays a central role, is made for the Forest God, the Great who is *tore* (Tore).

While the Tore festival is carried on chiefly by the hunting band, the women have the analogous *elima* festival, which takes place on the occasion of the first menstruation of a girl. It is a joyful festival that celebrates life (*elima*, vital force, power of the moon; Schebesta, 1950, II, p. 206) and offers the unmarried men access to the hut of the girls. Here again, song is most important, along with general instructions by a midwife (Turnbull, 1961, p. 159; 200; 1965, p. 71 f; 132 ff.; Schebesta, unpubl.)

Although information concerning the *elima* festival is relatively scanty, its existence is a further indication that cult and ritual form an integral part of all other aspects of life. Joy, sorrow, love, meaning, and hope permeate each other in such a way that they become manifest only in the smaller or larger breaks of everyday life. It is the world of the mythic which, in the process of myth and mythology, holds things together and sheds its formative light on spontaneous prayers, playful ceremonies, and customary behavior – and also on magic performances and attitudes.

5.3 *The Magic of the Bambuti*

Since the villagers cultivate an explicitly magical style of life (including witchcraft and black magic), the Bambuti traditions in this area become all the more visible. There is no case of purely individual and destructive black magic known among them. Since the social milieu is group oriented and depends on cooperation, it looks unfavorably on all attempts that might indicate antisocial behavior and private power. Turnbull describes, for instance, a hunting medicine, made from various parts of an antelope (1961, p. 94). This medicine may well be used for communal purposes. To stick an antelope horn filled with the paste in the ground near the family fire is considered, however, antisocial and selfish. If the same medicine is used during the *begbe* hunt, everyone accepts it. Thus it is not magic as such, which is rejected, but a special form of magic.

Forms of magic that are generally accepted range from fears, based on mythology and usually related to ravines, caves, streams, rocks, and atmospheric phenomena but also expressed in various taboos, to protective and fortifying rituals. As we noted earlier, the transition between magic and religion is fluid. Since the magic power is given by *tore* (Schebesta, 1932, p. 221), or since it was *ba'atsi* who told them to blow the *segbe* pipe (Schebesta, 1936, p. 125), it is impossible to attribute the ceremonies definitively to either magic or religion. The whole attitude of the Pygmies during a thunderstorm (a special occasion for magical practices) shows the basic conviction that they cannot change the situation if *epilipili* does not want to do so. Ultimately they keep very quiet (Schebesta, 1950, II, p. 70 f), and, as Turnbull remarks (1965, p. 58), recognize man's inability to control the weather. Thus even such apparently magical performances as the adjuration of a thunderstorm cannot be said to lack all religious (propitiatory) character. Moreover, how is it possible to know whether the smearing of the temples and the eyes (as is done during the *begbe* hunt following previous prayers to *kalisia*) is the figurative expression of hope, which is accompanied by the conviction that all depends on *kalisia*, or the positing of a cause that has its necessary effects? The same question remains in most cases, since the presence of the mythic also means the presence of power, of creation, of God. Man may refer to this world at any place and any time: by spitting in the direction of the chameleon; by a vine bracelet, which is worn to maintain and to gain power; by the sound of the *segbe* pipe. That magic is involved – or, that it is not lacking in such cases – becomes quite obvious, when the *segbe* pipe for instance, which usually is hung around the owner's neck, serves also as a container for objects belonging to another person upon whom he wants to exercise control (Schebesta, 1932, p. 72; 1950, II, p. 105 f), or when this pipe (also used during the hunt) is made of the wood of bushes that the animal in question prefers (Schebesta, 1950, II, p. 106). In such cases the scheme of cause and effect based upon a mythological know-how is all too apparent.

In the sense described, magic ceremonies accompany the Bambuti from birth to death. When a child is born, juice of the *pempe* fruit, which is mixed with various ashes, is given to him (Schebesta, 1932, p. 188). Libation ceremonies take place (Turnball, 1965, p. 129). In the case of a twin birth, one of the babies may even be killed, for it is dangerous to have twins (Schebesta, 1941, II, p. 407 f). The remains of the umbilical cord are worn by the child so that he may grow. Paint, colors, amulets, and vine bracelets are used as a sign and guarantee of protection (Schebesta, 1932, p. 218; 1936, p. 145; 1941, II, p. 308; 1950, II, p. 110; Turnbull, 1965, p. 130). Magical spells are used to insure love, fertility, or sterility (Schebesta, 1941, II, p. 398 f., 1950, II, p. 110). Powerful instruments that are applied for magical purposes, in addition to the *segbe* pipe, are rattles and branches (Schebesta, 1950, II, p. 108), dancing tufts, and fans (*lekombo, gbea-gbea*, etc.; Schebesta, 1932, p. 70; 1950, II, p. 107).

In addition to smearing various ashes and pastes over the eyes, the heart, and the stomach, the hunter also avails himself of a special blessing ceremony performed by his wife. She cuts small slits into his forehead and rubs the ashes of the *rofo* tree, mixed with her own spittle, into the wound (Schebesta, 1950, II, p. 111; Turnbull, 1965, p. 130).

It would seem that the elephant hunt developed its own magical complex, special magical rituals and attitudes, which are in marked contrast to the rest of traditional customs. On the eve of the hunt there are specific dances, along with libation ceremonies. During the night the hunters must not have intercourse. Early in the morning they swallow a vomiting medicine (*lenga*), etc. The hair of the elephant's tail and its eyes are used for secret medicines. If the hunter gives them away, he will be killed or injured (Schebesta, 1941, II, p. 138 ff).

The variations and combinations of these and similar customs are infinite. There are also some hints of practice of ordeals and the search for omens (Schebesta, 1950, II, p. 114). But here the indication is that the Bambuti also know how to handle the practices of the villagers, whereas they do not really engage in these things themselves. It therefore seems to be unnecessary to examine this complex further. More important are the forms of societal magic, which emerge especially with regard to the social and economical conflict between the villagers and the forest people. Yet, since this process is again largely a religious one, or is carried out with the help of religious means, it belongs to the general theme of the relationship between religion and the social order.

6. RELIGION AND THE SOCIAL ORDER

As the analysis of Bambuti mythology has already indicated, there is no doubt about the social implication of these data. Since the mythology and its enactment (religion) furnishes the meaning for the (forest) world and its life, it permeates the structures of society by inner necessity. However, it is not merely the structure as such that is supported by religion. Rather, is it the happiness of the individuals in the group and their mutual help and support that matters here. This is well expressed in a prayer to *kalisia*: 'Please give us a successful hunt, for then we will be happy!' (Schebesta, unpubl.). The eldest, in whose *megbe* the presence of the godhead becomes manifest, is respected and protected by religious sanctions in his traditional functions, but only as long as he does not seek his own benefit. Moreover, there is not only a mythological account of punishment of disobedient or disloyal children, but also of irresponsible adults or parents. (Schebesta, 1941, II, p. 322 ff). It would seem that the component related to personal spontaneity in the Bambuti mythology is too strong to be set aside in favor of institutional generalities that would give the institution a magical self-sufficiency.

This situation changes when economic power is concentrated in the hands of individuals. Here, religion becomes the most welcome and practical instrument to solidify (legitimize) the social descent between the different groups – a process that can be easily seen in the cultural and social conflict between the villagers and the forest people. As Turnbull points out, the villagers try very hard to integrate the Bambuti into their symbolic system, thus sanctioning the economic and cultural submission of the Pygmies.

Since the strongest religious feelings of the villagers are manifested in case of marriage and death, they are anxious to 'familiarize' the Bambuti with the respective traditions, particularly because the Pygmies show a relative lack of interest in this matter. As yet, their success has been limited. After all, it is the group and not the patriarchal family that is significant for the Bambuti culture. And *tore*, who in the mind of the villagers is the God of death and evil, is for the Bambuti the God of life. Thus the death rituals, customs, and ideas have not gone beyond the stage of a formal adoption, if they have been adopted at all. This holds true also of the myths that describe the adventures of a Pygmy in the underworld (Schebesta, 1950, II, p. 90 ff). Formally they express the Negro mentality, while the content describes the forest world of the *befe* and of *tore*.

The villagers were more successful with their *nkumbi*, the institution and festival of initiation, which represents a kind of synthesis between the genuine tribal initiation and the adopted or surviving Pygmy Tore (Schebesta, 1941, II, p. 467 ff; Turnbull, 1965, p. 63 ff). In contrast, 'initiation' among the Pygmies seems to be a highly informal act. When a boy kills his first game, the father boils the heart of the animal and presses it, together with the bow, into his hand. From now on he belongs to the Tore, who will introduce him into the various aspects of life.

The *nkumbi*, which occasionally is said to have been introduced by the mythological mother *amaima*, who first circumcised the girls, but when they died, allowed them to try circumcision on the boys, takes place in a forest camp in an interval of a couple of years. Women have no access. The boys are introduced into the customs of the tribe which is the first purpose of this institution, for circumcision is not practiced everywhere. The songs they learn and sing are strictly confined to the forest. Most important for the institutionalization and sanctioning of the social situation is the blood brotherhood (*kare*) between Pygmy boys and Negro boys. Both are supposed to help each other, to respect their totem, to form the bond between the two cultures.

Although the Bambuti do not take this ceremony too seriously (Schebesta, 1941, II, p. 475) – they call it 'stupid and empty' (Turnbull, 1965, p. 69) – their resistance can be only a temporal one, because they do not have the economic strength to withstand the 'friendship' of their economically superior neighbors. As the example of the so-called Village Basua shows – a group of Bambuti that has become sedentary – the new socio-religious structure will take over as soon as the former economic background has ceased to exist (Schebesta, 1941, II, p. 452 ff). The strength of the milieu-bound mythology of the Bambuti culture will also be its weakness in this intercultural struggle, which transforms the basic openness of the religious life into the magic compactness of fear-inspiring institutions. Yet, as the same example of the Village Basua shows, no final word can be said about the religion as such, which even in the form of a socialized pragmatism reveals clearly a reality that is essential in man's encounter with his own being.

5

The Religion of the Artic Hunters.
The Eskimos

We know of no other people who have adapted to such an extreme environment as the Eskimos. As might be expected numerous explorers and anthropologists have been and still are deeply interested in this arctic culture, which extends from the Aleutian Islands and the tip of Siberia in the West to the shores of Greenland in the East. But despite a well-established Eskimology, dating from the end of the last century, the cultural map of the (ca. 50,000) Eskimos still shows many blank spots. This holds true especially with respect to an adequate interpretation of their religion. On the other hand, since this religion belongs to a culture that survived under most unfavorable conditions, it calls for special attention and treatment in a study that is primarily concerned with the basic features of religious life.

1. LIFE AND RELIGION AMONG THE ESKIMOS

According to the archeological evidence,[1] the origin of the Eskimos has to be sought in the Old World. Probably at the end of the Upper Paleolithic, and perhaps in the region of Kamchatka, a branch of Old World hunters adopted an economy based chiefly on hunting sea mammals. Influenced by the waves of migration that passed through the Bering Strait region, this culture adapted itself to the marginal conditions of the arctic environment and finally survived in the recent Eskimo groups, scattered today over more than 6,000 miles. Archeological reconstruction, which agrees by and large with the results of comparative ethnology and linguistics,[2] indicates strongly that the recent Eskimo culture is

1. See Wendell H. Oswalt (1967, p. 36 ff). This book offers a very good summary of old and recent findings and theories concerning the origin and recent stratification of the Alaskan Eskimos.
2. See A. Gahs (1928, pp. 231 ff, 258 ff); Kaj Birket-Smith (1948, p. 221 ff). There are indications that Eskimo may be related to the Uralic and even the Indo-European languages. See W. Thalbitzer (1952).

to be considered as the achievement of a deep-ranging endogenic development. Although such a view does not necessarily permit conclusions concerning the religion of this culture, since archeological artifacts are inadequate sources for religious ideas, it justifies at least an interpretation that recognizes the various cultural areas[3] as concrete specifications of one basic unity and cultural paideuma. As in the case of the ergological elements, the differential distribution of which becomes meaningful in the light of the historical genesis, the symbolic patterns have to be envisioned as representations of an ideational reality which in a confined framework became highly specialized throughout the millenia.[4]

Except for the whale-hunting communities in the Bering Strait, who occasionally lived in permanent villages of up to 500 people, the Eskimos never developed a hierarchically structured society. Rather, they formed groups of several more or less independent households (nuclear families, plus dependents), which fused or separated for economic as well as emotional reasons, such as boredom, quarrels, or the need for companionship. Apart from the central regions, where they built snow houses (igloos), they used to hibernate in multifamily dwelling units that were rectangular houses, built partly underground, and with a four-post roof construction that offered patterns for the description of the universe. During that part of the year when they adopted a more nomadic way of life, they lived in dome-shaped or conical tents.

3. From a linguistic point of view we have to distinguish between the Inupik-speaking Inuit (all the groups that live between the Yukon River and the Atlantic) and the Yupik-speaking Yuit in Siberia and Alaska, and the language of the Aleutian-Eskimos, who form a very mixed population and culture. From an economical point of view we have to distinguish between coastal Eskimos and inland Eskimos, and those who rely upon both environments. Besides this distinction we also have a geographical one, namely a distinction that follows cultural areas: The Angmagssalkik Eskimos in eastern Greenland, the Westgreenlanders, the Polar Eskimos in the Thule district, the Labrador-Eskimos, the Baffinland Eskimos, the Caribou Eskimos west of Hudson Bay, the Iglulik and Netsilik Eskimos on the Melville and Boothia Peninsula, the Copper Eskimos around Coronation Gulf, the Makenzie Eskimos, the Point-Barrow Eskimos, the Nunamiut south of Point Barrow, the Bering Strait Eskimos, the Koniag on the Kodiak Island and the Chugach in the Gulf of Alaska (Pacific Eskimos), the Asiatic Eskimos, and finally the Aleutian Eskimos. A final distinction is that according to the linguistic subgroups. *Cf.* Birket-Smith (1948, p. 288 ff).

4. In addition to the works already mentioned, the following will be used or mentioned in this study: F. Boas (1888), E. S. Carpenter (1956), N. J. Gubser (1965), Ake Hultkrantz (1962), M. Lantis (1947, 1950), G. M. Marsh (1954), Knut Rasmussen (1908, 1926, 1927, 1929, 1930), W. Thalbitzer (1928), E. M. Weyer (1932). For a general introduction into Eskimo life, see also G. de Poncins (1941). Since the Eskimos today have been influenced significantly by Christian missionaries, the exposition employs mainly the past tense in its description.

Community life was centered around the communal or ceremonial house. The *karigi*, as it was called in Alaska (also *kazigi, kashgee, qazge, qalgi, qaggim*), served as a ceremonial center, as workshop, and occasionally as a sleeping place for the men and for visitors. It also served as a place for entertainment, as well as for deliberations dealing with vital problems of the community, such as the settlement of quarrels and the punishment of antisocial behavior. Such punishment ranged from social isolation to the death penalty. Usually the ceremonial hut was owned by the whole community. It was only among the whale-hunters in northern Alaska, whose economy favored the accumulation of wealth and power in the hand of the few *umyak* (whaleboat) owners, that the *karigi* became the more or less exclusive property of a single family or group.

Though neither chieftainship, nor a clearly described role of the eldest has been typical, the Eskimos always recognized individuals who by their strength and intelligence were the temporal leaders of their community. They called such a leader, who was very often, though not necessarily, a shaman, *isumataq*, 'he who thinks'. He was the first among equals, recognized as long as he was a successful hunter and leader.

The economic base that made life possible in the arctic environment was hunting and fishing, with special emphasis on whale, small sea mammals, and caribou, depending on the regions in which the groups lived. The so-called Caribou Eskimos were completely dependent on the reindeer or caribou, and on the fish of inland waters. Consequently, they formed a typical inland culture. Other groups depended entirely on a sea-mammal or coastal economy, while still others exploited both resources. Despite the fact that the latter economy might have been the common foundation of the others, the Eskimos conceived of the relationship between sea and land as antagonistic. Various taboos reinforced and perpetuated the distinction between both realms: The meat of land and sea animals could not be cooked together; weapons had to be purified, etc.

As important as hunting and the manufacture of the kayak, harpoons, and all the other specialized hunting equipment made by the males, was the hunter's clothing, prepared by his wife. 'The man is that hunter whom his wife makes', is a saying of the Polar Eskimos that characterizes the vital importance of the woman's domestic work. This also included the preparation of the meals and everything connected with it. Activities such as skinning and cutting up the game were done by either males or females. In this respect the limits were fluid. When seen within the whole culture, however, the division of labor points to a further polarity. It is the polarity between the inward world of the home and the outward one of game and hunting. Though opposed to one another, both worlds were equally important for sustaining life. As with the land-sea relationship, many taboos were directed at this polarity and opposition. Thus, the husband was greatly affected by the taboos of his wife, which were many in respect to menstruation and childbirth, while the wife had to adjust to various taboos concerning the husband's hunting and the game. This was especially true in case of the first successful seal or walrus hunt of her son, which was also marked by a ceremony. Similar recognition was given on the occasion of the girl's first menstruation.

The existence and coordination of mutual taboos was necessary because of the various antagonistic forces in and through which life continues, and which must be kept in an equilibrium (see Rasmussen, 1926, p. 381 f). According to this world-view nothing could be worse than to disturb this equilibrium of powers (Birket-Smith, 1948, p. 206). The greatest danger of life lies in the possibility that human food consists completely of 'souls' (Birket-Smith, 1948, p. 210). In the context of the symbolic life this might be understood as a distortion of the equilibrium (harmony) of the universe, in which the inward turned outward, while the meaning of things had been lost at the expense of their mere existence. Observation of the taboos was therefore a supplicatory as well as a precautionary measure, which offered security in the midst of frightening conditions and destructive forces.

An additional characteristic of the Eskimo culture in general is revealed in their trade patterns. Since the highly specialized equipment for hunting and living required both coastal and inland materials, survival demanded the exchange and acquisition of goods. The successful hunter, and also the efficient woman, tried therefore to gain trading friends. Such a partnership usually turned into a lifelong friendship that was expressed by the exchange of wives and also by ceremonies, gift exchange, and festivals with singing contests. In Alaska invitations were sent by two messengers for the so-called Messenger Feast. In the beginning of winter the guests came with loaded sleds. Ceremonies with mask dances continued for weeks. Finally, when the guests left, all ceremonial materials had to be burned. The bones of land animals also had to be burned before the sea-hunting season could be opened.

The interdependence of life and religion which has been indicated in the trading ceremonies and their respective ceremonials, is best understood when we consider some of the major events in the life of an Eskimo. Birth, as the beginning, is marked by many taboos concerning the mother, the child, the house, the household, and game. The mother was not allowed to call the hunted game by its real name, nor was she permitted to eat raw meat – an act that seems to have been regarded as a kind of communion with the forces of nature – nor could she or her husband participate in public ceremonies during the year following the birth. To avoid excessive birth pains, the woman in labor was taken to an isolated hut, where she gave birth either with the help of a woman shaman or alone. The mother had to cut the umbilical cord herself. If the mother died, everything had to be burned. If the infant died, complicated rituals were necessary, and numerous taboos had to be observed by the mother and her household for the entire year. Immediately after birth the infant received his first dress, which had to be changed and buried after some days. A part of the dress, however, was considered a highly protective amulet, and this was to be worn on special occasions during one's whole lifetime. In Alaska, birth was celebrated either by a feast that the happy father gave for his companions, or by a sweat-bath for the men of his ceremonial house, or simply by the distribution of gifts, which, as elsewhere, was thought to be a power-gaining ritual.

Explorers and investigators are unanimous in reporting that the Eskimos are fond of their children. They give them toys and entertain them with stories and fairy tales, which also serve an educational purpose. Nevertheless, infanticide, especially of girls, was relatively frequent. Even cannibalism occurred in times of complete scarcity of food.

Naming a child was most important and was occasionally done before the child was born. Without a name, or more accurately without a name-soul (which does not indicate the sex of the bearer), a human being was not complete. The name-soul left the person at death and waited to be incorporated again in a newborn child. Usually, the name of a deceased relative was chosen. It was also customary to use the names of all the persons who had passed away since the last baby was born.

Similar to this idea of the reincarnation of the name-soul was the belief that the souls of the game, if certain taboos and rituals were observed, would return to their dwelling place and be incorporated into new animals. Thus, the head of a slain bear would be placed facing the land in order to express this consciousness, and to enact its respective purpose.

Young people were usually considered ready for marriage after the girl's first menstruation and when the boy was able to maintain a family. Couples often passed through three or four trial marriages before a final settlement was achieved, both sexes having equal rights in divorcing the other partner. Marriages between close relatives were forbidden. Among the Bering Strait Eskimos, persons with the same protective amulet or fetish, which conferred a particular unity between the person and the power that it symbolized, were not permitted to marry. Though no fixed patterns existed, the consciousness of the male line seems to have been predominant. Both polygamy and polyandry were occasionally practiced. The marriage ceremony itself was very informal.

If sickness occurred, it was usually considered the result of the failure to observe taboos. In such cases the shaman held a divination ceremony, during which the patient had to confess his sins (broken taboos). Confessions in front of the shaman and an audience were the basic condition for the patient's improvement. Changing the name-soul could also be very effective. More serious illnesses were caused either by the intrusion or loss of the soul, usually the work of a malevolent wizard. In such a situation the shaman had to remove the foreign body, that is, to regain the soul by sending his own soul in search of it. If he could not bring it back or substitute an animal soul for it, the sick man was bound to die. Besides the shaman's intervention in case of illness, his help was also asked when a visit to a trading friend was planned, when the movements of the game had to be determined, or when misfortune afflicted the group.

The long winter nights, during which people had to live mainly on the surplus they had been able to store in the previous season, were occupied by mending old equipment or making new, by carving toys and symbols (idols), by telling stories in a ritual fashion, by entertainment, by the composition and singing of songs in which a friend or adversary was ridiculed, and by reflection and musing. All these activities were realized in a sphere of magico-religious feelings and ideas. Especially the knowledge of secret songs and singing in general formed an integral part of the various activities. The shaman, for example, needed a singing audience to support the flight and combats of his soul. The stories dealt with successful and unsuccessful hunters, great shamans gifted with strong magical powers, dwarfs and giants, legendary peoples and their interferences with the life of man. The storyteller did not face the audience but looked toward the wall, apparently a magic precaution required by the stories.

Although the rituals and taboos connected with death were relatively fixed, the ideas about the deceased were rather vague. Death, as such, does not fall outside the framework of conflicting events. A myth from Greenland, which mirrors quite clearly the acquiescing view of the experienced (Hultkrantz, 1962, p. 406), tells about a dispute of two beings who finally decided it would be best for man eventually to die. Since that time, man has to die. Thus death seems to turn into a matter-of-fact event that is not to be feared more than other things. To paraphrase an Eskimo woman: I know nothing about death. All I have experienced is life. Either death is the end of life, or it is a transition to another form. In either case there is nothing to be feared (Rasmussen, 1908, p. 127). This attitude largely explains why old people who are no longer able to maintain a household eventually may ask to be killed, or why it is not unlawful to kill them, or why suicide is considered not a crime but an effective way to enter the land of joy and happiness. If we judge from our point of view, we may also say that severity gives its own perspective to life and death.

If a person was expected to die, he was taken into an isolated hut. If he or she died in the dwelling house, everything had to be destroyed. Mourning and taboos, like abstinence from festivals, were connected with death, especially in the case of relatives who had touched the body. The corpse of the deceased was either buried or exposed in the tundra or on the beach. A great part of his personal property was destroyed and placed in the grave. Class differences in burial did not exist except for some groups in Alaska, where social stratifications were more complex.

The Eskimos distinguished two or three places to which the immortal soul could go: Heaven, the land under the earth, and a place just beneath the surface, where murderers, unkind people, and witches lived a very sad life. But as we have noted, the ideas about the hereafter are not clear and are often contradictory. Those concerning the soul itself can be summarized as follows. Some groups believed that the life-soul remained for four or five days with the body, after which it disappeared, while the free soul (name-soul) might stay nearby until it was incorporated into a newborn child. Others believed that the surviving man left in his totality the place after some days and passed by way of the galaxy into the land of the deceased. Such journeys were, to a certain degree, described in the soul voyage of the shaman. Those who arrived in the bright land of the living found everything in abundance, while those who went to the land below had to live by the sacrifices that (in Alaska) were offered during the memorial feast, a ceremony that took place from one to three times a year. The 'Great Feast to the Death', which was celebrated there at intervals of four to ten years and which could last for weeks, 'was held in order to free the souls of the deceased from the earth forever' (Oswalt, 1967, p. 228). Still others believed in the return of the deceased as a newborn child or in his transmigration into an animal. Several souls even might unite in the same infant. Finally, we find the idea that the dead turned either into malicious ghosts or into benevolent guardians who protected the newborn child until his soul was strong enough to survive. These latter ideas are interrelated with the conception of the name-soul.

The functional completion of practical attitudes toward death is expressed in the various rituals and taboos concerning the death of an animal, especially those that were hunted for the first time in a season. They were performed on the analogy of the customs referring to human departure, each animal being given its specific ritual. Since such performances were actually enacted to appease the 'owner' of the species, it is perhaps not too far-fetched to interpret the death ceremonial as the expression of honor and esteem toward the 'owner' of man and mankind.

The question that arises immediately with this interpretation is the nature of this 'owner', namely of 'God', as the metasymbolic center of all symbolic life. Thus far we have dealt with taboos, the mythological land below and above the earth, the equilibrium of the forces achieved through the observation of rules, souls, and ghosts or legendary beings. At first glance it might seem that the Eskimos lived in a world filled with magic forces but without a God as highest being and absolute Lord, that they lived in a whirlpool of conflicting principles that eventually destroy any meaning to life, making it consist of senseless antagonisms and ultimate absurdity. Since this problem can be adequately settled only in the light of the mythic consciousness of a culture, we must consider the general structure and meaning of the respective mythology. In the case of the Eskimos, however, the mythology is not easy to grasp. At least there is no off-hand indication of a body of narratives that could be easily identified as mythology Thus, before we can hope to find the basic features of the mythic consciousness that characterizes Eskimo culture, it will be necessary to widen the horizon of empirical facts by considering highlights of their cultic performances and an institution whose impact on the Eskimo culture can hardly be overemphasized, namely, shamanism. But first, let us discuss the relationship between their religion and ethics.

Such phenomena as the taboo conscience, infanticide before the child has been named (before he has become a full person), blood vengeance, the killing of the aged, exchange of wives, all of which are common or even traditionally required among the Eskimos, could suggest a complete lack of ethical behavior, that is, a way of life untouched by a religious consciousness. But such a conclusion would not only fail to take into account the difference between worldviews but also the all-important fact which is the sustenance of life.

A myth of the Nunamiut, who live as caribou hunters in northern Alaska, and who are relative newcomers to this area, summarizes the characteristic ideas quite well, although the main figure of the myth probably has been borrowed from the Indians (Gubser, 1965, pp. 29–32). A giant named *aiyagomahala* created their ancestors and taught them all the skills essential for survival. He instructed them also in the art of trading. One day *aiyagomahala* came to the Eskimos of Point Barrow, who invited him to their *karigi*. They gave him a whale skin and blubber. In return, he sent a large herd of caribou, then he left. After his return to his people, he taught them the use of the stone lamp,[5] and how to build a *karigi*. He also arranged trading connections between the inland and the coastal people. Before he left he told them to take care of one another.

This myth focuses on four points: Hunting skill, trade, the *karigi* and care for one another. At the same time, it presents them as aspects of one texture, the ultimate bond of which is care for one another. Such care was realized in times of scarcity, when game had to be distributed to all members of the group and not only to the hunter's own household and, in times of abundance, when generous gifts could be expected by everyone. The custom of adopting orphans, the special, protégés of the owners of the moon, or of *sila*, the force of the air and the weather, the praise of the protection of the weak as pious behavior in the legends, all point in the same direction. Thus, if it is true that legends at least touch the sphere of religion, the relation between religion and (ethical) behavior has to be understood as one of the basic conditions of Eskimo life, which transforms at least a good part of a formally magical mode of life into the stummering prayer of a struggling mankind. This, of course, does not concur with the justification of such actions as infanticide, even if the name-soul ideology offers a legitimate explanation and reason to do so, but it certainly removes them from the ethical judgment of a culture that exists under better conditions. As anthropologists we cannot look at man from the viewpoint of the zoologist, nor can we do it with the eyes,

5. The stone lamp was essential for all Eskimos, though some inland groups apparently gave it up because they did not have the necessary supply of blubber. They consequently had to endur the harsh winters in unheated huts.

of the moralist. We have to find our stance between the two extremes of neutral, but ultimately man-despising, and thus, misinterpreting observation and absolutist evaluation, which in the form of condemnation and mindless self-sufficiency equally leads to misapprehension and biased interpretation. Perhaps the words of an Eskimo woman, at the end of a series of instructions in the Christian religion, explains the Eskimo attitude toward life better than learned reflections: 'I have never doubted that there was a good God. Twice, in the excess of my suffering, I had cried with all my strength "there must somehow be someone who does not do evil. Where is he? May that One hear me". I thought of a powerful spirit, more powerful than the others, but good. I loved him without knowing who he was. I seemed to see him, I had such need of him' (Turquetil, 1929, p. 64).

2. BLADDER FEAST AND FALL CEREMONIAL

Apart from everyday performances such as hunting rituals, especially on the occasion of the first game and the year's first walrus, polar bear, and caribou, the observance of taboos, death rituals, and to a certain degree also the trading ceremonials, two feasts have to be mentioned that exhibit in larger context the beliefs and attitudes with which we have become acquainted so far. They are the Bladder Feast among the Yuit tribes in Alaska and the Fall Ceremonial, or Light Ritual, among the Inuit speaking Eskimos. The whale-cult, which included numerous and complicated rites, especially among Alaskan Eskimos, may be omitted here because of its highly specialized character. Its basic features are more or less identical with those found in the Bladder Festival.

Each year the bladders of all the animals killed in the hunts were saved (Birket-Smith, 1948, p. 210; Lantis, 1947, p. 53, ff). The bladder was believed to be the place where the 'owner' (*inua*) of the animal lived. During the festival, usually held in December, when the moon was full, the bladders were inflated, painted and hung in the ceremonial house. They were honored by food, songs, occasionally, by silence, mimic mask dances and dances with paddles, during which the participants formed different groups, each belonging to a certain animal. Such ceremonies were considered as carrying out instructions once given to a human hero by the 'spirits' of the animals. The feast reached its climax with all the bladders being submerged through a hole in the ice, and with the shaman asking for a successful hunt for the next year. Also returned to the sea were skulls and bones of the animals. In this sense the Bladder Feast may well be interpreted as a restoring act, that is, as a formal sacrifice on the part of man, so far as the idea of equilibrium is at stake. When those ceremonies were ended, the participants purified themselves with smoke or by taking a sweat-bath. An exchange of gifts was also part of the festival.

The Fall Ceremonial (Boas, 1888, p. 195 ff; Rasmussen, 1929, p. 123 ff) was held among the Central Eskimos in late fall, when nature became unfriendly again. At this time the spirits of the dead try to lay hold of people. Other spirits attack the dogs. And the shamans (*angakoq*) have much work to do. The worst spirits of all are *sedna* and her father, who dwell in the depth of the sea. It is the task of the most powerful *angakoq* to drive them away. This is done in a figurative ceremony, during which *sedna* is lured by a magic song to a 'seal's breathing hole' in the ceremonial hut. The main *angakoq* harpoons her, but finally she gets away by a desperate effort. This marks the beginning of the festival. But people still must be on their guard against her rage. They protect themselves by wearing small pieces of the first garment they wore after birth.

The next morning, after the community has been aroused by a group of men, the crowd divides into two parties: Those born in winter and those born during summer. In an open place they hold a tug of war with a rope of sealskin to determine whether good or bad weather will prevail during the subsequent period. The ceremony that follows is a libation ritual during which the participants, headed by the oldest man and woman, tell their name and place of birth. Afterward, two gigantic masked figures stalk out of a hut and approach the assembly. Their first task is to match men and women, who are to remain together as husband and wife for the following day and night. After that they invoke the good north wind, which brings fair weather and ask the south wind to stay away. By now, both figures are attacked and 'killed'. When the participants leave them to get their cups from the huts, the figures awake to a new life, and they are approached again. This time, however, they are not attacked, but men and women ask them about their respective futures. The day ends with a ball game.

Some modifications of the ceremony are to be noted among other groups. Instead of the shaman's harpooning ceremony, the two figures, masked as a man and a woman, perform a knife rite. During the libation ceremony everyone's thoughts turn to *sedna*, wishing for good. An exchange of gifts may be added. Among the inland groups the *sedna* ritual is replaced by the killing of the evil spirit of the deer. Among other groups the main task of the two masked figures consists in blowing out the fires, which have to be rekindled anew. It is also reported that all participants may disguise themselves. In respect to the exchange of wives, Birket-Smith remarks (1948, p. 183) that, in case of an impending catastrophe, this procedure is obligatory, probably because the change of identity confuses the evil forces.

Sedna, whose conjuration forms a highlight in the festival, plays an important role in the mind and shamanistic rituals of the Central Eskimo. One legend (Boas 1888, p. 229) describes her as an old man's daughter, who, after refusing all suitors, married a dog by whom she produced ten offspring, five human and five canine. When her father killed her husband she sent the dogs into his hut, and they gnawed off his feet and hands. In revenge, he threw her overboard when they were in a boat together. When she grasped at the edge of the craft, he cut off her fingers. As they fell, they turned into seals and whales. To escape the vengeance of her father she sent her children away. They became the forefathers of the Eskimos (the humans), the Europeans and other peoples (the dogs); a conclusion which on the one hand pays tribute to the vital function of the dog, while, on the other, may be interpreted as an expression of the integration of new data (the Europeans, etc.) into the established world of Eskimo tradition. As might be noticed, this integration does not lack a tint of ridicule.

In another version (Boas, 1888, p. 175 ff) *sedna*, who again refuses all suitors, falls in love with a fulmar, who leads her to believe that he lives in a very beautiful place. She goes with the seabird and immediately discovers the deception. In her troubles she sings for her father who comes and kills the fulmar. When they escape, the fulmar's brothers stir up the sea. *Sedna's* father, thinking only of saving himself, throws her overboard. But she grips the edge of the boat. The father cuts off her finger joints, which are transformed into whales, seals and groundseals. Then he takes her back into the boat. Ashore, *sedna* calls her dogs, which gnaw off the father's feet and hands. In his rage her father curses her. As a result the earth opens and swallows all of them. Since that time they live in the depths of the sea and in the land of the dead, where *sedna* reigns. In times of scarcity, the shaman has to pay her a visit and to cleanse her from the dirt and the impurity of sins (broken taboos) that have accumulated on her. Because of a huge fierce dog or of a cripple who wants to catch his soul (as he does with the passing dead), such a journey is very dangerous.

Although the *sedna* complex is not fully described or exhausted in these two accounts, enough is presented to make the Fall Ceremonial intelligible. Both the harpooning rite and the knife ritual refer to *sedna*. But while the first ceremony refers to the *sedna* myth and works as an act of protective magic (thus separating the rite from the rest of the performance), the knife ritual shows many signs of enacted recollection. In addition, the *sedna* myth continues through the rest of the ceremony. People 'keep her in their minds'. The myth thus forms an integral part of the whole festival, which mirrors the antagonism of the universe, in which day and night, good and evil spirits or forces, man and woman, life and death are interwoven.

3. SHAMANISM

A phenomenon that cannot be separated from the religious or symbolic life of the Eskimos is that of shamanism. Though the institution seems to fall outside the framework of a primitive culture, it nevertheless is one of its possibilities inasmuch as it may be interpreted as a socio-religious transformation of certain psycho-somatic conditions which characterize human nature. Indeed, shamanism among the Eskimos is basically marked as a primitive institution. As such it lacks a social superstructure with a distinctive independent and institutional development. This does not imply, however, that the role of the shaman and his impact on the symbolic stratification of the culture can be dismissed. On the contrary, the final analysis of Eskimo mythology will largely depend on the existence of this 'office'.[6]

A shaman (*angakoq* among the Central Eskimos, *tonralik* in Alaska) in the widest sense is a person (male or female), who has a helping spirit. Since various protective and helping spirits (*tunraq*) are gifted with different powers, no *anga-koq* or *tonralik* is equal to another. A first class of shamans consisted of those who

6. Since Paul Radin (1937) draws many of his conclusions regarding primitive religion from the shamanistic phenomenon in general and that of Eskimo shamanism in particular, some brief comments seem appropriate. For him Eskimo shamanism is a 'well integrated system' (p. 52 ff) designed to keep the contact with the supernatural exclusively in the hand of the angakok, and to manipulate and exploit the sense of fear of the ordinary man. Therefore 'it can be said that angakok as a thinker has adjusted himself completely to the attitude of his less sensitive fellow-tribesmen' (p. 54). That this tendency and others similar to it do exist cannot be denied. But to emphasize them to the extent to which Radin does implies a failure to appreciate the mythic dimension and the mythological 'environment' characteristic both of the shaman and his alleged 'victim'.

had a personal relationship to their spirit or spirits (Balicki, 1963, p. 380 ff) They were the real shamans who had a bright fire in their chest (Birket-Smith, 1948, p. 216) and who were able to make the shamanistic voyage to *sedna*; to the land of the bears; to *sila*. To the type of the *krilasoktoq* (also *qilalik*) belonged those (usually women) who were able to perform divination rituals by head lifting. No special training was necessary for them. Their helping spirits were often the benevolent ghosts of dead relatives. Finally, a third class was formed by the *angatkungaruks*, the lesser shamans. Their helping spirits were not strong and were only able to perceive the whereabouts of evil forces.

The shamans did not form secret societies, nor were there clear boundaries between them and other people. Special power (*suungan* in Alaska) could be acquired by everyone. This does not exclude the fact that some individuals tried firmly to control their community. If they went too far, however, it was quite possible that they would be killed by the group or by competing shamans. At any rate, shamans themselves distinguished between true shamans, i.e., between people who gained their shamanistic function because they were gifted by nature, and those who relied chiefly on the effectiveness of tricks. As Rasmussen (1929, pp. 54–55) reports: 'We shamans of the interior have no special spirit language and believe that the real shamans do not need it. . . A real shaman does not jump about the floor and do tricks, nor does he seek help by the aid of darkness, by putting out the lamps, to make the minds of his neighbors uneasy. For myself, I do not think that wisdom or knowledge about things that are hidden can be sought in that manner. True wisdom is only to be found far away from the people, out in the great solitude, and it is not found in play but only through suffering. Solitude and suffering open the human mind, and therefore a shaman must seek his wisdom there.'

The vocation of a shaman was basically a matter of the spirits, that is of *sila*, the comprehensive power of the universe itself. Being aware of his new status through a dream or a vision, the candidate usually joined older shamans who instructed him for several (up to 15) years. The famous case of Igjugarjuk, as reported by Rasmussen (1929, p. 55 ff), may serve as an example. When everyone knew that Igjugarjuk should become a shaman because of his dreams, his father-in-law, who was a shaman himself, took care of him. He brought the young man into a small, isolated snow but. Here he had to stay for 30 days, and was allowed to drink only a mouthful of warm water after 5 days, and then again after 15 days. Only when the next 10 days were over was he permitted to eat again.

During all this time there was only one thought in his mind, that *pinga* (the moon god, or *sila*) should take possession of him and own him. Toward the end, a white woman, whom he often saw from then on in his dreams, was sent to him by *pinga*. 'She came to me from Pinga and was a sign that Pinga had now noticed me and would give me powers that would make me a shaman.'

Though the vocation of a shaman is a personal matter or event, his role or function is basically a public one. He participates in and leads the public ceremonies. The curing of a patient is also public to the extent that an audience participates and supports the shaman by songs and answers. Similarly, his lonely walks through ice and snow, during which he waited to be seen by *sila* and instructed about the future, or his journeys to *sedna*, to the moon, and elsewhere, during which his body lay in trance, are made in the interest of a household or of the whole community. During his flight to *sedna* in times of trouble, for instance, the audience had to stay with his body, while his soul encountered all the dangers of the trip in order to contact and appease the mighty goddess and to ask her to release the animals. A public confession of broken taboos ended the ceremony after his return (Rasmussen, 1929, p. 123 ff). On the other hand, there have been divination ceremonies, which by the sound of the shaman's drum and the darkness of the hut or tent turned into trickery ending in a general jugglery. Nevertheless, it seems that the Eskimos themselves were highly aware of the difference between shamanism as part of the community life (the transition between symbolic and magical attitudes being fluid) and black magic, where shamanistic power was used for destructive purposes.

Loneliness under extreme conditions, together with a strong concentration on its meaning, apparently is to be regarded as an element of Eskimo culture which can properly be called the feature of reflection.[7] Especially Rasmussen's reports show ample proof of this feature of reflection. When an Eskimo from Alaska, for example, tells us (1926, p. 506) that the old ones offered themselves up because of the equilibrium of the universe and for infinite and unfathomable things, one might believe that he was hearing one of the Chinese sages. An Eskimo's remarks on seeing New York might remind one of Sophocles remarks on the power of man: 'Nature or Sila, the world, and the universe which the shamans believed to keep in order, is great. But are not men greater?' (Rasmussen,

---

7. The reflective, meditative aspect of Eskimo culture is not necessarily pro-shamanistic. In at least one case a man is known who was, as Oswalt (1967, p. 224 f) describes him, 'an anti-shaman, an iconoclast, and a non-believer in supernatural powers'.

1927, p. 387). Another reflected: 'Why must there be snow and storms and bad weather for hunting, for us, who must hunt for our daily food, who seek meat for ourselves and those we love?... Why must my old sister suffer pain at the end of her days?... Even you cannot answer when we ask you why life is as it is. And so it must be. Our customs all come from life and are directed toward life; we cannot explain, we do not believe this or that; but the answer lies in what I have just told you. We fear! We fear the elements ... cold and famine and sickness ... Not death, but the suffering. We fear the souls of the dead, of human and animal alike. We fear the spirits of earth and air. And therefore our fathers, taught by their fathers before them, guarded themselves with all these old rules and customs, which are built upon the experience and knowledge of generations... We do not know how or why, but we obey them that we may be suffered to live in peace. And for all our angakoks and their knowledge of hidden things, yet we know so little that we fear everything else' (Rasmussen, 1929, p. 55 ff).

The importance of taking this reflective consciousness into consideration can be illustrated if we examine a statement such as 'no bears have come because of the absence of ice, and there is no ice because of too much wind, and (there is) too much wind because men offended the powers' (Weyer, 1932, p. 241). Taken literally, this statement is a syllogistic expression of a magic mind. Except for the final premise it is consistent and in accord with the facts. In the light of a consciousness, however, that is aware of the conditioned character of customs and traditions, this final premise must, perhaps, not be interpreted as a mistaken reality, but as the recognition of a relationship between man and *sila*, in whose absolute symbolism such statements begin to make sense. What seems to be magical – i.e., a misapprehension of reality by taking its substitutes for real – turns out to be an expression of wisdom which has experienced and understood that meaning and absurdity remain the permanent confrontation of human beings. 'And so it must be.'

Although they were accustomed to reflection, there are no indications that the Eskimo shamans broke through the mythological boundaries of their culture by systematizing its various aspects, i.e., by developing a theory of the symbolic conditions of man and world. In this respect they are of no help to the present analysis. We can only conjecture what the basic patterns of this mythological boundaries are. But since the conduct of life itself is framed by and framing the myth of its being while it contains the mythic consciousness of a culture at least in its lived ideas, which are indeed adequate symbols of human uncertainties,[8] it should be possible to gain a reflective understanding of these ideas and their respective mythology if we view them as the expressions of a human situation.

4. ESKIMO MYTHOLOGY

If we summarize the symbolic data gathered thus far, we can categorize them as follows: (1) The Eskimos use charms (amulets, songs, formulas, fetishes, medicines, and destructive substances when performing black magic)[9] and follow traditional rules (taboos) as a part of the maintenance of life. Although the magical element seems to be predominant in this behavior, personal and supplicant aspects cannot be completely dismissed. (2) The world is populated by ghosts, spirits, legendary dwarfs, giants, and numerous other beings. They are addressed by the shamans with various degrees of intensity (conjuration, divination, protection, supplication). (3) The ceremonies show the everyday world of the ordinary man and the world of the shaman interrelated in an operational texture of actions and reactions. Its comprehensive aspect seems to be manifest in the idea of *sila*. (4) Interfering with these three aspects of the symbolic world is the idea that everything has its 'owner' or *inua*, 'its man' (*inua* expresses the third possessive person of *inuk*, man, person; Birket-Smith, 1948, p. 205). The most important of the owners mentioned were either *sedna*, the owner of the sea animals, or *silap inua*, the owner of *sila*, the owner of the universe, of air, weather, and intelligence. (5) The idea of the soul remains unclear. Is it the owner of the body, which in addition has its own life potentialities? Although Birket-Smith assumes that soul (*tarneq*) and *inua* are two different phenomena, a concept like that of a lost soul and the association of the soul with man's shadow and breath seem to indicate an affirmative answer to our question (1948, p. 206; see also Hultkrantz, 1962, p. 373).

8. See Lantis (1950, p. 319). Lived ideas are not so much expressive beliefs as they are their basis or ground. As beliefs they may be (Lantis says 'perhaps') symbols of such uncertainties, depending on the reflective attitude toward them. But as lived ideas they form part of life's integral totality and are synonymous with the truth of life as articulated in its very continuation.

9. Woman also use tattoos on the chin, cheeks, above the eyebrows, the breasts, the arms and legs (Birket-Smith, 1948, p. 156). In Alaska the community occasionally was subdivided into a group that was associated with 'things of dead people' and another that was connected with 'things of women in childbirth and menstruating women' (Oswalt, 1967, p. 218).

The question that arises from this texture of lived ideas is that of their inner connection and consistency, including the problem of God and the specific meaning of the idea of God within this framework. Usually these questions are indirectly answered by the mythological narratives about the beginning. In the case of the Eskimos, all reports agree that creation myths or cosmic myths are relatively rare, if not entirely absent. The world is simply there. This experience seems so overwhelming that one feels no need to ask how it came into being. Only in Alaska have creative motifs, which probably go back to the Indians, been adopted and developed (Oswalt, 1967, p. 210 ff). Even then they are usually confined to actions of a limited scope and do not describe universal events in the unlimited beginning. Thus we must first understand why the Eskimos lack creation myths; and then we must try to determine the context of the ideas already mentioned, interpreting them within this context. If we follow these two lines of reasoning, it can be hoped that they will lead us by mutual clarification and verification to a concept of Eskimo mythology. The fact that creation myths could be adopted at all is at least an indication that the idea of creation is not altogether alien to Eskimo mentality.

The basic experience that leads man to the conception of myths is above all his 'being-there'. It is the experience of a presence in which he and things are or become real and distinct while witnessing at the same time their intricate togetherness. This experience is complicated and its awareness necessarily obscured insofar as it anticipates in a certain sense the encounter with this presence and the possibility of this encounter. This implies that man relies already upon the mythic condition when he forms the first sound of meaning. In this sense we can say that the mythic is *a priori* and indispensable. It precedes its imaginative or reflective transformation and evaluation into narratives or conceptual explanations of the world, or the sustension of its meaning in rituals and cult. In order to understand a certain culture as a typical emergence of mankind, we therefore have to seek the special circumstances or modality of man's 'being-there'. In the case of the Eskimos we are more or less immediately caught by the arctic conditions of their environment. It is the world of ice and snow, of endless waters and bare lands, of a clear distinction between the dwelling place and the open. It is a world in which the dependence of life upon life is more clearly expressed than anywhere else. And despite the changing seasons it is a world of great statics.

But though this consideration may produce an emotional empathy, it hardly allows for a convincing theory if no definite signs can be found to indicate how the Eskimos themselves responded to their world. It seems that we can find such a sign if we try to see the same world together with the language by which it has been articulated. As Birket–Smith explains, one of the most characteristic features of Eskimoan is its tendency to connect word with word, to change and modify the meaning of a word by enlarging it through suffixes (1948, p. 86 ff). As in the art of the Eskimos (1948, p. 178), element is added to element without transferring them into distinctive unities: The language emphasizes extension rather than intension. This appears especially in the word *uvanga*, 'I'. Literally translated it means 'here-mine', 'here is what concerns me'. Returning to the experiences of presence and the present as that which lies at the root of the mythological process, we are justified in distinguishing between a 'being-there' modality that is intensive and thus stresses presence and the present with regard to its depth in time, and another modality that is extensive and emphasizes the spatial character of the world. While an intensive modality is congenially received by a mythology that can trace things back to actions that stand at the beginning, an extensive modality points to the comprehensive character of presence and the present. The past as such does not primarily matter, since it is the extended texture of the 'now', the equilibrium of forces, that counts. Moreover, while the intensive mode of experience, according to its very nature, turns our attention to the becoming (or growing) of the 'now', the extensive mode can be expected to emphasize the having, or possession, of the 'now'.

If we accept this speculative distinction between intensive and extensive presence-experience and presuppose that the latter, as suggested by language, is indeed the predominant modality in which the Eskimos encounter world and being,[10] the symbolic data begin to appear in a new light. Especially the idea of an owner can now be understood as that mythological category, in which the comprehensive meaning of man's presence experience becomes intelligible as the hypostatic expression of an otherwise indefinite perception of existence. It is the 'owner' who concretizes the all-at-once so that orientation becomes possible. This distinction also shows that the Western concept of soul belongs to a type of mythology diametrically opposed to a mythology that emphasizes extension

10. In order to avoid too much of a constructive application of the two modalities we have to realize that both spring from one and the same source, i.e., man in his world. For this reason, we can except that any mythology participates in both modalities, giving the one preponderance over the other. If Webster's etymology of the English personal pronoun 'I' is right (Indo-European base *eĝ(h)om*: probably meaning '(my) presence here'), we have here an example of a shift from an extensive to an intensive mode of experiencing presence and the present.

rather than intension as the basic experience which structures the respective world-picture. Moreover, the lack of 'historic efficacy' which is mentioned by A. Hultkrantz (1962, p. 368) as a typical feature of Eskimo culture, can be understood in a similar way as an inherent condition of this type of mythology in which the static and timeless 'now' of the symbolic figures (Carpenter, 1956, p. 1 ff) becomes conceivable as the medium of their existence. This does not imply that the Eskimo mythology is undramatic. The antagonism of the present and the self-alienation of nature in sustaining life are, within the setting of comprehensive extension, analogues to such decisive events as creation and the origin of culture, which characterize an intensive view of man and world. In this sense the idea of an equilibrium in the universe, expressed by the antagonism of elements and owners, becomes revelant as a polar completion and interpretation of the myth-giving experience of 'being-there' and not simply as the conclusion of shamanistic reflections. Finally, we can say that a narrative, with the tendency to actualize the depth of time, must be alien to a 'mythology' that is rooted in an experience dominated by the mode of extension rather than intension. The tales of dwarfs, giants, half-humans, legendary beings and powerful heros which abound among the Eskimos and which reflect more the ups and downs of the present landscape than the decisive events of the beginning can consequently be interpreted as a kind of synthesis between a mythology of intensive narration, where the flux of the narrative mirrors that of time itself, and that of extensive awareness, where words must be understood as the almost simultaneously present abbreviations of unfinished sentences.

Among the Central and Greenland Eskimos the most important figure of everyday life is *sedna*, the Old Woman, or the Lovely and Glorious Lady. She is the owner of the mammals, and if she is offended by the sins of men, she closes the ocean. This description of *sedna* reflects a clear and distinct notion. And since it is the shaman who derives spiritual as well as social advantage from it, we may presume that his reflective work has left its imprint on the original myth. Indeed, the distinctness ceases when we compare the *sedna*- myth with other figures and with the customs of other groups.

According to the reports collected by Boas (1888, p. 175 ff) *sedna* is occasionally considered as a good spirit, who gives both seals and deer, though in other accounts she hates the deer. We also hear that *sedna* or *sanaq* had lived on earth but ascended to the moon (*takaq*). According to the common version the genesis of the moon has to be seen as the result of a fight between sister and brother, which broke out when he abused her. Both were lifted up and became sun and moon. Now it is the brother and now the sister who is associated or identified with the moon. (In Alaska tales are reported that trace the genesis of the two heavenly bodies back to the intervention of the Raven; Oswalt, 1967, p. 212 ff).

In another version, *anguta, sedna*'s father, created the earth, the sea, and the heavenly bodies, while his daughter made the animals and vegetables. Accordingly she is a protective divinity and supplications are addressed to her. In the west and also in eastern Greenland, it is the moon, that is, the one who has his dwelling there, who is the lord of all animals (Thalbitzer, 1952, p. 40 ff; Hultkrantz, 1962, p. 378 ff). He is insulted by the breaking of taboos. In Alaska the moon is represented by a huge mask that hangs in the ceremonial house. It is now interesting to note that the same figure exists among the Central Eskimos as the *tornaq* of the *gaggim*, the owner of the dancing house, whose touch may be deadly (Boas, 1688, pp. 189, 228).

The ambivalence between 'below' and 'above' (even the happy land of the deceased is now below, and now above), between man and woman (the moon-person is now female, now male), continues in the polarity between sea and land: The Pacific Eskimos knew *imam-shua*, the owner of the sea animals, and *nunam-shua*, the owner of the land animals. According to the Caribou Eskimos, *pinga*, the Caribou Mother, was not only the owner of the reindeer but also of all land animals. She lived, like *sila*, somewhere in the universe, but nobody knew where (Rasmussen, 1930, p. 48 ff). In Labrador the Eskimos believed in a male owner of the sea and a female owner of the land animals. The owner of the land animals was thought of as a giant caribou or as a white bear.

If we synthesize these various aspects, which could easily be multiplied, they show a clear interrelation, with a strong tendency toward functional identity and substitution respectively. The mythological concept that agrees most with this idea of a functional identity and substitution as expressed for instance by figures such as *sedna*, the Moon, the Caribou Mother, is *sila* (also *hila* among the Inuit; *sla, tla* among the Yuit). According to Thalbitzer (1928, p. 390 ff), the word *sila* covers such phenomena as the open space in front of tne house, air, weather, storm, wind, world and also intelligence and cleverness. A person that is wise, for instance, has *sila*. Similarly the vision that proves the vocation of the shaman is supported by *sila*. Like everything else, *sila* has also his, her, or its, *inua*, though *silap inua* and *sila*, i.e., the owner and what is owned, largely coincide. *Silap inua*, whose sex is usually undetermined, is responsible for good and bad weather.

He wants man to observe the rules of existence. Like the moon, who may be considered as the 'eye of the world' (Marah, 1954, p. 29) or of *sila*, he is the protector of orphans, whom he may endow with special power. Occasionally *sila* is identified with wind and snowstorm, with sun and weather.

If we accept the words of one of Rasmussen's shamans (1927, p. 386), the idea of *sila* or *silap inua* can be summarized as follows: There is a power, called *sila*. No simple words can describe this wonderful spirit. Only through the forces that frighten man can *sila* be heard, but he may reveal himself also through sunshine, a calm sea or through playing children. In good times and as long as man does not abuse life, *sila*, whom no one has seen, retreats to his infinite void. His dwelling place is so mysterious that he is away and present at once.

Though this explanation of *sila* clearly shows the work of a strong reflective mind, the basic ideas fit into the whole of Eskimo religion and close the circle of symbolic and myth-becoming or myth-making behavior, in which fear is not only one emotion among others but the medium in which the world of the mythic makes contact with the present world under the premise of a comprehensive presence. As among other pre-reflective cultures and peoples, the world of the factual is immediately associated with the meaning of being-there. The style of this association works as the myth that animates a culture in its function and task to sustain life and to bestow duration upon the transmission of its elements. While such associations are elsewhere concentrated and personalized in the God who created heaven and earth in the beginning, the Eskimos accomplish their association by differentiating the 'now-and-there' and correlating it in the idea of owners. Consequently, everything has its owner: Man, the animals, and also stones and places, sleep and dream, and above all, the universe and its intelligence. Thus a lived myth pays its respect to the drama of life by rules that are followed and rites that are performed. It is significant in this context that the Eskimos honor the *inue* (owners) of rapids and big stones with a silent sacrifice. Similarly, the idea that the owners experience reincarnation and that the rituals prepare and reflect this process becomes understandable as a rational inconsistency, by which a basic insight is meta-rationally confirmed. Finally, the *sila*concept confines and releases in the light of the human – only man 'has' – the various aspects of the universe in the totality of its mythic foundation, giving them the inner coordination that is vital for all cultural life.

In summary, we may say that the world in which the Eskimos live and that seemed at first a magic and more or less depersonalized world, turns out to be a cosmos that, in the image of man, reveals everywhere the signs of this image because it mirrors, though not a highest or first being, a comprehensive reality whose first and foremost symbol is no other than man himself. *Sedna*, the Moon, the Caribous Mother, and even *sila* become identified moments in the myth-giving extension that prevails in the intervals of such concretizations. The distance between man (as he appears) and the foundation of his being (as he longs for) is effected, maintained and mediated through the lived myth that turns such figures into beings which are open and responsive to man and human behavior. The idea that, strictly speaking, man and world have not been created, is counteracted by a consciousness which knows that both man and world are owned. In this we may see the essence of Eskimo life and existence.

6

Three Facets of Primitive Religions

In the previous two chapters an attempt has been made to describe the religious situation of two most divergent paradigms of primitive cultures. Though dealing with many details in an abbreviated form only, we nevertheless were guided by the intention to get hold of the whole situation. We wanted to get as comprehensive a picture as possible. In this chapter we will shift our interest from emphasizing as we might also say, the correlation between culture and religion to paying attention to certain facets of religion in primitive cultures. While recognizing the fundamental significance of the correlation between culture and religion we will not set it into prominence. Instead we will concentrate on the tension between heaven and earth as it becomes apparent in the tradition of Asian Negritos, on the universalization of totemic ideas in Australia, and on the awareness of 'self-love' and 'doom' in the religion of one of the all too many dissolving cultures in Eastern Brazil.

1. THE TWO WORLDS OF THE ASIAN NEGRITOS

The Negritos, previously mentioned as the most significant among the Asian gatherers (see above, p. 81) can (or could) be found in the Philippines (the Aëta), on Great and Little Andaman (the Andaman Islanders) and in Malaya (the Semang). Although their development was interrupted by various migrations in Southeast Asia, through which their present culture was shaped, foreign influences were not strong enough to destroy the basic features of their nomadic or semi-nomadic life. Even in the social and religious field, where the differences that developed among these three groups are most evident, basic similarities have been preserved (cf. Nippold, 1936; Cooper, 1940).

A number of valuable monographs have been written on the religion of the

Negritos that offer sufficient data for a comprehensive study.[1] But since it is not our intention to cover here the religious life of these groups in its entirety, only the general traits of the Negrito religion will be outlined, with special emphasis on some of the mythological and cultic patterns of the Semang.[2] But first some introductory remarks on the economic and social situation of the Negritos are in order.

The economic life of the Negritos, which is based on gathering natural food resources, changes in accordance with the specific conditions of their environment. Apart from the gathering of vegetables, which underlies their economy in general, fishing dominates in the Philippines. The Andaman Islanders practiced both fishing and hunting[3] depending on the location (seashore or interior) of the group. For hunting, the Semang today use the blowpipe, which replaces the traditional bow and arrow. They add only smaller animals to their diet.

Apparently none of the groups ever developed a typical hunter's mentality. Only the Aëta groups are known to associate the godhead with the hunt and to express this attitude by presenting a piece of the heart and liver to the Lord of the thunder, or to the Forest itself.

Since class differences and the subordination of one of the sexes have not developed, men and women have equal rights and the process of production

1. The Andaman Islanders, who today are either extinct or, as on Little Andaman, on the verge of extinction, have been described mainly by E. H. Man (1932), A. R. Radcliff-Brown (1933), and Lidio Cipriani (1963). The main sources for the religion of the Aëta, who are the most numberous of these groups, are M. Vanoverbergh (1925–30, 1937–38), J. M. Garvan (1964), P. Schebesta (1957). The religion of the Semang Negritos, who have been the most thoroughly investigated of all groups, is reported mainly in the works of H. V. Stevens (1892), W. Skeat (1900), I. H. N. Evans (1937). P. Schebesta (1957).

2. There are two reasons why special emphasis is laid upon the Semang religion. 1) Since many religious ideas of non-primitive cultures have been assimilated especially among these groups, the transformative process that took place reveals basic patterns of primitivity in the manner upon which the cultural substratum has been functionally integrated. 2) The Semang offer one of those examples which have often been cited as a 'proof' for a people without religion. For instance, J. de Morgan (1885, p. 13) writes: 'Les Négritos de Pérak n'ont pas de religion. ... Quelques auteurs ont dit que les Sakeyes croyaient aux esprits. Ce fait est faux; les vrais Négritos n'ont point de superstitions.' This and similar statements are many. One reason for this is obviously the fact that primitive cultures do not recognize sharp boundaries between the various aspects of life. As Radcliffe-Brown (1933, p. 405) puts it in respect to the Andamans: 'It is not possible, in the Andamans, to separate a definite entity which we can call religion from things that may more appropriately be regarded as art, morality, play, or social ceremonial'. Combined with a superficial acquaintance, this certainly accounts for many 'myths' about 'Primitive Man'.

3. The most important animal that is the object of hunting is the wild boar, *sus andamensis*, which was probably imported, along with pottery, by a farming culture 3000 years ago.

follows the natural division of labor. The men are chiefly responsible for hunting and fishing, while the women take care of the children, the collecting of fruits and other food. But men may also turn toward gathering, depending on the circumstances. The erection of the hut or the shelter involves both sexes.

The basic social unit is the local group, which consists of several related families which own its territory. The group is headed by an eldest member, who is the first among equals. An individual with special skills and leadership may take over some of the functions of the eldest. Each family is autonomous and has its own shelter, under which its members prepare meals and sleep. The shelters may be so constructed that they form separate enclosures under one huge circular roof. The use of the same common language is the basis for whatever 'tribal' consciousness exists. Occasional gatherings of several groups serve religious and entertainment purposes, without special political implications. Marriages are usually monogamous, although divorce is frequent. One way to take care of orphans or displaced children is through adoption. Strong laws of avoidance allow only for exogamic marriages. The marriages themselves are usually based on mutual sympathy and affection. As in any other society the love spell is frequently used to prompt such feelings. The best guarantee for maintaining the social order is provided by the religious traditions, which are simple, yet effective.

1.1 *General Traits of the Religion of the Negritos*

The religious traditions are basically determined by the consciousness of a supreme reality (being), which is called upon by such names as *puluga, bilika, tara, daria* among the Andaman Islanders; *apo katawan, apo kilad, abog, tolan dian* among the Aëta; and *taped'n, karei, keto, moltek* among the Semang. This supreme being is associated with the sun (light) and especially with the thunder, which, as its hypostatic appearance, occasionally is identified with the godhead itself. There are basically two worlds, the world of mortal men (*orang mati*) and the world of the immortals (*orang hidop*). The *orang hidop* are invisible divine beings, although they blend or even identify themselves with visible phenomena such as thunder, trees, flowers, places, insects. Despite many traits that are similar to those of the *orang hidop*, the godhead suprasses them all in its almighty power and strength.

Taboos and ethical laws are sanctioned by the godhead, who, as among the Pygmies, is merged also in the culture hero and the first man.

Besides the more 'negative' contact with the other world as established by the various taboos, a 'positive' contact is found in the person of the medicine man (shaman) or priest. He heals, or even destroys, with the help and power of divine beings, by means of a crystal given to him by the godhead.[4] When he dies he becomes a son of god. To contact the divine world, the medicine man must return to the region whence he came, that is, to the world of dreams. He then becomes one of the *éenoi*, the *orang hidop* who populate the regions beneath the godhead.

The bones of the deceased are considered powerful among the Andamans and some Aëta groups and are carried around by the people. The land of the deceased, who live far away in a large country full of fruit trees, can be reached over the rainbow bridge. Hence, the rainbow is a greatly feared sign of the other world.

It seems that the 'needs' for magic are mainly met by the medicine man. Apart from the various magic and semi-magic customs that form part of his functions, magic seems to be confined to the use of amulets and ornaments, that are applied to the body and to various bamboo instruments. Such bamboo ornaments occasionally work by representing mythological events. In comparison with the Indonesian population, we are told however, that there is an 'almost total lack of superstition and magic (Vanoverbergh, 1925-30, p. 157). The idea that a bird or birds play a role in the origin of man points to a kind of class totemism, although no special development of totemistic relations seems to have taken place.

1.2 *The Mythology of the Semang Negritos*

From a comparative point of view, the Semang mythology shows a clear influence of many elements of Indonesian and Hindu mythology (see Skeat, 1900, p. 85 ff; Schebesta, 1957, II, p. 116 ff). However, to be operative this influence pre-supposes certain conditions on the side of the one who receives. The one who gives can do so only if there is someone else capable of accepting. There must be a predisposition on the part of the receiver. That such a predisposition existed and still prevails becomes clear if we consider some of the basic features of Semang mythology. In line with the generative character of their tradition, Semang mythology must not be equated with a rationally balanced and stabilized system

---

4. This crystal is a mysterious stone which either is implanted in the chest of the shaman by the godhead, or which by divine guidance can be found in certain plants.

of mythological narratives. As in case of the Bambuti Pygmies it shows its consistency in the dynamics that connects the narratives with one another and within themselves.

One of the main mythological *figures* is *karei*, the thunder (see Evans, 1937, p. 138 ff; Schebesta, 1957, II, p. 110 ff). But *karei* is also the sun, which produces the thunder. Thus he is the thunderer and the thunder at once. Besides *karei* there are his servants, that is, his wife and his sons. Together with all the other divine or semidivine beings (*ćenoi*) they live in the sky where they eat the fruits from the heavenly trees. The seeds and peels that fall down to earth become fruit trees for men. *Karei*'s wife is *manoij*, who lives below the surface of the earth. They unite in the lightning flash. Their children are *taped'n, begreg* and *takel*. *Karei* has made everything, the animals, the plants, and finally man.

In another account it is *taped'n* (elsewhere the mediator between God and man) who is responsible for all creation. *Taped'n o'de semuá* – Taped'n made everything.' *Karei* is considered as somewhat evil because he demands the sacrifice of man's blood if he trespasses his law. *Taped'n* and *karei* may exchange roles, though it seems that *karei* in his role as the thunder-hypostasis of the godhead is, historically, a later substitute; the tendency indicated here is typical in the Semang mythology. Without going into further details, the narratives on *taped'n, karei* and the other members of the divine family can be summarized as follows. There is a strong awareness of the mythic origin of all things. Yet like the godhead itself, who may assume many shapes, none of the mythological figures can be fixed. They substitute and replace each other without altering the fact that the world as it exists is the result of events that are taking place in an eternal mode and that give meaning to heaven and earth even before such meaning is predicated. Thus, it is easy for *karei* or *taped'n* to ascend to heaven and find wives there; to come down to earth and kidnap the two daughters of *agag*, the crow, to obtain wives; or to become associated with the sun and the moon, or with insects, flowers, rocks. The decisive events take place on an already existing earth that nevertheless is created by the mythological beings. Ultimately, however, nobody has seen the immortal God, who sees everything.

This tension between heaven and earth, the visible and the invisible, the identical (sun, moon, thunder, trees) and the nonidentical (*karei, taped'n, manoij, takel*, who associate with or turn into one another) points to the ineffability of the divine by means of figurative accounts. But it is also expressed in the distinction between the language of man and the *lingua sacra* of the *ćenoi*.

The latter is the language used by the *hala* (shaman, medicine man, priest) during cult performances in which he contacts the divine world. To the extent that he is a *hala*, man himself is a part of the world of the *ćenoi*, who are headed by *taped'n* the greatest of all *halas* (*taped'n* is *keto*, the light itself, whose eyes are sun and moon).

Many detailed accounts are woven into this general texture of a mythic consciousness. We hear about the creation of the earth from an immense ocean, upon which *ya laning* (*manoij*, the tortoise) was swimming. We become aware of how *terhob'm*, the dung beetle, brought the earth out of the slime; how various animals (which are, of course, powerful *halas*) shape the earth; and how *karei* and his brother *taped'n*, disappeared into the sky, leaving behind them the *Batu'Rib'm*, a lonely single mountain, which connects the heavens with the earth, for it actually is the navel of the earth. The mythological accounts connected with the *Batu'Rib'm* are manifold.[5] They cover motifs extending from the origin of water from the rainbow to the belief that the mountain one day could collapse. Such an event would be the beginning of a universal catastrophe. At the moment, however, it is kept in order, and with it the whole universe with all its cycles of life by the *hala dalog'n*.

The origin of man, though as certain as the origin of the world, is not described in any well-defined way. Some accounts tend to identify the two brothers on the mythic sea with a brother and sister who procreate the various (Semang) peoples. Today, however, these two beings have changed into a mountain with two peaks. Changing into various figures is believed to be one of the faculties of a *hala*, that is, of the godhead. Another chain of mythic legends tells about the emergence of man from fruits. *Taped'n* and *manoij* descend to the earth. *Manoij* dreams about a child. *Taped'n* gives her a fruit, which turns into the baby boy *capong* (rhinoceros bird). The same thing happens again. The baby girl is *paig*, the tortoise. Both become the ancestors of men, who are the grandchildren of *taped'n*.

The replacement of the fruit with a figure of clay formed by *taped'n* points toward a further mythic conception, the emergence of man from rocks and stones. These originators (ancestors) are also the culture heroes.

The complementary conceptions of God and man, the *orang hidop* and the

---

5. Although it is not as impressive, the *Batu' Rib'm* can be easily compared with the Shiprock Peak near Gallup, New Mexico, which has played a similar role in the mythology of the adjacent peoples.

orang mati, man and wife, power and weakness, man and animals (the latter were once human beings) finds its expression in various myths. Besides their etiological function, they indicate that the underlying, paideumatic experience of the Semang is chiefly associated with and dominated by the life of plants, namely, of fruit trees. Even the origin of fire is occasionally linked to the origin of plant life, even though it is commonly believed to descend from an animal (culture hero). Finally, however, this paideuma is fostered by the immediate connection of the world of man and that of the *orang hidop*, a connection of which man is reminded by the voice of thunder. The significance of thunder is particularly expressed in the sacrifice of blood and the pano celebration.

1.3 *Blood Sacrifice and Pano Ritual*

The lasting answer-in-action that completes and maintains the divine creation and its inherent order if it has been disturbed, is the sacrifice of blood (Stevens, 1892; Skeat, 1900, p. 204; Evans, 1937, p. 180 ff; Schebesta, 1957, II, p. 78 ff). If a member of the group has been killed by a tiger, or more often, if a thunderstorm passes the camp, man is reminded of his duty. If he should not listen to this reminder and be oblivious of the required ritual, it would be disastrous for the entire world. The sacrifice is usually carried out by a woman who has transgressed one of the divine laws or taboos. In her action she represents the whole community. If the thunderstorm lingers, or in the case of a death by a tiger, other women and also the men join the ceremony.

The person in question cuts both legs with a knife or bamboo splinter and tries to catch the blood as it flows down into a bamboo container, where it mingles with water. Some of this mixture is poured to the ground with the words: 'Go to the earth, go to *manoij*.' The rest is cast toward the angry sky or the sun with the words: 'Go to the sun; go away; *karei*, it is enough, I do not have any further debt.' Besides these abbreviated formulas there are also fuller invocations: '*Ye*, Grandmother *manoij*, go to heaven and tell your grandsons *karei* and *taped'n* that I pay my debt.' Or: '*Ye*, there below, I cast my debt to *ped'n*, I pay, I am not presumptious.' Or: 'I pay my debt, *Ye*, *ped'n*, take it away, I pay.' Or: 'I present blood for the sun. Let it be enough. Stop it!'

The debt in question refers to various taboos that have been disregarded. The taboos themselves chiefly reflect the mythological texture as associated with birds, animals, insects, plants.

The blood is accepted by the godhead, but it is not a gift for *taped'n*. Rather, it flows to an underground lake where *manoij* lives. From there it nourishes the fruit trees and supports their growth and fertility.

Although this sacrifice seems to be performed as a protective measure against the thunderstorm, to interpret it this way is to miss its proper meaning: The recognition of the godhead and the world as narrated by myth; and the restoration of an inflicted order, which otherwise would cause a diminution of fertility. This does not mean, however, that the ceremony may not approximate a magic ritual, especially if it lacks the mythic background in its entirety, as is the case among the neighboring Senoi. With them, it is not the act that counts, but its correct performance. The Semang themselves occasionally try to ward off the thunderstorm by blowing and whistling against the angry sky and by wearing protective amulets.

An indication that a cosmic interpretation of this sacrifice is correct is given in the taboo of the leech. This creature is taboo because it is considered a messenger of the godhead sent to bleed man, thus making human blood a part of the mythology as such.

A second performance that sheds light on the entire religious scene is the *pano* ritual. The celebration itself takes place only occasionally, and it is centered at the conical *pano* hut, built by the women at the edge of the camp.

In preparation, the participants, including women and children, decorate themselves with colors, verdure, and flowers. After sunset the *Hala*[6] and his assistant enter the *pano* hut carrying fire and incense. In analogy to the mythic accounts, the incense cloud will carry the *hala* to the heavens.

As soon as the two men have entered the hut they begin to sing. As Evans (1937, p. 194) describes it, 'sounds of grunting, whistling, growling, shouting,

---

6. Although the *hala* institution belongs to the general complex of Indonesian shamanism, many differences can be noted. The kind of spirits (*ćenoi*) with whom the *hala* works is largely different. He acts in the name and power of God, who is his and the *ćenoi*'s father. The *ćenoi* themselves are the servants, the messengers, and grandchildren of the godhead, who support him. He is not the master of these friendly beings, but one of them, who has been chosen by the godhead. Thus, the mythic beings and lastly God himself work rather through him than he through them. Beside the animistic and magic constituents, a theistic component is most typical and essential for the Semang *hala*. The *hala*, who serves his community as priest and mediator – as the Semang say, 'we do not know how to pray, only the *hala* does' – does not stress this position to gain a social status. Rather, he tries to keep it a secret. It is only after his death, when his soul goes straight to *taped'n* and when he turns into a *ćenoi*-tiger (the hypostatic symbol of *taped'n*) that all the world will know that he was truly a great *hala*. In addition to these characteristics the *hala* does not work with ecstatic techni-

singing, chest-beating and slapping with the hands on the walling proceeded from the inside before he began his chants under the inspiration of the Chinnoi.' Then the *hala* becomes a mythic being (*čenoi-hala*) by turning his personality into the sound and language of the *čenoi*.

The arrival of each *čenoi* is marked by an improvised song, in which the form though not the content is a matter of the moment and situation. The crowd around the hut answers in a refrain. The main *čenoi* is the *bidog*, the Tiger-*čenoi*, who is the guardian of the *hala*, God himself.[7] As soon as he is in the hut, people may ask him different questions, turning the ritual into a kind of an oracle. Enjoyment and entertainment are not excluded in such moments. Basically, the purpose of the ritual is communion with God and his divine world, the assurance of the support of the *čenoi* for the human community and for those who are ill.

When all *čenoi* have visited the *pano* hut and the *hala* has accomplished his ascent into heaven, the performance ends. Dancing, spectacles, and festivities, however, continue. The mytho-religious consciousness identifies itself again with ordinary life, which, after all, forms only part of the mythic whole.

2. THE TOTEMIC RELIGION OF AUSTRALIA

Together with all other 'stone-age' cultures, the Australian sparked special interest in the once-ardent debate on the origin of religion. But, as in the case of so many other primitive cultures, the ethnographic reality revealed that the theories proposed tended to be a self-reflection of the minds of the scholars proposing them rather than an adequate interpretation of empirical data. While

---

ques. He is not a necromancer but an 'exorcist of God' (Schebesta, 1941, II/2, p. 136). Even the special language he uses during his performances (actually an archaic Malayan) is rather a sacred language than a secret one. Though a special institution, Semang shamanism is generally characterized and distinguished by the tendency to comprise the various elements of symbolic life and culture, and thus, of forming an integral part of the mythology as a comprehensive entity. In a certain sense we may even say that it works as a non-institutional institution. The assimilation of shamanistic ideas by a primitive culture apparently works to the effect of turning them into an 'asymetrical' phenomenon.

7. It may be noted here that the Aëta also have a nightly celebration (*talbong*), in which the eldest (and not necessarily a shaman) symbolizes *apo katawan*, the Aëta equivalent of *taped'n* (Schebesta, 1941, II/2, p. 255).

such theorists as Spencer, Frazer, Tylor, Hartland and others were convinced of the inferiority of the religion of the aborigines, such men as Lang and Schmidt looked upon them through the glasses of an over-rationalized picture of man, or, as in the case of Durkheim, through those of a reductionist hypothesis.

It cannot be the purpose of this study to attempt a thoroughgoing and comprehensive interpretation of the Australian cultures and religions.[8] Yet since their traditions offer the most complex and comprehensive realization of the totemic idea, we shall try to outline the main patterns of an endogenic history. This does not imply that 'totemism' is the whole or even the beginning of Australian religion, nor does it maintain that it is a mechanism invented by the social body (as an autonomous organism) in order to survive. It starts from the assumption that the totemic idea represents a possibility of the religious consciousness, which, like all other ideas, can be adopted, developed and used as a means to support and, to a degree, to perpetuate social processes and values. A strong argument in favor of this interpretation is given by the uneven distribution of totemistic[9] patterns as part of the social structure, although the final word on society and totemism can only be spoken after a thorough examination of these two complexes themselves. The same holds true for the relationship between religion and totemism. The discovery of an All-Father (*baiame, bunjil, nurunderi, daramulun, munganngaua*) among the southeastern groups, which aroused so much controversy in the interpretation of Australian religion, should not be considered an exception – E. B. Tylor tried to explain the Australian high gods as a result of Christian influence (1891, p. 283 ff) – but as an indication of the mythic context in which totemic heroes could become predominant. As more recent investigations show, the idea of a supreme 'sky being' cannot be restricted to the southeastern tribes but seems to be or to have been part of the general background of Australian religion (see Elkin, 1964, p. 225 ff; Strehlow, 1964, p. 723 ff; Stanner, 1963, p. 239 ff; Eliade, 1966, Part I, p. 124 ff).

Whatever the historic circumstances and minutiae may have been that effected the 'idea of God', the mythic transformations and transmutations throughout the process of various associations and images indicate strongly the presence of the

---

8. Recently such an attempt has been made by Mircea Eliade in a series of articles that were published in the *History of Religions*.

9. In order to distinguish between totemism as the expression of certain ideas integrated into the general conduct of life and totemism as a (social) theory, we use the adjective 'totemic' when referring to the lived idea and 'totemistic' when the theoretical or systematic implications of this idea are at issue.

amythic-mythic divinity, in which totemic interpretations as well as rituals and social values are equally connected with the cult and association of god(s) and goddess(es). Similarly, they show the futility of each attempt to identify the divine exclusively with one of its associations, be it that of the All-Father or ancestral hero, or others, since they (the idea of an All-Father included) recall basically nothing but the mythic awareness of the ineffable in the affective experiences of man. In order to understand the totemistic issue we must therefore outline its mythic foundation (totemic idea). We may then specify its ramifications and finally trace some aspects of its practical applications.

2.1 *The Totemic Myth*

The Aborigines are highly aware of the fact that behavior as well as thought must be enshrined in a myth in order to gain validity. Otherwise 'it is regarded as merely man-made and of no great importance' (Elkin, 1964, p. 209). This is also true in respect to various expressions of totemistic behavior and customs. They are the reminder and even the reactualization of basic and primordial conditions, which became decisive for the present. 'The myth is life-giving' (Elkin, 1964, p. 215). It is the dimension in which the cycle of life returns to its origin, rendering meaning to man and world alike.

The accounts of this 'cycle of meaning' can be of a more fundamental kind or slanted toward the specific. As an illustration of the first, we shall refer to the Aranda and Unambal myths of origin (see Spencer and Gillen, 1927; Strehlow, 1947, 1964; Lommel, 1952). As an example of the second type, an account from the Dieri will be presented (Elkin, 1964, p. 209).

Though the indefinite existence of the earth is nowhere a problem that concerns the Aranda mythology, there is a strong and vivid conception of the beginning. When everything lay in eternal darkness and embryonic slumber the beings beneath the surface of the earth woke up and broke through the layer that covered them. The sun rose from the ground and light filled the earth. The beings that 'had been born out of their own eternity' (*altjirana nambakla*) appeared in many shapes and manifestations, as plants, animals, and humans (Strehlow, 1964, p. 727). Metamorphosis was a basic part of their mode of existence. These beings began to wander over the surface of the earth. They shaped the landscape, created men, and taught them what was necessary for life. When they had fulfilled their task and exhausted their strength and energy, they returned to their original state, marking the sites of their disappearance or leaving behind them their identity in rocks, trees, and *tehurunga* objects, that is, cult sticks.

Before they disappeared death was brought into the world through some of their deeds, giving those who remained all the labor and pain we know today. The sites where they emerged and disappeared are sacred centers, which must be avoided on pain of death, except for special ceremonial occasions. Even then only the initiated are permitted to approach them.

The events of the beginning still continue in the beings that live today. They are effective in the genesis (conception) of man and in the inherent order that connects the metamorphic states of all that is (totemic idea). But they regain their true meaning only to the degree that man discovers, revitalizes and develops his initial genesis and creative relations. Such a reenactment of the beginning is possible because each human being not only possesses the mortal soul that comes to him with the fetus as a result of intercourse but is also a reincarnation of the effervescent life of the beginning (spirit children).

This beginning is unity and plurality at once. The world is prior to each creative act. But at the same time it gains meaning and even reality only in those instances in which one of the primordial heroes acts. *Numbakulla*, for example, whose name means 'out of nothing', 'always existing' (see Spencer and Gillen, 1927, I, p. 355 ff), traveled to the north, made mountains, rivers, plants, animals. He also created spirit children (*kuruna*), concealing them first in his body. Later, he inserted *kurunas* into *tehurungas*, which he had stored in a cave. The result of this creative act was the emergence of the mythical ancestors. He taught them how to perform all the ceremonies connected with his various deeds and with the totemic relations he made manifest. Finally he planted a pole (*kauwaauwa*) and anointed it with blood. He asked the first ancestor to follow him when he climbed upon the pole. But because of the blood, the man could not follow. Therefore, he went alone, drew up the pole, after he had climbed up on it, and was never seen again.

Though different in its basic design, the mythology of the Unambal entails an interpretation of man and world that is similar to that of Arunta mythology. In the beginning only earth and heaven were there. In the earth lived *ungud*, the great snake, while *wallanganda* abode in the sky (Milky Way). He made everything by pouring water on the earth. But only because (or when) *ungud* 'made the water deep' could rain and life come into being. In order to achieve this creative event, *ungud* and *wallanganda* 'dreamed' the beings of the beginning. *Wallanganda* projected them first as painted images of plants and animals, then sent them as real beings all over the earth. He still continues to send such 'spiritual germs' to the earth. The images themselves (*wondjina*), which are symbolically identical with the rain, were found by *ungud*, who endowed them with the proper organs during a 'creative dream' at the bottom of the waters. Even today each body of water still belongs to a *wondjina*. After the *wondjina* were found and inspired by *ungud*, they wandered over the earth doing what we already know of the other 'dream-time' heroes. When they left, they lay down on the 'wet rocks', where their 'impressions' produced the primordial rock paintings. Since then, they live beneath the earth and in the waters that belong to the rock paintings. The 'child germs' (*jallala*) they produce are found by the father during a dream and again during a dream projected into his wife. They are a part of *ungud* and thus, immortal like *ungud* him(her)self. At this point the borderlines between the godhead and man become fluid. The *wondjina*, which man repaints from time to time, are not alien to the human being, but are his true self. 'I am going now to refresh and invigorate myself; I paint myself anew, so that the rain can come' (see Eliade, 1967a, II, p. 227). Similarly the *wondjina* of plants and animals, which stem from the same source as man, need man's intervention in order to maintain their true reality as expressed in the paintings. The destiny of mankind is their fate too. Thus the world will continue only as long as man continues in his awareness of the beginning.

While the mythology of the Arunta and Unambal outlined thus far gives the general reason for man's primordial union with everything that has form and life in nature and points to the basic meaning of such phenomena as the *thurunga* and *wondjina*, the following myth, which comes from the Dieri, offers an example for the concentration on a single and more or less accidental fact as established in the general framework of tribal mythology.

The dreamlike hero Paltira stole a mortar and pestle. Since he could not lift the dish, he sang a song, which caused a wind to lift the stone and to move it onto his head. He carried the stone to the Parachilna district, where it can still be found today. The songs Paltira used are sung at the present time in order to make the wind blow, each wind having its special song. But only the men who have the wind for their *mura-mura* (cult totem) can sing those songs successfully. It was in memory of Paltira that groups living far from the Parachilna district came to this site to obtain stone slabs.

Australian mythology offers a rich hunting ground for the labyrinthine details of formative events in the beginning, but space does not allow us to trace them further. The few examples are paradigmatic enough to shed light upon the totemic presuppositions of a totemistic culture and cult that developed in the context of the basic patterns of this mythology.

2.2 *The Totemistic Culture*

The emergence of man as a being conscious of himself is, for the Australian Aborigines, founded on and realized in the discovery of their dream-time. The metamorphic dream-time and multioriginal ancestral hero conception is not only complete enough to include through numerous variations the facts of man, life and the world, it is also adaptable and universal enough to specify and affect the meaning of every human situation. This meaning is formally expressed through the awareness of a basic, though modified, togetherness (totemism) of all that is. If we follow the terminology proposed by E. P. Elkin (1964, p. 143 ff), we can distinguish between totemistic forms, which result from situational circumstances such as individuality, sex, moiety, section and sub-section, clan, locality, and subject-object relations (multiple totemism). Each of these various situations in which man necessarily exists is marked by having its own specific and distinct relation to the primordial events and metamorphoses.

In order to gain access to the complete meaning of the totemic and totemistic complex, we cannot be content with this formal or classificatory aspect, even though it may permit us to establish a system of algebraic patterns (see Lévi Strauss, 1949, 1967b). Rather, we have to turn to the impact the 'forms' and 'formal relations' have on the various situations in their functional unity. In this sense we can distinguish between the social, the cultic, the cosmological, and the 'assistant' functions of the totem conception.[10]

In its social function, the totemic idea offers the framework for the structure of the society. The result is a social stratification shaped in totemistic patterns. When, for instance, man and his totem form one 'flesh' or 'meat', it logically

---

10. Elkin (1964, p. 148 ff) distinguishes between a social, cult, conception, dream, classificatory, and assistant totemism. Since the functions of conception, dream, and classification are largely part of the cult system on the one hand, while, on the other, they commonly share in the interpretation of man and world, it seems more appropriate to emphasize this second aspect, inasmuch as it indicates the cosmological dimension of totemism.

follows that a marriage between two individuals with the same totem (the same flesh) is incestuous. This shows how totemic ideas can serve as principles of solidarity and social grouping.

In its cosmological function the totemic idea becomes a principle of explanation and classification. It explains natural processes (conception, for example) or offers a method of classifying various phenomena such as lightning, thunder, rain, clouds, hail, winter, the moon, the stars, animals, plants, and even society (thus blending with the social function). In its 'assistant' function the totemic idea is used as a principle for gaining the special powers needed by the shaman, the medicine man and sorcerers. With the assistance of the totem, man becomes able to do things he could not do otherwise.

In all these cases we are not dealing, however, with completely independent functions. In their distribution as well as in their meaning-giving role, they point toward a common origin: The mytho-cultic complex which from both theoretical and practical points of view may be considered as the core of this totemistic culture. The understanding of the cult complex is therefore the foremost condition for an appropriate approach toward a religion realized in a totemistic framework.

2.3 *The Totemistic Cult*

The present experience of life is necessarily incomplete as long as there is no actual awareness of its relationship with the dream time. Thus, the aborigine's search for personal perfection and completion becomes a search for his place in the setting of the primordial world. Since this world is not obvious, but mysterious, like dream and death, two stages can be distinguished: The initiatory stage and the stage of self-realization. In the first, the individual man learns about his own glorious beginning and true identity, while in the second, the initiated regains and deepens his primordial fullness of being by celebrating his own and the world's historic events and by actively participating in the process of life and nature (increase ceremonies).[11]

Since initiation is structured by its purpose and goal, the special features and

11. See Elkin (1964, p. 171) where he distinguishes between initiation rites, historical rites, and increase rites. Since there is a strict distinction between those who are initiated and those who are not, the historical and increase rites can be regarded as two aspects of the new state in which the initiated finds himself, that is, as a man who has found his true self. He is now in a state where he remembers what he has done, and by remembering becomes capable of resuming and of continuing his primordial task.

the highlights of this rite are very instructive for interpreting the mythology and the myth underlying the whole totemistic system. Although the details of the initiation rites differ in various parts of Australia, the general outlines are very much the same (see Elkin, 1964, p. 171 ff). Prescinding from the fact that the western groups usually believe 'in a sky culture hero or all-father who instituted initiation and now watches over what is done', whereas the central and western groups believe that the culture heroes watch over the ritual 'from beneath the surface' (Elkin, 1964, p. 178), the stages can be summarized as follows (Elkin, 1964, p. 179, ff): (1) Taking the novice: A ceremony during which the separation of the novice from the camp and the woman is ritualized. Red ochre or human blood is used to paint the boy, who is going to leave the profane world for the sacred one. (2) The welcome and combat of guests. Before initiation becomes effective all quarrels have to be settled among the participants. A welcome ceremonial (in public *corroboree* ground) was followed by a combat scene that was supposed to settle all disputes. If someone was killed during this ritual, a cannibalistic feast disposed of the body (burial ritual). As the intent of the combat ritual shows, the world of the sacred is a world of peace and cooperation. All animosities of the profane world have to be left behind in order to enter it. It is a moral idea. (3) The preliminary ceremonial. The candidate's entry into a new stage is ritually prepared. 'The candidate must act, and is treated as though he were lifeless' (Elkin, 1964, p. 180). (4) Ritual bodily operations The death (rebirth) symbolism of the preceding ritual is continued by tooth-avulsion and/or circumcision, cicatrization, the removal of a finger joint, perforation of the septum, and, in regions where no relationship is seen between intercourse and conception, subincision (the penis is cut open to the urethra from underneath (Elkin, 1964, p. 173). The humming of the bull-roarers recalls the voice of the all-father. (5) Period of seclusion. The candidate is introduced into the sacred and secret world of the 'tribe'. He is dead to ordinary life. The period of seclusion may take a year or more. (6) The blood ceremony. The initiated is anointed with blood from the arm of an older man. Together with a special song, the blood consecrates the newly initiated. (7) Fire ceremony. An ordeal and act of purification, which is continued in the next step. (8) The washing and return ritual. 'The newly initiated is welcomed as one returned from the dead' (Elkin, 1964, p. 184).

The ritual procedure of the initiation, which from the viewpoint of those who are already initiated is interpreted as a reenactment of a dream-time event, is significant in various respects. Its proximity to death rituals and death itself gives special emphasis to the experience and meaning of this phenomenon (Eliade, 1967b, III, p. 65 ff). The infinite void of death, which tries to annihilate the meaning of man's existence, for such is the heritage of consciousness no matter where it emerges, is sustained by relating it to 'blood' and 'sound' and by rendering it sacred, that is, as belonging to another world and mode of existence. In the symbolism of man's blood[12] (including the factors of sex, fertility, birth and rebirth), strength, endurance, and courage come forth as part of the texture of being, provided that it is seen in connection with the sound (song and myth) of the beginning as symbolized in the bull-roarer, which is used during the operations and which represents (together with the other symbols) the personal principle of individualization and meaningful multiplicity. They are like the new name that is given to the candidate during his initiation, *churinga*, that is, parts of the dream-time, the undifferentiated *logos* (see Stanner, 1956, p. 51) of all that is and matters today. The world of the sacred, in the secrecy and seclusion of the ceremonies, is set apart from the everyday world, but nevertheless contains the latter's true meaning.

Thus initiation is not just a process through which a child gains the social status of an adult; rather, it creates a new consciousness in which mythology and present behavior merge into one unity ('monototemism') and each person begins to achieve his specific truth. Adulthood is indeed the presumption of death as part of a consciousness that knows about the beginning and the meaning of the present. This consciousness is like truth itself the mythological and ritual self-realization of man as accomplished through the recognition of historical events in the structure of the society, the observation of rules (taboos) regarding natural and cultural phenomena, the cultic reactualization of metamorphic relations in totem communions, the actualization and 'dreaming' of new myths as part of necessary adaptations to changing circumstances.[13] They

---

12. There is also an initiation rite for girls (see R. M. and C. H. Berndt, 1954, and M. Eliade, 1967b, p. 82 ff). Nonetheless this is much simpler than that of the boys. The reason seems to be the conviction that women are by nature closer to the mystery of life. In mythological language it is said that they 'possessed all the sacred rituals before they were taken from them by the men' (Eliade, 1967b, p. 87; see also Elkin, 1964, p. 190 ff).

13. Like other primitive cultures, the Australians try to integrate modern conditions, including the Christian message, into their 'old' system. That they do it by 'discovering' new myths, does not only underline the vital importance of mythology, but also the generative character of tradition in primitive culture. *Cf.* R. Berndt (1962), Eliade, 1968, p. 256 f).

are the basic, though unreflected expression of the consciousness that 'living as a human being is in itself a religious act' (Eliade, 1967a, II, p. 222). The ceremonies that are performed outside the framework of initiation rituals are indeed the continuation of its specific impetus: To achieve truth in and through the (re-)discovered dream-time.

There can be no doubt that totemism shapes and forms the religious life; or better, we are confronted with a cultural system that is qualified by the relationship between man and animals, plants, natural and cultural objects and the stratifying impact of these relations on society and individuality. In the whole context of its mythology, however, totemism cannot be considered the core of this religion insofar and to the extent that it is religion. If we try to describe the meaning of this religion we better speak of the tangible modality, the face value 'illusion' (see Levi-Strauss, 1967b, p. 225) of a consciousness, whose essence comes forth as mytho-magism. There are divine beings, fertility goddesses, totemic and cultural heroes, who continue to exist in their creative metamorphoses of mountains, plants, and animals. Since these beings are recalled in cults and celebrations, the religion that integrates them can be said to be totemistic in its outlook and totemic in its realization. Insofar, however, as the personal life that is projected into and also found in the mythic beings and mythological figures, is leveled by turning it into the dream-time itself, it is not the totemic content of the mythology, but its understanding that puts religion into its proper perspective. '*Baiame* say so' becomes identical with '*altjira, djugur, ungud*', the dream-time (Elkin, 1964, p. 225). Man does not participate in the mythic reality, but he is a part of it. Instead of maintaining the heterothetic character of the mythological associations and 'saving' them in their primordiality, they become reified as 'part' of the present world. Though magical manipulations with objects and formulas also exist, especially in the hands of medicine men and sorcerers, they have to be separated from cult, which does not manipulate objects but myths.[14] In comparison with the modalities of the myths in other cultures, we can also say that the Australians did not socialize their

---

14. This is underlined in cases where, owing to the destructive influence of modern civilization, the meaning of the mythic background ceases to shape the cult performances. Fertility dances, for example, begin to lose their total significance and turn into 'exclusively erotic' performances which apparently function as 'magical means' for the participants' erotic life. *Cf.* C. H. Berndt (1950, pp. 59, 70).

mythology but mythologized their society and finally their culture. Thus, the problem of Australian religion is not so much the idea of God but the truth of myth and mythology.

3. RELIGION IN THE DISSOLVING CULTURE OF THE KAINGANG (BRAZIL)

Thus far we have approached religious phenomena in the framework of traditions that were more or less stable. At least there were no indications that these traditions had thoroughly changed in recent history. Since it is the intention of this study to deal with religion in the functional and ontological as well as in the historical context of cultural dynamics, it seems appropriate that we also analyze the meaning of religion under culturally extreme conditions.

An example of such a situation is provided by a group of Kaingang Indians (Botocudo) in Brazil, who have been thoroughly investigated by J. Henry (1941). The group in question lived at the time of the investigation in the government reservation of Duque de Caxias (Santa Catarina). From the cultural-historical point of view, it was a more or less artificial situation, since in their lives divergent tribal elements had been mixed. But even under this condition a *modus vivendi* had to be found, which shows perhaps better than a well-established cultural situation the vital and basic meaning of the symbolic, and especially the religious, dimension.

When the Kaingang of Duque de Caxias (and we will be speaking only of them, not of other Kaingang groups) were 'pacified' in 1914, they counted between 300 and 400. In 1932, when Henry arrived, they had been reduced to 106 individuals. Because of influenza and other illnesses, and also their suicidal aggression against one another, they presented 'a picture of social tragedy', a culture that was dying through its own hands (Henry, 1941, pp. xii, xiii).

Although the group subsisted partly through small farming, it still spent half the time hunting and gathering. Thus Henry had considerable opportunity during his stay (which ended in 1934) to study the traditional way of life, which considered the tapir not only as the most important food but also as the very symbol of subsistence (1941, p. 14).

Before we turn, however, to a detailed description of this way of life and its symbolic implications, it seems appropriate to outline the religious background to which the present symbolic structure, or more accurately its elements, can be traced. Because of the destructive development of the surrounding cultures during the past centuries, and also because of a lack of comprehensive studies, it cannot be emphasized enough that such an outline has only a tentative character, at least so far as cross-cultural connections are concerned.

3.1 Religious Ideas of the Gé-speaking People

Like the Timbira, Kayapo, Aluen and other tribes, the Kaingang belong linguistically to the so-called gé (also gê or jé) family, which in turn has been considered a subgroup of the South American marginal culture (see Cooper, 1942). Although these 'incipient cultivators' (practicing hunting, gathering, and rudimentary horticulture) have recently been subdivided into several areas,[15] they show enough similar traits in their symbolic structures to be taken as a more or less loose unit, at least if we restrict our treatment to the gé-speaking tribes.

Since a marked hostility toward neighboring villages and tribes is or was typical of the gé-speaking peoples, the sociopolitical structure did not reach beyond the level of village organization. In this framework, however, it ranges from bands with exogamic moieties to occasionally large villages (400 to 700 individuals), with dual organization, age grades and feast groups. People lived in either individual or multi-family huts and were matrilineally oriented. Rich and complex rituals, often connected with log races and mask dances, marked all major events, especially deaths. Shamanism existed but was unevenly developed among the various tribes. Great care was taken in raising the children. The couvade[16] was only one expression of the mystic unity between parents and their children. Work was rather evenly distributed between the sexes.

The main figures in the mythology (see Lowie, 1946; Nimuendajú, 1939, 1942, 1946, 1948; Haekel, 1953; Baldus, 1952; Zerries, 1954) of these groups were the Sun and the Moon, which appear on the one hand as culture hero and his trickster, both of whom created man by throwing pairs of gourds into the water. Their mythic relationship is reflected in the dual organization, the Sun and the Moon people and the sociocultic antagonism that ties them together. On the other hand, they can be considered as hypostases of the godhead itself,

---

15. See E. Galvao (1967, p. 169 ff). According to this map, the gé-speaking people belong mainly to areas VI and X.

16. *Couvade* (Fr.: couver, to hatch), a custom where the father goes to bed 'as if for labor' when his wife is giving birth.

whose presence continues in the sunlight during the day and in the moonlight during the night. 'Then Sun said to Moon: "Now our children are all married. Come, let us go!" "Yes!" Moon agreed, "Let us go! You shall light up for them by day, and I by night!" Then they assembled all the people in the plaza and Sun spoke: "My children! Now I am going off with my godchild!" And Moon replied, "Well then, let us go, my godfather!" Then both rose to the sky' (Nimuendajú, 1939, pp. 164 f).

Sun and Moon were both called upon. Lunar festivals were held at the time of a new moon. The Moon was invoked to promote the growth of plants. During a lunar eclipse the Moon was asked to look upon his wife (a girl lifted by an old man toward the Moon) and not to die. If he appeared in human shape, it was at night and with the intention of having intercourse with a menstruating woman. Thus there was an unmistakable difference between the moon as a celestial body and the Moon as a mythological and cult symbol.

The same difference, only more pronounced, can be noted between the physical sun and the sun god. This not only accounts for the predominance of the sun over the moon but also suggests that the idea of a myth bound godhead might be opposed to the awareness of a personal God, or at least that we have to take this distinction into consideration when we analyze the mythological setting of religious life. The Sun is called upon as father or grandfather in case of sickness and at the opening of various seasons. He is asked to protect the game; he is asked for rain, for a good harvest, for the increase of wild plants and the like. One prayer asks the grandfather to protect all animals and to let them grow so that they can be eaten by man (Nimuendajú, 1946, p. 71 f). The sun is remembered in all circular patterns, the house, the plaza, the radial paths, and the round meat pies that are eaten at festivals. The Sherente knew a ritual for times of drought in which a post was erected upon which men climbed in order to pray to the Sun, their creator, who, as indicated by the drought, was angry with them.

Striking examples of the mythic-amythic and therefore personal position of the sun god are given in various dreams and visions. One vision, which reminds one involuntarily of Exodus 3:4 ff, was told to Nimuendajú (1939, p. 136): 'I was hunting... All along the journey there I had been agitated and was constantly startled without knowing why. Suddenly I saw him standing under the drooping branches of a big steppe tree. He was standing there erect. His club was braced against the ground beside him, his hand he held on the hilt.

He was tall and light-skinned, and his hair nearly descended to the ground behind him. His whole body was painted, and on the outer side of his legs were broad red stripes. His eyes were exactly like two stars. He was very handsome. I recognized at once that it was he. Then I lost all courage. My hair stood on end, and my knees were trembling. I put my gun aside, for I thought to myself that I should have to address him, but I could not utter a sound because he was looking at me unwaveringly. Then I lowered my head in order to get hold of myself and stood thus for a long time. When I had grown somewhat calmer, I raised my head. He was still standing and looking at me. Then I pulled myself together and walked several steps toward him, then I could not go any further for my knees gave way. I again remained standing for a long time, then lowered my head and tried again to regain composure. When I raised my eyes again, he had already turned away and was slowly walking through the steppe...'

In addition to this mythoreligious sun-moon complex the world and the life of the gé-speaking people is chiefly shaped by ideas and rituals that center around the man-animal-plant and the man-soul relationship. Though such relations are more or less autonomous, they occasionally show connections with the Sun-Moon conception. The world is populated by spirits, shadows, images, souls and other independent beings, which are collectively termed as *me-galõ* (*Apinayé*). The sound of the bull-roarer also belongs to them. Their presence gives access to the wide field of hunting and planting rituals, of shamanistic visions and interventions, of metamorphic events, and the various forms of white and black magic. Beings such as the souls of the dead and those of animals and other objects are usually benevolent, provided they are treated in the right way. The medicine man (*vayangá*) and the shaman (*akó lo-čwudn*), who have special connections with this world, act as intermediaries, for example, when a temporary loss of the soul threatens the life of the individual or when the counsel of the invisible world is needed. Though the one or other of the *me-galo* may take a predominant position (the jaguar or tapir, for instance, or the star-woman, who gave the maize plant to man), the general function of this concept seems to be to lay the foundation of a magicoreligious unity, in which the diverse elements of the world endure by becoming part of the mythological metamorphoses and the indefiniteness of the mythic.

As an illustration of this interpretation, which shows at the same time a basic ambivalence in this 'sun-culture', it will suffice to present the myth of the Red-haired People: 'In the easternmost end of the world, where the sun rises, there lives a red-haired people. Since the sun rises close to them, they suffer severely from his blaze and live in bitter enmity with him. Every morning at sunrise they shoot arrows at him, but with averted faces since they cannot bear the light and the burning heat. But the sun rises very rapidly, so they always miss him. So they decided to fell the post that supports the sky in order to make the sky topple down and prevent the sun from following his course thereafter. They chopped and worked away till the pillar was worn quite thin. Then from fatigue they had to stop, and when they returned to their task the chopped-away portion had grown anew and the pillar was as thick as before. They are still at it today' (Nimuendajú, 1939, p. 180).

3.2 *General Traits of Kaingang Religion*

In comparison to the social structure and symbolic background of the gé-speaking peoples outlined above, that of the Kaingang shows a marked decline when viewed from a morphological point of view. While the differentiation and general structure of the society was almost lost, the social body survived by emphasizing the principle of the mystic parent-child relation, and by extending it at the same time to the whole of that body. This means that the ultimate framework for human existence is provided by the band or the extended family, in which close bodily contact guarantees social security, and not by the tribe or the village. Within these limits the individual grew up with few restrictions, but with almost no prospects. As noted, we are dealing here with a culturally extreme situation.

Marriage was quite informal, forbidden only between parents and children and brothers and sisters. The 'almost amorphous social life' (Henry, 1941, p. 43) was held together by the woman's household, which in turn was based on the considerations of close bodily contact, food and sex. Most significant in this context is the linguistic equation between eating and cohabitation. Both acts were designated by the same word (Henry, 1941, p. 53). As a result, polyandrous and even joint marriages were relatively common. While sexual liberty among groups such as the Apinayé was permitted only on the occasion of few cultic events and in an institutionalized framework, it was the rule rather than the exception among the Kaingang. Without the interference of an institutionalized and thus traditionally sanctioned leadership, the bands massacred one another. They accepted invitations, although they knew that they would end in murder and assassination. One may ask here what the symbolic structure of this (circum-stantial) culture was; a culture whose people lived in a world without bounda-ries, protected merely by open shelters, built only when absolutely necessary; a people, for whom every human being that did not live in their life-community was just a 'different thing', inspiring fear and violence alike (Henry, 1941, pp. xii, 14, 68).

Though the Kaingang have a ceremony in which two men seated opposite each other shout legends syllable by syllable (Henry, 1941, p. 126), the myths recorded by Henry are hardly revealing. They do not show any 'consistent ex-pression of motives that are dynamic in the Kaingang culture.' (1941, p. 127). All they indicate are the following ideas: A long time ago their ancestors came out of the sea and over the mountains; the animals were involved in wars and the tapir was tricked; food taboos came into being through the metamorphosis of human beings into animals (which for that reason were not permitted to be eaten); and shadowy men named their ancestors (Henry, 1941, p. 128). More important to the Kaingang were those stories and legends that commenced with the words: 'They were angry and they fought...' or 'They wanted to kill them and invited them to a feast...' (Henry, 1941, p. 132). But while these stories of feud and murder are illuminating as to the general mood and disposition of the Kaingang, they furnish no substitute for the symbolic significance of myths. To come to grips with this dimension we must therefore analyze the various symbolic patterns of behavior, including the psychological self-evaluation that is concomitant.

There is no word to express a divine presence as incorporated in sun and moon. Nevertheless, it is said that the moon comes and helps in sickness (Henry, 1941, p. 73). In the context of the preparation for hunting, the hunter may show his bow and arrow to the moon with the words, 'Moon, I give you my bow!' (Henry, 1941, p. 93). During an eclipse of the moon, people say, 'Moon, show me your big heart, do not die. I see you about to die; stop! Moon, be courageous!' (Henry, 1941, p. 94). Similarly, the sun is called upon, 'My relative, show me your big heart! Be strong!' When it has rained too long they say, 'Sun appear...' (Henry, 1941, p. 95). Comparing such utterances with the Sun-Moon-God traditions of the gé-speaking people, the conclusion seems justified that we are dealing with religious elements that survived as superstitious or magic traditions, for there is no indication that these 'prayers' have any significant impact on the general conduct and meaning of life. The same is suggested when we analyze the soul-ghost-spirit complex that is predominant in the entire life of the Kaingang.

The Kaingang believe in various beings, who together with the soul (*kupléng*) are collectively called *nggiyúdn*. They are thought of as monsters and are associated with forms such as those of the tapir, horse, and pig, but they may also appear as human beings. It is especially their sexual desire visibly displayed by an enormous penis and large testicles that makes them dangerous for man. They may also destroy man by shooting, crushing or devouring him. '*Yóin*', the most terrible of all, 'kills people, because he is a different thing and never calls men "my people" ' (Henry, 1941, p. 70). Occasionally, however, they not only exchange their roles and functions but even become benevolent. *Yóin*, for instance, becomes a man's hunting companion. In such roles they show great affinity to the 'soul' world of the animals and of everything.

The 'spirits of the natural world', as Henry translates the word *nggiyúdn* in this context (1941, p. 71), dwell everywhere: In trees, under water, in rocks and cliffs, in the sun, the moon and the stars, in wind and storm and finally in the various animals. They reduplicate the world as seen by the eyes of man. The Indians fear them, but they in turn also fear the Indians. If man encounters them, he has to respect their wishes. Then they may turn into a hunting companion, or a guardian, with whom foo dis 'shared'. They help the shaman (who, unlike other people, always sees his companion) to cure disease and to bring back a soul that is going away. If man does not take notice of such encounters, it is dangerous for him. 'Whoever turns away from quarry pointed out by a spirit is bound to fall ill and die' (Henry, 1941, p. 76). The 'spirits' of the species control the game. They let some of their animals out to be killed by man. If too many or too few of them are killed, they keep them hidden and animals become scarce (Henry, 1941, p. 76). Besides this kind of soul, there are also souls of arrows. If lost arrows, for instance, are not found, the 'soul' would come and kill the hunter (Henry, 1941, p. 14).

There is no doubt that we are dealing here with the conception of the owner of animals. At the same time, this idea is extended to everything – as the example of the arrow's soul shows – and thus points to an indefinite equilibrium between man and world in which man's own being becomes the implicit measure of all that is experienced. The key word to this mentality is the Kaingang's own interpretation of the *nggiyúdn*; it is the things 'talking' (Henry, 1941, p. 132). Though no further explanations are given to this conception by the Kaingang themselves, it becomes more understandable if we apply the interpretation as it is given by the Kaliña, a tribe that lives as far away as Guiana.[17]

The Kaliña believe (see Goeje, 1944, p. 4) that the *aula* (word, language) of each species (*wala* - melody) existed from the beginning and that it was just this *aula* that created every visible thing. Each *wala* in the visible world is complementary to the *wala* (melody) that gives life to it. Or as the Kaliña express it, 'If there were not a spirit that makes everything in its specific shape, there would be nothing'. It is the same sound that brings structured variety into the visible world. It is the language of men and things that shows the basic unity of the world.

For the Kaingang, who share this basic concept that everything has its 'talking', the conscious experience of a world full of 'different things' can be expected to be counterbalanced by the metaconscious 'awareness' of a basic unity. This awareness actually appears in the responsive meaning of hunting rituals and in the compulsive character of words and other forms of magic. Similarly the concepts and rituals surrounding birth and death are both a responsive and a compulsive expression.

3.3 Between Self-love and Doom

It is not only in the field of rituals and magic that metaconscious 'awareness' can be recognized. This holds also true on the psychological level, which reveals, as suggested by the conflicting character of conscious and metaconscious 'awareness', a deep-rooted tension and contradiction. On the one hand, we have the idea of *waikayú*, the self-love expressed in the compassion for the family and especially the children, who are considered an extension of one's self (Henry, 1941, p. 113 ff). Yet too much *waikayú* is dangerous, since it becomes destructive when the interests of the other members are suppressed. On the other hand, such interests are necessary for the sake of family survival. The 'tradition' that tries to maintain both principles, embodies these conflicting factors and becomes *yôkthé*: Guilt. The result of the *waikayú-yôkthé* relation appears as a kind of metaphysical or religious resignation. It is expressed in the concept *lu*,

---

17. By mentioning the Kalina here we do not mean to imply that there is a genetic relationship between them and the Kaingang, for a relationship of this kind is not the concern of our study. What matters is the morphological similarity; this is significant to the extent that it throws light on the symbolism of the Kaingang.

which can be translated by fate, doom, destiny, necessity. Phrases such as 'I shall go dancing to meet my *lu*', or 'my *lu* kills me' speak for themselves (Henry, 1941, p. 120).

The hunting rituals mentioned earlier usually consist of an address to the dead animal. The tapir's windpipe, for example, is wrapped in vine and in 'tapir's raw food' (the animal's main food supply). Before this bundle is burnt, the tapir's *kuplêng* (soul) is addressed by the words 'Look at your fine heart-bundle. I want to do the same with you - so stand looking at me' (Henry, 1941, p. 85). The intention is that the dead animals may influence their brethren to come out and be killed.

In this context the function and the meaning of the word itself is as important as the conception of an animal-*kuplêng*. When uttered, a word is irresistible (like being itself) and thus effective. For the same reason, the words (thoughts) that one attributes to others are in their receptive state as real as if they were uttered by them; this is a suggested source for 'preventive' murder. Thus, if the *kuplêng* (or storm, thunder, or other 'beings') has been addressed, it is forced by the power of the word to comply.[18] The Kaingang thus project their own 'fear of refusing' (Henry, 1941, p. 87), into the world of symbolic realities, which in turn offers the condition for such a behavioral pattern.

The 'tapir's raw food' is not only effective in words, it also has a special vital power that is applicable to each situation, since everything stems from the 'supernatural' (Henry, 1941, pp. 83, 84). (It would also seem that we must attribute a superior position to the tapir's *kuplêng* among those of the other animals.) It plays a role as a preventive and medicine in cases of illness and in critical situations. When, for instance, a child under twelve years has died, the 'tapir's raw food' is spread over the infant, while his soul is asked to return to the mother's womb (Henry, 1941, pp. 23, 83). It is also used in connection with other hunting rituals. A 'fledgling hunter', for instance, must not eat of the tapir he has killed unless he has been initiated through a ritual meal into which the tapir's 'raw food' has been blended (Henry, 1941, p. 86).

The conception of a magic union as expressed in the word-thing relation and in the symbolic universality of (the tapir's) vital power is also tangible in various magic rites that operate mainly with the symbolism of sound, water, fire, stone

---

18. This explains also why the shaman uses only an indirect language (Henry, 1941, p. 78) when speaking about his 'office'.

and bodily contact. They furnish the general background of various forms of magic (imitative, contagious, divination), the detailed presentation of which can be omitted in this context, since it does not offer any further insights into the mythic world.

From the point of the *lu*-consciousness we can understand that the Kaingang are more concerned with the fearful aspects of the invisible world and reality than with the comfort that could be found there for the present situation (Henry, 1941, p. 75). Thus the event of death becomes not only the focus to which their thoughts return over and over again but is also the inducement and occasion for the most elaborate rituals of the Kaingang culture. In a certain sense this process of concentration on death is already anticipated by the complex rituals that surround the event of birth.

It will suffice to mention some aspects of the birth ritual. When a child was born (Henry, 1941, p. 194), the placenta and a part of the umbilical cord were wrapped in medicinal herbs (*cf.* the tapir's heart bundle), placed in a small basket and sunk in a stream. The infant was submitted to various rituals with herbs and water, and cords were laid around his feet. After some time the parent gave a big feast during which the cords were removed with accompanying singing and put into running water together with the umbilical cord. At the age of two, the child's lips were pierced and a lip plug inserted. The festival was supervised by the ceremonial parents of the baby and culminated in a ceremony during which the child was carried through a circle while the Water's Talking was called upon. A play on the hunting ritual ended this ceremony. Besides these performances many more magical rites accompanied the growth of the child.

The most threatening danger to life is the loss of one's soul (a complete soul-loss being the ultimate cause of death) (Henry, 1941, p. 180). If the soul (*kuplêng*) has left the body, it continues to stay nearby calling (like the invisible monsters) for the souls of those with whom it lived before. 'She died because her (dead) husband called her' (Henry, 1941, p. 67). People react to this threat to security and self-love by anger but still more by protective rituals. In an outburst of frantic fear and anger a man may beat the trees, calling upon the *nggiyúdn*: 'If I see you I will kill you. . . You are vicious and kill all the time'.[19]

19. Henry (*ibid*). A similar behavior as reported for the Fuegians (W. Koppers, *Der Urmensch und sein Weltbild*), seems to indicate that we are referred in this context to the former idea of an owner godhead. In case of the Fuegians, man is angry with God (*watauinéwa*) because he has taken a child. He dreads to revenge himself by destroying *watauinéwa*'s property.

The death rituals consist of two parts. The first is the burning of the corpse, accompanied by various supplications in which the deceased (*kuplêng*) is asked to go away. When, for instance, wax and meat have been put into his hands, people may say: 'Take it and go away.' While they pound against his chest they ask the *kuplêng*: 'Leave your children... Speak well of me... Do not be *vai*.'[20] Children may add: 'Mother, leave me and go' (Henry, 1941, p. 68). When the corpse is burnt, the bones (interpreted as the Sun's feces) (Henry, 1941, p. 187) are buried and a little hut is erected over the place. All rub themselves with clay and stone, saying: 'I am going to be like the old stone – I am never going to die' (Henry, 1941, p. 187). Those who helped erect the pyre and burn the corpse are submitted to additional rituals. When all these ceremonies (during which singing has a very important role) are finished the group leaves the camp (Henry, 1941, p. 66). The old firebrands are thrown away and new fire is kindled (Henry, 1941, p. 187). The widow or widower is sent into isolation.

The second part of the death ritual (Henry, 1941, p. 181 ff) is celebrated when the widow or widower is brought back from isolation (a period of three to four weeks). During this time she (he) was subject to many 'cleansing ceremonies', which now reach their culmination, accompanied by the sound of songs and the whirl of gourd rattles. The ceremony is called *angjidu* (feast of rattles). Again, their purpose is to get rid of the *kuplêng*. Through a reversal of customary acts the community tries to obliterate the identity of its members.[21] After a few more days of dancing and singing the feast will end with a ritual meal of tapir meat. Death, as experienced and expressed in these ceremonies, is not a matter of immortality. It becomes a question of body identity. On the other hand, the *kuplêng* becomes a part of the *nggiyúdn* and thus a 'different thing' (Henry, 1941, p. 68). On the other hand the principle of *waikayú* (self-love) still prevails and continues. The deceased wants to lure the living away from their world because he wants to be united with them. He loves and pities the living, but the living fear him (Henry, 1941, p. 67; see also the role of the fulmar in the Sedna myth, p. 202). Moreover, the living actually have to protect themselves against this extended antagonism, and this seems to show the essence

20. This word seems to be a concept indicating all the harm a *kuplêng* can inflict on the living. See Henry (1941, p. 85 ff).

21. It should be noted that the food, for instance, is given by those who have an opposite paint design, which indicates a mythic differentiation of mankind. Theoretically people with the same design were not allowed to marry (Henry, 1941, p. 176).

of their culturally extreme situation, by (magical) rituals and also by describing the world of the deceased to be as sad as possible. It is a world in which honey tastes like water and where no meat but the grubs in rotten wood (Henry, 1941, p. 95) can be eaten. Doom (*lu*) is not just a temporary feeling; rather, it is the god-less 'God' (*lu*) that becomes predominant when a culture begins to dissolve.

In summary we may say that in comparison with the other primitive cultures we have described, the Kaingang are a people or group whose religious symbolism shows signs of dissolution that are similar to the signs of dissolution in the culture itself. Even if it is not possible under present conditions to discuss the exact historical development and its causal genesis, a basic interrelation between cultural identity, human integrity and religion becomes visible. None of these aspects can be reduced to factors other than the totality of man himself. He is the reality that has to be brought into perspective if we are to grasp the meaning of cultural data. That, at least, seems to be the indication of a culturally extreme situation.

7

Patterns of Primitive Religion

No matter how perfect his culture, man is uncertain about birth and death, about the today and the tomorrow. His quest for meaning, which is a response to this predicament, is like language, thought and all the other symbols in which he recognizes himself, particular and universal at once. Its demands continue now and forever.

Basically, everything is included in man's search for meaning. Crisis and decay, joy and accomplishment, everything that man experiences is human to the extent that it is linked to the symbolic reality we call culture. The world that has been touched by man not only gives identity to him but is also transformed in the light of this identity. There is a dimension of depth as the result of man's presence to himself, the world and to others.

The depth of the symbolic dimension constitutes a field and cluster of symbols that is marked by this very condition of man. The actual and correlational existence of these symbols in the cultures studied in this work not only permits us to sum them up under the title of religion, but also to deal with them as a universal phenomenon. As for the protoculture religion becomes manifest as a primordial phenomenon. To remove it would be to deny man's character as the initiator of meaning, and thus would be to deny true humanity to every being that speaks, asks and understands.

The religious phenomena in primitive cultures, however, do not present themselves, as do the so-called world religions, within a doctrinal system and a set of ideas that claim universal or cross-cultural recognition. Rather, the universality of primitive religion can be seen more in its function than in its content in the cultures of gatherers and hunters, and, to a certain extent, in that of planters and pastoral nomads. Despite many historically related elements, such as rites and mythologies, the religious life of these peoples shows a certain spontaneity in which the analogous universality of man reflects itself in accordance with his specific situation. The historic reality of religious phenomena is not like that of tools and social inventions. They do not continue or change like the environment and the means of production, but like man himself, by being continuously re-created through cultural participation. The universal reality of primitive religion is its continuous becoming and is thus neither identical with institutionalized traditions nor restricted to specific cultural situations. It emerges wherever a human being exists. Since no human act is self-sufficient, religion, which receives its *raison d'être* by revealing and thematizing this insufficiency, is necessarily bound into the developing nature of man himself. But while it changes its appearances with the cultural modification of man, it maintains its formative uniqueness by connecting him with the origin of his being as a person. As a part, or more accurately as the core, of man's personal life, religion is not reducible to specific self-subsistent and objective phenomena. Its reality is rather that of a polar field in which the phenomenal reality is structured and restructured, depending on the mutual influences between the field itself and its stratification at a given time. As a result of this condition, two forms of religious patterns can be distinguished. On the one hand there are those patterns that display a certain order in the phenomena themselves. The symbols are interrelated and thus can be combined and classified in accordance with similar or predominant traits in their relationship. As outlined in chapter three, there are specified cults and mythologies, cosmic and biological symbols, sacred objects and places, gods, spirits, and ghosts. They are, so to speak, the external face of religion in primitive cultures. On the other hand are those patterns through which the phenomena, and consequently also the phenomenal classifications, come into being. They are the patterns in which religion originates and participates in the totality of man's reality by turning into symbols of his ultimate condition and originating dimension.

In the course of interpreting primitive religion, we have to keep both these aspects in mind. In line with the analysis of culture, however, and in accordance with the category of primitivity, we must give a preferential treatment to the second aspect. Religion presents itself primarily as a genetic problem. It is interwoven with the process of culture genesis and, like culture itself, is always in the making. To understand its meaning in this horizon, that is, in the horizon of a universal humanism, implies therefore that we attempt to trace and to outline the texture of its continuous origination. Otherwise we shall not only fall short of obtaining the meaning of religious phenomena and their interrelation, but the study of primitive religion also becomes an absurdity.

The dynamic reality of religion in primitive cultures is obvious when we consider its differential universality. Although the interpretation of religion as a genetic phenomenon implies its universality, it is not simply that of concepts and clearly defined symbols, but of existence. Like existence itself, it is deeply involved in a process of selection and specification, which as already mentioned can be understood as the result of an interaction between certain factual conditions such as environment, social structure, emotions and the human response to these conditions by archetypal reactions, namely, by reflection and intuition. The universality that results from these conditions differs, like man himself, from situation to situation. At the same time it maintains the identity of the relation that brings it into existence. It is influenced by various factors, yet is not constituted by them. In a word, it is differential. Consequently, differential universality is not just a description, but a basic pattern, in which primitive religion emerges and presents itself in the religious phenomena of primitive cultures.

The differential universality of primitive religion implies that it appears in a variety of symbols that are bound together in some sort of basic relation and structuring dynamics. Thus far, this relation is still undetermined. In order to identify it, we must analyze the fundamental condition of religious life. Since the mythologies in primitive cultures offer a kind of synthesis of divergent religious phenomena, we shall begin our search for this relation by analyzing the meaning and function of mythology. The result of this analysis, which will be covered later, is the discovery of the theogonic consciousness as the condition of primitive religion and the postulate of a mythic unity (*unio mythica*) as its initial realization.

The theogonic consciousness as the fundamental relation of the religious life develops in two directions. On the one hand, it points toward God or the God-person as the ultimate content of mythology and religion; on the other, toward man as its ultimate condition. The first aspect is supported by an independent analysis of man's situation as a personal being. It is the outcome of accepting 'primitive man' as existing consciousness.

The same can be said of the second aspect of the theogonic consciousness. The turn toward the ultimate (as *unio mythica*) is integrated into the cultural situation and is thus interwoven with the process of hominization as the achievement of meaning through participation in this reality. As a result, religion has to be interpreted not merely as a part of culture, but also as immanent polarity in the process of cultural realization. The same holds true also from the point of view of sheer survival as a human being, as a being whose reality is bound up with consciousness and conscience. As a consequence, the problem of primitive religion and its emergence in many primitive religions has to be correlated with the understanding of the mythic unity. Apart from a possible typology that results from the analysis of such understanding, the pattern of hominization also includes a fundamental distinction between religion and magic, which affects the whole of symbolic life and not merely some of its aspects.

If there is a final word on religion in primitive cultures, then it is the demand of treating and interpreting each religious situation in the light of a philosophical theory of religion, which covers in principle the whole of humanity and not merely some of its facets.

1. The Differential Universality of Primitive Religion

Whereas the analysis of man's symbolic existence exposes a dimension that is ultimate and universal, it is for the study of concrete examples that this theoretical assumption is verified and put into the right perspective. Each of the four cultural types examined in this study reveals a sphere of actions, values and concepts, that cannot be explained by the immediate context in which they become specific. They interrupt the course of daily events that center around the sustenance of life and thus point to a dimension other than the world of empirical connections and interactions. They point rather toward themselves as they are rooted in the dimension of the beginning, of meaning in the deeds and modes of life, and of the future as a sign of happiness and completion. While this dimension is basically the same in its demands and genetic function, it is nowhere completely identical in its concrete appearances and meta-empirical interactions. These differ in response to the circumstances of the various situations of life and world, not just according to their functional modifications. This can be seen if we compare some of the symbolic expressions (theoretical and practical symbols) in the cultures of gatherers, hunters, planters and pastoral nomads.

1.1 *The Culture Hero*

A first example of this kind is presented in the idea of the culture hero and in those cult performances that refer to this idea. Since the accounts of his function and deeds are attuned to the world as it is known to the various traditions, they change in detail from group to group. But since he stays at the beginning of each culture, there are strong typological similarities: The culture hero is related to the techniques necessary for successful gathering and hunting, for the acquisition of cultivated plants and the equipment for their effective cultivation and use, for the discovery of how to breed animals. In addition to the local differences and typological similarities, we also observe features that are perhaps best characterized as morphological similarities and that exist on a cross-cultural level. For instance, the culture hero may be identical with the creator God, or with the first ancestor, or with both; he may be identified with a certain animal (the chameleon, rabbit, crow) or a visible phenomenon (moon, sun). He often appears as a divine child or son of God, born under miraculous circumstances. Very often the culture hero reveals antagonistic features, as he may appear together with a twin brother or an opponent (trickster) who may work against him. Other similarities appear in the way cultural products originated or were acquired: They were given by chance or mistake or they were acquired by robbery, often connected with a walk in heaven or in the underworld. In the case of the coexistence of two cultural types, the equipment of the one culture, such as bows and arrows, may be given because of sacrifices from the products of the other, such as corn. Most impressive is the acquisition of cultural existence by the death of the culture hero. The god or goddess (divine child, a totem animal) dies and is born again as a cultural plant, as an animal or the like.

The morphological similarities are not restricted to one cultural type but are cross-cultural phenomena. They often exist, as in case of the Bambuti, side by side. Usually, however, one of the features becomes predominant and thus centers the symbolic life around its existence. While one type of culture favors the acting culture hero, others are more impressed by his existential interference with the process of life. The cult is then not so much intended to remember and to reactualize the events of the beginning as it is to integrate the individual or the life of the group into the mysterious processes of fertility, birth, death and rebirth. As one of many consequences of such a paideumatic attitude, human sacrifices are relatively frequent in the latter case. Among pastoral nomads and hunters, for whom gathering is only secondary, the cultural object (cattle, horse, reindeer, bear, seal) tends to become symbolically self-sufficient. The sacrificial animal is a substitute for man and/or god.

In summary and without tracing these ideas on the culture hero and bringer of blessings any further, we may say that they represent a pattern that is modified by the various cultural situations. Despite these modifications, the pattern discloses cross-cultural and cross-typical similarities that point to a universal condition. By being interwoven with the cultural processes, it appears, however, not as a unifunctional but as a differential universality.

1.2 *Prayer and Taboo*

By associating the idea of a culture hero with the human response as this is expressed in various cults, we become aware of a system of interrelations whose final terms blend with the whole of man's life and culture. A symbol that expresses these interrelations, and thus points to them in a primary manner, is prayer. The emotional value of the present situation, the uncertainties of life and world, the meaning of success or failure of the day's work – all these factors operate in the formation of prayers. Gatherers pray for fruits and other edible things; they invoke their God or other invisible beings for help in serious situations; they express their gratefulness for a successful day. Such acts may be underlined by a sacrifice of a bit of the food that has been gathered to the being who helped find it. Since these acts refer to the sustenance and security (and/or insecurity) of life, they are as universal as life itself, provided that a similar mentality permeates this life. As Malinowski (1954, p. 42; see also Schebesta, 1968, p. 303) puts it: 'Food is the main link between man and his surroundings... by receiving it he feels the forces of destiny and providence.' Yet these acts are also as changing as the situations: The hunter is concerned with the game, the forest, the increase of the species. Planters and pastoral nomads are affected by the fertility of the field and herds. Dependence on seasonal rain is mirrored in a series of prayers and rain rituals.

The functional universality of prayer as affected by environmental and economic situations is qualified in many instances, which are neither restricted to a specific culture nor to a certain cultural type, though certain forms may be predominant. The quality of prayer changes with its mode; it can be supplicatory or magical, for instance. Whereas a supplicatory prayer – as for instance the invocations of the Bambuti – manifests an open consciousness in which the world is encountered in terms of an immediate personalism, magical prayer expresses a business-like and legalistic or even mechanistic attitude. Prayer frequently becomes a formalized and temporalized public act that requires verbal accuracy to be efficacious (*cf.* the Pueblo Indians, the Paleo-Indonesians, and others). Sacrifice as a concomitant symbol of an invocation becomes a more or less self-sufficient ritual (*cf.* the blood sacrifice of the Semang and the blood-ritual of the Sakai). Other forms of qualitative, but not functional, changes are in evidence when man calls upon an almighty being or when he enters into 'trading' with his ancestors, with semidivine superbeings. As in the case of many African peoples, life is secured by transactions with ancestors. It is only in situations of grave crisis that God is called upon, and this in its turn reveals a qualitative difference between the forms of prayer. Finally, the social structure does not remain without influence on the quality of prayer. There is, for example, a marked difference if the Bambuti eldest, or the Negrito shaman, or a secret society, or a Maori priest addresses an invisible reality. The spontaneous and situational cries of one instance become in the other an institutionalized and frequently highly sophisticated form of liturgy. At times, as with the Kaingang, for example, historical circumstances may influence the quality of prayers. Whereas the Apinayé call upon the sun and the moon as personal beings, the Kaingang address them in a way that is obviously a historical, formal survival of their tradition, without any genuine awareness of a personal relationship. In connection with the qualitative character of prayers mention ought also to be made of curses, which reveal a mode of negative and destructive coercion.

As these examples illustrate, prayer, although universal in its function, is differentiated by ideational, emotional, social and historical circumstances. The same is true of taboos and ethical imperatives, which can be understood as a type of behavioral or attitudinal prayer. By adhering to ethical codes man responds to the ultimate conditions of his existence and thus gains, as he does through prayer, some meaning of life. Although these ethical responses are usually intended to preserve the social structure, they are also subject to specific cultural and emotional developments that transform them into a kind of magical self-sufficiency. Taboos are observed because the gods and the forces of the universe, as reflected in mythology, require their observation. The entire process is subject to the influence of shamans, chieftains, secret societies, social groups and history; because of these divergent influences, there is a great deal of variation in the quality and distribution of prayers.

1.3 *Divine Being*

The symbolism that expresses more than any other the complexity of the differential universality of primitive religion, that is, of religion in its origin, is that of the divine being in general.[1] In its mythocultic interrelation this symbolism also reaches more aspects of life and world than any other form of behavioral and ideational relations, including those mentioned thus far. Although one of the goals of this study is to propose a comprehensive and genetic analysis of the meaning of the divine being, it is not necessary to do so for the moment. For the present it is sufficient to emphasize that people refer to invisible beings in whom man's symbolism is ultimately terminated. By bestowing these beings with such powers that they become ultimately responsible for the existence of certain things, or even of all things, and/or for the events of life, man's consciousness presents and reveals itself in the idea (and cult) of God or of divine being.

One way of conceiving divine being is by associating it with the immediate conditions of the economy and the environment. Gatherers and hunters refer in their ideas, values, and actions to the 'Lord of the forest' or to the 'Forest' itself, to the God and gods (owners) of the animals or to the animal itself. They are impressed by the frightening and marvelous manifestations of their environment and blend them with their ideas about the divine being. Planters are influenced by their fields and plants, by the fertility of the earth and its mystique. They associate the divine being with sun and earth, with rain and wind. Pastoral nomads approach the godhead in terms of experiences that they have had with their livestock and their specific way of life.

The list of these associations could be augmented and specified in accordance with the situational data. Since the economic and environmental conditions in these cultures are related more or less directly to all aspects of life, the impact of these associative ideas on the cult as the symbolic self-interpretation of man is equally comprehensive. But economy and environment are not the only factors that contribute to the specific qualifications of the divine being. Paideumatic and social experiences, historical relations and symbolic patterns interact with one another and have an effect on the idea of God if this is viewed from a morphological perspective. To see this we need only mention those ideas that refer to God as the creator or initiator of life and history, as the first ancestor, or as father and mother. Similarly influential are such experiences and ideas as those of a basic antagonism within the godhead between omnipotence and limitedness, between life and death. Other indications of this are such notions as the inter-

---

1. The expression *divine being*, as its grammatical form suggests, may be understood as divine person, that is, as *a* divine being, or as the mode of being that pertains to the divine. In the following discussion this grammatical ambivalence will be maintained by purpose.

relationship between celestial symbols (sun, moon) and the godhead, as well as the symbolism of such objects as water, blood, sexuality, the cosmic tree, the tortoise, etc. These symbols are not bound necessarily to a certain culture and economy but exist cross-culturally. But in their symbolic universality and immediacy they are subject to the processes of cultural development, wherein individual and social interests are deeply affected by environmental, economic and historical factors.

The idea of a father God, for instance, is favored in cultures that for economic reasons generally emphasize the role and function of the patriarch. The sky god of the pastoral nomads not only projects and justifies the *patria potestas* or the father-son relationship but also becomes as impersonal as this patriarchal power. The culture of planters, where a matriarchate is frequently institutionalized, instead concentrates the idea of God in the figure and cult of the mother goddess. However, in both instances there is no rigid identification. The idea of divine world parents, of the sacred wedding, or of conflict between heaven and earth, are further ways in which basic experiences of the divine being are conceptualized chiefly among the planters. The antagonism of God as giver of life and as killer is mirrored here in the universalized polarity of the sexes. As the example of the Negritos shows, such ideas may be introduced through historical contact situations, or they may survive, as is probably the case with the cosmic mythology of the Asian pastors.

The differential transformation of the idea of God or the divine being by and in interrelation with certain cultural processes can also be seen when the ancestors (and not only the first one) take over most of the functions of the godhead and thus outline the patterns of cult (manism), or when the indefiniteness of mythological figures is structured and realized (cult) in accordance with a highly distinct social order (polytheism) or environment (local deities, owners). The formative function of man's reasoning power in the genesis of religion becomes manifest when individuals such as the shamans, or groups such as the Polynesian priests, try to traditionalize and to ritualize visionary or highly speculative ideas about God. In all these instances the symbolic dimension, though absolute in its existence, is submitted to the historical and genetic situation of mankind. The destiny of man as a cultural being is interrelated with that of the God to whom he responds, and vice versa. And, if we take the quest for the hereafter also into consideration, the destiny of man's soul is similarly interrelated.

The actual fact that religious phenomena can be found among all the primitive cultures we know can perhaps be understood as a cultural epiphenomenon, whether we interpret it as a means for the maintenance of the economic or social processes or as a form of the irrational that is typical for a mankind not yet 'advanced'. In such instances, we would have to expect, however, that the various phenomena could be reduced either to themselves as a mechanically functioning set of elements or to an identifiable sphere other than their own. Their distribution would have to proceed, then, either by complete dissimilarity, and then the term 'religion' would be a cross-cultural absurdity, or unambiguously in accordance with its foundation. Against this theoretical view there remains, however, the empirical and comprehensive differentiality and cross-cultural similarity of the religious data, which points to a unique and unfounded sphere or dimension. We have therefore to conclude that primitive religion does indeed exist, that religion is a primary datum of man. Like rationality and symbolism, it is not object-bound, but only object-related. As such, it shows a basic relationship to all aspects of *homo existens*, whose undifferentiated experience as *homo religious* takes shape in ideas, images, objects, rules and actions. They reflect and embody the total concept of man's basic insufficiency, which characterizes the depth of his existence and which emerges in as many instances as does his existence.

1.4 *Primitive Religion and Religious Phenomena*

The universality of primitive religion is rooted in the multidimensional universality of man as a cultural being. Like existence and culture, it appears in a variety of forms. In its countless manifestations it is realized and shaped by the creative aspect of human existence, by thinking and experience, no less than by the conduct and actual conditions of life. The indefinite totality of being as presupposed by a reflective consciousness is opposed to and complemented by the presence of the divine as it is encountered in the total awareness of man. Reality as encountered by the senses vanishes into the dimension of divine being. The field between these two poles, that is, between being and divine being, offers the fertile ground for the genesis and formation of religious phenomena. This, in turn, requires that the independent and basic universality of religion becomes subject to the cultural processes, to its advances and truth as well as to its declines, aberrations, or dissolutions. Religion becomes phenomenal in a variety of religions, which are differentially interwoven with the many situations of man. This means that culture and religion are both affected by the human person, who exists on the borderline between finiteness and infinity and thus provides the foundation of differential universality.

The meaning and function of primitive religion as seen against the horizon of its differential universality can be outlined as follows. On the one hand, we have the subconscious, conscious, and metaconscious modes of human experience, which translate what they encounter into their specific language. On the other hand, there are the factual conditions surrounding man: Environment, biological and social needs and challenges, archetypal and paideumatic affections, emotions and volitions, historic conditions, the quest for meaning – in a word, the content of his experience. Since the modes of experience and the creative powers of man are interrelated, the united whole that comes into being is the cultural process itself. The same whole, when it is experienced and symbolized in its origin and in the polar relation of being and divine being, appears as religion. Since neither experience nor symbolization is restricted to a specific form or object, religion is manifested as a genetic phenomenon that grows and develops with the whole of a culture. But since it is not bound to a specific aspect of an existing culture, it may also turn into a kind of subculture or even anticulture that will follow its own ways, independent of established patterns of existence or even in opposition to them. As a genetic phenomenon it is interwoven with all the factors that form and specify the situation. If, for instance, a visionary and semiconscious type of thinking and experience becomes predominant, it will affect the whole outlook, as can be seen among the Australian aborigines. The same can be said about the economic, social, emotional and other factors. The paideumatic experience of the Forest and the Moon among the Pygmies, of the Sky and All-father among the pastoral nomads, of sexuality and fertility among most of the planters affect and shape the whole of the religious system. In all these cases religion appears as a kind of balanced system of symbolic interrelations, in which the objects, images, ideas and rules mentioned above have been selected throughout the cultural processes in such a way that they have mutually influenced themselves and the selective processes as well.

From this point of view we can see that the study of religion must not disregard the cultural context but has to refer to its situational character and significance. It is equally clear that religious life has to be expressed in a distinct, although not necessarily separate, complex or cluster of ideas, insights, experiences, actions and values. The genetic interpretation of religion envisages the possibility of the divine or sacred being as the final horizon of the differential universality of primitive religion, and of God as the most distinct concentration or symbolic expression of precisely the same universality. In other words, we must now look for the content of religion, for the general denominator that mediates between the symbolic expressions of life and world and their interrelation with the depth of man's existence.

Both the idea of God as the focal point of the religious life and the comprehension of the divine being as its universal and absolute horizon are synthesized in mythological narratives. Consequently the analysis and understanding of primitive mythologies seems to be an adequate means for coming to grips with both these aspects. With this we can take up once more, but now from an opposite direction, the line of reasoning that was indicated previously (see Ch. 3) by linking the sacred with the personal on the basis and by means of mythology.

2. The Theogonic Significance of Primitive Religion

If we interpret religion as a cultural complex with fairly distinct boundaries, we can then appreciate the various mythologies as attempts to interrelate the different aspects of this complex and to bring them together into a functional whole. The mythic narratives give verbal expression to the consciousness that man has of his own origin, of the origin of social groups and institutions and of different cultures. Within the context of mythology life becomes livable as a certain tradition; the appearance of things and the perception of events are brought into perspective. Reality and emotion work into one another. In brief, mythology attempts to close the functional gap between symbol and reality, between meaning and actual existence.

2.1 *Functional Truth and the Interpretation of Myth*

This functional theory or vision of mythology has the advantage of covering most of the empirical data. Also it permits a scientific description and analysis of mythological tradition. A mythology once given and initiated stabilizes the divergent forces that affect the community of beings that, because of consciousness, are in one way or another concerned with meaning, happiness and ever-growing fulfillment. For that reason mythology is neither cosmology, nor poetry, nor allegory, nor history, although elements of all these categories may be included. Likewise we must exclude a purely psychoanalytic interpretation of mythology. There are certainly elements in each mythology that refer to man's sexual condition, to subconscious conflict situations and to an unconscious structure of the world. But this is only to be expected. Nevertheless, the simple fact that a mythology is linked to man's whole existence as a cultural being is sufficient proof that it bears on far more aspects of man's existence than those accounted for by psychoanalysis. As a functional medium for uniting divergent aspects of human existence, mythology shows a reality of its own. Myths are, so to speak, true or false, depending on their functional integration or disintegration with the whole of the cultural situation. Or, as Raffaele Pettazzoni (1950, p. 7) put it when analyzing the role of the coyote in North American myths, 'The life of a myth, which is at the same time its truth, is the life of its primordial world of formation and development. Independent from this life a myth may survive, but a surviving myth is no longer true, since it is no longer alive.[2]

The functional interpretation of truth and myth is certainly helpful for the distinction between myth and fairy tale. Like a myth, the fairy tale works with figures of fantasy, with unconscious and conscious projections, with 'legendary' beings and miraculous events. But in distinction from the lived myth, it has no total impact on the meaning of life; it is not an intermediary that embraces the practical symbolism (cult) as well. It is untrue, a false myth, though the borderlines may be fluid in some instances, especially when such myths show a deep moral significance, as in the case of many Eskimo legends. But the functional interpretation is inadequate as long as we do not know why life and myth are interrelated at all. Why is there such a strong interrelation that the destruction of cultural life coincides with the deterioration of the traditional mythology, as can be noted in so many instances? In other words, the factual interrelation between life and myth has only a classificatory and descriptive value as long as the emergence of mythologies and their specific content remain undiscussed. Thus, to give a satisfactory answer to the problem of mythological phenomena, on the one hand we must ask for the relation between their function and content, and on the other, for their impact on the cultural genesis of man. Only if this latter point is seen can there be an adequate approach to the phenomenological connections between myth and religion.

2. See R. Pettazzoni (1950, p. 7). See also R. Pettazzoni (1967, p. 21). As for the literature concerning the problem of myth, *cf.* Schelling (no date), Cassirer (1953a, 1953b), M. Eliade (1963, with literature, A. Anwander (1964), K. Bolle (1968), M. Fuhrmann (1971), J. v. Baal (1971), and W. Dupré (1972a)).

A step toward a solution of the mythological problem as a question that concerns not only some aspects of man, but the universal meaning of human existence, has been offered by the *structural analysis* of Lévi-Strauss.[3] By taking any given mythology as a specific form of language that exists above the ordinary linguistic level and not merely as a state of the mind that makes use of verbal expressions, structural analysis is able to seek the inherent logic of myths. It shows sufficiently that myths are not simply irrational utterances of an unbridled fantasy. But it does not solve the problem of the meaning of this language. The situation here is similar to that of the scientist who attempts a solution of the problems of his science by outlining the structure of the thinking he employs (which is certainly necessary for a sober approach to the problems at issue). In addition, structural analysis shows that some kind of orderliness (a presupposition of all scientific accomplishment) is present. But it will fall short if the analysis proceeds at the expense of experiences and reality. Like the functionalistic, the structuralistic approach becomes insufficient on the cross-cultural level, which implies and requires an analysis that recognizes the differential universality of the mythoreligious complex as an integral aspect of a universal humanism. To meet the requirement of a constitutive analysis, we must deal with the problem of experience as well as with that of objectified meaning (content). We not only have to consider the mytho-*logical* process but also the 'things to which it is applied' (see Lévi-Strauss, 1965, p. 106). As long as we do not listen to the mythologies and trying to interpret them as universal problems of mankind, we apply 'colonial' principles rather than those of hermeneutics, that is, we 'solve' partial aspects and neglect the fact that man's totality is involved.

Any attempt to understand mythology as a reality of its own, that is, as a reality that is effective beyond its functional significance, must acknowledge a basic and irreducible immediacy in the mythological accounts. Though we may use the term 'mythopoetics' to indicate the genetic character of a mythology, mythology is primarily not a poetic way of expression or a verbal exposition of rationally disclosed experiences – to say nothing of its interpretation as the stam-

---

3. See the work of C. Lévi-Strauss, in particular (1967a) and (1969). But also Schelling (no date, XI 89, footnote 2): 'Man könnte die Mythologie etwa auch mit einem großen Tonstück vergleichen, das eine Anzahl Menschen, die allen Sinn für den musikalischen Zusammenhang, für Rhythmus und Tact desselben verloren hätten, gleichsam mechanisch fortspielte, indes dasselbe Tonstück, kunstgemäß aufgeführt, sogleich seine Harmonie, seinen Zusammenhang und ursprünglichen Verstand wieder offenbaren würde.'

mering of a prescientific mind. Mythology, rather, *is* what it *says*. 'It is not allegoric, but tautegoric.'⁴ Whenever we speak of it, we either create a new mythology or try to translate it into a language other than its own.

Consequently, in order to safeguard the authenticity of mythological narratives, we must provide a theoretical framework in which narratives can express their message the way they do because they are understood as a universal mode of being human. Mythologies become real either by being expressed or enacted or by being received within a *human* situation. This means that the intermediary between myth and theory is man himself as a being who possesses language and understanding. In a word, the intermediary between myth and theory is man as person.

The most striking discovery of comparative mythology is the fact that certain mythic themes can be found the world over. People speak of invisible beings that influenced or are still influencing the situation. In nearly all primitive cultures there are accounts of the beginning of the world, of the destiny of the soul, and the like. In conformity with the differential universality of the religious complex, with which the mythologies are actually interwoven, we may postulate therefore a mythic dimension that is maintained throughout the changing situations of man. Since it is anticipated that this dimension is universal, it is necessary to think of it in the same way that we have to conceive of culture. The mythic dimension, or the mythic, must not be understood as the sum total of mythologies but as the common ground from which mythologies spring forth and to which rituals point back in their mythological implications. It is the dimension that continues when old mythologies wither and new ones emerge, or when they apparently disappear altogether. It is the dimension of anticipated integration that is at work wherever an individual or social body continues to exist. It is the dimension of indefinite meaning, which cannot be reduced by or in reflection, but which endures as the inherent certainty of all fundamental questions. As such, it shows a basic relationship to language, in which the inarticulate awareness of world and man is what is primarily articulated and communicated.

So far, this postulate and its interpretation are largely speculative. We have to turn to the mythologies themselves to analyze their ways of expression as well as what they say before we can attempt to secure the proper place of the mythic in

4. See F. W. J. Schelling (no date, p. 198). Schelling borrowed the term 'tautegoric" from Coleridge.

the horizon of human universalism. That mythology and language are inter-related (not only by the mere fact that both rely upon words but also by their sharing a common ground in such a way that they may form a mytho-linguistic unity) is strongly suggested in the case of the Bambuti mythology. But since the linguistic analysis of their mythology is still largely hypothetical, and since an actual and expressive mytho-linguistic unity is certainly the exception rather than the rule, it would not be reasonable to attempt a demonstration at this point. It may be considered, however, as a very significant hint.

Generally speaking, we can say that mythologies respond to basic conditions and questions of man. Among the themes treated in endless variation are the question about the beginning, the emergence of life, the acquisition of the means needed for the sustenance of life, the explanation of illness and death, of certain institutions and situations. These themes are universal as well as ultimate in their outlook. They are an expression of human existence, in which the visible is united with the invisible, the without with the within, the beginning with the end. If we look upon the myths from the point of the themes they are dealing with, they reveal an immediate proximity to the reflective questions of philosophy.

Like philosophy, mythology is concerned with the world and its existence, the presence of man in this world, the meaning of life and history, and what man has done and will do. It is concerned with personal togetherness and longing for immortality. But while philosophy tries to treat these themes by reflective thinking, the mythologies simply tell us how it is. Mythologies explain but do not demonstrate their explanations. They give reasons, but they do not search for them by proving their validity through systematic thinking. Thus we become aware of a division between two attitudes which, in fact, refer to the same situation. Despite the sameness in themes, philosophy seems to be on the opposite side of what mythology is able to accomplish, or more accurately of what can be accomplished in mythology.

In assessing the relationship between philosophy and mythology two points should be taken into consideration. The first is the fact that reflection relies upon experience, for which it cannot account but which it must use. There simply is no such thing as an empty structure of reason. The *a priori* character of a given knowledge and understanding is always an *a posteriori* discovery. Only if experience unites with reason and intelligence can reason become universal and thus a realization of meaning. The second important consideration is that of

being. Although philosophy tries to clarify the question of being, all its attempts
to do so show clearly that an indeterminate awareness of the meaning of being is
the continuous presupposition of the questions that philosophy raises and seeks to
answer. Even 'nothingness' is thinkable only as a momentary projection of the
mind on its way toward being.

These considerations have a twofold result. On the one hand, they show that
philosophy and mythology share a common ground if we look upon them from the
perspective of the themes with which they deal.[5] Thus, the division between
philosophy and mythology is only gradual and not basic. It is not only justifiable
to postulate a mythic dimension to human existence, it is necessary to do so in
order to appreciate the interrelationship between mythology and philosophy with
respect to the *a priori* character of meaning. Meaning relates to both, to the word
of a reflective process (*logos*-word), and to the word of tradition (*mythos*-word)
(see Dupré, 1973a). On the other hand, it is obvious that the analysis of concrete
mythologies cannot proceed unless there is some interpretation of experience and
its relationship to the human person. This brings us back to the mythologies
themselves, to their content and mode of expression.

2.2 *Myth and Meaning*

Mythologies make statements about the general condition of man and the world
by relating the present situation to their own. The mythical world of the beginning is extended into the present and affects the things of today in their meaning.
A mythology is a totality of meaning, unique in its symbols and acts, in its
figures and events, yet it always directs the emerging individuality of the here
and now to the unconditioned universality and presence of 'wherever' and 'whenever'. It is a meaning that is identical with the things themselves and yet far
away from them.[6]

The concrete mythologies express this relationship between meaning and fact

5. Since language is the medium in which thought and meaning originate and develop, this
common ground can be extended to include language. Consequently a mytho-linguistic unity, even if
its presence should not be discernible in existing languages, is at least a theoretical possibility, if
not a transcendental postulate. See J. G. Herder (1789), W. v. Humboldt (1836), E. Heintel
(1972); also Chomsky's (1969, p. 3 ff) concept of *linguistic competence*.

6. See the problem of the transcendental difference (above p. 27) and the present discussion
about the meaning of meaning both in philosophy and the phenomenology of religion. *Cf.* J. J.
Waardenburg (1972a).

in different ways. Their reality is that of creation, the unity of an eternal present with an eternal effectiveness. The invisible reality of the primordial and comprehensive time becomes visible in the continuous presence of man and world. The Australian aborigines speak about their dream-time, which they rediscover in visions and during the secret and sacred ceremonies of initiation. The Bambuti refer to the invisible, yet most effective (visible), power (*megbe*) in which things originate and grow. The totality of meaning that is encountered in the mythological stories and acts is expressed by a thoroughgoing interrelationship between the mythic figures. In their functions, and occasionally also in their names, they merge into one another. The creator-god becomes the first ancestor, the earth, the sky; the culture hero turns into God or the first ancestor, and vice versa. Metamorphosis is thus a universal category of the mythological figures that expresses the comprehensive reality of the mythic dimension.[7] The polarity of man's existence is mediated in the unique meaning of being-there.

The mythological figures, while becoming identified with the world, nevertheless preserve a fundamental 'otherness' from the world. God, the first ancestor, the culture hero have left the world or are in some way separated from it, although they may remain immediately associated with such phenomena as the forest, the chameleon, the moon, the *wondjina*, the bull-roarer, the drum, the rattle. Thy mythological reality, in other words, while deeply interwoven with the visible world, is fundamentally different from it. To express this mythic truth, the narratives make use of rationally inconsistent language. The Moon created the Moon (Bambuti); the Sun appears as a handsome human being while shining in the sky (Apinayé). The philosophical insight of the heterothetic existence of man is a foregone conclusion in the mythic narratives.

The first conclusion that we can draw from these instances as they exist in given mythologies is the necessity of interpreting mythology as a whole. Its relation to the present situation is not that of one event to another but that of a complex and complete reality. Mythology begins to have significance only when it is taken as whole because comprehensiveness and totality are the fundamental implications of its coming into being. In a negative sense, this implies that even the sum total of narratives, as they can be registered in a given cultural situation, does not exhaust the whole reality of the dimension from which they emerge.

---

7. See E. Cassirer (1953a, p. 91) who speaks of 'the law of the leveling and extinction of specific differences'.

Positively, this implies that the term 'mythology' should be extended to include not only the traditional word but also each gesture that responds to the mythic or unconditioned meaning of life and world. Mythology embraces the unconditioned dimension of all symbols and anticipates the completion of the process of symbolization. Consequently, man is not only the most symbolic symbol but also the irreplaceable myth, since it is he who actually anticipates the recollection of mythologies in the participant character of his existence. Whatever becomes meaningful for man, even if it is not expressed as reflection consciously mythic, is part of an actual mythology. This explains the universality of the mythic and its functional truth, and it also shows why myth and ritual are connected. To seek the priority of one over the other is a pseudo-problem, since it restricts the range of the mythic and thus reduces mythology to something that it is not.

The pertinent question here is the following: Does the inherent mythology of cult and custom correspond to the narratives and vice versa? If it does, it would explain why traditional mythologies can lose their immediate meaning or may disappear altogether. A mythology opposed to the present experience necessarily conflicts with this form of realization, and this is a phenomenon that we have noted in discussing Eskimo culture. The mythology, however, is preserved in the interrelations between symbolism in general and its mythic depth. Similarly, if the traditional symbolism dissolves (as occurred in the case of the Kaingang) the narratives become meaningless, for the structure of the mythic dimension (man's ultimate mode of life) has already changed. Finally, we can understand why a mythology continues without being traditionalized in the strict sense of the term. The mythic consciousness is in itself sufficient to recreate the same mythology in a more or less homogeneous physical and cultural environment (for instance, that of the Pygmies).

The second conclusion is that mythology must be interpreted as the expression of a primary experience. This resumes the reflections on the interrelation between *homo existens*, *homo symbolicus* and *homo religiosus* and the interpretation of religion as the result of a universal, though selective, process. In his heterothetic existence man is present to himself (the person) and to things (the world). By uniting both modes of experience he is aware of the 'fact' that there is something and that there is someone. This experience is filled and synthesized with the realization of events such as growth and decay, birth and death, work and support, individual and community. But it is also permeated by emotions such as fear and hope, hate and love, responsibility and guilt, authority and spontaneity, by archetypcal visions and dreams, and finally by the intuitions of meaning and ultimacy. 'Someone' and 'something' are therefore not separate facts but are concretizations of an all-embracing horizon of awareness, which perhaps can be best characterized as *coincidentia mythica* since it is constituted by the coincidental movements within the mythic itself. It is 'being' in the unity of the visionary, intuitive and reflective consciousness and thus the final foundation for all articulations. The mythic experience is primary experience, the condition of everything that may be experienced. In distinction to the reflectively analyzed modalities of being as inward presence (actuality), past (necessity) and future (possibility), or as outward thing (actuality), form (necessity) and matter (possibility), it unites the depth of time and space in the 'mythic' modality of *mythicity*.

It is in this latter mode of mythicity that the mythic dimension becomes the general condition of primitive religion. In its mediatory universality it not only offers the foundation for irrational-rational behavior, but it is also *theogonic*, in the sense that it opposes and unites God and the world as the mystery and the concretion of being and meaning. As the foundation of narration it bestows reality upon the figures of which mythology speaks and which cult enacts. Mythicity sets the consciousness free by bringing it into the horizon of ultimate communication, in which it comes forth as personal ground as well as metapersonal creativity. Its foremost statement is not an explanation of phenomena such as birth and death, but that God created heaven and earth in the beginning. It is the basic openness of man, in which the truth of the originating person is the truth of the mythic in its completion. Man's relation toward the mythic is, therefore, fundamentally a personal one. It enables him to be creative, to 'make' himself and his mythology, to be religious in the constitutive milieu of the life community. The mythological projection and the mythic emergence of man as an image of God or simply as a divine being (*cf.* the function of the first ancestor; man as the foremost myth) is not a fantastic self-deception of a presumptuous consciousness but an expression of the spontaneous truth of human existence. Mythicity is thus the condition while its initial transformation into myth and mythology might be described as the foundation of primitive religion.

2.3 *Mythicity, Consciousness and Religion*

In its complementary function with respect to consciousness in general, mythicity not only influences the ways of the human mind (as it is likewise influenced by them), but it also offers the basic aspects of the religious life – God and creation, the mythic Someone and Something – and is shaped in accordance with the responses to these aspects. Although this relation is, like the mythic itself, basically open to a formative process that is initiated by cultural history and is shaped by the many circumstances of man's factual existence, it nonetheless shows an inherent structure that embraces in a primary manner the ways of religion. The primary experience of the mythic dimension (our second conclusion) is thus related to its comprehensiveness (our first conclusion).

Mythicity is not just a universal no-man's land, a featureless *fluidum*. In its completion as *coincidentia mythica* it connects and unifies opposites. This implies, however, that a polar reversal is the continuous feature of its dynamism. The mythic God and the mythic creation are not only coordinated but reversed. God stays 'behind' his creation, and vice versa. The mythologies express this when they presuppose what they are going to 'explain'. The mythic completion simply precedes all specifications and momentary articulations, although such specifications and articulations are simply the forms and expressions in which it becomes manifest. The mythologies also express it when they describe a creative force that permeates the creation. It is the power of God as personal center that continues to shape the world, though the world has already been shaped by its creator. *Megbe, mana, manitu*, though different in detail when compared with one another are nevertheless similar insofar as they penetrate the world and are received by a person whom they endow with creativity and power. Finally the mythologies express it when they relate the world to the godhead by turning the facts of man, world and history into associations of divine appearance. The world behind the mythic God becomes the sacred manifestation of his presence. It is, in the terminology of the Negrito mythology, the world of the *éenoi* that is displayed between the ineffable God and man's effability.

To formalize the polar interplay of the mythic dimension, we can summarize these deliberations as follows: (1) The mythic someone (god) as opposed to the mythic something (creation) is reversed and united by turning God into Creation. Someone/something comes forth in the conception of the mythic force. (2) The mythic something (creation), which is opposed to the mythic someone (god), is reversed and united by turning Creation into God. Something/someone presents itself in the conception of mythological associations, that is, of the sacred and all its entanglements.

The consequences of this analysis of the *coincidentia mythica* are far-reaching. For instance, our previous definition (*cf.* above, p. 140) of religion as 'the totality of man's encounter with the sacred' must be reevaluated in the light of the preceding reflections, whether the 'sacred' is replaced by the 'mythic' or whether it is understood expressly as a moment in the process of mythic mediation and coincidence. At any rate, it is now obvious that from the point of view of primitive religion the sacred is not necessarily dialectically opposed to the profane. Rather the opposition is only potential, and its realization depends on a reflective interference of man. As the example of the Epulu Pygmies shows, the world of the Forest turns out to be the sacred world (a dialectically defined entity) when it is opposed to the (profane) world of the villagers – an opposition that is clearly associated with the cultural conflict and thus with a negatively definable difference between two economies and societies. If we consider the role of the sacred in the self-alienating process of the Kaingang culture (where it is a 'different thing') or in the processes of depersonalization as implied by food and social taboos and the various forms of magic, we become aware that the problem at issue relates to the whole of mythology and religion and that it must be indicated in the definition of religion.

Another consequence affects the relationship among mythicity, mythology and religion. Mythicity is the primary truth of man as a person, that is, as a being constitutively related to the life-community and to itself. The reality of man is his becoming: He gains his identity in a multitude of actions and reactions. He lives by speaking and thinking – in and through language. It is the mythic condition of man that makes this consciousness-giving relation of personal being possible. As we have said, the relation to the mythic enables man to be creative, to 'make' himself and his mythology. Since this relation is rooted in the ultimate depth of human existence, the process of creativity is not just a matter of specifying a given texture but also of an unrestricted transcendence. Man's becoming is not just the 'accumulation' of recollected presences but also and *a fortiori* the integration of his future as a constitutive dimension of his 'being-there'. Since it simultaneously contains God and creation, mythicity is the immanent content and foundation of man's consciousness, which for precisely this reason has been described as theogenic consciousness. Because of its coincidental immanence, however, mythicity inescapably initiates a process of transcendence. In its unconditioned reality and comprehensive function it turns (transcends) toward the visible as well as toward concrete imagination. But at the same time as it turns toward the concrete (in virtue of its originating and all-embracing primacy) it challenges the person-in-the-becoming to reverse this process of his mythic immanence and to transcend the visible, imaginational, and singular, and turn toward the invisible, ideational and universal. In other words, mythicity is not only the meta-empirical reality of man's consciousness, which assimilates the empirical world as the manifestation of meaning, but it also initiates a movement to leave behind all figures and mythological concretizations and to transcend consciousness in the medium of its ultimate conditions.

The inherent move of transcendence as rooted in the coincidental immanence of mythicity requires the not-mythic or amythic as the final outcome of reflection, a reflection brought about, however, because of the mythic. On the one hand, the mythic dimension is open to all the formative factors that may come together in a cultural situation. It is open to archetypal conditions, dreams and visions, emotions, sublimations, environmental, economic and social circumstances, and whatever their suggestions may be. It is open to volition, value, reflection and intuition alike. On the other hand, all these elements and their impact on man's situation are not simply matters of fact. They are swept along by a movement of transcendence or, since it is a movement from the ultimate and immanent to the concrete, by a movement of descent so far as consciousness is concerned. In the context of the person's attempt at finding himself, however, this mythological descent is subject to a basic reversal, to an absolute ascent, or to transcendence in the proper sense. Mythologies are therefore not only shaped in accord with the inherent structure of mythicity but also in accord with the human person's response to his immanent mythicity, that is, they are subject to man's intellectual responsibility or conscience, in which he either recognizes or distorts the transcendent movement as initiated in the depth of his being there. Thus, in order to speak objectively about mythicity and the actual realization of its demands (mythology and religion), the use of qualitative junctors to describe mytho-religious phenomena becomes necessary. Man may turn, for instance, toward the mythic God-person by seeing in the various mythological figures the translucent symbol of his hope and trust in the world and the meaning of being. Or he may treat his mythological presence as the subject of rituals and self-effective rules. He may relate to the mythic force by accepting its mythological manifestation as a gift and creative present of the godhead and thus, through its concrete significance, reach out to the ultimate God and his Creation, or he may consider it as a useful and/or dangerous means for achieving the immediate purposes of life. In all these instances, man has the choice either to accept his mythicity and to recall in its concretizations his ultimate and comprehensive origin, or to forget this origin and to distort it by equating the signs of its presence with the empirical conditions of his existence. Whatever the reasons for his actual decision, it becomes clear that in the latter case God, Creation, the Sacred, the mythic Force and their many translations turn into separate entities, into 'sacred' hierarchies, supermen or even monsters, into fate, and other constructions of man. The history of man as the process of human self-realization and and self-discovery or finding reveals, in the light of the mythic condition, the permanent possibility of distortion and self-alienation.

Mythicity as the condition of primitive religion determines its appearance as the initial realization of the theogenic consciousness. Primitive religion is therefore not identical with a certain set of ideas, rules, prayers and rituals but rather with the process that binds them together and gives them direction at a given moment of culture history. The intersymbolic dynamics and reality of primitive religion has therefore both a practical and a theoretical significance. From the practical and objective point of view (the functional approach), it can be understood as the integration of the mythological figures and concretizations in the total conduct of life. Primitive religion is here simply the theogonic consciousness as it is realized in the total articulation of life itself. From the theoretical and subjective point of view (the humanistic approach), it can be interpreted as the concentration of the mythological symbols toward their mythic origin and a-mythic meaning. Primitive religion comes forth as the initial reversal of man's symbolic existence toward the transcendent and comprehensive horizon of the theogonic consciousness. In any case, it is that act of man in which he finds God by finding himself. Both aspects indicate therefore basic patterns of primitive religion.

2.4 *Unio Mythica*

Before we turn to a discussion of the God- and Man-finding patterns in primitive cultures and their interrelation with primitive religion, it remains to resume the problem of magic. In chapter three we considered magic as a complementary, and to a certain degree necessary, aspect of religion. We came to this conclusion by contrasting the process of religion with that of personalization. While this analogy and transformation is still valid, its content can be reevaluated in the light of the preceding reflections on mythology and mythicity as a universal condition of man. The fundamental relationship between mythicity and consciousness presents religion as a process, the reality of which, though universal as this basic relation itself, is nevertheless subject to the natural as well as the cultural circumstances of human existence. Since this process is essentially interwoven with the genesis of the person and his conscience, it is in principle an open and therefore unpredictable process. This does not exclude the possibility of singling out specific modes of behavior or response. If we intend to analyze the God-finding pattern of primitive religion, we have already anticipated such a possibility. The problem here is not that of typological structures but the necessity of qualifying the religious process as a whole and of evaluating it by the opposite and universal characterization of self-finding and self-alienation or, as we may also say, as religion proper and magic.

It is true that a qualification of this kind is based upon empirical conditions. The fact of consciousness implies that of mythicity, and mythicity reveals itself as the basic tension of the human person in which man becomes capable of projecting himself, of acting as a responsible being. The absolute demands of mythicity reveal actual incompleteness and possible deviation and distortion. In keeping with the human situation and the coincidental structure of mythicity, there is always an opposed or reverse movement in the constitution of the person, whether it continues as an immanent possibility of man's process-being, or whether it becomes a goal in itself. Thus magic, as we may call the impending presence and realization of this movement, is as universal as religion. Although we need not inquire here why such an opposed development must take place, we must ask how it is related to religion. Is it indeed complementary to religion and, if so, in what sense?

Both processes, the transcendent movement and its reversal, originate in the immanence of the theogonic consciousness of man, which is not only polar in its content (*coincidentia mythica*) but also in its relation. The polarity of the person, which has been mentioned, can be understood as the empirical expression of a meta-empirical factual condition of man. In this sense, religion and magic are already mediated by sharing the same origin. They are complementary to one another insofar as the ultimate character of the process in which both of them share remains by necessity in the tentacles of finiteness. The ultimate significance of the theogonic consciousness and its symbolic realization (religion) is limited by the finite relationship of precisely the same symbolism (magic). What is over-looked in this dialectical interpretation of religion and magic (the formal value of which cannot and will not be denied) is the non-dialectical thrust of mythicity.

As the dimension that mediates between the terms of understanding (someone/ something as related to mankind and world), mythicity is not subject to negatively opposed divisions and subdivisions but shows a fundamental integrity that is shared by the elements and the process of communication. It is neither thesis, nor antithesis, nor synthesis, but the common ground of the dialectical process which precedes and exceeds all dialectical oppositions, just as the presence between persons goes far beyond the terms and words that are employed to articulate its meaning.

Mythicity is relevant for man not only because it gives access to the theogonic dimension but also because it brings consciousness upon this existence in the first place. That means that there is a factual unity in which religion as well as magic, thinking as well as conscience, values as well as volitions, are united in a 'yet' undifferentiated manner. Being a complex of its own, the *unio mythica* as we may consequently call this 'yet' undifferentiated reality, can be considered as the remaining minimum of integration in the diversified streams of life. The *unio mythica* can be reduced by the dissolving factors of reflection and cultural life but never removed, for its removal would still presuppose, and thus introduce again, its existence as being possible. From the viewpoint of religion and magic, we can therefore say that there is a sphere in which both processes come together because they originate from it. It is a sphere in which the achievement as well as the deficiencies of the theogonic consciousness cease to exist, as in the case, for instance, when a cult turns into the wordless song and the purposeless play of sheer existing. Consequently, mythicity as the condition of primitive religion is also its reality to the degree that both are interwoven into the *unio mythica*.

For the actual understanding of primitive religions, however, it is important to see that the extent and undifferentiated complexity of the *unio mythica* cannot be determined *a priori*, nor is it identical in the various cultural situations. The degree to which the *unio mythica* is real depends on many factors, among them on the intensity of historical differentiation and on its challenges to the individual and the community. In this sense it may be that the religious life in a primitive culture is largely identical with its *unio mythica*. This at least is suggested by the more or less total interwovenness of the various areas of life. But there is no justification for calling such an identity a *unio magica*, as Mensching does, at least not if we approach the religious phenomena from the point of view of mythicity. This does not exclude the possibility that magic and religion are inextricably interwoven in a given culture, or that magic predominates over religion. It is not, however, the *unio mythica* but a mixture of religious and magical elements to which we are referring in such an instance. If we intend to describe the *unio mythica* as it is real in many primitive cultures, we may rely upon the proximity between the mythic and the person as realized in such a situation. In this case, we could describe a situation in which the *unio mythica* is more or less unrestricted in its impact on the religious life as that of an immediate or 'numinous personalism' (J. Haekel).

Returning to the question whether magic is complementary to religion or not, and if so in what sense, we can answer now as follows: Seen from a purely theoretical point of view, their complementarity is that of a dialectical opposition. There is a rational gap, in which the finite cannot be united with the infinite, although the one cannot be thought of without the other (see Hegel, 1968, p. 8 ff). From the practical point of view, which of course goes back to the theoretical approach, magic and religion are complementary in respect to the *unio mythica*. It is because of the fluidity of the extent of this unity in a given situation that the borderlines between magic and religion become fluid in themselves. In this sense it may be said that magic is indirectly complementary to religion. In their theoretical opposition as well as in their practical mediation, however, religion and magic are concomitant phenomena in the historical process of hominization. They are, for this reason, not restricted to certain cultures or peoples.

3. THE THEISTIC OUTLOOK OF PRIMITIVE RELIGION

Mythicity as the origin and point of reference of mythological symbols, and finally of all symbolic gestures, is co-original with the human person. Its universal condition affects more than just one or another aspect of life. Indeed all aspects of life are bound up in their entirety by the dynamic and polar constitution of the mythic dimension.

Mythicity is disclosed in a factual process of descent, in which the invisible reality of man and world is associated with the visibility of things and images by the mere presence of consciousness. Consequently, mythicity must be understood as the universal condition for the quest of meaning and for the formation of rational hypostases, words and concepts, sentences and propositions. Mythicity is also manifested in a spontaneous process of ascent, in which the relational whole of the visible associations and images is transcended in the direction of their mythic invisibility and amythic, personal significance. The mere presence of consciousness is associated with the conscious search for the meaning of the present and the conscientious response to the present sought. In consequence of the ultimate 'something' and 'someone' as the immanent polarity of the present and the response to it, mythicity turns out to be the initial realization of theogonic consciousness and reality. The *unio mythica*, in which the processes of descent and ascent are primarily interrelated, thereby becomes both the practical and the theoretical description of primitive religion. It is the initial reality of primitive religion.

The differential distribution of ultimate symbols and modes of behavior throughout the context of primitive cultures made it expedient to see religion in those aspects of man in which the universal quest of his existence is interwoven and synthesized with his historical and cultural becoming. Now the discovery of mythicity and the *unio mythica* explains why this empirically suggested and theoretically postulated conclusion is philosophically necessary. As the primary datum of existing consciousness, primitive religion is neither an *epiphenomenon* of the cultural processes nor a *phenomenon* in the true sense of this term but the fundamental and (as *unio mythica*) the autonomous relation that is involved in the process of personal becoming. It is the metaphenomenal condition in the genesis of the religious phenomena that unites them with the whole of culture by giving them a distinguishable identity. Whenever we speak about these phenomena, including the conception of God, we must keep this condition in mind.

For this reason it would be methodologically wrong to raise the question of a monotheistic conception of God in the protoculture, which by definition is culture in its origin. Since this question implies that of polytheism, and thus presumes a certain degree of cultural and ideological differentiation, it necessarily misunderstands protocultural conditions. Likewise, we can say that the question about an a-religious or purely magical stage in the development of man is beside the point because it denies the universality of consciousness and personality as expressed by the mere fact of language. Equally to be rejected is the presumption that the idea of God is absent on the protocultural level, and that, if it is present in a culture, it is only explicable as the result of a 'long' development. Although this interpretation of protocultural conditions does not necessarily deny the existence of religion, it nevertheless distorts the protocultural completeness of mythicity and thus implies a distorting reduction of the *unio mythica*. Since the reduction of the *unio mythica* must be interpreted as the result of cultural and ideological differentiations, this theory actually deals with a secondary and not with the primary 'stage' of culture, but this is what it is intended to do. Besides such theoretical constructions there remains the fact of relatively undifferentiated cultures, and consequently the question of what they contribute to the understanding of religion in general and primitive religion in particular.

3.1 *The Divine Person*

Although an empirical understanding of primitive religion must take into account all available phenomena, certain complexes hold priority. Above all, it is the idea of God or of the divine person that is most important for the subject. The reason for this preference is factual as well as theoretical. On the one hand, there is, as has already been mentioned, an extensive distribution of phenomena closely related to the idea of the divine person. On the other hand, there is the unique meaning of the mythic someone in the initial polarity and movement of the mythic dimension. In contrast to the fundamental aspects of the Sacred, of Creation and of the mythic Force, the divine person is not only an integral part of the process of mythological descent and ascent but is also the final and only goal of (meta-mythical) transcendence. Since transcendence is the basic relation of the person and all personal acts, the divine person as presented in the texture of mythicity attains a unique position inasmuch as it becomes the mythic-amythic reality of man's freedom. Although he is symbolized in many ways and pictured by many images, God can be called upon because he is neither symbol nor image, but the transcendent pole of life as far as the person-in-the-becoming is concerned. He is, strictly speaking, the ineffability of man as a person, and all that can be said about him is already an explanation of the mythic awareness, whether it be that he created heaven and earth in the beginning, or that earth and man are there by being his possession.

We do not have to repeat here all the empirical data in order to verify the theistic outlook of primitive religions. In all the cultures we have discussed, the very existence of prayers or invocations, for instance, implies the presence of someone other than the living man. Since it is possible only to call upon a person, and prayer in its essence calls upon someone, the intentional reality of the religious life does include a personal aspect. The same can be said about mythology, when we look upon it from a purely matter-of-fact standpoint, that is, when we refer to it as a phenomenon distinct from mythicity. So far as it accounts for the human situation, the personal implications of this situation become in one way or the other retroactive for its own meaning. Because of the interpersonal projection of man, there is a need for the invisible person, whose presence is in some way responsible for something. That at least can be said to be indicated by the empirical data.

With this general and descriptive approach from 'outside,' a framework is established in which it becomes possible to synthesize the 'divine person', as found in the empirical situation, with its structural reality as discovered in the analysis of the relationship between mythicity and mythology. By understanding the 'divine person' not as a specific being but as an open category, which complies primarily with a psychological need for an interpersonal demand, we have found a classificatory instrument that permits us to collect the significant data in a new way and thus broaden the empirical base for the constitutive analysis. The advantage of this second approach consists mainly in that we do rely not only on the meaning of narratives (words) but also on that of behavioral expressions (deeds) and their corresponding affirmations.

Although there are as many ways as there are human situations in which the idea of the 'divine person' is realized, we reduce these realizations to a relatively small number of typical features. In this context it is to a certain degree necessary to repeat some of the remarks that have been made (see chapter three and above, p. 247). What matters at the moment is not so much the features themselves but the way in which they are approached and explained.

In analogy to man's encounter with man, we can distinguish between four aspects of the realization of the divine person. There is, first of all, the presence-experience of the other person, which is qualified by the ways of person-experience in general and also by spatial and temporal circumstances. There is, secondly, the implication of hypostatization. A person is present as a body, as a gesture, as a voice, as a deed. A third aspect is that of interpersonal relations. The other person is there for the sake of togetherness, of help and support. Persons are not by accident, but by essence, community-related. They define one another in mutual dependence. As for the life-community, we may think of situations where person and community merge into one another. On the other hand, as a consequence of this relation, persons become also subject of avoidance and manipulation. Finally, there is the aspect of interpretation. We think about the other person, his character, his reactions, his status, knowledge and intention.

Though all these aspects are infinitely interwoven with one another, they never-theless do help in the attempt to decipher the immediate situation and thus offer guidelines for the description of the problem at issue. The application, which we present as the dialectics of divine presence, will explain what is meant.

3.2 *The Dialectics of Divine Presence*

3.2.1 *The presence Experience of the Divine Person*

The features of the divine person that belong to this descriptive pattern can be reduced to the questions 'How is its presence experienced?', 'Where?' and 'When?'. Since the ideas about divine beings are handed down from generation to generation, one way to become aware of them is through tradition in general. The individual experiences the 'divine person' because he grows up in a certain human community and mythology. The invisible presence of the divine person is a part of the underlying yet tacit and undiscussed presence of cultural symbols and the mythic experiences of the life-community. 'God' is there because man has been brought up with his presence. We can say that this form of presence-experience, though unaccounted for in itself, is a universal mode of man, which may be more or less prolific in certain instances but which is nevertheless a funda-mental and a cross-cultural fact. It becomes specified, however, when it is con-nected with certain forms of experience. The presence of the 'divine person' may be associated, for instance, with the dream-(time) experience, or with ecstatic and visionary experiences. Emotions such as fear, wonder and joy, or the paide-umatic experiences of growth and decay, birth and death, are other instances in which the divine presence may become obvious. Also the possibility of intuitions, of value-experiences, must be granted as a means for becoming aware of the divine presence. In summary, such experiences can be interpreted as the subjective component in the process of divine presentation. As such, they necessarily escape exact objectification, although the psychology of religion has sufficiently shown (*cf.* W. James, G. Wobbermin, W. Gruehn and others) that it is possible to take them into consideration on a typological basis.

From an objective point of view, the presence of the 'divine person' can be connected with certain events, objects, and places: The rise of a thunder-storm, the appearance of the rainbow, the occurrence of disasters and wars. But play and work, birth, adolescence and death, not to speak of cult performances as such, are also events that are intimately related to the presence of the 'divine person'. The opening of a new season, the absence of rain or sunshine (in a word every significant alteration or interruption in the progress of time) all bear the immanent possibility of becoming an occasion for the presence-experience of the 'divine person'. The same can be said about places and celestial phenomena. The forest, the seas, certain sites, mountains, caves, the sun, the moon and the stars may become significant for the presence of the 'divine person'. The same is true of objects such as stones, plants and animals. Practically everything that exists under the sun may instigate the presence-experience of the 'divine person'.

Finally, we can distinguish between the modalities of the presence itself. 'God' may be everywhere. He is all-present and simply there. Or he may be far away (*deus otiosus*), present only in situations of absolute crisis. Usually, however, it is a limited presence, that is, it is more or less exclusively restricted to its temporal, spatial and objective associations. This leads us to the second aspect of the 'divine person', to the forms of its hypostatization.

3.2.2 *Hypostatizations of the Divine Person*

As we know from the reflection upon our concepts, presence as such cannot be thought of, although all thinking is mediated by it. Presence must be related to something else. The basic indefiniteness of the 'divine person' has to be identified with something other than itself. The range of such identifications is broad. One way is offered by the presence-experience itself. 'God' is the sky, the sun, the moon, the earth, the chameleon, the bear. As visible phenomena, however, these identifications are to a certain degree incompatible with the inward experience of the personal. They are therefore often substituted for or at least connected with the hypostatizations of precisely this inwardness – the soul, the figures of dream and imagination and, finally, ideas. The 'divine person' is identified with the deceased, whether the latter are independent entities or are merged in the idea of the first ancestor or in other hypostases of the godhead. Or the 'divine person' is identified with imaginary super-beings that are thought of in connection with significant aspects of life and the world. They 'own' the forest, the game, the water, the air, the village, the field. But again, the boundaries of their existence are often fluid; they merge into one another or blend with an indefinite 'divine' being. With regard to ideas, the 'divine person' may appear as all-father or all-mother, as the beginner, the power of life, as highest being or simply as the nameless someone. But also in this instance there is no strict definiteness of the 'divine person'. It is always subject to the merging process described in respect to the human situation and its interpretation.

3.2.3 *The Interrelation between Man and the Divine Person*

Since the human self-experience as a person reveals some kind of unconditioned element in the texture of causal relations (in terms of work the latter is known by each cultural group), the idea of a 'divine person' offers both psychological and theoretical reasons for securing the meaning of life without denying its apparent absurdities. The presence-experience of the godhead and its hypostatic identifications make it possible and even necessary to refer practically to this invisible 'thou' and thus to realize the meaning of life by establishing a system of interrelations (cult). In accordance with the indefinite presence of the 'divine' being, such interrelations may be equally indefinite. Everything that man does becomes in some way a part of that cult-system. Or it may be restricted to certain moments and actions, which in their turn are associated with the divine 'entities' or with their specific appearances. The result of this association is the development of distinct cult patterns in which the help of the 'divine person' is sought and its presence celebrated. This may be done in a mood of supplication (by recognizing the superior character of the divine as grace and goodness) or with the intention of manipulation (by implying a superiority of man through right knowledge) or with the feeling of obligation and duty. Even avoidance may become a way of interrelation. 'God' (and this is also the suggestion of the etymology of this word) is the one who is called upon or to whom sacrifices are offered. The 'divine person' becomes the measure of meaningful, customary behavior. And customary behavior determines the ways of response in respect to the divine. In this sense, we can say that each tradition bears its own religion.

3.2.4 *The interpretation of the Divine Person*

The relationship to the invisible 'person' is realized by actions that follow the logic of interpersonal behavior as well as of its identifications and the modalities of its presentations. Besides these factors we must include the interpretation of the 'divine person' and its hypostases as an active constituent of the religious complexes. Like the human person, the divine person is either good or evil; it is gifted with knowledge and power; it is affected by modes of behavior and reacts to them. By regarding or disregarding the demands of its presence, it will be honored or insulted, loved or hated. 'God' protects his children or he punishes them. He listens to them or refuses to do so. Such qualifications, which by themselves imply the ethical character of the 'divine person' (if we presuppose that the origin of ethics is seen in the constitution of the person), can be limited or universal, definite or indefinite. The divine person may be eternal and without beginning or may share these qualities only to a certain extent. Its knowledge and power are absolute or restricted and thus escape all human attempts to influence them, or, if restricted, are subject to the intervention of others, including man himself. By comparing the accumulated traits of the 'divine' character, the 'divine person' may also share a certain status or position. It may take a higher or lower rank in the divine hierarchy. Since these interpretations are also ideas, they can, of course, be used also as separate hypostases. The good God, for instance, is opposed or complemented by an evil one, the Mother God by a Father God, the dying God by a rising God. But even in these instances, which in turn indicate the basic unity of the personal component of religion, there remains the same problem of interpretation. It is the problem of the 'divine' as the attribute of the ineffable yet responsible 'person'.

By analyzing the religious problem in primitive cultures from the perspective of the 'divine person', we make two highly significant discoveries. First of all, it becomes obvious that no definite answer can be given about 'the' divine person. Its meaning is too situation-bound to be universalized in its character. Something like that is possible only on the speculative level, which is, however, not that of lived ideas. There is, of course, the possibility of a classificatory approach, as the typological descriptions we have given indicate. An approach of this kind may be helpful for a cross-cultural comparison, but it has no ontological value as far as the protocultural situation is concerned, unless it is taken in its entirety, that is, unless the classificatory patterns are understood as indications and ways of realization of one morphological process. But this leads us to the second discovery, which can be described as the total implication of the 'divine person'. Within the framework of presence-experience, identification, relation and interpretation, the 'divine person' not only gains its own momentary identity but also structures and stratifies the whole of religious life. It allows us to take the empirical data as morphemes, which in their interpersonal entanglement become indications of one universal process, that is, of the process of hominization. As such, and only in this sense, they become highly significant for the protocultural conditions of religion.

3.3 *The God of Primitive Religion*

Since the protocultural dimension must be interpreted, by virtue of its essence, in terms of the relationship between the undifferentiated and the differentiated, the indefinite and the definite aspects of life, we must look for such indications when analyzing a given phenomenon. With respect to the 'divine person', there are two moments of indefiniteness that are unseparable from but not reducible to one another. They are, on the one hand, the presence-experience of a personal reality, and, on the other, its immediate interpretation as power or mightiness. By complementing each other they constitute a field of tension in which man realizes their indefiniteness in definite figures (hypostases) and specific modes of behavior (cult). The 'divine person', which was first conceived as the categorical projection of a psychological need and an interpersonal demand, now becomes the terminal conception of a coincidental process between 'presence' and 'power'. In the primordial coincidence between the personal and the powerful, the situational restriction of the meaning of the 'divine person' becomes an unrestricted condition of man and his world-experience. Though subject to man's self-realization, it is always 'ahead' of its identifications and interpersonal realizations. Conversely, we can also say that the concretizations of this process (when connected) point beyond themselves toward a horizon of absolute transcendence and all-presentness. In their more or less broken unity, primitive religions reveal an unbroken unity of man, world and God, which can be understood as the final condition of primitive religion. The analysis of the 'divine person' here arrives at the same result as that attained by analysis of the mythic or theogonic consciousness. The God of primitive religion is the nameless one who is all-present.

Just as the coincidental interpretation of the process of primitive religions makes it possible to arrive at its immanent presupposition and implication of absolute transcendence and all-presentness, it also allows us, when reversed, to reinterpret the empirical data in the light of this implication. The complementary togetherness of the personal and the powerful is then not only an indication of the coincidence of these two aspects but also of their separation. In the concrete situation we can therefore expect that one of these two aspects becomes predominant. 'God' as power and 'God' as person (presence) detach from one another in a similar way as all other aspects do (that is, as presence, hypostasis, relation and interpretation). At the same time, however, such singularizations are not simply 'parts' of a scattered whole but combine and reflect their morphological origin. If we call the complex system that indicates absolute transcendence and all-presentness in the divine person *mono*theism and if we name the systematic restriction of the divine hypostases *poly*theism, we can also say that the concrete situation is that of a relative monotheism or relative polytheism. Both are identical so far as they are broken representations of the unbroken reality of primitive religion.

The relative structure of primitive religion, which is perhaps best expressed in the functional transition of the various hypostases of the divine person, not only allows for the theoretical exposition of the transcendent and all-present person but also makes it necessary to postulate a fundamental unity that permeates the processes of conceptual and practical specifications. It is a unity that has to be seen at the 'beginning' of the existing consciousness and, since it continues as its condition, at the 'end' of all cultural achievement. Between these two poles we have the whole scale of cultural modalities, in which the fundamental unity between man and world, the man-person and the God-person, is gradually realized, depending on the human response to the demands of its own existence. Since this unity is in its origin neither reflective nor simply emotional or irrational it can only be mythic. The theory of mythicity and the *unio mythica* merges with the theory of the divine person and all its implications. In the identity of their results, both theories verify each other. The idea of the *unio mythica* as the fundamental reality of primitive religion is therefore a valid instrument for its description and understanding.

Applying our previous analyses to the study of primitive cultures, we are now able to specify the modes of their relation to primitive religion as follows: (1) The closer a culture comes in its representation of protocultural conditions the more comprehensive will be the *unio mythica*. (2) The less broken or reduced the *unio mythica*, the more we can expect that the mythic polarities will coincide with one another, and vice versa. (3) The stronger the reflective attitude toward the *unio mythica* becomes, the greater becomes the gap between magic and religion. (4) Since the content of the mythic (the mythology) is gained by its descent toward visible associations and visible-invisible images (ideas), its transcendence can be realized only in respect to the divine person, who is not a thing or a content but a 'thou' that is called upon. The theistic outlook is therefore not only an accidental aspect of primitive religion but also a basic pattern of its realization throughout cultural processes. (5) Although the discovery of the theogonic consciousness and the *unio mythica* (fundamental unity) reveals a basic autonomy of primitive religion, its fundamental interrelation with cultural processes shows also that it cannot be treated independently from these processes, and vice versa. Being co-original with the process of hominization, primitive religion is not only influenced by this process but equally influences it. Its impact on the process of hominization thus becomes the final pattern of the realization of primitive religion and its transmutation into primitive religions and religious phenomena in general.

4. PRIMITIVE RELIGION AND ANTHROPOGENESIS

Thus far we have dealt with religious phenomena mainly in respect to culture (differential universality), to consciousness (theogonic reality) and to the person (hypostatic presence). The result is an interpretation of religious phenomena as aspects of a universal process that is constitutively interwoven with the reality of culture and mankind and thus as real as man himself. In his very existence and experience, as well as in his ability to respond and to make decisions, man is necessarily involved in the morphological development of religion. The situational synthesis that evolves from these conditions is a symbolic reality that both shapes man and is shaped by him. It is a correlational reality. As such, it opens the road toward a reversible and complementary or constitutive analysis. On the one hand, we can and must trace this reality (as has been done) toward its ultimate meaning. This process culminates in the theoretical outline of the God-person as the metaphenomenal condition of man as person and as religious being. On the other hand, we can and must trace this symbolic reality (as has yet to be done) toward its immediate meaning for the human being. Because of its phenomenal structure we must interpret religion in its impact on the actual condition of man. Both aspects are complementary and thus imply and require one another. They can be separated only for methodological purposes.

The question requiring attention now in order to complete our analysis is that of the meaning of religious universality for the particularity of man. What does man think about himself, how does he realize himself, and what is the impact of this process on religion and vice versa?

●

4.1 *Survival and Religion*

As a biological being man wants to and must survive. As a human being he fulfills
this basic drive consciously. Because he is aware of himself, he realizes the need or
drive within him toward synthesis. Consequently it is not enough for him and his
well-being to overcome economic and social difficulties by reasoning alone; the
condition for the exercise of this power is man's consciousness, and this brings all
human situations into a synthesis with the whole of life. Man wants to live and to
enjoy life and thus is in principle totally affected by the changing content of his
situation. In addition to economic and social uncertainties, he must overcome all
kinds of fear, especially that of death. His general well-being is not merely the
result of an optimal reduction of all forms of calamities but is largely dependent
on the realization of such drives as power and sexuality, play and work. The result
of this situation is a lasting gap between the demands of existence and the reality
of the empirical world. To overcome it, man has to relinquish the remedies of the
empirical world and to turn to those of a metaphysical fantasy, of a fantasy that
gives him the ideas of integrity and fulfillment by basing its figures and descriptions on the intuition of a fundamental synthesis of the divergent forces of life,
world and time. By integrating them into the texture of life, he finds a way to
survive as a human being. If we identify the goal of this process of integration
with the immanent and ultimate purpose of religion, religion can be considered
the culmination of man's attempt to master life. As such, it belongs to each
human being. It is the core of man's quest for himself as part of his will to survive
under the condition of his particular existence. Whatever the character of the
symbolic reality that bridges the gap between existential demands and the empirical world, it necessarily mirrors man's groping projection of himself. Paradoxically,
it even precedes this, inasmuch as it makes it possible through the implicit anticipation of a fundamental synthesis.

Like any other human effort, the religious can succeed or fail. It may be to the
advantage of one group and the disadvantage of another. It may be constructive
or destructive, depending on the way in which symbols are handled. In the context of primitive cultures, this religious function is manifested in the various
intercultural and inner-cultural situations. In the struggle with other cultures, it
becomes the main force of cultural identity, as can be seen in the case of the
African Pygmies and Australian aborigines or whenever a culture is about to be
overthrown. The decay of culture, as the examples of the Kaingang and many

others show, is connected with the deterioration of religious symbols. If a culture is overthrown by another culture or by altered economic, environmental, and social forces, religion is the factor that will stabilize the new situation. Here we have only to mention the efforts of the villagers to enslave the Pygmy hunters by integrating them into their initiation rites. The various forms of group-ideology, which guarantee the superiority of one group over another, are further expressions of this condition.

In all these instances religion is seen as an ambivalent reality. On the one hand, it is altered and specified throughout the process of history by the human needs and tasks that must be mastered and by the many goals that are to be pursued by individuals and groups. It is basically open to the creative imagination of man, as well as to his destructive imagination. On the other hand, nothing opposes change as strongly as religion sometimes does. By rendering customs meaningful, it justifies them and sanctions their continuation. As so many taboos show, it is here that man often becomes the prisoner of his own creations and the slave of those who enjoy the advantages of the system. Instead of realizing his freedom in the openness of religious transcendence, he turns to the imagined security of self-constructed formulas and traditions, including those of the concept of 'God'. Religion then becomes a strong barrier against all attempts of the mind to break out from its imposed world-structure.

In both instances we become aware of a fundamental choice in man's attempt to master life. It is the choice between an attitude that integrates the content of metaphysical fantasy without destroying its fundamental synthesis and an attitude that uses or refers to this content but rejects its unobjectifiable foundation. In keeping with our explanation of the transcendent character of the fundamental synthesis (the *unio mythica*), we can also say that it is the choice between religion proper and magic. Although both are functionally identical to the extent that they are both attempts to master life, religion does not close the gap between the demands of existence and the empirical world. Despite the mediatory figures of its mythology, it maintains its reality in the indisposability of the divine person. Its most expressive symbol is the supplicatory prayer. Magic, on the contrary, claims to close the gap by manipulating the same mediatory figures and ideas. Its primary symbol is the self-efficient formula and the right ritual at the right time.

Two things become clear in this analysis: (1) On the one hand, there is the rational and comprehensive character of religion and/or magic. As the culmination of man's encounter with the world, religion and magic are not only bound into his rational endeavors but also exceed all particular forms of human realization, including their own concretizations. The thrust that brings them into being is such that it escapes the effects of its very action. In this sense religion and magic are not a particularity of 'primitive man', although it may be granted that their total impact on human existence is perhaps much more obvious in primitive cultures than in our own. (2) On the other hand, there is the interrelation of this rational attempt with something like a metaphysical fantasy that is postulated with regard to the modes of survival.

While the meaning of metaphysical fantasy remains by and large indefinite in cultures with more or less definite philosophies and ideologies, it can be identified with mythology in primitive cultures. To complete the analysis of the relation between man and primitive religion, therefore, we have to reduce the question of this chapter to the problem of the relationship among thinking, mythology, religion and/or magic. But first there is still one other aspect of the impact of consciousness on the situation that must be mastered and that has left its traces in the formation of religious attitudes and traditions.

4.2 *Conscience, Adulthood and Priestly Existence*

We have said that man must master the problems and challenges of life within the conditions of his consciousness. These conditions are not only described by the transcendental fact of a metaphysical fantasy but also by the temporal conditions of recollection and expectation. Man remembers his life, and thus he has to face the problem of meaning inasmuch as this recollection shows that things could be different from the way they are. To be conscious of the world, therefore, includes the possibility of being aware of its apparent absurdities such as the struggle for survival, sickness, suppression, exploitations, mischief and, finally, death. In addition to this experience of evil as the negation of meaning in the objectivity of consciousness, there is also its affirmation in the subjectivity of conscience. Man faces the problem of meaning not only in the things around him but also in what he has done and is about to do. In its existential modality consciousness is interwoven with the process character of existence. It is bound into the evaluative texture of comparisons and statements and into the responsive structure of decisions and, finally, of being as such. In a word, it comes forth as *conscience*. Thus, the attempt to master life is in its consciousness-relation equally related to the latter's modality as conscience. To bridge the gap between existential demands and the empirical world, the metaphysical fantasy has to project an image of man, as can be seen in the various mythologies. These mythologies are expressions that account for the implications of his conscience. They deal with the problems of sin, guilt and duty, that is, with his failure to act as a human being, with the unavoidability of such failure and with the obligation to oneself and the life-community.

Though the awareness of these implications is largely integrated into the genesis of mythological patterns and thus points again to the problem of the interrelation between thinking, mythology and religion and magic, there is also an empirical-practical aspect that has a formative impact on the religious process.

Since conscience is essentially practical, its discoveries of actual distortion and possible integrity raise problems of personal and social interaction. Religious existence, like social existence, needs to be mediated; it implies a priestly (or charismatic) existence, that is, an existence that finds its integrity in and by the positing of symbolic acts and their transcendent meaning. This transcendent meaning can, of course, be neglected, forgotten or simply skipped, while the acts that are aimed at mediation are posited and continued. Instead of the priestly existence, we then envisage that of the magician. In the concrete situation it is usually impossible to decide to what degree a priest acts as a magician, or vice versa.

In its general meaning the priestly existence, like that of the magician, is not restricted to certain individuals. Basically, it has to do with everyone who participates in a cult performance or a magical ritual. As the examples of the Pygmies and many other peoples show, every adult person may function as a priest or a magician by meeting the customary obligations and rituals. By sharing the status of adulthood, man is aware of his position as mediator in the world around him. As one Pygmy expressed it, only stupid people forget sacrifices and prayers. Man grows into this world by becoming aware of the connections between birth and death, behavior and meaning. Among the Bambuti, for instance, the rites that mark the passage from childhood to adulthood are more or less informal. The first successful hunt or the symbolic touch by the moon (menstruation) indicates the new status. This is, however, the exception rather than the rule. Usually the initiation rituals are complicated and entail a marked difference between 'before' and 'after'. Like the various *rites de passage*, in which the metamorphic events of man and world are celebrated (birth, death, marriage, seasonal changes), initiation expresses a new status. It is the consciousness of adulthood, in which birth and death and the meaning of life are mediated in the existence of man as a new being (often symbolized by giving him a new name), as can be seen especially among the Australians.

While every adult may function as a priest in most of the cultures of gatherers and hunters, it usually is the eldest or the leader of the group who bears more responsibility than others. However, since the performance of cultic acts and magic presupposes a definite kind of knowledge and understanding, the idea of the priesthood or the magician tends to become more specific and institutionalized. The priest becomes a specialist. It is, as the Negritos express it, the *Hala* who knows best how to pray.

In conformity to the data of primitive cultures, we can distinghish two distinct types of priests or magicians. First are those who have been called by the godhead or by a divine being. Their career begins with some kind of visionary experience. Such experiences may be, as among North American Indians, obligatory for each individual who wishes to achieve human maturity or adulthood. Here again we have an indication that initially the priesthood is a general feature of religious man. In this case, the shaman (to use the Tungusic term that refers to this type of priest) is a person whose visionary experiences exceed those of the others. Second are those who have been chosen through social processes. The old men in Australia, the African priest of the earth, the leaders of sacred (and secret) societies, the Polynesian priests or the members of a certain profession (blacksmiths, porters) are examples of this second type of priesthood.

The two types of priesthood are not always clearly distinguishable. The shamans, for instance, may try to perpetuate their office by recruiting their sons as their successors. In any case, since knowledge is important, the learning process has to be organized in some way, and this gives new impulse to social structuralization. There are major and minor shamans and higher or lower priests. In addition to the knowledge required from the shaman or priest, there is also power, which is displayed in the effectiveness of his ceremonies. The consequence of this aspect is, for the specialist, the attempt to make his power secure by rendering his office and person an integral part of the religious and magic world. On the side of the social specialist (eldest, leader, chieftain), it is the attempt to share this power either by uniting the social and the religious office in his preson, or by becoming a part of the religious and magic world also, without exercising preistly functions. In the latter case, the chieftain is not only a person who is responsible for the maintenance of the social situation and process but also the symbol for the integrity of man and world. He becomes a cult object. Since this development points beyond the context of primitive cultures, especially in its form as sacred kingship, we need not trace it further here.

The need for mediation involves, as we have noted, knowledge and power in order to become efficacious. Not only does this account for the possibility of social tensions in the priestly existence, it also explains why the shaman or medicine man becomes the doctor and advisor of the group, or why witches, who are believed to have special faculties and powers, are so important in primitive societies. Since the consciousness of a priestly existence is clearly present, the 'extraordinary' individual is in himself a religious phenomenon, even when there is no priestly caste.

We should also mention the sorcerer or witch doctor. Unlike the medicine man or shaman, who rely very often on magical knowledge, he does not use this knowledge for the interests of the community but for selfish and destructive purposes. In this sense he can be considered a caricature of the priestly existence, a fact that becomes possible when magic loses all contact with the religious dimension.

The power that all these persons share and the knowledge they possess are based on the mythic conviction and experience of the community. In this conviction the empirical world is not divorced from its mythological interpretation but forms one basic unity. The causal process is therefore not restricted to empirical conditions but is equally interwoven with the mythological, especially if the transcendent presence of the God person, which introduces the unavailable (god) without removing the objectivity of the symbolic, is lost sight of. Consequently, the mythological symbols are not only efficacious with regard to the empirical world but also synthesize the logic of empirical processes with that of their own. This is certainly a reason why it is so difficult, if not impossible to come to grips with the details of a symbolic culture; for those who share it, it is a necessary and indisputable condition of truly human life, while those who observe it encounter an unaccustomed and, to a certain extent, bewildering entanglement of reality and the symbolic. In the context of such an empirico-mythical world, sickness, disaster and death are not merely the result of empirical causes but are equally attributable to influences of mythical or meta-empirical realities. Priestly and/or magical mediation becomes at this point a matter of a mythical struggle – or as we might also say, a mythological performance – in which the inward needs of man are overcome by mastering their outward projections (symbols), and in which the outward needs (sickness, for example) are interpreted as the result of inward distortions.

A most significant illustration of this situation is the flight of the Eskimo shaman to Sedna in times of grievances or his attempt to rescue a soul that has been lost, leaving the body in illness and in the agony of death. Apart from the fact that mythological ideas of man and the soul are rationalized and, from the point of mythic thinking, in some way demythologized, these ceremonies clearly show both elements. On the one hand, there is the cult performance, the confession of sins (broken taboos), and on the other, the mythical struggle, as when the shaman cleans away the dust that has accumulated on Sedna, or when he tries to catch the escaping soul. To accomplish this goal he has to fight, in collaboration with his invisible protector, against the evil forces of the world and of man, forces that are simultaneously empirical and ideational.

4.3 *Mythicity and Thinking*

There can be no doubt that man's rational attempt to master life and to gain personal and social integrity relies upon a world of images and ideas. These are the work of his fantasy, the momentary and spontaneous reflections of man's encounter with reality, and yet they have a life of their own. They form the world in which man discovers his own origin and that of all things and in which he takes refuge when his struggle for survival and search for meaning collapses in the face of his fears and troubles. It is a world he remembers joyfully when he detects the astonishing fact that he has survived and that life is worth being lived. It is also a world with which he operates for the well-being or ill-being of his own life and that of his fellow man. Though many factors can be listed that influence and determine the structure of this world, in its immediate reality it is (like existence itself) an unconditioned revelation. Man is there, and because he is there he has this world of his. This at least is the indication that comes forth if we connect the morphological differentiations that evolve in the general interrelation between religion and culture, or in a more specific phenomenon such as the priesthood, and trace them back to their undifferentiated roots.

Several factors point to an immanent and all-embracing unity that is mediated through man's metaphysical fantasy. Among them are the basic ambivalence of religion in the maintenance or alteration of the cultural processes, the differing ways of realizing religion by the person and society and the universal character of the priesthood with its tendency toward specialization. To understand religion as a cultural and personal phenomenon we must therefore rely upon the *unio mythica*. Since this is the comprehensive reality of the mythical mediation, it is not only the initial reality of primitive religion but also the theoretical and practical condition of man. It is the meta-natural and meta-cultural beginning that continues in the evolutive process of man and culture as the personal foundation of a universal humanity. In the light of this mediation, religion is not only hypothetically but also necessarily the culmination of man's attempt to master life, and whenever such attempts are made religion is involved in one way or another.

Since we have already tried to interpret the immediate content of the *unio mythica*, we must now reflect on its relationship to the rational process of history in order to put the theogonic consciousness and its cultural development in the right perspective.

In its mediatory function, the mythic dimension is not reducible to the work and power of reason, although it must be granted that reason has its impact on the formation of the mythological figures and events. For the mythologies are, as we have seen, not simply identical with the mythic dimension, but are the result of a translative process that takes place in and reflects the heterothetic movement of man's existence. To illustrate this relational complexity it may help to consider a symphonic performance.

There is a thorough contingency in the selection of instruments, the tonal systems and the score itself. In their genesis, however, and in their actual performance, it is rationality that assimilates the nonrational conditions and transforms them into an emotionally pleasing and rationally appealing unity. Nevertheless, there remains a preceding unity that is rationally inexhaustible. It is the unity of music itself, or the musical dimension, which appears in the silence of the symphonic intervals and rests, and which in the indefinite richness of its content makes it possible to create music and to listen to its creations, although it is reason that finally translates musical receptibility into the symbolic sound of an orchestral performance.

As has been explained, the mythic dimension is not reducible to one aspect of consciousness. It is the whole of consciousness that presents itself in the mythic dimension. For that reason we called the mythopoetic fantasy a metaphysical one, a fantasy that is possible and real because it is born by the entirety of the existing consciousness. Since thinking can be identified with those acts of consciousness in which it synthesizes its contents (experiences) by transforming them into a different modality of its existence (language as articulated thought), the mythic dimension and its content are necessarily (or always) related to the process of thinking. The thinking that emerges here is, however, neither emotional nor instinctive, neither rational nor theoretical. It is a form of thinking that is congruent to mythicity and in keeping with the immediacy of its function and origin. It is perhaps best characterized as mythic thinking because it relates the undetermined contents of the mythic dimension to that of object-consciousness and articulation in general.

Mythic thinking is neither alogical nor is it restricted to primitive cultures. Rather, it is the core of all forms of thinking in which they are connected to the *unio mythica* and to its interpersonal reality in a living community, where they are mediated, so far as their actuality is concerned. There is, of course, the possibility that the intensity and extent of mythic thinking or (if we look at its universal function) of the interpersonal consciousness of a life-community may vary from situation to situation. But more important than this aspect of mythic thinking, at least for the study of religion, is the fact that it has not only theoretical but also practical significance. This means that whenever thinking is realized, its possibility of being 'translated', that is, of being realized on different levels, is mediated in the *unio mythica*, which for that reason is simply the mediatory reality of culture itself. We can also say that mythic thinking has not as yet been differentiated into the processes of retention and expectation (protension). Its recollection (retention) and expectation (protension) are still united in the comprehensiveness of the mythic present. Thus if it is proper, from the structural point of view, to call the completion of the retentive relation *faith* and that of the protensive relation *hope*, then faith and hope are not yet differentiated, but they are both implicated in the unity of mythic thinking, which indeed serves as the condition of their possibility. The same can be said about the *ought* character of ethical and, in a certain sense, of logical propositions. The antecedent movement of transcendence in the *unio mythica* offers a comprehensive projection of the world and of mankind, relating the end of mankind to its beginning by taking it back into the unfathomable depth of the God-person who is both amythic and mythic.

Because there is such a close relationship between the *unio mythica*, primitive religion and mythic thinking, primitive religion is, strictly speaking, not a faith- or belief-system, although it must be interpreted as the underlying condition for a system of this kind. This helps to explain why so many primitive religions are capable of integrating heterogeneous religious elements, and why they are not inclined to propagate their religious system, as are religions that have a more or less identifiable founder. The submission of one group to the religious symbols of another, which can be observed frequently, does not contradict this, since this submission is primarily not a matter of religious convictions but of cultural assimilation. Similarly, we can say that primitive religion is not an ethical system, although it must be considered as the foundation of the latter. This explains why many of the mythologies of primitive cultures are so indefinite about the compensation of good and evil, about the destiny of the soul (as ethical subject) and about the hereafter (as ethical measure). For primitive religion what matters is that man is a divine being, that he is meaningful in his existence, and that this existence has undergone some disastrous events in the beginning that account for the difficulties today. As the Pygmies say, nobody knows what happens when man dies. It is true that various theories about the soul have emerged, that primitive religions speak about many principles of life, such as dream-souls and shadows, that they refer to the destiny of man in the hereafter and describe a land of the deceased, an underworld, the forest of the godhead and so forth. All these aspects of primitive religions may be interesting in their detail and are highly important for the actual working of a symbolic system or culture, but for the whole of religion and its foundation such ideas are secondary because they presuppose a mythic space in order to take shape. In its initial realization religion is not a matter of the hereafter but of this earth, whose meaning is guaranteed by the comprehensive awareness that God created it in the beginning and that it is owned. It is the realization that there is an answer to man's search for the meaning of the present and to his desire to understand the challenges of its experience.

Like the protoculture itself, the mythic dimension and the modality of mythicity are present as empirical ideas rather than as objective data. As empirical ideas, the mythic dimension and mythicity exist nowhere in their pure state or in any clearly definable isolation. They are subject to the processes of historical development, to the creativity it entails, and to the rational grasping whose purpose is the mastery of the urgent problems of life. In the immediate relation of mythicity to the situation we can distinguish between the following features: (1) On the one hand, we have such constituents as environment, economy, paideumatic experiences and language, all of which modify mythicity and define its content. (2) On the other hand, there is the conscience-related awareness of the mythic dimension, or what we have called mythic thinking. (3) In the third place, mythic thinking is qualified and specified by consciousness-related understanding, which in turn is met by the rational interpretation and application of its content. Since the so-called objective factors are more or less secondary in respect to the basic structure of the mythic dimension and the *unio mythica* (*cf.* the *coincidentia mythica*), the key problem that is left is concentrated in the qualification of mythic thinking, of its understanding as presupposed in the endless number of situational applications (rational interpretation), cult patterns and customs. Thus, the question that now has to be asked can be formulated as follows: What are the qualifications of mythic thinking in primitive cultures? Or, how is the *unio mythica* understood in primitive cultures?

5. Cultural Perception and the Dynamics of Primitive Religion

People in primitive cultures usually do not reflect upon the presuppositions of their actions and symbolic orientation. 'Our parents told us so' is a stereotyped answer to questions about the evidence of their tradition. A theoretical or transcendental understanding is thus not typical for primitive cultures. But then, what kind of understanding is it?

If we compare the symbolic culture of the Pygmies with that of the Australians, we can say that both people live their respective mythologies and that the mythological narratives are comprehensive. But while the Bambuti show an indefinite relationship to their mythology, the Australians have made a definite system of it. Man and world are integrated into the mythic accounts, not in their mythicity but as they are today. The mythic world is no longer the total and comprehensive otherness-identity of the present world but is part of it. It belongs to the rational explanation of the historic and geographic landscape. The present world does not participate in the mythic world but is an identifiable part of the myth itself. Two basically different modes of understanding are thus exemplified by the Bambuti and the Australian aborigines. On the one hand, we find a kind of intuitive awareness of the mythic world in which the real and the mythological merge without becoming separate parts or entities. It is a total diversity that, by the immediate association of the 'two' worlds, passes beyond all particularities in the unquestioned and undoubted presence of the godhead. We might say that it is the quality of mythic thinking itself that characterizes understanding here. As the problems of everyday life are encountered, the mythic world is rationally interpreted (*cf.* cult and magic) and thus identified with respect to, but not with, the empirical world. It maintains an intuitive and meta-rational life-integrity, which becomes manifest in the cultural fact that 'God' and 'Power' are basically one reality. On the other hand, (among the Australians) it seems that we have an awareness of the mythic world, in which its meta-rational life-integrity is more or less completely interpreted, that is, rationally specified and ordered. Understanding and rational securing are in a process of coincidence. The mythic and the empirical world are not really different. As a result, the mythological associations fall short inasmuch as they do not transcend the particularities of the empirical world but only synthesize them. They are not 'associations' but 'facts' beside facts. It seems to be a kind of understanding that gives rational and cultic meaning to the dream-time experience at the expense of personal integration and a balanced view of reality.

Both modes of understanding can be well distinguished in their final effects. By connecting the *unio mythica* with the empirical world, they pave the way for the practical, that is, the rational realization of mythical ideas. But while the first mode of understanding initiates a process marked by the basic openness of religion proper, the second entails a magical manipulation of the mythological contents. In case of the Bambuti and Australians we can also say that both ways of understanding result in a system that as for the mythology realized might be described in the first case as mythotheism and in the second as mythomagism. This does not mean that the Australians are unaware of divine beings or that the Pygmies would not be familiar with magical rituals. It only indicates that the rational translation and application of the *unio mythica* is dominated in the one case by an understanding that favors the indefiniteness of the divine presence, while in the other it is governed by an understanding that relies heavily on the definite content of the mythological reality.

While it cannot be doubted that there are two different modes of understanding that oppose each other, much uncertainty remains about their correct explanation. In accordance with the indefinite, yet most revealing, character of intuitions, we called the first mode of understanding an intuitive one. It indicates that the first mode of understanding has to be established on the intuitive side of the multidimensional reality of consciousness. It is on the intuitional or meta-conscious level, where mythicity (mythic thinking) and consciousness come together. But how can we specify the second mode of understanding? What is its relation to the first mode? Are there other modes between or in addition to them? From the point of view of its effects, the second mode of understanding could becalled the magical one. This terminology would have the advantage of underlining the universal character of magic, but it does not offer a satisfying explanation.

It seems that a solution can be achieved if we go back to the analysis of the 'divine person'. When we analyzed the presence-experience of the person, we said that it needs to be identified by associating it with identifiable phenomena, that is, by turning it into a hypostasis. The category of hypostatization, as it appears in this context, is a universal pattern of thought and language that is intrinsic to the structure of experience and personal being. If I speak about a person (and there is no other way to get 'hold' of a person than by speaking about and to him) I must relate my predication to something. This 'something' is not the person I address or about whom I am speaking but something else. Consequently, there are two ways of understanding which are different yet are real only in mutual relation. Since the mythic dimension is intimately connected with the genesis and the realization of the person, we can expect that these two modes of understanding are equally valid with regard to its translation.

By emphasizing the thing-pattern as the polar aspect of the experience and conception of the person and in continuation of the hypostatization of mythicity, which results in the appearance of concrete mythologies, we can conceive of the possibility that man also hypostasizes the mythologies, or at least parts of them. The result of such a double hypostatization would be an empirical integration of the mythological world, which is indeed the case if we look at the cultic and social elaboration of the Australian dream-time conceptions. What has been a hypothetical presumption becomes (at least in this instance) a reasonable explanation. In addition, it answers the question about the first mode of understanding and its relation to the second, since the intuitive awareness is fundamentally the core of personal experiences. To know that I am here, that I am thinking about the problem of experience, about a thou to whom I am speaking and who is speaking to me, about the flow of time and the total manifestation of the present, always implies a momentary intuition that is basically indefinite. However, it is in the light of this indefiniteness that I understand myself, the other person and everything that subsists. The two modes of understanding are for that reason not merely two unrelated possibilities but, as has already been indicated, belong together as one polar entity.[8]

The suggestion that the rational interpretation and application of the mythology might be preceded by an understanding that operates on the basis of hypostatization is not based solely on the Australian data. It seems that in the majority of cases of primitive religions this type of understanding is operative, provided that we do not consider it in a specific way but instead focus on its immanent polarity. Because of their foundation in the mediatory comprehensiveness of the *unio mythica*, all possible forms of translation are in some ways co-remembered, even though one of them becomes predominant. As has already been indicated, the hypostatic understanding may affect the whole of a given mythology or only parts of it. In the first case, the mythological world becomes a distinct and separate entity, which is in itself dialectically opposed to the non-mythical or to the profane world; but since it has been subject to hypostatization twize, it is at the same time a part of the empirical world. There are holy or sacred objects, places, times, beings and ideas. The sacred no longer complements the mythic God-person but is an independent quality. It has lost its personal relation and hypostatic dependence. The sacred as constitutive aspect of the myth in religion (*coincidentia mythica*) becomes a myth of its own, which is opposed to that of the profane but which in this opposition shares the basic implications of the latter.

The advantage of this understanding of the mythic dimension (and this holds true also for the scientific interpretation of this understanding) is without a doubt the fact that religion becomes by far more graspable. As aspects or even parts of a substance-like entity, religious symbols can be treated in a way similar to that by which tangible objects are treated. On the practical level, religion is not only related to society but becomes part of the world in which the society in question develops, or even a part of the society itself. In its dialectical otherness religion reflects the 'sacred' image that the society preserves of itself against the unrestricted freedom of the person. From the perspective of the empirical data of primitive cultures such an absolute transformation of religion into societal magic is the exception rather than the rule. It is a possibility that is indicated by the speculative understanding of hypostatization but only partially realized in the

8. As for a philosophical approach we mentioned previously the transcendental or theoretical mode of understanding. Properly speaking, this is not a third way of understanding, but is the result of the thematization and coordination of the two possibilities described in the text. Consequently, there is no philosophy that could disregard the basic polarity initiated in the divergent modes of mythological realization. If it does, they will nevertheless 'return' under the disguise of 'self-evident' ideology.

empirical situations of cultural processes (*cf.* the Australian aborigines and the taboos concerning Polynesian and African chieftains).

The second form of hypostatic understanding touches only parts of the mythic dimension, while total or complete hypostatization remains indefinite. The typological possibilities that we can conceive are theoretically identical with the types of hypostases mentioned above. To the degree that the second mode of understanding is concerned, however, they are not the immediate associations of mythic thinking with regard to the mythic dimension and the situation but double hypostatizations, that is, independent and substantial entities that have dissolved from mythic indefiniteness and polarity while being confronted by rationality and dialectical opposition.

Such understanding may be concentrated in various degrees on the different parts of the symbolic reality. The religious types that result from these analytically described processes have been emphasized at various times and occasions throughout the history of religious studies. In this context they may be roughly outlined as follows: If, for instance, the gods are hypostasized and conceived as superstructures of the empirical world, there is a religious system that tends toward the predominance of high gods and toward polytheism. If the divine character of man is stressed, and the dead are consequently put into the foreground, the system that results from this process is known as manism. The same might be done with ideas about the soul. We speak of animism. If vital force, nature symbols and cosmogonic ideas are stressed, we may speak of dynamism, nature worship and fatalism. As for totem-oriented systems, the mythological metamorphosis can be seen to have undergone a similar process.

Unlike the primary process of hypostatization, which corresponds to the first mode of understanding, the secondary process of hypostatization no longer expresses the comprehensiveness of mythic thinking. It becomes extensive rather than comprehensive. As a result, religion loses its rational indefiniteness, which is characteristic of mythic thinking, and becomes an identifiable system of traditionally fixed or institutionalized patterns of behavior. Its rational interpretation is no longer a translation based on the situation, but is rather a purposely directed modification of the mythological world. It would be wrong, however, to see a clear-cut conformity between the morphology outlined here and the empirical data in primitive cultures. Although the empirical data strongly suggest a structural similarity such as has been outlined here, the borderlines between an intuitive or open and a hypostatic or fixed understanding of the mythic unity are very fluid. There is no reason whatsoever to identify primitive religion, or even religion in primitive cultures, with one of them exclusively. In many planting cultures, for example, where clear distinctions are made between the mythological high-god hypostases, such distinctions are easily removed in the actual process of worship. The god to whom people refer is, though situation-bound, unrestricted in his actual presence. Instead of using the systematic term 'polytheism', it would be more in conformity with the actual intention of the worshipper to speak about *henotheism* in these instances. Similarly, we can say that the God-person who is addressed in a culture with an unrestricted or comprehensive mythology nevertheless bears the concrete features of his momentary appearance, which are definitely distinct from those of another situation. It is a kind of theism, that, from the point of view of its functional structure, shares unmistakable similarities with a henotheistic attitude. As we did in discussing the theistic outlook of primitive religion, we emphasize again the relational character of religious phenomena. This makes it necessary to introduce the term 'relative' as a key word in the description of primitive cultures (*cf*. relative monotheism; relative polytheism).

Perhaps more important for the analysis of primitive religions than the transitional and typogenetic aspects of the hypstatic complexes is the impact of the two modes of understanding on the structural distinction between magic and religion. Thus far we have spoken about magic in connection with the mediatory function of the mythic unity and the attempt to master life with the help of a metaphysical fantasy. What has been indicated as a possibility implicit in the analysis of the structural dynamism of the human being, particularly with respect to the synthetic function of consciousness, becomes a certainty from the viewpoint of applied or rationalized symbols. Since magic relies upon the anticipated completion of the process of hypostatization, the morphology that results from this analysis can be applied to magic as well as to religion.

Thus it is not the ritual as such or the manipulating of symbols that turns the mythic unity into magic but the interpretative attitude in and toward the symbolic dimension. Magic, as impending possibility, is thus implicitly given with the structure of personal experience. To overcome its inadequacy with respect to the person, man must turn to religion as that dimension of symbolic self-realization in which the hypostatic pitfall is overcome by the unfathomable freedom of personal intuition and transcendence. But while it is overcome in the theogonic dynamics of the human consciousness, its traces remain as the present signs of the religious projection. For that reason we must say that even a cult system that is centered on the idea of a highest being can be both a religious and a magical system. All depends on its relation to the mythic unity and the theogonic consciousness, on the one hand, and to the anticipated completion of a hypostatic understanding, on the other. Custom, tradition, belief-system (though they describe and reflect man's consciousness) do not have the final say about man as a person, his conscience and his freedom. In this regard we can only conjecture but not pronounce definitely. For the final word in the analysis of religion relates to the human person and all the implications of such a relationship. Even the mind of 'primitive man' has, then, to be granted its secrecy, mystery and uniqueness.

Since it is not possible to decide *a priori* if an actual situation is predominantly religious or magical, the interpretation of religion in primitive cultures is, as in every other situation, basically ambivalent. On the one hand, there is the singularity of each situation, which requires an adequate study of the community at issue; on the other hand, there is the uniqueness and universality of the human person, which is understandable only in a similar horizon in which the available data become indications (but never the building stones) for a reconstruction of the history-related inwardness of man. Otherwise we would become victims to the same type of understanding that is at the root of all magic expressions. This means that in order to manipulate the world by self-sufficient terms, we would become prey to the temptation of hypostasizing where no hypostatization can be permitted.

With respect to primitive cultures, the following picture can be given of the religious situation of man: As a being able to ask, to speak and to understand, man necessarily lives in a world of symbols. He shares them with mankind in general and with his life-community in particular. Throughout the process of symbolization, the symbols become necessary as mediatory instances of the realization of interpersonal relations and the person alike. Since the world of symbols is bound together in the process of homogenesis and is not merely the sum total of co-existing entities, a definite structure can be discovered in the general texture of symbolization. As a result, religion appears as a differential universality in a cluster of aspects that refer to the absolute character of the symbolic and of life. The mediatory dimension of the symbolic reality of man is in turn concentrated in the mythic unity as the absolute foundation for thought and action. It is a unity that while connecting the individuals in their life-community opposes them in the distinctness of their personal uniqueness. In its theoretical, as well as practical reality, the mythic unity reveals an immanent dynamism (*coincidentia mythica*). This brings man into a decisive relation with the final outlook of this dynamism, that is, with the God-person and, consequently, with the God-person in relation to man and world (religious symbolism). Religion becomes manifest as a primary datum of culture. Its initial realization as primitive religion is founded in the theogonic consciousness or the personal existence of man and is challenged throughout the processes of social togetherness and cultural survival. In its emergence in many religious phenomena, primitive religion is, like culture itself, subject to translative and alternative developments. It is opposed by its magical mirror image, where the same symbols are understood as if they were substances of the empirical world (hypostasized hypostases) and where the same symbolic acts are performed as if they were efficacious in themselves.

In summary, we can say that religion is not a construction of the human mind, although man's constructive power is obvious throughout the course of history. Nor is religion the result of impersonal processes, although such factors as environment, economy and social structure never cease to influence its genesis. Primitive religion leads us into the original condition of mankind and to its multi-relational modes of appearance. Man is born as a religious being whose existential truth is basically identical with that of his religion, and vice versa. That is the indication given by primitive cultures.

8

Primitive Religion and Modern Man

When we set out on the study of religion in primitive cultures we began by analyzing the meaning of culture and understanding. As it turned out we came to the realization that the comprehension of cultural data and phenomena must remain inadequate as long as we do not succeed in developing the principles that lead to the constitution of these phenomena. Since we do not know, however, of any device that would insure our having this constitution before we dealt with the phenomena themselves, we had to make it part of the initial question of this study. For methodological reasons we combined the question about religion in primitive cultures with that of primitive religion as a presupposition and universal implication of culture and religion alike. By coordinating the empirical and the transcendental, that is, by studying the empirical in the light of the constitutive difference between culture and cultures, the question of primitive religion became a sort of beacon that guided the study of religion in primitive cultures both in the form of anticipation and recollection. As anticipation primitive religion made us aware of the heuristic character of cultural studies. As recollection it drew our attention to the verificational self-critique of interpretation and understanding. So far the study stands on its own grounds.

If we ask ourselves, however, for the motivation of such a study, we cannot disregard the theories about the origin of religion as they have been articulated particularly in the nineteenth century. Accordingly, if we add now to the first question about religion in primitive cultures that about the significance of the results of this study and, in particular, the significance of primitive religion for modern man, we shall, in the first places, have to reassess those theories in the light of the previous reflections. In the second place we might then proceed to the further implications of primitive religion for the present situation.

1. Reassessment of the Studies on Primitive Religion(s)

The classical approaches to the problem of primitive religion did not primarily try to give situational and phenomenological accounts. The less they reflected upon the culture-producing effect of cultural studies, the more they were interested in integrating the available ethnoreligious data into their vision of man and mankind which was largely a product of evolutionism and rationalism. The interest in primitive cultures was at least partially determined by the question about the (chronologically) first stages in the development of man. A diachronical interest was thus displayed over against the synchronical mosaic of the world's cultures. The search for the origin of religion was understood as part of an inquiry into the chronological genesis of mankind.

There can be no question about the legitimacy of investigating the beginnings of mankind in a temporal or chronological sense and of asking about the religious expressions of the ages in question. The search for the physical or biological evolution of the species *homo sapiens* makes it necessary to formulate hypotheses concerning the development of culture as a meta-physical or meta-biological 'trait' of the species man. There is also a point in looking at existing stone (age) cultures, their tools, artifacts and burial customs, when formulating such hypotheses. Paradoxically enough, these matters are as important for the biological questions as the morphological findings of physical anthropology and paleontology. After all, man is not only a biological species but also a cultural being whose culture becomes part of his brain when seen from the viewpoint of function and survival. Consequently, if there are similarities between the remnants of former cultures and certain objects and aspects of cultures with which we have become acquainted in historical times, we may legitimately ask whether the documented context of these objects does not offer us a clue for the interpretation of these former cultures. But, as in every hypothesis, there are a number of premises and presumptions which have to be worked out and employed very tentatively, particularly when we extend them to the phenomena of religion. Moreover, since the significance of premises and presumptions must be sought in their application, we have to expect that they will have a definite impact upon the models in and by which they are applied. Within the frame of reference assumed as a working hypothesis, the beginning of the premises is evident. Otherwise we would not know what we were doing. But this alone is no reason to prevent us from reflecting upon this beginning in and throughout the process of its concretion. Though reality is implied by thinking, it is not thinking which creates reality, but rather reality that demands the *kenosis* of thinking in order to be understood and, on the basis of understanding, to be transformed into the world of man and culture.

The evaluation of the classical theories about the origin of religion can be developed along two lines of reasoning. In the first instance we may evaluate these theories in the framework of their own premises. Assuming that the general theories and presumptions are true, we may ask whether the conclusions that have been drawn from the available materials conform with the information that has been acquired subsequently on primitive cultures. In the second place we have to examine the premises on which the classical theories were based. We have to confront these theories with the meaning of primitivity, its philosophical significance, and the problem whether it will be possible to synthesize this significance with the empirically given. Both these aspects have to be present when we discuss the classical theories. In the end they will lead us to the point where we face the problem of culture history in general and that of the history of religions in particular.

From the viewpoint of the historical situation it was practically inevitable that the theories on primitive religion and the study of religion in primitive cultures developed in accordance with the information gathered from non-Western peoples. In this respect the history of religious studies presents already in its own development a critique of the various theories. Here again we may point to Ehrenreich's answer to the Pan-Babylonian school or to the search for a pre-animistic stage of religious development as a critical reply to Tylor's theory of original animism. The same holds true with regard to the introduction of social and functional aspects to which attention was called both by the field workers and by the newly emerging social sciences in Western traditions. Lévi–Bruhl's emphasis on the type of thinking exhibited by primitive peoples and the cultural differentiation evolving from the predominance of certain typological features is a further example of the manner in which new insights helped modify the theories. The ethnoreligious data used by E. B. Tylor, G. Frazer and their contemporaries, for instance, were drawn chiefly from sedentary peoples, whose economy is based on horticultural and agricultural conditions. No one can deny that a preoccupation with the soul and the ancestors is very common in this group of peoples. Their mythological world is well elaborated and traditionalized. Complex rituals with a strong tendency toward magical manipulation and formalization – a symbolic feature (value) that is concomitant with the idea of traditionalization – are characteristic for the cult life of these peoples. Yet, no cultural anthropologist today would suggest that mankind grew up with planting techniques as indicated by biblical myths (see Genesis 3:23; 4:2 ff, and others), or that the complexity of these cultures accurately reflected the primary conditions of cultural life, that is, of a situation where a minimum of tradition is provided to overcome with lasting success the alienation of nature that is due to the reduction of instincts and the emancipation of consciousness. The same can be said with regard to Lubbock's postulate of peoples without religion. Such peoples have never been found among contemporary 'primitives', if we preclude those studied on the basis of one-day acquaintance. As for Durkheim's thesis that the Australian aborigines are a paradigm of the most primitive society known today, comparative ethnology must also disagree. On the contrary, it would be very difficult to discover an equally sophisticated system of social organisation on the pre-political level. Thus, if it is true that more than 90% of the people who ever lived on earth were gatherers and hunters (see R. Lee and De Vore, 1968, esp. p. 3 ff), we have to examine all available forms of this culture type in order to discover the 'origin' of religion in the framework of the hypothesis of ethnological survivals and prehistoric remnants.

Even when we stay within the confines of evolutionistic theories, the overwhelming presence of gatherers and hunters in the ethnological picture has far-reaching consequences. It shows first of all that Spencer, Tylor, Frazer and many other scholars turned to speculation at a point where, according to their own premises, data were still available for penetrating further into the depth of time and the complex genesis of culture. In comparison with the situation of gatherers and hunters their constructions are based on highly differentiated forms of culture and religion, especially with respect to manistic and animistic ideas, magical techniques and the respective patterns of behavior. While these theories have some empirical validity with respect to phenomena on the level of incipient high cultures (village communities, archaic high cultures), they are very weak in accounting for data pertinent to the religious life of gatherers and hunters. Yet, according to the theoretical premises of these theories, gatherers and hunters should be of primary significance.

The second consequence of the predominance of gatherers and hunters concerns the type of religion that might have been at the root of religious development. As we have seen there has been a tendency to see the origin of religion either in a dynamistic or an animistic (manistic) or a theistic type of religion. As the data show, these types do exist among gatherers and hunters, but they are not isolated or negatively opposed to one another. They coexist in mutual interdependence. Moreover, when seen from the viewpoint of cultural contact situations and economical and social changes, there are indications of historically conditioned trends toward the predominance of one of these components. Consequently, if we speak of the 'origin of religion' within the framework of the classical theories we not only have to accept the data that are given, but we have to accept them in such a way that justice is done to this phenomenal situation. It is true that religion is functional, but this alone does not justify the conclusion that functionality exhausts the reality of religion. From the viewpoint of the so-called ethnologically old cultures[1] a lack of development or non-differentiation certainly excludes specialization in an economical and technological sense. But if we accept the facts we cannot deny a symbolic complexification that results from integrating the divergent aspects of life into a meaningful unity of cultural existence. In this sense we can say that 'in so-called "primitive" societies religion encompasses philosophy, theater, "science", ethics, diversion, and other behavior spheres which recent Western civilization has tended to segregate' (see Kluckhohn, 1965, p. xi). The facts of life are mediated in the translative unity of man and the life-community. Thus, if a judgment is to respect the data collected from the cultures of gatherers and hunters, one must say that the various components taken together interact in the constitution of 'primitive religion'. It is neither theism nor animism nor dynamism nor any other type of religious behavior which could account for the 'origin of religion' according to the data provided by the cultures of gatherers and hunters, but it is the interaction of several types with which we have to begin (see Schebesta, 1954, I, pp. 558, 561).

We need not emphasize that at this point the data suggest very strongly a revision of the speculative model that interprets them. Accordingly a third consequence refers to the understanding of man suggested by the cultures of gatherers and hunters. 'Primitive man' is not the rational abstractum the classical theories would have us accept as the empirically given. Instead, as any other speaking being, he shows a strong polarity in his behavior; a polarity, however, that is held together in his mode of personal existence. He is a being who has reached cultural

---

1. When we refer to ethnologically old cultures we do so with respect to cultures whose typological make-up reflects 'earlier' stages of human development, stages whose morphology has to be considered as transitory forms of the present development – a point which can well be made with regard to economy and technology.

stability by making use of the translative and synthesizing potency of his existence. Consequently, with Frazer and Preuss we may well say, that he is magic-
minded. But not only that. As Lang and Schmidt would insist, he is also a rationalist. If he is nota philosopher or a reflective thinker like Plato and Aristotle, this
does not imply that he is either childlike or a retarded being, incapable of reasonable thinking, as some theories may suggest. (On this question, see the particularly lucid remarks of Geertz, 1965; also Radin, 1927; Lévi–Strauss, 1968).
Neither can we legitimately evaluate this attitude toward myth and the mythic
dimension by comparing it to the attitude developed in the history of the Western
world. Since this attitude is basically alien to the situation of mythologies in the
cultures of gatherers and hunters, it will be necessary to understand these cultures
first in their general foundation before comparisons might be made. A culture
which has become accustomed to identifying myth with falsehood and which, on
the scientific level, has accepted euhemeristic and allegorical interpretations of
myths in a more or less unquestioning – and thus, unscientific – manner is not
capable of understanding primitive mythologies unless the whole phenomenal
complex is re-evaluated with regard to its comprehensive meaning in the constitutive genesis of man and culture history.

If the customs of primitive cultures are different from ours, it does not follow
that 'primitive man' is neurotic. Nor do the empirical facts suggest or justify a
procedure that fails to respect the polarity of his existence. Yet, this is the procedure involved when the meaning and dynamics of his life are reduced to
sexuality (Freud) or to society (Durkheim) or to economics (Marx). The stories of
promiscuity and the psycho-analytic Oedipus complex may be myths that respond
fairly well to a situation encountered by a modern psychiatrist, but there are
neither *a priori* reasons nor empirical indications that they cover equally well the
situation of 'primitives'. Here the old topic of the 'theoretical hunting ground'
displays once again the historical role bestowed upon it by the need of rationalist
ideology to corroborate its 'self-evidence' by projected empiricity (see Schelling,
no date, Vol. 11, pp. 56, 183).

If 'society' is predominant in the mind of Australian aborigines – a hypothesis
that presupposes its own theory on mind – it cannot be maintained that it is
equally so for the rest of the world's gatherers and hunters, nor can it be sufficiently demonstrated that the apparent difference between person and society is
only an illusion, similar to that between man and totem. From the viewpoint of
factual stability and effective survival the social community cannot be reduced

to a fight between the individual and the group. Even though such fights do exist, we have nevertheless to count on a personal or dialogical togetherness, in which the mythic unity of man comprises the interpersonal dimension of understanding (language) and support (life-community). Similarly, if the influence of work and economy on religion is strong in primitive cultures, it does not follow from the empirical data that work and economy 'produce' consciousness and its contents. On the contrary, when the situation is viewed in the light of the mythic dimension, we begin to realize that it is existing consciousness which enables us to 'understand' the particularities of man as a cultural being and which brings the cultural data including those of primitive cultures into perspective. In a word, the differential universality of religion in primitive cultures contradicts quite clearly a causal and total reduction of religion to external factors. When measured by the available data there are no clear-cut 'solutions' regarding the empirical genesis of religion.

Finally, the discovery that a complete human being forms the center of primitive cultures challenges the framework of an evolutionistic philosophy in at least two ways: (1) It shows that the hypothetical predictions and conclusions of evolutionistic theory are invalidated by the facts of existence. (2) It calls into question the premises of all those theories which anticipate an image of man that is alien to the one for which philosophy is searching under the conditions of a universal mankind. This universal mankind provides the basis of communicable experiences and of a universal humanism as the horizon of its theories. A critique within the premises of the classical theories turns – enforced by the logic of fact and interpretation alike[2] – into a critique of the premises themselves. If we turn to the empirical sphere, we may also say that the study of primitive cultures cannot eliminate, though it may modify, the attitude that guides the study of the so-called high cultures and of Western civilization. Man has to be taken seriously as long as we speak about man, i.e., about a being that speaks. To recognize man's humaneness is not a matter of philanthropy but a principle of hermeneutics. Wherever man emerges, he is not a zoological subject but a human being with all the contingencies, advantages, and disadvantages of this particular existence. The immanent critique of the classical theories on primitive religion and religions

---

2. See also C. Geertz (1965, p. 208), who expresses this inversion of logic and fact by distinguishing between models *for* and models *of*: 'The inter-transposability of models *for* and models *of* which symbolic formulation makes possible is the distinctive characteristic of our mentality.'

leads us to the same questions that have already been raised by the constitutive analysis of cultural reality. It falls back upon those who have developed those theories and who try to interpret them.

2. PRIMITIVE RELIGION AND THE HISTORY OF RELIGIONS

The basic premise with which we began, and which has gained momentum in the empirical context and throughout the course of this study, was the interpretation of man as a cultural, and in consequence as a complete, human being. In a more speculative language we spoke of the analogous universality and the universal analogy of man. So viewied it becomes impossible to consider the religious symbols and patterns of today's primitive cultures as more or less identical survivals of prehistoric times. Like all other cultures, primitive cultures have had their own history, their own pace and form of anthropogenesis – even though the depth and thoroughness of cultural change may have been considerably different, especially when an endogenic development took place in an independent environment. But even then a unilateral reduction of religion in connection with certain factors that may not have changed or, if so, only in a narrow framework, still would misconceive its differential variety, and, above all, it would forget that it is man as existing consciousness who realizes religious articulation. Therefore, no case can be made for a 'geological' reconstruction of the history of religions by coordinating the synchronic cultural 'layers' of today with their diachronic genesis in the past. The discovery of this principle by G. Soulavie (about 1800) was without a doubt a tremendous achievement in geology. If we apply it to cultural anthropology, however, we have to speak of an anthropological fallacy that mixes the treatment of man with that of the earth.

Yet, the rejection of a geological reconstruction of the cultural past does not exhaust the problem. The fact that we are dealing with cultural phenomena reveals both the variables and invariables of nature *and* of consciousness. In particular there is the invariable of consciousness, or, as we might also say, the open tautology of the human mind, which must be considered as an irreplaceable constant in the foundation of cultural development. As such it gives meaning to the interaction of the various factors that build up history, including those of time and its internal components. If history appears as constellation (M. Weber) and configuration (C. Kluckhohn) it is because of consciousness both as agent and as principle of recognition. Since there is consciousness, there is not only history as the result of morphological processes but also cross-culturality as a general trait of cultural data.

If we use the term 'invariable' in connection with consciousness, we do not claim that it is a mathematical or physical invariable, somehow akin to the constants in the formulas of physics. All we wish to express by this term is the particular stratification that is brought into being by the emergence of consciousness. In this sense we understand consciousness as a tautology that is one *and* all (*hen panta*). Though variable in itself – each human being is different, no 'word' is identical – consciousness becomes nevertheless invariable by opening and by closing once and for all the gap between being and nothing, between something and everything, between person and world. In universal analogy, man is the same to himself and to others; his being is that of analogous universality. It is because of this invariable that we are capable of communicating with one another and of relying, for instance, upon the rational constants such as logical identity and non-contradiction, or that we may talk of thinking and truth both as explicit and as implicit aspects of language and speech. Yet, its major impact on the human situation is not the implication of rationality but of history. Consciousness implies language and communication, and both of these reveal the horizon of culture history as the condition of self-objectification and of the quest and question of man's origin. As a result, each form of self-objectification (conscious articulation) becomes a sign or indication not only of what is meant but also of man's origin. In their achievement they are the visible memory of the conditions and circumstances that brought them into being.

The fact of cultural descent and differentiation within the context of self-objectification reveals, when judged against the background of the invariable of consciousness, the concretion of history as a morphological process in which each culture shows in its own way and with its own rhythm what the basic conditions might have been that initiated and continue to initiate the emergence of mankind. The speculation about the constitution of man on the basis of self-experience can and has therefore to be complemented by an imaginative reconstruction of anthropogenesis by means of the empirically given in such a way that they mutually limit each other in critique and completion. History as past (diachrony) has to be coordinated with the cultural present (synchrony) in such a way that fact and interpretation begin to 'meet' one another within a system of representative figures. Thus, while we reject the evolutionistic system of historical development on the basis of conciousness, we accept, on the same basis, the idea of a morphological history, in which the events and cultural facts of the present (incuding those of written and archeological evidence) refer to the process of origination as a universal condition of man. For reasons of objectivity our attitude toward the 'facts' of culture history has to be qualified, if not changed, inasmuch as we recognize in them the articulations of consciousness. Because we want to take them for what they are, we cannot content ourselves with face values.

When viewing the data of culture history in the light of the invariable of consciousness we always must pay attention to the fact that it is not a causal continuity (the geological model) that comes forth in and as history but a participational causality that brings it into being (the morphological model). Consequently, when we speak of 'ethnological age', we should not do so without distinguishing whether we refer to the age of 'surviving' elements, or to the 'age' of the culture as such. If we speak of 'age' in the latter sense, we must be aware that the word 'age' has to be used accordingly. If we want to maintain meaningful speech we should not understand it as a temporal or chronological term but as a symbol by which we refer to the primary conditions of culture. As a representative term 'age' is not a matter of years but of the proximity to the all- and ever-present beginning. It characterizes a cultural situation in which elements are functional but does not characterize the elements as such. If we neglect this difference we will fall under Hegel's verdict of confusing 'the primum as idea and reality of consciousness in accordance with its very conception' (Hegel, Suhrkamp ed., Vol. 16, p. 262).

If history is understood from this morphological viewpoint, primitive cultures must not be considered any longer as convenient hunting grounds for the 'verification' of ideologies, for scholarly curiosity, or as one more non-importance among others. On the contrary, they become significant in various respects. *First* they permit us on the basis of cross-culturality to clarify the meaning of religion as a universal pattern of human self-realization. In the configuration of the symbolic data they *secondly* point to primitive religion, or, as we might also say, to the constitutive presence of religion in the emergence of man, as an original datum of mankind. To the degree that primitive religion presents itself as a fundamental relation within the structure of primitive cultures, the latter offer us, in the *third place*, an indication of the content as well as of the modes of its realization and understanding. As for this study we became aware of the mythic unity of man and world, man and mankind, as general condition of religious origination, and myth and cult as ways of its enactment. We came to understand the idea of God, Creation, the Holy and the Mythic Force as constitutive features of divine being (mythicity), comprising God and man alike. Also the movements of descendence as enacted by man's metaphysical fantasy and of ascendence or transcendence as realized in conscience and person-giving behavior turned out to be essential for the concept of primitive religion. *Finally* primitive cultures give us an idea of magic and religion which characterizes them as outwardly complementary yet inwardly exclusive modes of primitive religion. This, in turn, explains why the historical process reveals a continuous oscillation between alienating progression and/or self-destruction on the one hand, and dialogical communication and/or de-activation or *Zweckbefreiung* on the other. It explains why history is characterized by a progression whose reason of progress is negative rationality and a process whose progression has reason (*Vernunft*) itself as the principle and measurement of cultural realization. In either case we come to understand that the philosophies of history contain and necessarily imply premises which are, even if a-theistic in their intention, fundamentally religious in their genesis and final outlook. They turn out to be mythologies that work with the materials provided by theoretical thinking.[3]

In short, if we analyze the problem of primitive religion in the light of a constitutive analysis of primitive cultures, we come to reject the premises of the classical theories because they do not recognize the cross-cultural significance of 'primitive man'. On the other hand, if we approach primitive cultures within the framework of a morphological interpretation of history, they give us indeed the 'elementary forms of the religious life'. As such – and here we agree with Durkheim (1965, p. 18 ff), although the forms he points out are in many respects different from those mentioned in this study – they become 'privileged cases' for disentangling the cluster of the history of religions. While they are verified to the extent that culture history falls into a pattern, they become hermeneutically significant for the study of religion by shedding light on the constitutive conditions of its genesis. Fact and speculation support one another if investigated and realized under the guidelines of universal humanism and culture history. But to get an idea of the meaning of universal humanism – which we understand here as the speculative extrapolation of cross-culturality indicating the conditions of its

---

3. Instead of mythology one could also speak here of logomythy.

possibility in the reality of language and consciousness – we cannot content our-selves with the data of documented history. On the contrary, if we emphasize the latter – for instance, in connection with the history of religious ideas – we are referred to the ethno-religious data as those symbolic instances that permit us to get hold of that particular background which, though present in any cultural datum, has undergone such a transformation that its apparent 'disappearance' became in itself a condition for the possibility of the so-called universal religions. The implicit anticipation of a universal humanism which takes shape in the inter-pretation of cultural data and which functions as the immanent criterion of veri-fication remains thus necessarily incomplete and, since the idea of completeness forms part of the adequacy of articulation, also remains inadequate as long as the quest for primitive culture does not become an essential feature of methodolo-gical awareness and procedure. If we are to understand the present predicament and its history, we must not forget – and here we may refer to what was said in the introduction – the cultural reality of 'primitive man'.

A focal point in the discussion of primitive cultures and the history of religions was (and still is for many scholars) the problem of a proto-revelation and proto-monotheism (see Cornélis, 1965, p. 17 ff). Although this problem has a long history – as far as I can see it was R. Bacon who introduced the thesis of a proto-revelation into the philosophical and theological discussion – it was W. Schmidt who brought it to the fore within the framework of cultural anthropology. A brief discussion of this question may illustrate the previous remarks on a morphological interpretation of history as suggested by the analysis of primitive cultures.

We pointed already to R. Pettazzoni's rejection of protomonotheism because of the misleading usage of this term (see above p. 53). Since monotheism was formulated with respect to polytheism, it belongs by definition to a specific period in the history of mankind. It has a specific historical milieu. Consequently, when asking for the proto-cultural conditions of man, we cannot disregard the historical setting as an implicit anticipation of the questions we formulate in connection with this term. As a result, the meaning of monotheism must be carefully re-evaluated and determined before we go on with the formation of hypotheses. We cannot transpose the monotheistic phenomenon into the proto-cultural horizon without concerning ourselves with the meaning of this transformation itself. What is needed is a morphological reduction of the historical situation in which monotheism has its proper place. From a formal point of view this means, how-ever, that the term loses its situational particularities. As proto-*mono*-theism it thus becomes non-sensical. In the perspective of protocultural conditions proto-mono-theism is as meaningful and as meaningless as proto-poly-theism. Yet, there remains the problem of an adequate interpretation of the monotheistic and poly-theistic complex (see Schelling, no date, 6 th and 8th lectures).

Since Schmidt connected his thesis of proto-monotheism with the idea of a proto-revelation we may ask whether the same critique can be applied to the latter term as well. This, of course, depends on how we understand the term 'revelation'. If we consider revelation as a personal relationship whose possibility depends on the existence of persons, our answer has to be in the negative. Since the idea of the person refers to a meta-historical constant,[4] the previous critique does not apply. As far as the the thesis of proto-revelation is concerned we cannot refute it on formal grounds.

One could, of course, exclude the hypothesis of proto-revelation on *a priori* grounds. In a similar way one could deny the possibility of a divine, that is, of a personal revelation during the process of history. But if one accepts the idea of revelation at all on account of man's ability to communicate, the hypothesis of a protorevelation still may have to be taken into consideration. In this case the question remains whether the ethno-religious data suggest such an assumption or not.

There is no support of this hypothesis as far as the ethno-religious data are concerned. The reasons for this position are basically the same as those presented against the evolutionist theories on the origin of religion. If we restrict the meaning of consciousness to its rational component, i.e., if we consider mythology as a deficient phenomenon in the history of mankind, then the ethno-religious data obviously support the hypothesis of a proto-revelation. In this case W. Schmidt's work offers ample proof for this hypothesis. But then we give a verdict against 'primitive man' as a person. As a result, the hypothesis forfeits the grounds upon which it rests. It becomes meaningless. For if mankind has to be de-mythized in order to find the truth of humanity and humaneness,[5] 'primitive man' cannot be fully recognized as a person. The possibility of revelation as a personal event remains without a sufficient base.

4. This does not mean that the person is a meta-historical figure in an exclusive sense. All it says is that within the constitution of person and history the person points, while belonging to history, at the same time beyond it.

5. We distinguish here between de-mythization and de-mythologization. In the sense of re-mythologization the latter is a permanent task, whereas the former is an impossibility that expresses the misapprehension of man as a mythological being.

The question which then arises is this: Do we have any right to such a restricted explanation and interpretation of consciousness as suggested by the self-proclaimed, anti-mythological bias of rationalism? As in all other cases of hypothetical presumptions, he right to do so depends not the least on the explanatory force and validity of the basic conceptions. Since 'primitive man' has to be addressed as a complete human being, we not only must explain how he got the idea of God but also what the implications of a restricted interpretation of consciousness are with regard to such phenomena as language, communication, learning, values, conscience, faith and so forth. Since the possibility of such phenomena can be sufficiently understood only if consciousness is interpreted in the light of mythic conditions, it not only follows that the historical exegesis of these terms needs primitive cultures as a referentail background in order to be adequate, but also that consciousness is in its very essence revelatory. Thus the mere fact that man appears in this world has implications of a proto-revelatory nature. For this reason there is no theoretical necessity to postulate a proto-revelation in W. Schmidt's sense. Even when speaking from the viewpoint of an accepted revelation in history, there is no need to appeal to a proto-revelatory event (in a strictly temporal sense) whose memory precedes similar events in the course of time and which has been kept alive in ethno-religious data. The emergence of the human person, whose revelatory being continues as the primary datum of religion, is reason enough to explain the conditions of historical development including that of the polytheistic as well as of the monotheistic complex. There remains the myth of proto-revelation but not the theory of a distinct event except in the sense of a theory of myth as such. Thus, while we refute a hypothesis that has been formed by the history of religions because of the data provided by primitive cultures, it is the acquaintance with these data that inspires us to bring history into a new perspective. Chronological sequence has to be synthesized with morphological structure.

Before we can go into a further description of this morphological structure, it will be necessary, however, to discuss the more philosophical aspects of this problem. After that we shall try to outline those features that characterize the so-called high cultures in contrast to the conditions of primitive cultures.

3. PRIMITIVE RELIGION AND PHILOSOPHY

The correlation between the human person and the constitution of religion as established by the analysis of primitive cultures is not only significant for the question of revelation as part of the historical beginning of mankind but also for the question of culture in general and the philosophy of religion in particular. If, for instance, the mythic dimension is as universal and all-embracing as the quest for meaning, no symbol can be thought of without being referred to it. Culture and idea, society and art, life and language, experience and consciousness, are, as van der Leeuw has pointed out,[6] basically mytho-religious in their beginning and final outlook. An understanding of these phenomena and complexities thus cannot forego the analysis of the mythic without giving up the basis upon which understanding and phenomenon both rest.

According to the available data it is not too difficult to verify this conclusion in primitive and even in archaic high cultures. The examples that were given offer ample proof for the importance and comprehensive function of mythology in substantiating the cultural process. However, the problem that arises in this centext is the question about the precise character and the extension of the significance of the situation presented by primitive cultures.

As we have already seen, the answer to this problem will differ considerably whether we proceed from the premise that 'primitive man' is a complete human being, or from the presumption that he lacks true humanity. Since we have discussed this matter at length, we need not belabor this point again. What we do have to ask now is the question about the conclusions that can be and must be drawn from the mytho-religious character of culture as it is manifest among primitive peoples. In this respect some additional remarks on thinking and mythicity may be helpful for understanding the full importance and philosophical actuality of the study of primitive cultures and their religion.

When we spoke about mythic thinking we did not say that this mode of thinking is the expression of a pre-human form of life or that it prevents man from conceiving adequately the emprirical world. On the contrary, we emphasized the fundamental character of mythic thinking as the foundation of mythopoetics as

6. See G. van der Leeuw (1963, Vol, 2. p. 679). By interpreting religion in the light of human fulfillment ('religion is the extension of life to its uttermost limit'), he indicates at the same time the essential unity between culture and religion. 'Ultimately, all culture is religious; and, on the horizontal line, all religion is culture.'

well as of all rational acts, including those of reflective thinking. Mythic thinking, as it is understood here, is not a deficiency of man's reasoning processes but the enactment of mythicity as the foundational unity of mythos, logos and being at once. It anticipates and substantiates the person and his relationship with the world. As such mythic thinking grows in and from the experience and thought-producing mediation between the modalities of consciousness and those of being.

As the dynamics of the meaning that interlinks man and things, mythic thinking cannot be expressed but only remembered in the fleeting genesis of thoughts, words and deeds. For this reason we are well capable of speaking about it but only under the condition of recollection. If we resume here the idea of the mythic unity, we may also say that mythic thinking can be described as the process that initiates the transition from a theogonic consciousness toward the community's God-consciousness and its realization in cult and purposeless deeds by tracing them back to the transcendent presence of the divine. Thus, if there is an all-embracing mytho-religious dimension in primitive cultures, it is not a sign of mental retardation, childishness or some other defect, but the expression of the person-giving function of primitive religion. In this sense we may thus say that primitive cultures are empirically significant for the transcendental 'reconstruction' of human existence.

As the analysis of mythology and mythicity has shown, mythic thinking must be understood as the constitutive relation of a consciousness that gains its identity ('invariability') insofar as it articulates and survives by speaking. Since it is thus at the root of all conscious articulation, it is as universal as thought itself. As such, it introduces the polarity and dynamism of the mythic unity (*coincidentia mythica*) and of primitive religion into the processes of thinking and rational behavior. It affects whatever emerges as a datum in the realization of consciousness and so provides in the forms of myth and mythologies the 'hologram' that permits us to have religious experiences.[7]

In its genesis the act of thinking is, like language itself, a mytho-religious act and thus subject to the movements of the mythic dimension and their transforma-

---

7. We use here the metaphor of the hologram because it provides an explanation for the 'programmation' of experiences on the basis of neurophysiological structures. If sexual experience can be explained on the basis of a psychological predisposition for certain 'figures', 'shapes', etc., we can expect that language and culture do something similar with respect to the reality mediated by them. See A. Vergote (1966).

tion into religion and magic. If we translate these reflections into the empirical situation, we can recognize there a twofold root of knowledge that is worked out in the historical realization of consciousness. The one goes back to religion, which turns thinking into the adoration of truth by exposing itself to the quest for meaning and to the world as it is. The other originates, as Frazer has pointed out, in magic as the attempt to manipulate the meaning of man and life by sealing off the openness and the uncertainties of man's origin in the certainties of self-sufficient, though illusionary, concepts and empirically effective formulas. Instead of dealing with the world as it is, man develops and employs his gnoseological faculties within the framework of his own constructions as the unexamined remnants of his basic quest for meaning and subconsciously established relations to the mythic dimension. The emergence of a theoretical interpretation of the world is counteracted by an ideological termination of culture and tradition. In the process of understanding and rational explication, the polarity of the mythic is both gained and lost in optimal and deficient modes of existence.

When judged in the light of personal constitution, magic and religion are in no way restricted to the articulations and data of primitive cultures. They continue in the gnostic manipulation of man and world as expressed in various ideologies and/or in the faithful search for truth and hopeful longing for salvation as realized and anticipated in the perennial efforts of philosophical and theological theory. If these efforts are supposed to be kept in line with the very conditions of their possibility, the analysis of primitive cultures is no less imperative for the study of religion as it is for the fundamental questions of philosophy and culture history. Since the elaboration of the implications of primitive religion enables us to uncover the possibility of comparative patterns both in the study of religion and of philosophy, primitive cultures can no longer be set aside as irrelevant curiosities. By recognizing them we come to understand that man has access to the world of religion and thought alike simply because he exists. We are, as we might also say, in principle capable of understanding culture history and religious phenomena and of philosophizing about them by comparing the variety of their manifestations and reducing them to their phenomenological genesis. Yet, while we handle this as a self-evident premise whenever we study other people, it is through the analysis of primitive cultures that we will be capable of corroborating this evidence, and of forming such a concept of its meaning that it can be critical and constitutive alike.

By concentrating on mythicity both as the condition of primitive religion and as the 'lesson' that is taught by primitive cultures, the latter become significant in two ways. *First*, primitive cultures turn out to be theoretically significant. As we have seen, their analysis is highly important for the question about the constitution of man and culture. Furthermore, they will give us an idea of the possibility of a theoretical stance with regard to the factual integration of the philosopher and theoretician into established traditions. As the condition of primitive religion, mythicity precedes religion proper as well as magic. At the same time it is not alien to man as person and thus is open for the freedom of research and investigation. Consequently, there is the possibility of a mytho-conscious position or attitude which is neither that of religion, nor magic, nor the dialectical synthesis of both. Rather it is that of the original freedom of the human person, who, by discovering his very conditions, is to commit himself to the search for truth under the restricting circumstances of history and contingency. It is the position that enables man to perceive the world in its appearance or phenomenality, and yet to interpret it in the light of the logos in which he himself develops by participating in the universality of mythicity and myth.

In the *second* place primitive cultures are significant from an interpretative point of view. If a reflective self-interpretation of man proceeding within the framework of a traditionalized belief-system (whether it is a theology, philossophy, or simply codified custom) has to expose itself to the protocultural meaning of primitive religion, if it is to understand itself within the horizon of mankind, it needs both contrast and an empirical foothold to begin with. It has to respond to the fact that its own experience and thinking are impregnated by the universal condition of mythicity, i.e., that the act of existence is the foremost fact and datum of revelation as well as of communication and understanding. For the sake of cultural perception the self-interpretation of man has to accept the idea that religions – including the so-called world religions – are not merely related and opposed to one another by factual co-existence, but that they are related and opposed to one another in the mediatory dimension of the mythic unity. As such, religions co-exist by representing different modes of participation in the origin of man. They are hermeneutically significant for and to one another presupposing we accept the mediatory dimension of the mythic unity. In addition, since this mediatory dimension is a theoretical necessity, primitive cultures, in which it finds empirical expression, become at least a practical convenience as far as the interpretation of culture history is concerned. From a categorical principle with respect to the constitution of culture history, primitive religion changes into an interpretative device if we consider its typological manifestations in primitive cultures.

On the basis of the idea of participation – an idea, which is forced upon us because of cultural pluriformity and personal unity – we do not only get a conception of the communicability of religious phenomena in general but also of the unity of the ethno-religious data in particular. In contrast to the non-primitive religions, primitive religions are basically similar to one another. They form a kind of homogenous whole that differs from those religious phenomena which have to be typologized within the context of high cultures. Although they are different as far as the results of culture history are concerned, they are similar again inasmuch as they indicate the genesis and dynamics of religious and, in a broader sense, of the symbolic life. In the context of culture history the analysis of primitive cultures becomes thus a hermeneutical instrument for interpreting the whole of cultural dynamics and for bringing those symbolic complexes into a perspective that developed within a different cultural framework. In their own ways of realization primitive religions shed light on the non-primitive religions and on the cultural complexes shared by them.

Concerning the interpretative significance of primitive cultures, a few remarks on Christianity may help to clarify this issue. It need not be emphasized that *mutatis mutandis* the same analysis could be applied to any other religious tradition that developed in documented history.

If we accept the belief in Jesus of Nazareth as the decisive principle of Christianity, we can say that the basic myth of this tradition – an expression that is justified on the basis of a thoroughgoing correlation between myth and cultural reality as we have come to understand it in the analysis of primitive cultures – is that about the manifestation of the God-person in Jesus as a historical human being. The acceptance of this myth raises two questions. The one refers to the immanent dynamics of its realization and interpretation. The other question refers to those elements and aspects of Christianity as an historical phenomenon which are secondary or even alien to its authentic message and basic thrust. The first question is most important for the philosophical and, from an inside point of view, for the theological interpretation of Christianity. The second question is indispensable from a functional point of view. For every complex that is alien to the immanent structure and movement of a given mythology contains elements of conflict which sooner or later will lead to the deterioration of the original myth and of the life community that bears witness of its message. From the viewpoint of the person as the final criterium of religious truth, it thus becomes necessary to demythologize those myths that have lost their integral function in the perpetuation of the life-community and to re-mythologize the scattered pieces of the authentic[8] myth, presupposing the presence of this myth as an intentional belief has not vanished altogether.[9]

Presupposing such a belief is given, the history of Christianity and its social manifestations, already and even prior to the awareness of primitive and other religions, offer by their own epochal differentiation indications for an authentic re-translation of the Christian message and myth. At the same time, however, unless we try to analyze the developing symbolism in the light of those complexities in which they became alive, i.e., in the light of a universal and morphological history, an authentic retranslation is also trapped by this very history. More often than not it is both familiarity and triviality that hinders us from seeing things nearby while the imagined perspective of the far off functions as an illusion that substantiates the mistakes of the present. The symbols in question may thus appear to be quite accidental and insignificant. What does it mean, for example, when the Roman Pope is carried around? When terms like 'Holy See', 'Holy Office', 'His Holiness' are (or were) used in many phrases and are or were part of customary behavior? Or when titles are displayed as sacred things? When the dialectical distinction between the sphere of the sacred and the profane is taken as a matter of (divine) course? Or when the letter substitutes any true search for meaning because it is too sacred to be infringed upon? Yet, when we trace these instances to their mythological context they no longer say wat theyꝗ appear to be expressing. They point to elements with which we became acquainted when studying the religions of primitive cultures. Moreover, since their integration into Christian tradition cannot be said to be mediated by primitive religion as such, we may even add that they turn out to have little or even nothing in common with the myth of Christ.

The functional discrepancies that do exist with respect to the myth of Jesus become even more distinct if we recall complexes like canon law and the various taboos; or when we think of the state-church relationship and its ideology in which constitutions and/or churches are deified; or of the sacralization of the

8. As for the philosophical meaning of authenticity see B. Boelen, 1968, p. 57 f.

9. It goes without saying that the possibility of a successful re-mythologization is primarily a matter of faith and not of philosophy, although philosophy may conceive of it as a possibility of its own enterprises in the horizon of mankind and with regard to a universal humanism.

hierarchic body; or the ritualistic interpretation of the cult performances, which more often than not are connected with a deep alienation between the community and the liturgy they (supposedly) realize. The struggle it took to overcome magical practices and power-structures during the age of reformation, the century-old refusal to introduce vernacular languages, the paternalistic interpretation of the service for the people of God and especially the many figures and symbols used by theology in describing man and world in their relationship to God – all these are further instances that can be mentioned and which demand an unrestricted analysis in the light of history. Finally we may refer to the adoption of the rationalistic interpretation (and thus, deformation) of those mythological accounts that have been selected and structured throughout the formation of the Bible (in particular, see Genesis, Chapters 1–11).

As for the question of the immanent dynamics of the Christian myth we are referred to the conduct of life in general and to mastering the problems of man through the symbolism and the realization of cult in particular. In the light of primitive religion, cult can be defined as the recollection and mediatory reactualization of the mythic condition of man, that is, as the celebration of creation and its decisive events or meaning with regard to the present situation. It is thus the purpose of cult to turn life and world into the sacrament of the divine presence in which man and being become meaningful in spite of the apparent absurdities of existence (see Van Gennip, 1973).

This movement from the mythic towards the sacramental transformation and discovery of life can also be observed in the Christian cult. With respect to the myth of Christ in which creation begins anew in Jesus of Nazareth,[10] the creative fulfillment is specified by Christ's coming and death as those decisive events that embrace and enact the meaning of life in its entirety. Consequently we have the basic sacraments of baptism and the eucharist as the mytho-cultic reactualization and mediation of life in Christ himself. The faithful is reborn into the new creation that begins with Christ (baptism). In the presence of the eucharist he remembers death as the sign of meaning and the beginning of immortal life in the mortality of an existence that is glorified in Jesus Christ. In addition to these basic sacraments, others relate the ups and downs of life to its absolute and

10. Even though we cannot agree with Freud's (1913) own interpretation of the totemistic patricide – apparently he himself does not see the mythological character of this rapport or narrative – it is only consistent, when he tries to describe the death of Jesus in terms of cultural beginning.

unbroken meaning. There is confirmation which, as reactualized initiation, solidifies the new beginning, confession which expresses its renewal, the anointing which prepares sinful and mortal life for its eschatological realization in grace and immortality, the ordination which supports the new creation in its sacramental and mediatory dynamics, and finally marriage, which in human unity carries out the togetherness of those who live the new community with Christ (church). In a word, the myth of Christ is not one among others (see 2 Peter 1: 11) but the totality of God and creation at once.

As the theothic culmination of sacramental existence shows, there can be no doubt that an adequate interpretation of the sacraments resulting from and subsisting in the Christian myth has to take place in the horizon of primitive religion in which the birth of man and the manifestation of the divine are originally mediated with one another. The total manifestation of the divine in Jesus Christ substitutes in a certain sense the God who, in the beginning, created heaven and earth. Consequently, if we want to explicate the meaning of the Christian myth, we cannot content ourselves with correlating this myth to particular aspects of the mythic dimension, for instance, to the figure of the culture hero. Instead, we have to contrast it with the total movement that structures the mythic dimension. Similarly we can say that an interpretation of Christian sacraments must fall short when conceptual tools are applied that developed from specialized mythologies or 'outworn hierophanies' (see Eliade, 1965, p. 6). At any rate from the viewpoint of this study the interpretation of Christian mythology with the concepts of an Aristotelian hylomorphism must make one suspicious presupposing one accepts the claim of the Christian tradition. Since Aristotelian hylomorphism cannot be detached from the moira myth of Greek traditions where the final meaning of being is secured in the impersonal necessity of matter and form, a respective Christian theology becomes something like a 'wooden iron'. Depending on how deep the implicit alienation actually reaches, we may even add that an Aristotelian sacramental theology had to become a kind of time bomb in the development of the Christian community.

We need not belabor the fact that one could go on with this analysis indefinitely. Both the theoretical and the interpretative significance of primitive religioin does not halt at any particular phenomenon. Its protological thrust reaches for the eschatological dimension of man as the end anticipated by the implicit polarity of the *unio mythica*. For this reason these few remarks may suffice as far as the interpretation of some selected aspects of Christianity is concerned. Yet this chapter should not be concluded without referring to the present situation and without attempting to outline at least the perspective that is brought to our age in the light of the results of this study.

4. PRIMITIVE RELIGION AND THE END OF THE WESTERN WORLD

Today we live in the unique situation of experiencing an epochal transition.[11] The cultural thrust of ancient civilization has reached a point where the results of culture history demand a revision of the forces that brought them into being. Because of the factual alienation of an industrialized culture we have been enabled to detach ourselves from the making of tradition on a theoretical level. As the example of Marxist countries shows, man has begun to forge his political and cultural future. Yet, as suggested by the same cultural paradigm, we are also confronted with the puzzling question as to whether we are not falling victim to our own forgeries. In view of the present predicament, I dare say that there is no real chance to avoid the destructive impact of utopian trivialities unless we pay full attention to the theoretical as well as to the interpretative significance of primitive cultures.

There are many achievements that characterize the present age. Yet, at the same time it is a critical age. The turmoil brought upon man and the prospects offered for the future are, at least, of utmost ambivalence and ambiguity. If we take this experience as a point of departure for evaluating the present situation, we state, on the one hand, nothing new. Crisis, the reality and vision of catastrophy, is part of the predicament of man which is structured by the logic of birth, death and the will to survive. It is a challenge whose demands extend from mere biological survival to a successful integration of man and world in ultimate symbols. Within this process individuals are needed to maintain, or, if the achievement of once-established traditions deteriorates, to restore it. But to do so, they have to rely upon the symbolism of the life-community, which, through symbolic expression and successful communication, stabilizes the opposing forces of the human situation. As such they become the elementary units of the cultural process into which they are integrated and/or by which they are transformed.

11. Many studies have been published on this most important question. See, for instance, A. Varagnac (1948), P. Ariès (1954), H. Freyer (1955), D. Oberndörfer (1961), R. Redfield (1963), R. W. Meyer (1964), Th. Roszak (1972), H. Trümpy (1973), and my own essay (1971) (parts of which I am using here).

On the other hand, if we ask for the type of crisis that characterizes the present age, we become aware of a most important distinction. First, we can distinguish a situation for which a given symbolism is basically adequate. In the second place we may discern a situation where the responses fall short of the demands of reality. In the first case, crisis will be a matter of circumstantial shortcomings. A restoration of the *status quo* will suffice to regain the harmony and balance needed for an optimal continuation of cultural existence. In the second case, however, restoration alone will not suffice. On the contrary, it may even add to the crisis. What is needed is no less than the creation of modified and even of new symbolic systems.

There can be no question about the significance of forming a judgment whether it is the first or second type of crisis we are dealing with. In order to avoid a misapprehension in this most important matter we thus have to ask for the criteria that permit us to form an adequate judgment. Since the cultural process wherein crises once matured have also to be overcome relies on elementary units that develop in time, two points have to be clarified when establishing the criteria for assessing the type of crisis we are in today. First, we have to ask for a proper understanding of the connection between life-community and social stability. In the second place, we have to try to get an idea of the historical frame of reference needed for bringing the present situation into the perspectives of culture history.

If we depart from the fact that life-community and society are interrelated in such a way that the changing constellation and integration (or disintegration) of the former in the societal superstructure describes the actual process of history, it need not be emphasized that the question about this correlation cannot be detached from the question about the proto-cultural conditions of human culture. As such, however, it refers us, as we have seen, to the situation of gatherers and hunters as the most representative example of these conditions. In order to trace the structures and principles that account for the present crisis-situation we have to 'reconstruct' by means of theory the genesis of the life-community and its transition into the societal superstructure, which, in practical respect, is best to be studied through an analysis of the cultures of gatherers and hunters.[12]

12. In line with M. Scheler's approach to the life-community (see M. Frings, 1969), Th. Luck-mann has recently tried to discuss contemporary religious problems by means of an analysis of 'archaic societies'. See O. Schatz (no date, p. 76 ff). What has been missed, however, in this most interesting attempt, is the difference between the cultures of gatherers and hunters and those of planters and animal breeders. See also Ch. 2

At the same time, however, that we make this methodological reference to the cultures of gatherers and hunters, we have also to pay attention to the fact that it was this cultural type that preceded the development of mankind prior to the neolithicum, i.e., when man began to toil the earth and to breed animals. On the basis of this new economy he became capable, at least in principle, of building villages and cities and thus of turning life-communities into societies. For this reason it is by no means a far-fetched assumption when we ask whether it is not perhaps the neolithic metamorphosis which offers us the key to the crisis of the present age. In either case, with respect to the question about the life-community as well as to the morphological 'reconstruction' of the neolithicum, we will be referred to primitive cultures both as representative examples for a protocultural analysis and as a typological recollection of the historical circumstances under which ancient civilization began to take shape.

At any rate, I do not think that the crisis we are facing today can be solved on the basis of restoration. In contrast to our forefathers we cannot associate history any longer with the idea of a continnous presence. They could afford the luxury of living in the myth of the perpetual calender. For them the tomorrow was measured by the experience of yesterday. Crisis was a matter of restoration and epochs a structural differentiation on the same basic conditions.[13] If, on the basis of the experiences of the past three centuries, we can no longer accept this view, we may even say that the processes initiated by the 'neolithic revolution or metamorphosis' are coming to their end in such a way that the humaneness of man, its articulation and future, are intimately connected with the process.[14] Following the suggestions worked out by Schelling in his philosophy of mythology,[15] we may even go one step further by speaking of a transcendental significance of the neolithicum. As we will see, this significance is closely interwoven with the idea of universality and its enactment into the cultural process during this period.

13. A good example for this view is Daniel 2, 31 ff. Here we see very clearly the awareness of epochal changes. Yet, what makes epochs different from one another is not their basic pattern of cultural development, but the people who act within that pattern.

14. See Teilhard de Chardin (1965, p. 214) who reports this idea as a suggestion made by the distinguished prehistorian H. Breuil. 'With his customary acute intuition, Henri Breuil said to me one day: "We have only just cast off the last moorings which held us to the Neolithic age".' The formula is paradoxical but illuminating. In fact the more I have thought over these words, the more inclined I have been to think that Breuil was right.'

15. See Schelling's (no date) concept of crisis in connection with the question of ethnogenesis, lectures 5 and the following ones.

As we have already pointed out, on the basis of the universal similarity of man we can distinguish between two basic forms of cultural reality, and, in consequence, of culture history. The *one* is that in which the meaning of man is tied up in and more or less absorbed by the challenges of an independent environment and the needs of the life-community. The type of history resulting from such a situation is that of an almost eventless self-sufficiency. The memory of the past concurs with that of the life-community. The epochal pattern reflects mythological inversion. Man responds to the demands of his nature by adapting himself to the possibilities of his environment and to the limitations imposed by social contact situations that are part of his environment. Typologically speaking we are referring to the historical dimension of gatherers and hunters who, more than any other cultural form of life, survive by living on and within the terms set by their environment. The *other* form of cultural reality is characterized by man's attempt to overcome the independence of his environment. The immediacy of existence as an expression of the necessities of nature is broken up by a reflection which projects its own goals and plans its own future. The meaning of man is correlated with his own spontaneity as an individual and the events that qualify and modify this individuality. Man no longer responds directly to the fundamental terms of the environment but interferes with them by rendering them part of his own spontaneity and planning. His integrative participation in and his social existence as life-community becomes interrupted. Man becomes part of (the) society. The empirical borderlines of the life-community tend to lose their distinction in the wider fabric of the societal superstructure.

Man entered this second form of cultural reality when he turned to the cultivation of plants and to animal breeding. Since this period is that of the neolithicum, the transition itself might be described as 'neolithic metamorphosis' or 'revolution'. Although we neither know the precise time nor the concrete conditions that gave birth to the neolithic metamorphosis, we nevertheless can indicate what happened in this period of transformation. The data relevant to such an analysis are partially provided by the records of history and archeological findings, partially by cultures which realized their own time by a pace different from the one of the so-called high cultures. In addition there are the cultures of gatherers and hunters, which, for reasons developed throughout this study, have to be granted their own pre-neolithic dimension of historical time. As such they are paradigmatic.

If we try to outline the neolithic metamorphosis from the vantage point of primitive cultures the following picture begins to take shape. In accordance with the first form of cultural reality one of the most significant features of these cultures is the more or less total integration of all instances of their situation. The power of an independent environment is, when measured by the symbolic system that guarantees survival, just too strong to permit much of an unintegrated margin. The cultural equilibrium necessary for survival under the conditions of a gathering and hunting economy is of such a delicate nature that a breakdown becomes inevitable unless every situational instance is attuned to it. This explains why the various cultural situations of gatherers and hunters show such a great morphological similarity to one another, although genetically they are often as divergent as human groups can be. It also explains, why practically none of these cultures could survive colonial interference and/or the contact with Western civilization for some length of time. Changes in the economical process are under such circumstances not just peripheral alterations. On the contrary, by dint of the established and *de facto* harmonized correlation between individual, community, economy and so forth, alterations in the economy, which otherwise function as barriers against eventual changes in the definition of individual and community, are likely to be destructive as far as the identity of culture and tradition is concerned. Or, if such alterations grow from within – as it happened during the neolithic metamorphosis – we can expect that they free human energies which hitherto have been absorbed by the struggle for survival and the immediate needs of person and life-community. Presupposing the necessary economical changes are taking place, we thus have to count on a development in which the individual gains a potential distance from the concretion of his life-community which permits him to render this very community an object in the projection of goals and a factor in the realization of the these respective goals.

Within the context of the emerging conditions of the possibility and – since these conditions are interdependent with the cultural process – of the reality of socio-functional differentiation and political synthesis, leadership in particular assumes a new function. It concurs with goal-projecting activities and thus becomes tied up with the reflective fantasy that accounts for the development of socio-functional structures under the 'new' economical conditions. As a result, the individual no longer stands as a whole *vis-à-vis* the life-community in the sense that the latter finds its realization through a total integration of the individual

– as is the case by and large under the conditions of a gathering and hunting economy – but becomes part of the social structure in the function and role he selects or is selected for. It is a process in which the natural alienation due to the psychological make-up of man assumes lasting forms, comparable to those of cultural duration. Alienation by culture becomes an impending possibility to the extent that the individual, or even groups of individuals, may live at the expense of others by reason of institutional stratification. The advantages granted by the community to 'parts' of its 'body' are likely to become disproportional as far as their service to the community's continuance and well-being is concerned. At any rate, the reality of the (life-)community is limited and transformed by that of the society. The independent environment of nature as a limiting force is partially curtailed and partially augmented by the reality and the idea of society and societal structure.

When we say that the neolithic changes in the economical system were likely to release forces which in the previous situations had – for reasons of the emprical necessity imposed upon man by objective factors – no chance to become operative, we have to add that we do not know on this basis what the actual impact of these forces will be on the development of culture. For the sake of logical stringency in the deduction of these forces, we have to concede that their actual synthesis in the reality of culture history remains theoretically open. We are dependent on the factual data provided by the study of culture-history. It neither is nor can it be the intention of reflection to deduce *a priori* the concretion of history. After all it is not thought that makes being, but being that encounters itself in thought, although both modalities must coincide with one another along the borderline of mutual dependence and autonomy. For this reason the study of history is neither identical with the mere confirmation and reporting of what we assume to be facts and data, nor is it the self-sufficient reconstruction of their development by concepts associated with them. Rather it is the interpretation of the human situation in the horizon of both being *and* thought. What makes history possible is the situation which, as the comprehensive word of existence and culture, precedes the historical articulations in the deeds and thoughts of man. As such the human situation can be turned into and represented as a symbol of recollection and expectation. To understand history is tantamount to understanding ourselves in whatever instances of the given we are and can be aware of. What we have to search for is the projection of lines of development in which we synthesize the synchronic contrasts of typoloicgal comparisons with the diachronic contrasts of empirical succession. Here we can and must concede that the conditions of the possibility of history are at the same time those of its interpretation. In describing and reconstructing history we have to understand ourselves both as products of history and as meta-historical 'constants' that observe history (see Gadamer, 1965, p. 246 ff).

By sharpening this line of thought with regard to the problems of the neo-lithic metamorphosis, we thus can say that we must connect the syntheses of cultural situations that emerge 'after' this metamorphosis with those that pre-ceded them in the light of the possibilities reflected in both of them. When seen in this manner we become aware that the reflective fantasy contents itself with a limited number of inventions and techniques. Once made, they are continued for centuries and even millenia. It is the 'neolithic paradox' (Lévi-Strauss, 1968, p. 13) that all the conditions for modern scientific development were practically provided from the beginning of this metamorphosis. And yet, it was only 'recently' that man began to realize their possibilities. What we observe is by and large a non-reflective cultivation of reflection as far as tech-niques and inventions are concerned.

The question that arises here is that about a possible account for the paradox which, under the premise of the analogous universality of man, must be evalu-ated as a historical fact. If we contrast the social organization of gatherers and hunters with that of tribal organization among planters and animal breeders we observe a definite alteration on the social level. Whereas the group, being more or less identical with the extension of the life-community and with the function of an eldest as mediator in communal quarrels, characterizes the social situation of gatherers and hunters, planters and animal breeders find their social identity within the tribe and the village-community. In the transition from group- to tribal organization the community thus experiences a socio-functional structuralization that results in the institutionalization of leadership. There is the office of the chieftain, of the 'king' and/or of a ruling stratum. Since these alterations have to be correlated with the economic system, and since we know the historical sequence of economic development, we do not have to restrict their description to the situation of contemporary cultures, but it may equally be applied to the neolithic metamorphosis. Even though the discovery of plant-ing techniques might have been a genial coincidence, the accumulation of the harvest provided in principle the conditions of the possibility of a development that eventually resulted in the existence of society. In this sense it is not the intention, but the deed, synthesizing being and thought, which makes history.

In stating the possibility of societal reality we gain access to the principles presupposed by our own cultural situation. For, once initiated, the societal development became subject to terms, and thus, also to possibilities that did not exist 'before' but which are still in existence today. Yet, if we synthesize the experience of contemporary tribal societies with the evidence provided by prehistory, the neolithic metamorphosis cannot be simply identified with the beginning of ancient civilization. Although the conditions for this beginning are there, the newly initiated process of societal development at first closes upon itself. It comes to rest in tribal communities that co-exist on an indefinite level. Except for some minor modifications, it would seem as if nothing had changed. Nevertheless, the 'scientific' paradox of the neolithicum is retained in the social phenomenon of tribal existence. While trying to come to grips with the neolithic metamorphosis, we have to accept the idea that the neolithicum is not only a period in which certain techniques come into use but an historical epoch that stands for itself. That is, when speaking of the neolithicum we are, in fact, not only referring to a sequence of ages marked by certain tools or certain economical and social changes but to a particular dimension of culture history. As such the neolithicum marks a style of life. The neolithic metamorphosis does not turn into the incipient high cultures but comes to rest in its own cultural form.

If we ask now for the circumstances that brought the archaic high cultures into being – the conditions of this possibility were, as we have seen, already provided by the neolithic metamorphosis — we could point to a variety of reasons. However, since the answer to this problem is above all a matter of archeological evidence, it would not make sense to invoke here the study of primitive cultures. But apart from this kind of a problem there is nevertheless another question about the beginning of archaic high cultures where the reference to this study is well in place.

If we ask ourselves what happened with the neolithic response to economical alterations when taken over by incipient high cultures, it soon becomes clear that something is amiss with this solution. First we can observe that tribes begin to expand, partially by integrating other (related) communities, partially by subjecting them to their superior power. While the socio-functional differentiation grows, mankind enters the dimension of political history. In the second place we have to note, however, that this new turn did not end the neolithicum as an historical epoch. Instead, the values and patterns of orientation that emerged with the village-communities and the tribes remain basically the same. If they change as a result of the immanent logic of events and inventions, they are set up again in the same 'old' framework. What is taking place is a process in which universal validity is bestowed upon the given structures of a social situation which, in turn, becomes the self-evident measure of intercultural contacts. The paradox of reflection that has been retained throughout the development of an indefinite tribalism becomes thus manifest as the paradox of the politico-social self-interpretation. The thrust of tribal tradition is in essence extended to whatever is deemed to be human and worthwhile to live with. The socio-symbolic reality is reflected or universalized on a non-reflective level. The stages reached in the realization of politico-social universalization do not alter the symbolic attitudes with which they were initiated. As can be seen from the history of Egypt, whenever a new dynasty begins, its development is interlinked with the propagation and universalisation of one's own tradition.

What we observe here in this interplay of morphological alteration and historical sequence is a tribal universalism functioning as a dominating frame of reference for man's socio-political self-understanding in the development of archaic high cultures. Universality is envisioned because ways of life are set as goals by man's reflective fantasy, but the vision itself is absorbed in the restrictions of tribal traditions.

When taken over by the archaic high cultures, the neolithic response misses somehow the full impact of the logic implicit in the idea of universality. Since tribal orientation continues, the new historical thrust does not cut the cord that connects it with the neolithicum. It creates its own paradox and develops within it. In principle universality is not the measure of the tribal, but the tribal is the measurement of the universal. Though initiated by the idea of universality the movement of the archaic high cultures bears its own end within its beginning. In essence it remains a tribal affair.

If we accept this idea of tribal universalism the history of the high cultures begins to fall into a pattern. Although the why of tribal universalism, while being a cultural reality and becoming an ethical issue of man's future, retracts itself into the indefinite depth of anthropological and historical genesis, it nevertheless gains meaning as a referential frame. Tribal universalism becomes significant as the description of patterns that characterize and polarize the how of cultural realization within the practical and ideological genesis of documented history. As a basically paradoxical synthesis it prepares us to expect all sorts of cultural contradictions. Moreover, since the true dimensions of a contradictory beginning can be said to become visible when the initial thrust reaches its very perfection, the idea of tribal universalism not only permits us to ask for the end of this movement but evaluates it also as a turning point in culture history.

If we reopen at this point both the question about stability and the symbolic value of the present age, we first can say that stability has been one of the foremost tasks in the neolithic metamorphosis. At this juncture of cultural existence mankind came up with the world construction appropriate to the tribe. This tribal world construction was, however, not simply discontinued in the succeeding development of archaic high cultures. On the contrary, it remained effective and became part of the paradox of tribal universalism. In the second place we therefore should ask ourselves whether the tribal world construction has been replaced since then? Because of the epochal significance of tribal universalism this question cannot be eliminated from a serious attempt at bringing culture history into a perspective. Moreover, it if should turn out that mankind has not yet experienced the end of tribal universalism, then it goes without saying that the question about crisis and stability today cannot be separated from that about this end.

Assessing the present situation in the light of these deliberations, two observations receive conclusive status. On the one hand we can point to many instances in the history of civilization that run counter to the tribal world construction. Yet, at the same time we have to add that no final success has been granted to these efforts. Since this result is in line with the idea of tribal universalism, we may assume that the thrust of this paradox has not yet lost its vigor. On the other hand we can point to the potential and factual destructiveness of modern civilization. If we understand this development as a kind of culmination of universalism in the name of and according to the tribe, it is fair to say that the paradoxical thrust that gave birth to archaic high cultures is reaching its end. Consequently, the crisis in question is not the one of the restorational type, but it is an epochal crisis in a radical sense. In either case we are led to the neolithicum both as the key to our age, its crisis, and stability problems, and as the historical place where we have to search for the forces that brought us into being.

As for the first observation three references might be singled out to substantiate our conclusion. There is no instance that is more closely connected with the idea of universality than learning and knowledge. And indeed, among the criteria that describe the concept of the high culture, there is without a doubt that of institutionalized learning and script. Yet, ever since this thrust of learning and knowledge became culturally effective, there has been the counter-movement of absorbing this thrust in the framework of socio-functional differrentiation, if not in and by institutionalized elitarianism. As the history of the university shows (see W. Dupré, 1973b), the fight between the tribal initiation school (today we may speak of vocational training) and a life-style formed by and understood for the sake of insight has never been settled. As a matter of fact, the present crisis that has befallen the universities in the free world is not the least due to the development that they were and still are to become institutions for everyone. Yet as long as the symbols of a tribal world construction are still valid, mankind is not – and cannot be – willing to pay the price for the luxury of this enterprise, even though it has turned out to be a necessary luxury.

The second example refers to the idea of democracy. Although democracy was not the political form the archaic high cultures began with, it is nevertheless an implication given with the transgression of tribal borderlines. Yet, while democracy did indeed eventually develop in the ancient city, it not only took more than two millenia until its idea met somewhat general acceptance, but the acceptance itself remained tied up with the tribal myth of self-sufficiency and superior value. In contrast to the demoncratic development in our own age, we have to point only to phenomena such as the fascist state with its ideology of the super-tribe that conquers the world, or the communist party culture where the tribal superstructure is autonomized at the expense of the life-community, or in general, the constellation of the present power-centers and the ideology that keeps them in existence. Although one has to concede that it is difficult to see how the implicit tribal universalism could be, or could have been, overcome in the various constellations of political history, the fact of its paradoxical presence throughout this history cannot be disputed. Nor can we claim to have overcome it today. On the contrary, the contradictions that are in line with its thrust have reached proportions never experienced before.

In the third instance we may refer to the history of religion. Since the question of religion has been of foremost concern in this study, it should be permitted to be more complete in discussing this case than in the previous two instances.

When seen from the viewpoint of survival, religion can be understood in a double function. On the one hand it can be interpreted as an achievement through which man becomes capable of bearing the burden of existence. Birth and death, suffering and joy, failure and success, threat and trust, all these instances of human life are mediated with one another in the ultimate symbols of myth, cult and life itself. Religion in this sense renders meaning to man under the conditions of the life-community. It enables him to accept the necessities of life as a human being. Religion is to be understood as the symbolic structure in which the humaneness of man receives lasting expression. As such it shares in the truth of man as a human being.

On the other hand, and in consequence of the logic of survival, religion can be interpreted as a symbol of transition. Meaning is not only given, it *has* to be accepted. Like existence itself, religion is not tailor-made. Its synthesis with life in the humaneness of man is mediated by the distance of persons who constitute and are constituted by the life-community. By its very constitution religion recalls in the expression of accepted meaning the genesis of this acceptance. Consequently, the *search* for meaning and truth is essential to the reality of religion inasmuch as it is religious.

Yet, while the search-for-meaning component of religion in the life-community is by and large absorbed in the continuation of life itself, it becomes a force of its own in a situation of socio-functional differentiation. Religion is set free as the search for truth and meaning – but, also, as a potential subject of human purposes. Consequently, when seen in the context of the neolithic metamorphosis and the transition of tribal world constructions into archaic high cultures we not only observe the universalization of the search for meaning but also the tribal expansion of accepted meaning and their functional manipulation by leaders, groups and the society as a whole. There is in a certain sense one line from the religious submission of conquered tribes by ancient civilizations to the propagation of 'faith' and 'ideology' in modern times. The fact that the universalization of the search for meaning develops within the framework of tribal universalism not only raises the paradox implicit to universalization under such conditions but also shows a peculiar contradiction with respect to the 'founders' of universal religions Thus, while the neolithic metamorphosis provides in principle the cultural condition for the possibility of religious founders and the universalization of their work, it also opposes the realization of such a beginning along the lines of its initial impetus: A contradiction that, no matter how we are prone to evaluate it, must lead sooner or later to social conflicts and symbolic disturbances. If we apply these deliberations to the particular circumstances of the traditions that are directly related to the genesis of the present world, that is, to the traditions of the Western world, many of its conflicts become understandable. In the previous section we have already pointed to certain religious phenomena that developed within Christian traditions, although their proper context differs considerably from that of the Christian myth. At this point the contribution of primitive cultures consisted mainly in providing a device to reveal these discrepancies. Now, that is, from the viewpoint of tribal universalism, another aspect can be added.

Christianity which clearly distinguished between Caesar, God and the conscience of the person[16] in such a manner that their socio-functional integration was no longer a matter of course, necessarily had to be considered as a threat against the *pax romana* and the stability achieved by this symbol. As a metapolitical movement, it nonetheless carried political value in a system whose structure was rooted in religious dimensions articulated in definite symbols.

Yet, when Christianity had sufficiently expanded it was eagerly subjected and eagerly subjected itself to the forms of tribal universalism. Christianity became state religion (under Theodosius I); the sacraments the prerequisites of citizenship (Theodosius II) and the bishops enjoyed their role as judges of the emperor. Heretics who appealed to the truth of the gospel as a justification of their particular way of life were persecuted in the name of orthodoxy and the common good established along the lines of the sociopolitical synthesis of Christianity. Nonetheless, the forces of tribal oppression neither overcame the resurgance of heresy, nor did they entirely succeed in replacing the gospel by juridical canons. On the contrary, religious persecutions and wars finally and *de facto* dissolved into a world of distinct creeds and ecclesiastical organizations. Religious persecution in the name of Christ and the universality of his message has turned into absurdity on the basis of its very achievements. The stabilization of society through the socio-political assimilation of Christian tradition along lines of a neolitchic mentality has become a factor of disillusionment, although – and perhaps because – it still continues to exist in self-confined instances. Because of the particular circumstances of Christianity, the separation between church and state has become a necessity of sectional co-existence, although the acceptance of the state – and this becomes particularly clear in the political

---

16. See Mt. 22:21 and also the dissent raised against the established ecclesiastical authority by the apostles.

situation of a so-called atheistic emancipation – is still achieved by symbols functioning in the frame of neolithic religion and tribal world constructs.

Thus, when seen from the viewpoint of the history of Christianity and judged according to the idea of tribal universalism, the present age turns out to be a continuation as well as a cessation of neolithic structures. Stabilization along the lines of neolithic religion still works, but both the universalization of the search for meaning as initiated by primitive Christianity and the religious situation of the present are a contradiction to and, to the extent what they are real, a cessation of its meaning.

If we summarize these arguments concerning our first observation – arguments that could easily be corroborated by many more instances – it is clear that the idea of the university, of democracy, and universal religion are indeed, when realized, phenomena that do not fit into the tribal world construction. Yet, if we want to understand them in their concrete history, we have to place them in this construction even up to our own age. The idea of tribal universalism and the paradoxical thrust of its enactment is thus a referential frame that is still valid today. If we maintain nonetheless that the cultural dimension marked by this dynamics of tribal universalism is reaching an end, it is because the second observation of which we have spoken cannot be separated from the first one.

As for the second observation we have, on the one hand, to concede that the destructiveness of the World War II for instance, was not sufficient to destroy the paradoxical thrust of tribal universalism as an epochal principle. If we think of the restoration of Europe or the liberation of the colonies in the aftermath of this event, one can say that this catastrophy was only a price for progress, and that the tribal universalism once more has proven its historical viability. On the other hand we must not forget, however, that the potential and factual destructiveness of the present culture is not only more comprehensive than it has ever been before, but also that it has reached its utmost limit. Today mankind is, in fact, capable of destroying itself and the planet upon which it lives. On the basis of values set forth by tribal universalism the weapons have been constructed which can accomplish this 'feat' at any time. In addition, if the ecological disturbances that are equally embedded in this value system are continuing at the same rate, the same goal will be reached by 'peaceful' means within a foreseeable time period. At this point, the neutrality that is appropriate to the observer of history, reaches a definite end.

There is no need to go into further details. If we try to assess the present age in the light of culture history and its constitution – a constitution, whose principles are won through the analysis of primitive cultures – we can say that ours is the crisis of an epoch that has *almost* reached an end. Since the type of this crisis is fundamental, restoration of the traditional ways of living will not do. They can only prolong the process of final destruction. Yet, as long as this end is not final, there is still a chance for a new beginning. Although no recipes for the future can be given, the fact that we are dealing with cultural processes is enough of an indication that a solution cannot be found if we do not come to a fair evaluation of the situation where it all began. At this point we are clearly referred to the study and the analysis of primitive cultures. As such it is indeed, and in a more serious sense than E. B. Tylor (1958, p. 24) would have expected, 'an important guide to the understanding of the present and the shaping of the future'.

References

ALLPORT, G. W. (1958), *The nature of prejudice.* New York, Anchor.
ANWANDER, A. (1964), *Zum Problem des Mythos.* Würzburg.
ARIÈS, P. (1954), *Le Temps de l'histoire.* Monoco.
AUSTIN, J. (1962), *How to do things with words.* William James Lectures. Oxford.

BAAL, J. V. (1971), *Symbols for communication: An introduction to the anthropological study of religion.* Assen, Van Gorcum & Comp.
BAAREN, Th. P. VAN (1960) *Wij mensen: Religie en wereldbeschouwing bij schriftloze volken.* Utrecht, Bijleveld.
BAIRD, R. D. (1971), *Category formation and the history of religions.* The Hague, Mouton ('Religion and Reason', No. 1).
BALDUS, H. (1952, 1955), 'Supernatural relations with animals among Indians of Eastern and Southern Brazil', *Proceedings of the 30th International Congress of America.* Cambridge.
BALIKOI, ASEN (1963), 'Shamanistic behavior among the Netsilik Eskimos', *The South Western Journal of Anthropology,* 19: 380 ff.
BELLAH, R. N. (1969), 'Religious evolution', in: R. Robertson (ed.), *Sociology of religion.* Baltimore, Penguin Books.
BERNDT, C. H. (1950), *Women's changing ceremonies in Northern Australia.* Paris.
BERNDT, H. (1960), 'The concept of primitive', *Sociologus,* 10 (1): 50–69.
BERNDT, R. M. (1962), *An adjustment movement in Arnhem land: Northern territory of Australia.* The Hague, Mouton ('Cahiers de l'Homme', No. 2).
— and C. H. BERNDT (1954), *The first Australians.* New York.
BETTELHEIM, B. (1954), *Symbolic wounds: Puberty rites and the envious male.*
BIDNEY, D. (1967), *Theoretical anthropology* (second augmented ed.), New York.
BIRKET-SMITH, KAJ (1948), *Die Eskimos.* Zürich.
BOAS, FRANZ (1888), *The central Eskimo.* Washington. (Reprinted 1964, University of Nebraska Press).
— (1938), *The mind of primitive man.* New York.
BOELEN, B. J. (1968), *Existential thinking.* Duquesne.
BOLLE, K. (1968), *The freedom of man in myth.* Nashville.

CAILLOIS, R. (1939), *L'Homme et le sacré*. Paris.
CAMPBELL, J. (1968), *Creative mythology*, vol. 4 of *The masks of God*. New York, Viking.
CARPENTER, E. S. (1956), 'The timeless present in the mythology of the Aivilik Eskimos', *Anthropologica*, III. Ottawa.
CASSIRER, E. (1953a), *Language and myth* (tr. by S. K. Langer). New York, Dover.
— (1953b), *The philosophy of symbolic forms* (tr. by R. Mannheim). New Haven.
CHOMSKY, N. (1969), *Aspects of the theory of syntax*. Cambridge, Mass., M.I.T. Press.
CIPRIANI, LIDIO (1963), 'Altertümlichkeit und Bedeutung der Kultur der Andamaner', in A. Vorbichler and W. Dupré (eds.), *Festschrift P. J. Schebesta*. Vienna-Mödling.
CODRINGTON, R. H. (1891), *The Melanesians: Studies in their anthropology and folk-lore*. Oxford.
COOPER, J. M. (1929), 'The origin and early history of religion', *Primitive Man*, 2: 33.
— (1940), 'Andamanese-Semang-Eta cultural relations', *Primitive Man*, 13 (2).
— (1942), 'Areal and temporal aspects of aboriginal South-American culture', *Primitive Man*, 15 (1*2).
CORNÉLIS, E. (1965), *Valeurs chrétiennes des religions non chrétiennes*. Paris.

DIAMOND, S., ed. (1964), *Primitive views of the world*. New York, Columbia.
DOUGLAS, M. (1970), *Purity and danger: An analysis of concepts of pollution and taboo*. Harmondsworth.
DOZIER, E. P. (1956), 'The concept of "Primitive" and "Negative" in anthropology', pp. 187-202 in *Current Anthropology* (A supplement to *Anthropology Today*), ed. by W. L. Thomas. Chicago, University Press.
DUPRÉ, L. (1972), *The other dimension*. New York.
DUPRÉ, W. (1962), 'Von der dreifachen Bedeutung der docta ignorantia bei Nikolaus von Kues', *Wissenschaft und Weltbild* (Vienna), No. 15, p. 264 ff.
— (1962-63), 'Die Babinga-Pygmäen', *Annali del Pontificio Museo Missionario Etnologico*, 26: 9 ff.
— (1963), 'Die methodologische Bedeutung von Sprache und Mythos und das Weltbild der Bambuti', p. 85 ff. in A. Vorbichler and W. Dupré (eds.), *Festschrift P. J. Schebesta*. Vienna-Mödling.
— (1971), 'Beyond the secular and the sacred', pp. 202-250 in H. Loiskandl (ed.), *Man in society: Facts and visions*. Dubuque.
— (1972a), 'Wahrheit und Mythos', pp. 73-100 in G. Heinz-Mohr (ed.), *Arger mit der Wahrheit* Köln.
— (1972b), 'Wat is religie?', in E. Schillebeeckx and T. Schoof (eds.), *Toekomst van de religie: Religie van de toekomst?* Utrecht, Spectrum.
— (1973a), 'Mythos', in H. Krings *et al.* (eds.), *Handbuch Philosophischer Grundbegriffe*. Munich.
— (1973b), 'Universiteit en herstrukturering', *Tijdschrift voor Theologie*, 13: 34-57.
DURAN, G. (1968), *L'imagination symbolique* (second ed.). Paris

DURKHEIM, E. (1967), *The elementary forms of the religious life* (tr. by J. W. Swain). New York, The Free Press.

EBERLE, O. (1955), *Cenarola*. Olten.
ELIADE, M. (1963), *Myth and reality*. New York.
— (1965), *Patterns in comparative religion* (tr. by R. Sheed). Cleveland, Meridian Books.
—, *History of Religions*. (1966), 'Australian Religions', Part L, Vol. 6 (No. 2, Nov.), 108–134; (1967a), Part II, Vol. 6 (No. 3, Feb.), 208–235; (1967b), Part III, Vol. 7 z(No. 1, Aug.), 61.90; (1967c), Part IV; Vol. 7 (No. 2, Nov.), 159–183; (1968), Part V, Vol. 7 (No. 3, Feb.), 244–268.
— (1967d), 'Crisis and renewal in the history of religions', in M. E. Marty and D. G. Peerman (eds.), *New theology*, No. 4, New York.
— (1967e), 'On understanding primitive religion', in G. Müller and W. Zeller (eds.), *Glaube, Geist, Geschichte: Festschrift für E. Benz*. Leiden, E. J. Brill.
— (1973), *The quest: History and meaning in religion*. Chicago, University of Chicago Press.
ELKIN, A. P. (1964), *The Australian aborigines*. New York.
EVANS, I. H. N. (1937), *The Negritos of Malaya*. Cambridge.
EVANS-PRITCHARD, E. E. (1967), *Theories of primitive religion* (second ed.). London.

FABIAN, J. (1963), 'Der Sippenälteste bei den zentralafrikanischen Bambuti nach den Forschungen Paul Schebesta', p. 35 ff. in A. Vorbichler and W. Dupré (eds.), *Festschrift P. J. Schebesta*. Vienna-Mödling.
— (1971), 'Language, history and anthropology', *Phil. Soc. Sci.*, I: 19–47.
FERM, V., ed. (1950), *Forgotten religions*. New York, Philosophical Library.
FERRÉ (1969), *Language, logic and God*. New York, Harper Torchbooks.
FORTMANN, H. (1971), *Inleiding tot de cultuurpsychologie*. Bilthoven, Ambo.
FOSTER, D. (1967), *Die Welt der Symbole* (second ed.).
FRANKFORT, H., et al., (1946), *Before philosophy*. Chicago.
FREUD, S. (1913), *Totem und Tabu: Einige Übereinstimmungen im Seelenleben der Wilden und der Neurotiker*.
FREYER, H. (1955), *Theorie des gegenwärtigen Zeitalters*. Stuttgart.
FRINGS, M. S. (1969), *Person und Dasein: Zur Frage der Ontologie des Wertseins*. The Hague.
— (1971), *Zur Phänomenologie der Lebensgemeinschaft*. Meisenheim am Glan.
FROBENIUS, L. (1898), *Die Weltanschauung der Naturvölker*.
FUHRMANN, M., ed. (1971), *Terror und Spiel: Probleme der Mythenrezeption*. München.

GADAMER, H. G. (1965), *Wahrheit und Methode* (second ed.). Tübingen.
GAHS, A. (1928), 'Kopf-, Schädel- und Langknochenopfer bei Rentiervölkern', *Festschrift P. W. Schmidt*. Vienna.
GALVAO, E. (1967), 'Indigenous culture areas of Brazil', in J. H. Hopper (ed.), *Indians of Brazil in the twentieth century*, ICR, Studies 2, Washington.

GARDAVSKÝ, V. (1969), *Gott ist nicht ganz tot; Ein Marxist über Religion und Atheismus.* München.

GARVAN, J. M. (1964), *The Negritos of the Philippines* (ed. H. Hochegger). Vienna.

GEERTZ, C. (1965), 'Religion as a cultural system', in W. A. Lessa and E. Z. Vogt (eds.), *Reader in comparative religion: An anthropological approach* (second ed.). New York.

GELLNER, E. (1959), *Words and things.* London.

GENNIP, P. A. VAN (1973), *Het offer: Aspecten van den vorm.* 's-Hertogenbosch.

GOEJE, C. H. DE (1943), 'Philosophy, initiation and myths of the Indians of Guiana and adjacent countries', *Int. Arch. for Ethnography,* 44, 4.

GOLDENWEISER, A. (1931), 'Totemism: An essay on religion and society', in V. F. Calverton (ed.), *The making of man: An outline of anthropology.* New York.

GOLDHAMMER, K. (1960), *Die Formenwelt des Religiösen: Grundriss der systematischen Religionswissenschaft. Stuttgart,* Kröner.

GOODE, W. J. (1951), *Religion among the Primitives.* Glencoe, Ill., Free Press.

— (1955), 'Contemporary thinking about primitive religion', *Sociologus* 5(2): 122–132.

GROSS, B. R. (1970), *Analytic philosophy: An historical introduction.* New York, Pegasus.

GUBSER, N. J. (1965), *Nunamiut Eskimos: Hunters of caribou.* New Haven – London.

GUSINDE, M. (1942), *Die Kongo-Pygmäen in Geschichte und Gegenwart.* Hall.

— (1948), *Urwaldmenschen am Ituri.* Vienna.

HABERMAS, J. (1967), *Zur Logik der Sozialwissenschaften.* Tübingen.

HAEKEL, J. (1952), 'Der heutige Stand des Totemismusproblems', *Mitteilungen der Anthropologischen Gesellschaft* (Vienna) No. 82.

— (1953), 'Neue Beitrage zur Kulturschichtung Brasiliens', *Anthropos,* 47'48.

HARTLAND, E. S. (1914), *Ritual and belief: Studies in the history of religion.*

HEGEL, G. W. F. (no date), *Vorlesungen über die Philosophie der Religion I* (Suhrkamp ed.).

— (1952), *Phänomenologie des Geistes.* Hamburg, Meiner.

— (1962), *Glauben und Wissen.* Hamburg, Meiner.

HEILER, F. (1962), *Die Religionen der Menschheit in Vergangheit und Gegenwart* (second ed.). Stuttgart.

HEINTEL, E. (1958), *Hegel und die Analogia Entis.* Bonn.

— (1968), *Die beiden Labyrinthe der Philosophie: Systemtheoretische Betrachtungen zur Fundamentalphilosophie des abendländlischen Denkens.* Vienna-Munich.

— (1972), *Einführung in die Sprachphilosophie.* Darmstadt.

HENRY, JULES (1941), *Jungle people: A Kaingang tribe of the highlands of Brazil.* Richmond.

HERDER, J. G. (1789), *Über den Ursprung der Sprache.* Berlin.

HERRMANN, F. (1961), *Symbolik in den Religionen der Naturvölker.* Stuttgart, Hiersemann.

HOWELL, A. Irving (1955), *Culture and experience.*

HULSTAERT, G. (1963), *L'étude des Congo et de leurs Pygmoids',* p. 7 ff. in A. Vorbichler and W. Dupré (eds.), *Festschrift P. J. Schebesta.* Vienna-Mödling.

HULTKRANTZ, AKE (1962), 'Die Religion der amerikanischen Arktis', pp. 357–415 in *Die Religionen Nordeurasiens und der amerikanischen Arktis*. Stuttgart.
HUMBOLDT, W. VON (1836), *Über die Verschiedenheiten des menschlichen Sprachbaues*. (In *Schriften zur Sprachphilosophie*. Werke III, 1963, Stuttgart.

JAMES, E. O. (1938), *Comparative religion*. London.
JENSEN, A. E. (1960), *Mythos und Kult bei Naturvölkern: Religionswissenschaftliche Betrachtungen* (second ed.). Wiesbaden. (English tr. by M. Th. Choldin and W. Weissleder, *Myth and cult among primitive peoples*. Chicago, Ill., University of Chicago Press, 1963.)
— (1966), *Die getötete Gottheit*. Stuttgart.
JEVONS, F. B. (1896), *Introduction to the history of religion*.
JOSET, P. E. (1948), 'Buda Efe ba: Contes et légendes Pygmées', *Zaire*, 1 (2): 25–66 and 137–157.
JULIEN, P. (1954), *Pygmeeën*. Amsterdam.
JUNG, C. G. (1912), *Wandlungen und Symbole der Libido*.
— (1940), *Psychologie und Religion*.
JUNG, C. G. and K. KERÉNYI (1941), *Einführung in das Wesen der Mythologie*. (English tr. by R. F. C. Hull (1963), *Essays on a science of mythology*. New York, Harper Torchbooks.)

KAINZ, F. (1967), *Psychologie der Sprache* (fourth ed.). Stuttgart.
KAWABATA, YASUNARI (1968), *Snow country* (tr. by E. G. Seidensticker). New York, Berkeley Medallion.
KING, W. L. (1954), *Introduction to religion*.
KLOSTERMAIER, K. (1960), 'Das Problem des Ursprungs der Religion', in P. J. Schebesta (ed.), *Ursprung der Religion*. Berlin.
KLUCKHOHN, C. (1942), 'Myth and rituals: A general theory', pp. 144–158., reprinted in W. A. Lessa and E. Z. Vogt (eds.), *Reader in comparative religion: An anthropological approach*. New York, Harper and Row, 1956. Also pp. 137–167 in R. A. Georges (ed.), *Studies on mythology*, Homewood, 1968.
— (1965), in W. A. Lessa and E. Z. Vogt (eds.), *Reader in comparative religion: An anthropological approach* (second edition). New York.
KOPPERS, W. (1951), *Primitive man and his world-picture* (tr. by E. Raybould). London, Sheed and Ward.
KRINGS, H. (1964), *Transzendentale Logik*. Munich.
KROEBER, A. L. (1920), 'Totem and taboo: An ethnologic psycho-analysis', *American Anthropologist*, 22.
KROEBER, A. L., and C. KLUCKHOHN (1952), *Culture: A critical review of concepts and definitions*. Cambridge.
KUES, Nikolaus von (1964–67), *Philosophisch-Theologische Schriften*, 3 Vols. (Latin and German; trans. and ed. by D. and W. Dupré). Vienna.

LANGER, S. K. (1951), *Philosophy in a new key.*

LANTIS, M. (1947), *Alaskan Eskimo ceremonialism.* New York.

— (1950), 'The religion of the Eskimos', in V. Ferm (ed.), *Forgotten religions.* New York. Pp. 309–339.

LEE, R. B. and I. DE VORE, eds. (1968), *Man the hunter.* Chicago.

LEEUW, G. VAN DER (1937), *De primitieve mens en de religie.* Groningen, Wolters.

— (1963), *Religion in essence and manifestation,* 2 Vols. (tr. by J. E. Turner). New York, Harper Torchbook.

LEHMANN, F. R. (1930), *Die polynesischen Tabusitten.* Leipzig.

LÉVI-STRAUSS, C. (1949), *Les Structures élémentaires de la parenté.* The Hague, Mouton.

— (1963), *Totemism.* Boston.

— (1965), 'The structural study of myth', in T. A. Sebeok (ed.), *Myth: A symposium.* Midland Books.

— (1967a), *Structural anthropology* (trans. C. Jacobson). New York, Anchor Books.

— (1967b), *Totemism* (tr. by R. Needham). Boston, Beacon Press.

— (1968), *The savage mind.* Chicago.

— (1969), *The raw and the cooked* (tr. by J. Weightman). New York.

LEUBA, J. H. (1912), *A psychological study of religion: Its origin, function and future.*

LÉVY-BRUHL, L. (1921), *Primitive mentality.*

— (1949), *Les Carnets de L. Lévy-Bruhl.*

LOISKANDL, H. (1966), *Edle Wilde, Heiden und Barbaren: Fremdheit als Bewertungskrieterium zwischen Kulturen.* Vienna.

LOMMEL, A. (1952), *Die Unambal. Ein Stamm in Northwest-Australien.* Hamburg.

LOMMEL, H. (1965), *Die Welt der Frühen Jäger.* Munich.

LOOFF, H. (1955), *Der Symbolbergriff in der neueren Religionsphilosophic und Theologie.* Köln.

LOWIE, R. H. (1924), *Primitive religion.* New York, Boni & Liveright. Second, revised ed., New York, Liveright ('The Universal Library'), 1948.

— (1946), 'The Northwestern and Central Ge', *Handbook of South American Indians,* Vol. 1, pp. 477–517. Washington.

LUCKMANN, Th. (no date), p. 76 ff, in O. Schatz (ed.), *Hat die Religion Zukunft?*

MADER, J. (1965), *Die Logische Struktur des Personalen Denkens.* Vienna.

MALINOWSKI, B. (1925), 'Magic, science, and religion', in J. Needham (ed.), *Science, religion and reality.* New York, Macmillan.

— (1926), 'Myth in primitive psychology', pp. 66–119, in W. R. Dawson (ed.), *The Fraser Lectures, 1922–1932.* London, Kegan Paul.

— (1954), *Magic, science and religion and other essays* (Thirtd ed.). New York, Doubleday.

MAN, E. H. (1932), *The Andaman Islanders* (second ed.). London.

MANNERS, R. A. and D. KAPLAN, eds. (1968), *Theory in anthropology: A sourcebook.* Chicago.

MANNHEIM, K. (1972), *Ideology and utopia: An introduction to the sociology of knowledge.* London, Routledge.

MARCEL, GABRIEL (1951), *Being and having* (tr. by K. Farrer). Boston.
MARETT, R. R. (1932), *Faith, hope and charity in primitive religion*. New York.
MARSH, G. H. (1954), *A comparative study of Eskimo-Aleut religion*. Fairbanks.
MARWICK, M. (1970), *Witchcraft and sorcery*. Harmondsworth, Penguin Books.
MARX, K., and ENGELS, F. (1958), *Über Religion*. Berlin.
McLENNAN, J. F. (1869-70), 'On the worship of animals and plants', *Fortnightly Review*.
MENSCHING, G. (1959), *Die Religion. Erscheinungsformen, Strukturtypen und Lebensgesetze*. Stuttgart, Goldmann Taschenbuch.
MEYER, R. W., ed. (1964), *Das Zeitproblem im 20. Jahrhundert*. Bern–München.
MONTAGU, A., ed. (1968), *The concept of the primitive*. New York, Free Press.
MORGAN, J. DE (1885), *Exploration dans la Presqu'île Malaise: Journal de Voyage*.
MÜLLER, W. (1961), 'Die Religionen der Indianer Völker Nordamerikas', in W. Krickeberg, H. Trimborn, W. Müller and O. Zerries (eds.), *Die Religionen des alten Amerika*. Stuttgart.
MUNSON, T. (1968), *Reflective theology: Philosophical orientations in religion*. New Haven–London.
MÜRI, W. (1931), *Symbolon*. Bern.

NEWMAN, J. H. (1959), *The idea of a university*. Garden City, N. J., Doubleday.
NILSSON, M. (1934), *Primitive religion*. Tübingen, Mohr.
NIMUENDAJU, C. (1939), *The Apinayé*. Washington.
— (1942), *The Serente*. Los Angeles.
— (1946), *The Eastern Timbira*. Los Angeles.
— (1948), *Handbook of South American Indians*, B. A. E. Bul. 143, Vol. 3. Washington.
NIPPOLD, W. (1936), *Rassen und Kulturgeschichte der Nigritovölker Südostasiens*. Leipzig.
NORBECK, E. E. (1961), *Religion in primitive society*. New York, Harper.

OBERNDÖRFER, D., ed. (1961), *Wissenschaftliche Politik. Eine Einführung in Grundfragen ihrer Tradition und Theorie*. Freiburg.
OSWALT, WENDELL H. (1967), *Alaskan Eskimos*. San Francisco.
OTTO, R. (1964), *The idea of the holy: An inquiry into the non-rational factor in the idea of the divine and its relation to the rational* (tr. by J. W. Harvey). New York, Galaxy.

PARRINDER, E. G. (1971), 'Religions of illiterate people', in C. J. Bleeker and G. Widengren (eds.), *Historia Religionum: Handbook for the history of religions*. Leiden, E. J, Brill.
PETTAZZONI, R. (1950), 'Die Wahrheit des Mythos', in A. E. Jensen (ed.), 'Mythe, Mensch und Umwelt: Beiträge zur Religion, Mythologie und Kulturgeschichte', *Paideuma* (Bamberg), IV. English tr. 'The truth of Myth', in *Essays on the history of religions* (see below).
— (1967), *Essays on the history of religions* (trans. H. J. Rose; second ed.). Leiden, E. J. Brill.

PLATTEL, M. (1970), *Utopie en kritisch denken*. Bilthoven, Ambo.
PISKATY, K. (1957), 'Ist das Pygmäen werk von Henri Trilles eine zuverlässige Quelle?', *Anthropos*, 52.
PONCINS, G. DE (1941), *Kabloona*. (Bantam Books, 1971).
RADCLIFFE-BROWN, A. R. (1933), *The Andaman Islanders* (second enlarged ed.) Cambridge, Cambridge University Press. (Reprinted in Free Press paperback edition, New York, 1964).
— (1952), *Structure and function in primitive society*. London, Cohen & West. (First Free Press paperback edition, 1965).
RADIN, P. (1927), *Primitive man as philosopher*. New York, Appleton. Enlarged ed.: New York, Dover Publications, 1957.
— (1937), *Primitive religion: Its nature and origin*. New York, Viking Press. Enlarged ed.: New York, Dover Publications, 1957.
— (1950), *Die religiöse Erfahrung der Naturvölker*. Zürich, Rhein Verlag.
RASMUSSEN, KNUT (1908), *The people of the polar north*. London.
— (1926), *Thulefahrt*. Frankfurt.
— (1927), *Across arctic America*. New York.
— (1929), *Intellectual culture of the Iglulik Eskimos*. Copenhagen.
— (1930), *Observations on the intellectual culture of the caribou Eskimos*. Copenhagen.
RATSCHOW, C. H. (1947), *Magie und Religion*.
REDFIELD, R. (1963), *The primitive world and its transformation*. Ithaca, N. Y., Great Deal Books.
REINACH, S. (1905), *Cultes, Mythes et Religion*.
RICŒUR, P. (1968), 'Hermeneutik der Symbole und Philosophisches Denken', *Kerygma und Mythos* (Hamburg), pp. 44–68.
RINGGREN, H. and A. V. STRÖM (1967), *Religions of mankind, today and yesterday* (tr. by N. L. Jensen). Philadelphia.
ROHEIM, G. (1932), *Psychoanalysis of primitive culture types*.
ROSZAK, TH. (1972), *Where the wasteland ends: Politics and transcendence in post-industrial society*. New York, Doubleday.

SCHATZ, O., ed. (no date), *Hat die Religion Zukunft*.
SCHEBESTA, P. (1932), *Bambuti, die Zwerge vom Kongo*. Leipzig.
— (1934), *Vollblutneger und Halbzwerge*. Salzburg.
— (1936), *Der Urwald ruft wieder*. Salzburg–Leipzig.
— (1938), *Die Bambuti-Pygmäen vom Ituri: Geschichte, Geographie, Umwelt, Demographie und Anthropologie*. Brussels.
— (1941), *Die Bambuti-Pygmäen vom Ituri*. Vol. II/1, *Die Wirtschaft der Ituri-Bambuti*; Vol. II/2, *Das soziale Leben*. Brussels.
— (1949–50, 1954–55), Unpublished notes.
— (1950), *Die Bambuti-Pygmäen vom Ituri*, Vol. II/3, *Die Religion*. Brussels.
— (1952), 'Das Problem der Pygmäensprache', in W. Koppers, R. Heine-Geldern and J. Haekel (eds.), *Kultur und Sprache*.

— (1953), 'Wanderungen und Schichtungen der Völker im "Herzen Afrikas"', *Kongo Overzee*, 19: 63 ff.

— (1954), 'Die Religion der Primitiven', in F. König (ed.), *Christus und die Religionen der Erde*, Vol. 1, Viena.u

— (1957), *Die Negrito Asiens*. Vienna–Mödling. (Vol. 2, Part 2, Religion und Mythologie.)

— (1963), 'Colin M. Turnbull und die Erforschung der Bambuti-Pygmäen', *Anthropos*, 58: 209–223.

— (1967), *Portugals Konquista-mission in Südost-Afrika*. Steyl.

— (1968), 'P. W. Schmidt's Studie über den Totemismus der äquatorialen Waldneger und Pygmäen', in Anthropos-Institut St. Augustin (ed.), *Anthropica, Gedenkschrift zum 100. Geburtstag von P. W. Schmidt*. Bonn.

SCHELER, M. (1954), *Der Formalismus in der Ethik und die materiale Wertethik*, Works, Vol. 2. Bern.

— (1960), *Die Wissensformen und die Gesellschaft*, Works, Vol. 8. Bern.

SCHELLING, F. W. (no date), *Philosophie der Mythologie*, Works, Vol. 12.

SCHILLEBEECKX, E. (1972), *Geloofsverstaan: Interpretatie en kritiek*. Bloemendaal.

SCHLEIERMACHER, F. (1965), *On religion: Speeches to its cultured despisers* (trans. J. Oman). New York.

SCHLESINGER, M. (1912), *Geschichte des Symbols*. Berlin.

SCHMIDT, W. (1910), *Die Stellung der Pygmäenvölker in der Entwicklungsgeschichte der Menschen*. Stuttgart.

— (1964), *Wege der Kulturen* (ed. J. Henninger). Studia Instituti Anthropos, Vol. 20, St. Augustin.

SCHUMACHER, P. (1950), *Die Kivu-Pygmäen*. Brussels.

SEARLE, J. (1969), *Speech acts: An essay in the philosophy of language*. Cambridge.

SKEAT, W. (1900), *Malay magic*. London.

SPENCER, B., and F. GILLEN (1927), *The Arunta: A study of stone age people*. London.

SPENCER, R. F. (1963), 'Fate and freedom in primitive religion', in D. Bidney (ed.), *The concept of freedom in anthropology*. The Hague, Mouton.

STANNER, W. E. H. (1956), 'The dreaming', p. 51, in T. A. G. Hungerford (ed.), *Australian signposts*. Melbourne.

— (1963), 'On aboriginal religion', *Oceania*, 33: 239 ff.

STEVENS, H. V. (1892), *Materialien zur Kenntnis der Wilden Stämme auf der Halbinsel Malakka* (ed. A. Grünwedel). Berlin.

STREHLOW, T. G. H. (1947), *Aranda traditions*. Melbourne.

— (1964), 'Personal monototemism in a polytotemic community', p. 723 ff, in *Festschrift für A. Jensen*, Vol. 2, Munich.

TEILHARD de Chardin, P. (1965), *The phenomenon of man* (tr. by B. Wall). New York.

THALBITZER, W. (1928), 'Die kultischen Gottheiten der Eskimos', *Archiv für Religionswissenschaft* (Leipzig), pp. 364–430.

— (1952), 'Possible early contacts between Eskimo and Old World languages', p. 50 ff, in S. Tax (ed.), *Indian tribes of aboriginal America*. Chicago.

TILLICH, P. (1961), 'The religious symbol', in S. Hook (ed.), *Religious experience and truth*. New York.

TRILLE, H. (1932), *Les Pygmées de la foret équatoriale*. Münster.

TRÜMPY, H., ed. (1973), *Kontinuität-Diskontinuität in den Geisteswissenschaften*. Darmstadt.

TURNBULL, C. M. (1959), 'Legends of the Bambuti', *IRAI*, 89 (1): 58.

— (1960), 'Field work among the Bambuti Pygmies, Belgian Congo, Preliminary report', *Man*, 60: 50-69.

— (1961), *The forest people: A study of the Pygmies of the Congo*. New York, Doubleday.

— (1965), *Wayward servants: The two worlds of the African Pygmies*. New York.

TURQUETIL, A. (1929), 'The religion of the central Eskimo', *Primitive Man*, 2 (3'4): 64.

TYLOR, E. B. (1891), 'Limits of savage religion', *JAI*, 21: 283 ff.

— (1958), *The origins of culture*, 2 vols. (Arranged by P. Radin). New York, Harper Torchbook (Orig.: [1871], *Primitive culture. Researches into the development of mythology, philosophy, religion, art and custom*, 2 vols. London.)

VANOVERBERGH, M. (1925-30), 'The Negritos of Northern Luzon', *Anthropos*, 20, 24, 25.

— (1937-38), 'The Negritos of Eastern Luzon', *Anthropos*.

VARAGNAC, A. (1948), *Civilisation traditionelle et genres de vie*.

VERGOTE, A. (1959), 'Le Symbole', *Revue Philosophique de Louvain*, 54: 197-224.

— (1966), *Psychologie Religieuse*. Brussels.

VORBICHLER, A. (1963), 'Zu dem Problem der Klasseneinteilung in Lebendiges und Lebloses in den Pygmäen und Waldnegerdialekten des Ituri', p. 23 ff, in A. Vorbichler and W. Dupré (eds.), *Festschrift P. J. Schebesta*, Vienna–Mödling.

— (1965), *Die Phonologie und Morphologie des Balese*. Glückstadt.

WAARDENBURG, J. J. (1969), *L'Islam dans le miroir de l'Occident* (third ed.). The Hague, Mouton ('Recherches méditerranéennes, Etudes' No. 3).

— (1972a), 'Grundsätzliches zur Religionsphänomenologie', *Neue Zeitschrift für Systematische Theologie und Religionsphilosophie*, 14 (3), 315 ff.

— (1972b), 'Religion between reality and idea: A century of phenomenology of religion in the Netherlands', *Numen*, 19 (2'3): 128-203.

WACH, J. (1958), *The comparative study of religions* (ed. with introduction by J. M. Kitagawa). New York, Columbia University Press.

WALLIS, W. D. (1939), *Religion in primitive society*. New York, Crofts.

WELLEK, R. and A. WARREN (1970), *Theory of literature* (third ed.). London, Penguin Books.

WEBER, M. (1920-21), *Gesammelte Aufsätze zur Religionssoziologie*, 3 vols. Tübingen, Mohr.

— (1963), *The sociology of religion* (trans. E. Fischoff). Boston, Beacon Press.

— (1968), 'Die "Objektivität" sozialwissenschaftlicher und sozialpolitischer Erkenntnis', *Methodologische Schriften* (ed. with introduction by Johan Winckelmann). Frankfurt a. M.

WEYER, E. M. (1932), *The Eskimos*. New Haven.

WIDENGREN, G. (1945), 'Evolutionism and the problem of the origin of religion', *Ethnos*, 10: 57–96.

WIPLINGER, F. (1961), *Wahrheit und Geschichtlichkeit*. Freiburg.

WISSE, S. (1963), *Das religiöse Symbol*. Versuch einer Wesensdeutung. Essen.

WOLFF, K. H. (1968), *Versuch zu einer Wissenssoziologie*. Neuwied.

ZERRIES, O. (1954), *Wild und Buschgesiter in Südamerika*. Weisbaden.

Index of Authors*

---

* See also Bibliographical Appendix, pp. 112—116, and References, pp. 339—349.

Index of Names and Subjects